YOU DECIDE!

Current Debates in Contemporary Moral Problems

BRUCE N. WALLER

Youngstown State University

PEARSON

Longman

New York   Boston   San Francisco
London   Toronto   Sydney   Tokyo   Singapore   Madrid
Mexico City   Munich   Paris   Cape Town   Hong Kong   Montreal

Publisher: Priscilla McGeehon
Senior Marketing Manager: Ann Stypuloski
Production Coordinator: Virginia Riker
Cover Design Manager: Nancy Danahy
Cover image courtesy of Getty Images, Inc.
Manufacturing Manager: Mary Fischer

Library of Congress Cataloging-in-Publication Data

Waller, Bruce N., You decide! : current debates in contemporary moral problems /
Bruce N. Waller.
    p. cm.
  ISBN 0-321-35446-X
  1. Ethical problems. I. Title.
BJ1031.W295 2006
170--dc22   2005013128

Please visit our website at http://www.ablongman.com

ISBN 0-321-35446-X

TABLE OF CONTENTS

PREFACE

Controversy over ethical issues is a familiar feature of our world and our society, and this book explores a number of those controversies by presenting opposing positions in the strongest possible form. Each topic is briefly introduced, and a few questions are posed; then a forceful, persuasive, and interesting argument is offered for each side, each argument framed directly by a leading advocate of that position. Following each debate is a brief note of some recent events relevant to that issue, and finally some sources for those wishing to explore the issue further.

The book is made up of 16 debates, with an advocate for each side, making a total of 32 papers altogether. The issues range over some of the deepest and most contested issues facing our world, our society, and ourselves as individuals. They include such perennial standards as capital punishment, and pornography; more recent controversies over campus speech codes, campaign finance reform, conscription (the draft), and use of performance-enhancing drugs by athletes; and such deep and difficult issues as animal rights, cloning, and abortion.

As you read these debates, you may become convinced that one side is right and the other wrong—but you will have also read an opposing view that gives you something substantial to gnaw on and dispute. Or, you may decide that there is something to be said for both sides. You may find you can detect areas of agreement where perhaps the argument participants themselves saw only uncompromising conflict. Perhaps you will conclude that there are strong arguments on both sides, that the issue is one for further reflection, and that you aren't really sure which position is right. Psychologists call that a state of cognitive dissonance, and note that people often find it rather disturbing; it is not, however, fatal, and it may even have some benefits. Even if your views do not change, you may gain a better appreciation of the opposing perspective, and perhaps a better understanding of the arguments favoring your own view. And if you approach the arguments honestly and openly, you may find that some of your views will change—and surely change is not always a bad thing.

My debts are many. I have had the great good fortune of working in a very supportive department of philosophy and religious studies at Youngstown State University, a department that features a rich variety of perspectives and personalities in a warm and cordial atmosphere. They have all provided me with ideas, insights, new questions, and new ways of seeing old questions, and I am deeply indebted to Chris Bache, Walter Carvin, Stephanie Dost-Barnhizer, Brendan Minogue, Mustansir Mir, Gabriel Palmer-Fernandez, Charles Reid, Tom Shipka, Donna Sloan, J-C Smith, Linda "Tess" Tessier, and Victor Wan-Tatah.

I owe a very special debt of gratitude to Joan Bevan, whose amazing efficiency and constant good cheer provide the Sun around which our entire department orbits; and also to Justina Rachella, her very able assistant; and to James Sacco, research assistant in Islamic Studies who is wonderfully wise in the ways of editing.

The librarians at Y.S.U. have been enormously helpful in finding copies of articles, obscure books, and valuable research databases, and in many other ways. Special thanks to Ellen Banks, George Heler, Amy Kyle, Jean Romeo, and Kevin Whitfield.

Among my many other faculty colleagues who have offered suggestions and insights are Rebecca Barnhouse, Stephen Flora, Keith Lepak, Dan McNeil, Gary Salvner, Lauren

Schroeder, Mark Shutes, Charles Singler, Paul Sracic, Homer Warren, Bob Weaver, and John White.

Academic colleagues at other universities have been very helpful in offering ideas for topics and readings, and broadening my understanding of many of the topics covered; among them are Nawal Ammar, Richard Double, George Graham, Bryan Hilliard, Robert Kane, Lia Ruttan, and George Schlesinger.

Thanks to a number of friends who have discussed these and many other issues with me, including Fred Alexander, Allen Behsheim, and Jack Raver.

The editorial staff at Longman Pearson have been a delight to work with: always helpful, excellent suggestions, patient guidance, invariably supportive. Special thanks to Priscilla McGeehon, Ted Knight, and Stephanie Ricotta.

Many thanks to the warm and gracious people at the Beat Coffeehouse next to the Y.S.U. campus, whose delicious hot doses of caffeine have kept my brain waves happily stimulated.

Special thanks to my students at Y.S.U., whose enthusiasm for ethical discussions is always a source of insight, delight, and inspiration.

My wife, Mary Newell Waller, has discussed many of these questions with me, been particularly helpful on issues related to psychology, and given her warm and constant affection. My sons, Russell and Adam, have talked with me about these questions—sometimes willingly—and have always been a profound source of both joy and pride, and their auto insurance, music lesson fees, and tuition payments inspired the writing of this book.

Thanks to the following reviewers who read and commented on earlier drafts of this book.

Thomas D. Carroll
  Middlesex Community College
Craig Derksen
  University of Maryland at College Park
Joshua Golding
  Bellarmine University
Dr. William H. Hardy
  Tennessee State University
Joan Whitman Hoff, Ph. D.
  Lock Haven University of Pennsylvania
Dr. Kristen Intemann
  Coastal Carolina University
Kang Na
  Westminster College
Steve Odmark
  University of Nebraska at Lincoln
S. Ron Oliver, Ph. D.
  Embry-Riddle Aeronautical University
Thomas Peard
  Baker University
Eric Stiffler
  School: Western Illinois University

INTRODUCTION

Abortion, capital punishment, hate speech—these are controversial topics, and people often have very strong feelings about them. This book is dedicated to the idea that talking about these issues, and even arguing about them, is a worthwhile enterprise. Anyone who has observed the confrontations between pro-life and pro-choice advocates may doubt that anything can be gained by such debates; still, in the right circumstances the debates may be productive. Those circumstances must include an effort by both sides to play fair, and fair play in debate involves a few obvious rules. First, personal abuse is not effective argument. Calling your opponent an idiot, impugning her motives, or attacking his integrity may provide some fleeting satisfaction. But such *ad hominem* attacks are not merely bad manners, they are also *flawed arguments*: They commit the *ad hominem fallacy*. An *argument* must be judged on its merits, and the virtues or vices of the arguer are *irrelevant*. Suppose I give an argument for why driving while intoxicated is wrong: It places others at risk; it is easily avoided; it jeopardizes your own safety for no good reason. Later you see me stagger out of the tavern, stumble into my car, and then weave off down the street. I am a hypocrite, true enough. But that is no reason to reject my argument: The arguments of hypocrites must be judged on their own merits, just like the arguments given by paragons of virtue. If you discover that you were mistaken, and the drunk driver you saw only looked like me, my argument is not suddenly restored to health. It's still the same argument, whether the arguer is drunk or sober. When a defense attorney argues that her client should be found not guilty, then as a juror you must consider her arguments carefully. It doesn't matter whether she is defending her client out of love of justice or love of money: The argument is the same, whatever the motives of the arguer. Of course if an attorney is presenting her arguments strictly out of love of justice and not for pay, that would be an excellent reason to nominate her for a humanitarian award. But it is *not* a legitimate reason for concluding that the attorney's arguments are good, nor that the greedy ambulance chaser's arguments are bad.

Not all ad hominem arguments are fallacious. There are circumstances where ad hominem arguments are legitimate and relevant. For example, if I am giving *testimony*, then it is very important to know that I was bribed, or that I am a notorious liar. Or if I invite your friend out for dinner, it is perfectly legitimate for you to warn your friend: "Don't have dinner with Bruce; he's obnoxious and rude, his dining manners would embarrass a shark in a feeding frenzy, he tells boring stories and only wants to talk about himself." All of that is ad hominem, but perfectly legitimate and valuable information that would be valuable to know if you are considering having dinner with me (or hiring me, or loaning me money, or voting for me). But when we are *arguing* with one another, then my manners, my motives, my hypocrisy, and my arrogance are all irrelevant: my argument must stand or fall on its own merits.

A second fallacy to avoid is the *strawman fallacy*: the fallacy of distorting or exaggering or misrepresenting your opponent's position in order to make it easier to attack. It is after all, much easier to attack a strawman than a real man. Like the ad hominem fallacy, it is depressingly common in debates about important ethical issues. Pro-choice advocates sometimes attack their opponents as people who favor the murder of infants and small children. *Perhaps* there is some pro-choice person somewhere who actually favors such a view, but it is certainly not the view of most pro-choice advocates, who believe that a woman should have the right to control her own body and thus the right to abort a fetus growing inside her; but such a right obviously would not extend to murdering a child that is outside the womb. Pro-choice advocates sometimes accuse their pro-life opponents of not only wanting to ban abortions but also pushing for a ban on all artificial means of birth control. *Some* opponents of abortion do take that view (the Pope, for example); but it is certainly not the position of most pro-life people. That extreme position is much easier to attack, and representing the pro-life movement as a movement to ban artificial birth control is a strawman fallacy. Again, those who favor capital punishment sometimes represent the abolitionist view as a compaign to do away with the justice system altogether. But most who oppose capital punishment do want laws enforced, and they do not favor eliminating prisons or even life imprisonment. From the other side, those who favor abolition of capital punishment sometimes represent their opponents as wanting to execute small children for committing crimes. Though some supporters of capital punishment may favor the execution of children, that is obviously not the position of most. In both cases the more extreme strawman target is easier to hit, but hitting it won't score any points or change any minds.

Flailing away with strawman and ad hominem fallacies is not likely to convince anyone. It can, of course, inflame the sentiments of those already holding your position. Perhaps that is why ad hominem and strawman fallacies are so common on talk radio shows. But such fallacious attacks and distortions only make the opposing sides more intransigent, and make it increasingly difficult to carry on an intelligent argument.

If you sincerely want to communicate with someone who holds an opposing view, and perhaps even convince that person to change her view, then you are more likely to succeed if you adopt the *principle of charity.* Try to represent your opponent's position in the strongest possible form, and honestly consider your opponent's strongest arguments. That way your opponent is more likely to consider what you say, since you will be addressing the views she actually favors, rather than a strawman distortion she can quickly dismiss.

Another common form of argument is the *slippery slope argument.* This argument claims that the step you are taking, or the policy you are considering adopting, is not in itself such a bad thing; but that this first step will inevitably lead to further steps down a *slippery slope* to arrive at a disasterous end. Such arguments are prominent in discussions of euthanasia: It may seem like a good idea to allow physician-assisted suicice of competent consenting adults suffering from painful terminal illnesses, but it will inevitably lead to the killing of persons who are judged by others to be better off dead and who have not chosen to die (or in more extreme versions, it will lead to Nazi genocide). Slippery slope arguments are common, and they can be legitimate and effective. Unfortunately, they are often difficult to evaluate: After all, it's difficult to predict the future.

How do we evaluate slippery slope arguments? Cautiously. Obviously there are some dangerous slippery slopes, and we would be wise not to step onto them. A few cigarettes probably won't do any harm, and won't significantly increase your risk of cancer or emphysema; but the problem is, a few cigarettes are enough to get accustomed to inhaling smoke, and that smoke contains the very highly addictive drug nicotine, and once you develop nicotine addiction it is very difficult to stop smoking, and the effects of long-term smoking—greatly increased risk of many forms of cancer, heart disease, emphysema—are very severe. That seems to me a legitimate slippery slope argument, a slippery slope argument that offers a worthwhile and plausible warning. On the other hand, consider this argument from James Watt, the Secretary of the Interior under Ronald Reagan: "[The environmentalists'] real thrust is not clean air, or clean water, or parks or wildlife but the form of government under which America will live. Look what happened to Germany in the 1930s. The dignity of man was subordinated to the powers of Nazism. The dignity of man was subordinated in Russia. Those are the forces that this thing can evolve into." Obviously if our concern for cleaner air evolved into Nazism, that would be a disaster; but there is not the slightest reason to suppose that Nazism is a likely result of efforts to reduce air and water pollution. To avoid the slippery slope fallacy, you must do more than merely speculate about some distant disaster. Legitimate slippery slope arguments must do more than point to some eventual catastrophe, and more than merely list a few steps that might lead to such a catastrophe. Legitimate slippery slope arguments must give good, valid reasons that such steps and such an outcome are the likely result of the policy under consideration. A slippery slope argument does not have to conclusively prove that the catastrophic outcome would inevitably follow. No slippery slope argument could meet that standard. Slippery slope arguments can give valuable warnings, but the warnings given should have some plausible grounds.

If you wish to thoughtfully examine controversial issues, it is important to play fair and avoid fallacious arguments. Second, whenever you are dealing with arguments, it is essential to determine as carefully and precisely as possible exactly what is at issue: What exactly is the *conclusion* of the argument in question. Obviously you cannot evaluate an argument successfully if you aren't sure what the argument is supposed to prove. Suppose that Joe is on trial for murder, and the district attorney argues that the murder Joe is accused of committing was the most brutal, and vicious crime she has seen in twenty years as as a district attorney. The arguments the district attorney gives may be very effective in proving that the crime was vicious. The question at issue, however, is whether Joe committed the crime. The district attorney's argument does nothing to establish the conclusion that Joe is guilty. But suppose that we have a different situation: Joe has been found guilty of the murder on the basis of solid evidence, and now we are in the separate sentencing phase of the trial: The jury must decide whether this crime was so bad that it deserves the death penalty. At this point the district attorney's arguments about the horrible nature of the crime will be relevant. The moral of the story is simple but essential: When evaluating an argument, *start* by determining exactly what the conclusion is. Not only will that help you distinguish relevant from irrelevant reasons, it will also avoid lengthy and useless disputes in which the arguers are simply arguing past one another.

When the conclusion is clear, then it is much easier to detect and avoid another common fallacy: the famous *red herring* (or *irrelevant reason*) *fallacy*. The red herring fallacy occurs when someone uses a point that is *irrelevant* to the question at issue to distract from the real question. In the example above, the district attorney emphasizes how vicious the crime was, but the *question* is whether Joe committed the crime. The district attorney is dragging a red herring across the trail of the argument. If the jurors are not careful to stay on the trail of the actual conclusion, they may easily be led to the conclusion that the crime *was* vicious and convict Joe on the basis of that irrelevant reason. Red herring arguments are a common ploy, and all too often they are successful. If we are arguing about whether homosexuals should have the same rights as heterosexuals (to serve in the military, or have sexual relations, or marry), then someone is likely to bring up the problem of child sexual abuse as grounds for denying homosexual rights. Child sexual abuse is a terrible thing and may leave lasting psychological scars on its victims. But it has nothing to do with the issue. Child abuse is terrible, whether committed by homosexuals or heterosexuals or bisexuals; but horrible as it is, it is completely irrelevant to the question of whether consenting adult homosexuals should have the same rights as consenting adult heterosexuals. If you keep your eye on the conclusion, on the actual question at issue, then such red herring distractions are less likely to lead you astray.

The topics debated in this volume are profoundly controversial, and the debates can be long and intense. Avoiding fallacious arguments and being fair to opposing views and arguments is an essential step in considering the issues effectively. But even when we are scrupulously fair, deep disagreements may remain. One reason the disputes are so difficult to resolve is because disputants may be approaching the issues from very different ethical perspectives. When you are deciding *exactly* what is at issue in each debate, it is essential to take into consideration some basic differences among ethical theories.

When you approach an ethical issue —for example, the issue of physician-assisted suicide, or euthanasia—what basic perspective do you bring to that issue? Suppose you are a physician. Your competent adult patient is suffering from a debilitating fatal disease, and he asks you—thoughtfully, freely, and deliberately—to assist him in ending his life more swiftly and with less suffering. He asks you to provide a lethal combination of drugs that will bring a swift and painless death. Should you grant or refuse his request? Of course in most places in the United States it would be illegal for you to grant your patient's request, and doing so might cost you your medical license, and might result in a felony conviction, but leave the legality question aside for a moment and imagine this is your free choice to make. Should you grant your patient's request, or would it be wrong? Think—*how* would you decide?

As you thought about your answer to that question, did you think in terms of *rights* and *principles*, or did you think in terms of *consequences*? These are two very different ways of thinking about the same problem. Perhaps you thought this way: My patient is a competent adult, and competent adults have the basic right to make their own decisions about their lives, and so this patient has a right to end his life if that is his free choice. Or perhaps you thought along different but still similar lines: It is always wrong to purposefully cause the death of a human being, and so I must not grant this patient's request. The most famous champion of this ethical thinking about rights and principles was Immanuel Kant, and this view is commonly called *Kantian*.

In sharp contrast to the Kantain approach to ethics, perhaps your thinking was *consequentialist*. In that case, you were considering the *consequences* of results of this act. You might have thought: This person is suffering, and a lethal drug would end his suffering and would not have any bad consequences, so obviously I ought to meet his request. Or on the other hand, perhaps you thought: Giving this person such a drug might look like a good idea, but a policy of allowing doctors to assist people in ending their lives might lead to abuses and to decreased patient trust in their doctors, so the long-term consequences outweigh the benefit to this particular patient, and so I should refuse his request. Either way, you based your decision on the *consequences* of your act: If the overall consequences are good, then the act is right.

From the Kantian perspective, consequences carry much less weight: If this patient has a basic right to choose a swifter death, then that right must be honored even if it does not produce the best overall consequences. (If I have a *right* to smoke, then it is wrong to prevent me from smoking even though such prevention would produce much better results and might even save my life.) One prominent version of consequentialism is *utilitarian* ethics. There are many varieties of utilitarian ethics, but the basic idea is this: The right act is the act that produces the greatest balance of pleasure over pain for everyone involved. Since most consequentialists are utilitarians, the two terms have come to be used almost interchangeably. However, they are not quite the same: For example, someone who believes that what makes an act right is determined by the consequences for the ruling class and the nobility (*not* the consequences for *everyone*) would be a consequentialist, but not a utilitarian.

A utilitarian is neither self-centered nor short-sighted. The utilitarian believes that the right act is the act that produces the greatest overall benefit for everyone. The benefits for myself count, but they do not count for any more than the benefits to anyone else. And the long-term benefits and harms are just as important as the short-term: The pleasures of a night of heavy drinking must be weighed against the pains of a hangover, the distant damage to my liver, and the hazards my behavior poses for myself and others.

If you are trying to decide whether your own views are more Kantain or consequentialist, ask yourself this: Can you think of a case in which the overall and long-term *consequences* of an act would definitely be good and desirable, but the act is still *wrong* or *unfair*? If so, then you are probably closer to the Kantian perspective than the consequentialist.

A third approach to ethical questions is the *contractarian*. In this view, the acts that are right—and the rights that people hold—are set by a social *contract* that we accept. It is wrong to steal: Not because there is some rational or God-given principle against stealing, and not because stealing has bad long-term consequences, but because we agree that in our community stealing is something we do not want to allow. I might quite like to steal from you; the problem is, I wouldn't like it at all if you stole from me. And the only way I can get you to agree not to steal my property is to also agree that I will not steal yours. Of course, we didn't literally sit down and draw up all the rules of our social contract; rather, contractarians think in terms of what rules it would be reasonable for all of us to adopt, what rules we—as reasonable self-interested people—would accept as mutually beneficial. A rule against stealing meets that requirement; and so, from the contractarian perspective, stealing is wrong.

The Kantian, utilitarian, and contractarian all focus on what act or policy is *right*. For all those views, the basic question of ethics is: What should I do? What act is right? The *virtue* theory approach to ethics asks a different sort of question: What sort of *person* do I want to be, and what policies and practices produce virtuous persons? Suppose you have promised to tutor me for tomorrow's math exam, but you have an opportunity to do something that is more fun. The Kantian will ask what act is *right*, or what is *fair* in this case. The utilitarian calculates which act will produce the greatest balance of overall benefits for everyone. The contractarian examines what system of rules we have agreed to follow. But the virtue theorist asks: Do I want to be the sort of person who breaks a promise to a friend? From the virtue ethics perspective, deciding to break a promise is not just an isolated ethical choice. Instead, what we do shapes the person we become. If I practice dishonesty, then I become a dishonest person. If I practice generosity, then I become a generous person. If I am act in a miserly and greedy manner, but tell myself that deep down I am really a generous person, then I have simply added self-deception to my self-ishness.

When thinking about the patient who requested a lethal drug, some people will want more information. From a Kantian or utilitarian perspective, such details may seem irrelevant: No matter who this patient is, if he is a competent adult then he has the right to make his own decision. Or alternatively, no matter who this person is, it is always wrong to purposefully cause the person's death. From the utilitarian view, no matter who this person is, his suffering counts the same as anyone else's. From a completely different perspective, however—*care ethics*—who the person is may be very important. In this way of thinking I have special obligations to my friends and family and loved ones that are different and distinct from the obligations I have to others. That is not to deny that I have obligations to strangers: For example, the physician has an obligation not to kill the patient against his will, even if the patient is a perfect stranger. But—from a care ethics perspective—the physician may have a special obligation to honor the request of a special friend, an obligation that would not extend to a stranger. From the care ethics perspective, ethical theories that treat all questions as impersonal calculations of rights or contracts or consequences neglect a basic and vital element of our ethical lives.

Thinking about the varying approaches to ethics may help you avoid confusions, and may help you to think more carefully about the controversial ethical questions in the pages that follow. But the ethical theory you favor may not dictate the conclusion you will draw on a specific issue. A contractarian and a Kantian may agree on the question of affirmative action, while two utilitarians may find themselves deeply divided.

Though philosophers often favor a single approach to ethics, and strongly oppose all competing views, most people are not so steadfast. You may find yourself adopting a virtue ethics perspective for some questions, while a Kantian approach seems to work better for others, and perhaps some combination of Kantian and utilitarian seems appropriate in still another context. Whether such an eclectic approach is legitimate, or instead lands you in contradictions and confusions, is itself a controverisal issue. In any case, it is important to be aware of the distinctly different approaches that people take toward ethical issues so that a dispute between a utilitarian and a Kantian does not become hopelessly muddled.

As you examine the divisive ethical issues in the following pages, the task may seem daunting. The topics debated are the subject of deep differences, and the debates have often raged for many years—in some cases, many centuries. And not only are the specific issues controversial, but even the basic approaches to the issues—such as utilitarian, Kantian, and contractarian—are also in dispute. In addition, there are many fallacious arguments lurking to mislead you. Still, if you keep your wits and keep your passion under control, you will find it interesting to explore these issues carefully and systematically. You may discover better arguments for the positions you favor. You may discover that positions you oppose are not quite as ridiculous as you once thought. Who knows? You might even change your mind.

1 CAMPUS SPEECH CODES

Protection Against Intolerance *or* Destruction of Free Speech?

PROTECTION AGAINST INTOLERANCE

ADVOCATE: Andrew Altman, Professor of Philosophy, Georgia State
   University

SOURCE: "Liberalism and Campus Hate Speech: A Philosophical
   Examination," *Ethics,* volume 103 (January 1993)

DESTRUCTION OF FREE SPEECH

ADVOCATE: Jonathan Rauch, writer for *The Economist,* author of *The Kindly
   Inquisitors: The New Attacks on Free Thought* (Chicago: University of
   Chicago Press)

SOURCE: "In Defense of Prejudice: Why Incendiary Speech Must Be
   Protected," *Harper's Magazine,* May 1995

The issue of hate speech brings into conflict two basic values for university communities: on the one hand the value of unfettered free speech; on the other, the value of tolerance, nondiscrimination, and inclusiveness of diverse groups. The second value, obviously, is more recent: Not long ago campuses were almost exclusively the privileged preserve of affluent white males. Perhaps the belated recognition of the value of university diversity has made campus communities more sensitive to its importance—both as a value in itself, and as a factor in enriching education, and exploration and creativity.

Most of us value the civil right of free speech as well as the civil rights of oppressed minorities. During the battle for their civil rights, African-Americans found the First Amendment protection of free speech provided a vital protection of their right to demonstrate and protest. In those circumstances, the values of free speech and civil rights for all and an end to discrimination were a powerful and united force. But what happens when free speech is turned against the values of diversity, tolerance, and inclusiveness, and is used to tear down those values? What happens when hateful racist epithets are hurled at minority groups on college campuses? This problem is severe, since we usually regard free speech as almost absolute, otherwise it is not really free: Freedom to say only what is approved is not freedom at all.

It is not surprising that old allies have split over this issue, and advocates of free speech sometimes find themselves aligned with groups they detest. Long-time champions of civil rights rise to defend the venomous and hate-filled free speech of intolerant hate groups: Anthony P. Griffin was dismissed from his position as general counsel of the Texas NAACP after he argued a free speech case on behalf of Ku Klux Klan members.

On college campuses the tension is severe. Respect for free speech, open inquiry, tolerance for unpopular ideas, and unfettered argument are essential for serious inquiry. On the other hand, rich campus diversity, with people from varied backgrounds and a variety of experiences presenting new perspectives and challenging entrenched ideas is also of great value. Intolerant hate speech is an attack on that diversity. Vartan Gregorian, President of Brown University from 1989–1997, expressed his belief that the two goals can be reconciled: "Intellectual independence and social responsibility are not mutually exclusive. Our universities have been, are and must remain open intellectual communities. They also have an obligation to protect the safety and dignity of our students and their right to learn without intimidation or fear." A number of universities have drafted campus speech codes that place some restrictions on speech—particularly hate speech—in the interest of promoting a comfortable and welcoming atmosphere for campus diversity. Should all colleges and universities adopt such restrictions on speech?

POINTS TO PONDER

➤ Does your school have a speech code? Has it generated controversy? Has it undergone revision?

➤ Andrew Altman is an advocate of free speech, but he favors making a narrow exception of speech that should not be tolerated on campus. How does he define that exception?

➤ In Altman's policy, the same word or words might be permitted in one context, but banned in another context. How is that difference specified? Is the difference sufficiently clear that it could be used in drawing up a campus speech code?

➤ Altman intends his hate speech policy to apply to racist, sexist, and homophobic slurs, but does not believe it should be extended to prohibit "speech that demeans on the basis of physical appearance," because such verbal attacks "are not used to treat people as moral subordinates." Assume for a moment that you accept Altman's basic hate speech policy and his justification for it; do you think it should also be extended to include the physical appearance speech that Altman excludes?

➤ Jonathan Rauch states that he is certainly not in favor of prejudice, but that he *is* in favor of intellectual pluralism, and that "permits the expression of various forms of bigotry and always will." Altman would also permit "the expression of various forms of bigotry," but would not allow other kinds of expression. Would Rauch be satisfied with the range of free expression that Altman allows, or would he find even Altman's narrow restriction of bigoted speech-acts unacceptable?

➤ Rauch states that "the modern anti-racist and anti-sexist and anti-homophobic campaigners are totalists, demanding not that misguided ideas and ugly expressions be corrected or criticized but that they be eradicated." Does that characterization fit Altman?

Campus Speech Codes:
Protection Against Intolerance

ANDREW ALTMAN

INTRODUCTION

In recent years a vigorous public debate has developed over freedom of speech within the academic community. The immediate stimulus for the debate has been the enactment by a number of colleges and universities of rules against hate speech. While some have defended these rules as essential for protecting the equal dignity of all members of the academic community, others have condemned them as intolerable efforts to impose ideological conformity on the academy.

Liberals can be found on both sides of this debate. Many see campus hate-speech regulation as a form of illegitimate control by the community over individual liberty of expression. They argue that hate-speech rules violate the important liberal principle that any regulation of speech be viewpoint-neutral. But other liberals see hate-speech regulation as a justifiable part of the effort to help rid society of discrimination and subordination based on such characteristics as race, religion, ethnicity, gender, and sexual preference.

In this article, I develop a liberal argument in favor of certain narrowly drawn rules prohibiting hate speech. The argument steers a middle course between those who reject all forms of campus hate-speech regulation and those who favor relatively sweeping forms of regulation. Like those who reject all regulation, I argue that rules against hate speech are not viewpoint-neutral. Like those who favor sweeping regulation, I accept the claim that hate speech can cause serious psychological harm

to those at whom it is directed. However, I do not believe that such harm can justify regulation, sweeping or otherwise. Instead, I argue that some forms of hate speech inflict on their victims a certain kind of wrong, and it is on the basis of this wrong that regulation can be justified. The kind of wrong in question is one that is inflicted in virtue of the performance of a certain kind of speech-act characteristic of some forms of hate speech, and I argue that rules targeting this speech-act wrong will be relatively narrow in scope.

HATE SPEECH, HARASSMENT, AND NEUTRALITY

Hate-speech regulations typically provide for disciplinary action against students for making racist, sexist, or homophobic utterances or for engaging in behavior that expresses the same kinds of discriminatory attitudes. The stimulus for the regulations has been an apparent upsurge in racist, sexist, and homophobic incidents on college campuses over the past decade. The regulations that have actually been proposed or enacted vary widely in the scope of what they prohibit.

The rules at Stanford University are narrow in scope. They require that speech meet three conditions before it falls into the proscribed zone: the speaker must intend to insult or stigmatize another on the basis of certain characteristics such as race, gender, or sexual orientation; the speech must be addressed directly to those whom it is intended to stigmatize; and the speech must employ epithets or terms that similarly convey "visceral hate or contempt" for the people at whom it is directed.

On the other hand, the rules of the University of Connecticut, in their original form, were relatively sweeping in scope. According to these rules, "Every member of the University is obligated to refrain from actions that intimidate, humiliate or demean persons or groups or that undermine their security or self-esteem." Explicitly mentioned as examples of proscribed speech were "making inconsiderate jokes... stereotyping the experiences, background, and skills of individuals,... imitating stereotypes in speech or mannerisms [and] attributing objections to any of the above actions to 'hypersensitivity' of the targeted individual or group."

Even the narrower forms of hate-speech regulation, such as we find at Stanford, must be distinguished from a simple prohibition of verbal harassment. As commonly understood, harassment involves a pattern of conduct that is intended to annoy a person so much as to disrupt substantially her activities. No one questions the authority of universities to enact regulations that prohibit such conduct, whether the conduct be verbal or not. There are three principal differences between hate-speech rules and rules against harassment. First, hate-speech rules do not require a pattern of conduct: a single incident is sufficient to incur liability. Second, hate-speech rules describe the offending conduct in ways that refer to the moral and political viewpoint it expresses. The conduct is not simply annoying or disturbing; it is racist, sexist, or homophobic.

The third difference is tied closely to the second and is the most important one: rules against hate speech are not viewpoint-neutral. Such rules rest on the view that racism, sexism, and homophobia are morally wrong. The liberal principle of viewpoint-neutrality holds that those in

authority should not be permitted to limit speech on the ground that it expresses a viewpoint that is wrong, evil, or otherwise deficient. Yet, hate-speech rules rest on precisely such a basis. Rules against harassment, on the other hand, are not viewpoint-based. Anyone in our society could accept the prohibition of harassment because it would not violate their normative political or moral beliefs to do so. The same cannot be said for hate-speech rules because they embody a view of race, gender, and homosexuality contrary to the normative viewpoints held by some people.

If I am correct in claiming that hate-speech regulations are not viewpoint-neutral, this will raise a strong prima facie case against them from a liberal perspective. Contrary to my claim, however, Thomas Grey, author of Stanford's hate-speech policy, argues that his regulations are viewpoint-neutral. He claims that the policy "preserves practical neutrality—that is, it does not differentially deprive any significant element in American political life of its rhetorical capital.... The Right has no special stake in the free face-to-face use of epithets that perform no other function except to portray whole classes of Americans as subhuman and unworthy of full citizenship."

I cannot agree with Grey's contentions on this score. The implicit identification of groups such as the neo-Nazis and the KKK as insignificant presupposes a value judgment that is not viewpoint-neutral, namely, that the views of such groups have no significant merit. If Grey claims that he is simply making the factual judgment that the influence of these groups on the political process is nil, it is not clear why that is relevant (even assuming its truth—which is debatable). Certainly, such groups aim to become significant influences on the process, and their use of language that would violate Stanford's rules is a significant part of their rhetoric. In fact, I will argue later that the use of such language is tied in an especially close way to their substantive moral and political views.

Grey might be suggesting that our public political discourse does not tolerate the sorts of slurs and epithets his rules proscribe: public debate proceeds with an unwritten prohibition on that kind of language. Such a suggestion is certainly correct, as can be seen by the fact that racists who enter the public arena must rely on "code words" to get their message across. But from the racists' point of view, this is just further evidence of how our public political discourse has been captured by "liberals" and is biased against their view.

Viewpoint-neutrality is not simply a matter of the effects of speech regulation on the liberty of various groups to express their views in the language they prefer. It is also concerned with the kinds of justification that must be offered for speech regulation. The fact is that any plausible justification of hate-speech regulation hinges on the premise that racism, sexism, and homophobia are wrong. Without that premise there would be no basis for arguing that the viewpoint-neutral proscription of verbal harassment is insufficient to protect the rights of minorities and women. The liberal who favors hate-speech regulations, no matter how narrowly drawn, must therefore be prepared to carve out an exception to the principle of viewpoint-neutrality.

THE HARMS OF HATE SPEECH

Many of the proponents of campus hate-speech regulation defend their position by arguing that hate speech causes serious harm to those who are the targets of such speech. Among the most basic of these harms are psychological ones. Even when it involves no direct threat of violence, hate speech can cause abiding feelings of fear, anxiety, and insecurity in those at whom it is targeted. As Mari Matsuda has argued, this is in part because many forms of such speech tacitly draw on a history of violence against certain groups.[1] The symbols and language of hate speech call up historical memories of violent persecution and may encourage fears of current violence. Moreover, hate speech can cause a variety of other harms, from feelings of isolation, to a loss of self-confidence, to physical problems associated with serious psychological disturbance.[2]

The question is whether or not the potential for inflicting these harms is sufficient ground for some sort of hate-speech regulation. As powerful as these appeals to the harms of hate speech are, there is a fundamental sticking point in accepting them as justification for regulation, from a liberal point of view. The basic problem is that the proposed justification sweeps too broadly for a liberal to countenance it. Forms of racist, sexist, or homophobic speech that the liberal is committed to protecting may cause precisely the kinds of harm that the proposed justification invokes.

The liberal will not accept the regulation of racist, sexist, or homophobic speech couched in a scientific, religious, philosophical, or political mode of discourse. The regulation of such speech would not merely carve out a minor exception to the principle of viewpoint-neutrality but would, rather, eviscerate it in a way unacceptable to any liberal. Yet, those forms of hate speech can surely cause in minorities the harms that are invoked to justify regulation: insecurity, anxiety, isolation, loss of self-confidence, and so on. Thus, the liberal must invoke something beyond these kinds of harm in order to justify any hate-speech regulation.

Liberals who favor regulation typically add to their argument the contention that the value to society of the hate speech they would proscribe is virtually nil, while scientific, religious, philosophical, and political forms of hate speech have at least some significant value. Thus, Mary Ellen Gale says that the forms she would prohibit "neither advance knowledge, seek truth, expose government abuses, initiate dialogue, encourage participation, further tolerance of divergent views, nor enhance the victim's individual dignity or self respect."[3] As an example of such worthless hate speech Gale cites an incident of white students writing a message on the mirror in the dorm room of blacks: "African monkeys, why don't you go back to the jungle." But she would protect a great deal of racist or sexist speech, such as a meeting of neo-Nazi students at which swastikas are publicly displayed and speeches made that condemn the presence of Jews and blacks on campus.

Although Gale ends up defending relatively narrow regulations, I believe liberals should be very hesitant to accept her argument for distinguishing regulable from nonregulable hate speech. One problem is that she omits from her list of the values that valuable speech serves one which liberals have long considered important, especially for speech that upsets and disturbs others. Such speech, it is argued, enables the speaker to "blow off steam" in a relatively nondestructive and nonviolent way. Calling particular blacks "African monkeys" might serve as a psychological substitute for harming them in a much more serious way, for example, by lynchings or beatings.

Gale could respond that slurring blacks might just as well serve as an encouragement and prelude to the more serious harms. But the same can be said of forms of hate speech that Gale would protect from regulation, for example, the speech at the neo-Nazi student meeting. Moreover, liberals should argue that it is the job of legal rules against assault, battery, conspiracy, rape, and so on to protect people from violence. It is, at best, highly speculative that hate speech on campus contributes to violence against minorities or women. And while the claim about blowing off steam is also a highly speculative one, the liberal tradition clearly puts a substantial burden of proof on those who would silence speech.

There is a more basic problem with any effort to draw the line between regulable and nonregulable hate speech by appealing to the value of speech. Such appeals invariably involve substantial departures from the principle of viewpoint-neutrality. There is no way to make differential judgments about the value of different types of hate speech without taking one or another moral and political viewpoint. Gale's criteria clearly illustrate this as they are heavily tilted against the values of racists and sexists, and yet she does not adequately address the question of how a liberal position can accommodate such substantial departures from viewpoint-neutrality.

Gale contends that existing legal rules and regulations against sexual and racial harassment in the workplace should serve as the model in terms of which campus hate-speech regulations can be justified. Those rules are based on an interpretation of Title VII of the Civil Rights Act of 1964, outlawing discrimination in the terms and conditions of employment, and they prohibit a hostile or offensive work environment. But there are three problems with appealing to these harassment rules. First, almost all legal cases involving claims of a hostile work environment have required more than simply hostile verbal conduct for a finding of a violation. Second, it is doubtful that the context of a student at a university is sufficiently similar to that of a worker in the workplace to assume that the exact same rules should apply for both settings. Freedom of expression is far more vital to the role of the university than it is to that of the typical workplace, and so it is reasonable to think that university rules should be less restrictive of expression. Third, even if the university context is sufficiently similar to that of the typical workplace, Gale's invocation of the existing rules covering workplace harassment begs the crucial question of whether the current interpretation of Title VII itself involves an unjustifiably sweeping departure from viewpoint-neutrality.

I do not assume that the principle of viewpoint-neutrality is an absolute or ultimate one within the liberal framework. Liberals do defend some types of speech regulation that seem to rely on viewpoint-based claims. For example, they would not reject copyright laws, even if it could be shown—as seems plausible—that those laws are biased against the views of people who regard private property as theft. Moreover, the viewpoint-neutrality principle itself rests on deeper liberal concerns which it is thought to serve, Ideally, a liberal argument for the regulation of hate speech would show that regulations can be developed that accommodate these deeper concerns and that simultaneously serve important liberal values, I believe that there is such a liberal argument. In order to show this, however, it is necessary to examine a kind of wrong committed by hate speakers that is quite different from the harmful psychological effects of their speech.

SUBORDINATION AND SPEECH ACTS

Some proponents of regulation claim that there is an especially close connection between hate speech and the subordination of minorities. Thus, Charles Lawrence contends, "all racist speech constructs the social reality that constrains the liberty of non-whites because of their race."[4] Along the same lines, Mari Matsuda claims, "racist speech is particularly harmful because it is a mechanism of subordination."[5]

The position of Lawrence and Matsuda can be clarified and elaborated using J. L. Austin's distinction between perlocutionary effects and illocutionary force.[6] The perlocutionary effects of an utterance consist of its causal effects on the hearer: infuriating her, persuading her, frightening her, and so on. The illocutionary force of an utterance consists of the kind of speech act one is performing in making the utterance: advising, warning, stating, claiming, arguing, and so on. Lawrence and Matsuda are not simply suggesting that the direct perlocutionary effects of racist speech constitute harm. Nor are they simply suggesting that hate speech can persuade listeners to accept beliefs that then motivate them to commit acts of harm against racial minorities. That again is a matter of the perlocutionary effects of hate speech. Rather, I believe that they are suggesting that hate speech can inflict a wrong in virtue of its illocutionary acts, the very speech acts performed in the utterances of such speech.[7]

What exactly does this speech-act wrong amount to? My suggestion is that it is the wrong of treating a person as having inferior moral standing. In other words, hate speech involves the performance of a certain kind of illocutionary act, namely, the act of treating someone as a moral subordinate.

Treating persons as moral subordinates means treating them in a way that takes their interests to be intrinsically less important, and their lives inherently less valuable, than the interests and lives of those who belong to some reference group. There are many ways of treating people as moral subordinates that are natural as opposed to conventional: the status of these acts as acts of subordination depend solely on universal principles of morality and not on the conventions of a given society. Slavery and genocide, for example, treat people as having inferior moral standing simply in virtue of the affront of such practices to universal moral principles.

Other ways of treating people as moral subordinates have both natural and conventional elements. The practice of racial segregation is an example. It is subordinating because the conditions imposed on blacks by such treatment violate moral principles but also because the act of separation is a convention for putting the minority group in its (supposedly) proper, subordinate place.

I believe that the language of racist, sexist, and homophobic slurs and epithets provides wholly conventional ways of treating people as moral subordinates. Terms such as 'kike', 'faggot', 'spic', and 'nigger' are verbal instruments of subordination. They are used not only to express hatred or contempt for people but also to "put them in their place," that is, to treat them as having inferior moral standing.

It is commonly recognized that through language we can "put people down," to use the vernacular expression. There are many different modes of putting people down: putting them down as less intelligent or less clever or less articulate or less skillful. Putting people down in these ways is not identical to treating them as moral subordinates, and the ordinary put-down does not involve regarding someone as having inferior moral standing. The put-downs that are accomplished with the slurs and epithets of hate speech are different from the ordinary verbal put-down in that respect, even though both sorts of put-down are done through language.

I have contended that the primary verbal instruments for treating people as moral subordinates are the slurs and epi-

thets of hate speech. In order to see this more clearly, consider the difference between derisively calling someone a "faggot" and saying to that person, with equal derision, "You are contemptible for being homosexual." Both utterances can treat the homosexual as a moral subordinate, but the former accomplishes it much more powerfully than the latter. This is, I believe, because the conventional rules of language make the epithet 'faggot' a term whose principal purpose is precisely to treat homosexuals as having inferior moral standing.

I do not believe that a clean and neat line can be drawn around those forms of hate speech that treat their targets as moral subordinates. Slurs and epithets are certainly used that way often, but not always, as is evidenced by the fact that sometimes victimized groups seize on the slurs that historically have subordinated them and seek to "transvalue" the terms. For example, homosexuals have done this with the term 'queer', seeking to turn it into a term of pride rather than one of subordination.

Hate speech in modes such as the scientific or philosophical typically would not involve illocutionary acts of moral subordination. This is because speech in those modes usually involves essentially different kinds of speech acts: describing, asserting, stating, arguing, and so forth. To assert or argue that blacks are genetically inferior to whites is not to perform a speech act that itself consists of treating blacks as inferior. Yet, language is often ambiguous and used for multiple purposes, and I would not rule out a priori that in certain contexts even scientific or philosophical hate speech is used in part to subordinate.

The absence of a neat and clean line around those forms of hate speech that subordinate through speech acts does not entail that it is futile to attempt to formulate regulations that target such hate speech. Rules and regulations rarely have an exact fit with what they aim to prevent: over- and underinclusiveness are pervasive in any system of rules that seeks to regulate conduct. The problem is to develop rules that have a reasonably good fit. Later I argue that there are hate-speech regulations that target subordinating hate speech reasonably well. But first I must argue that such speech commits a wrong that may be legitimately targeted by regulation.

SPEECH-ACT WRONG

I have argued that some forms of hate speech treat their targets as moral subordinates on account of race, gender, or sexual preference. Such treatment runs counter to the central liberal idea of persons as free and equal. To that extent, it constitutes a wrong, a speech-act wrong inflicted on those whom it addresses. However, it does not follow that it is a wrong that may be legitimately targeted by regulation. A liberal republic is not a republic of virtue in which the authorities prohibit every conceivable wrong. The liberal republic protects a substantial zone of liberty around the individual in which she is free from authoritative intrusion even to do some things that are wrong.

Yet, the wrongs of subordination based on such characteristics as race, gender, and sexual preference are not just any old wrongs. Historically, they are among the principal wrongs that have prevented—and continue to prevent—Western liberal democracies from living up to their ideals and principles. As such, these wrongs are especially appropriate targets of regulation in our liberal republic. Liberals recognize the special importance of combating such wrongs in their strong support for laws prohibiting discrimination in employment, housing, and public accommodations. And even if the regulation of

speech-act subordination on campus is not regarded as mandatory for universities, it does seem that the choice of an institution to regulate that type of subordination on campus is at least justifiable within a liberal framework.

In opposition, it may be argued that subordination is a serious wrong that should be targeted but that the line should be drawn when it comes to subordination through speech. There, viewpoint-neutrality must govern. But I believe that the principle of viewpoint-neutrality must be understood as resting on deeper liberal concerns. Other things being equal, a departure from viewpoint-neutrality will be justified if it can accommodate these deeper concerns while at the same time serving the liberal principle of the equality of persons.

The concerns fall into three basic categories. First is the Millian idea that speech can promote individual development and contribute to the public political dialogue, even when it is wrong, misguided, or otherwise deficient.[8] Second is the Madisonian reason that the authorities cannot be trusted with formulating and enforcing rules that silence certain views: they will be too tempted to abuse such rules in order to promote their own advantage or their own sectarian viewpoint.[9] Third is the idea that any departures from viewpoint-neutrality might serve as precedents that could be seized upon by would-be censors with antiliberal agendas to further their broad efforts to silence speech and expression.[10]

These concerns that underlie viewpoint-neutrality must be accommodated for hate-speech regulation to be justifiable from a liberal perspective. But that cannot be done in the abstract. It needs to be done in the context of a particular set of regulations. In the next section, I argue that there are regulations that target reasonably well those forms of hate speech that subordinate, and in the following section I argue that such regulations accommodate the concerns that underlie the liberal endorsement of the viewpoint-neutrality principle.

TARGETING SPEECH-ACT WRONG

If I am right in thinking that the slurs and epithets of hate speech are the principal instruments of the speech-act wrong of treating someone as a moral subordinate and that such a wrong is a legitimate target of regulation, then it will not be difficult to formulate rules that have a reasonably good fit with the wrong they legitimately seek to regulate. In general, what are needed are rules that prohibit speech that (a) employs slurs and epithets conventionally used to subordinate persons on account of their race, gender, religion, ethnicity, or sexual preference, (b) is addressed to particular persons, and (c) is expressed with the intention of degrading such persons on account of their race, gender, religion, ethnicity, or sexual preference. With some modification, this is essentially what one finds in the regulations drafted by Grey for Stanford.

Restricting the prohibition to slurs and epithets addressed to specific persons will capture many speech-act wrongs of subordination. But it will not capture them all. Slurs and epithets are not necessary for such speech acts, as I conceded earlier. In addition, it may be possible to treat someone as a moral subordinate through a speech act, even though the utterance is not addressing that person. However, prohibiting more than slurs and epithets would run a high risk of serious over-inclusiveness, capturing much speech that performs legitimate speech acts such as stating and arguing. And prohibiting all use of slurs and epithets, whatever the context, would mandate a degree of intrusiveness into the private lives of students that would be difficult for liberals to license.

The regulations should identify examples of the kinds of terms that count as epithets or slurs conventionally used to perform speech acts of subordination. This is required in order to give people sufficient fair warning. But because the terms of natural languages are not precise, univocal, and unchanging, it is not possible to give an exhaustive list, nor is it mandatory to try. Individuals who innocently use an epithet that conventionally subordinates can plead lack of the requisite intent.

The intent requirement is needed to accommodate cases in which an epithet or slur is not used with any intent to treat the addressee as a moral subordinate. These cases cover a wide range, including the efforts of some minorities to capture and transvalue terms historically used to subordinate them. There are several different ways in which the required intent could be described: the intent to stigmatize or to demean or to insult or to degrade and so on. I think that 'degrade' does the best job of capturing the idea of treating someone as a moral subordinate in language the average person will find familiar and understandable. 'Insult' does the poorest job and should be avoided. Insulting someone typically does not involve treating the person as a moral subordinate. Rather, it involves putting someone down in other ways: as less skillful, less intelligent, less clever, and the like.

The regulations at some universities extend beyond what I have defended and prohibit speech that demeans on the basis of physical appearance. I do not believe that such regulations can be justified within the liberal framework I have developed here. Speech can certainly be used to demean people based on physical appearance. 'Slob', 'dog', 'beast', 'pig': these are some examples of terms that are used in such verbal put-downs. But I do not believe that they are used to treat people as moral subordinates, and thus the terms do not inflict the kind of speech-act wrong that justifies the regulation of racist, sexist, or homophobic slurs and epithets.

It should not be surprising that terms which demean on the basis of appearance do not morally subordinate, since the belief that full human moral standing depends on good looks is one that few people, if any, hold. The terms that put people down for their appearance are thus fundamentally different from racist, sexist, or homophobic slurs and epithets. The latter terms do reflect beliefs that are held by many about the lower moral standing of certain groups.

ACCOMMODATING LIBERAL CONCERNS

I have argued that regulations should target those forms of hate speech that inflict the speech-act wrong of subordination on their victims. This wrong is distinct from the psychological harm that hate speech causes. In targeting speech-act subordination, the aim of regulation is not to prohibit speech that has undesirable psychological effects on individuals but, rather, to prohibit speech that treats people as moral subordinates. To target speech that has undesirable psychological effects is invariably to target certain ideas, since it is through the communication of ideas that the psychological harm occurs. In contrast, targeting speech-act subordination does not target ideas. Any idea would be free from regulation as long as it was expressed through a speech act other than one which subordinates: stating, arguing, claiming) defending, and so on would all be free of regulation.

Because of these differences, regulations that target speech-act subordination can accommodate the liberal concerns underlying viewpoint-neutrality, while regulations that sweep more broadly cannot.

Consider the important Millian idea that individual development requires that people be left free to say things that are wrong and to learn from their mistakes. Under the sort of regulation I endorse, people would be perfectly free to make racist, sexist, and homophobic assertions and arguments and to learn of the deficiencies of their views from the counterassertions and counterarguments of others. And the equally important Millian point that public dialogue gains even through the expression of false ideas is accommodated in a similar way. Whatever contribution a racist viewpoint can bring to public discussion can be made under regulations that only target speech-act subordination.

The liberal fear of trusting the authorities is somewhat more worrisome. Some liberals have argued that the authorities cannot be trusted with impartial enforcement of hate-speech regulations. Nadine Strossen, for example, claims that the hate-speech regulations at the University of Michigan have been applied in a biased manner, punishing the racist and homophobic speech of blacks but not of whites.[11] Still, it is not at all clear that the biased application of rules is any more of a problem with rules that are not viewpoint-neutral than with those that are. A neutral rule against harassment can also be enforced in a racially discriminatory manner. There is no reason to think a priori that narrowly drawn hate-speech rules would be any more liable to such abuse. Of course, if it did turn out that there was a pervasive problem with the biased enforcement of hate-speech rules, any sensible liberal would advocate rescinding them. But absent a good reason for thinking that this is likely to happen—not just that it could conceivably happen—the potential for abusive enforcement is no basis for rejecting the kind of regulation I have defended.

Still remaining is the problem of precedent: even narrowly drawn regulations targeting only speech-act subordination could be cited as precedent for more sweeping, antiliberal restrictions by those at other universities or in the community at large who are not committed to liberal values. In response to this concern, it should be argued that narrowly drawn rules will not serve well as precedents for would-be censors with antiliberal agendas. Those who wish to silence socialists, for example, on the ground that socialism is as discredited as racism will find scant precedential support from regulations that allow the expression of racist opinions as long as they are not couched in slurs and epithets directed at specific individuals.

There may be some precedent-setting risk in such narrow regulations. Those who wish to censor the arts, for example, might draw an analogy between the epithets that narrow hate-speech regulations proscribe and the "trash" they would proscribe: both forms of expression are indecent, ugly, and repulsive to the average American, or so the argument might go.

Yet, would-be art censors already have precedents at their disposal providing much closer analogies in antiobscenity laws. Hate-speech regulations are not likely to give would-be censors of the arts any additional ammunition. To this, a liberal opponent of any hate-speech regulation might reply that there is no reason to take the risk. But the response will be that there is a good reason, namely, to prevent the wrong of speech-act subordination that is inflicted by certain forms of hate speech.

CONCLUSION

There is a defensible liberal middle ground between those who oppose all campus hate-speech regulation and those who favor the sweeping regulation of such speech. But the best defense of this middle ground requires the recognition that speech acts of subordination are at the heart of the hate-speech issue. Some forms of hate speech do wrong to people by treating them as moral subordinates. This is the wrong that can and should be the target of campus hate-speech regulations.

1. Mari Matsuda, "Legal Storytelling: Public Response to Racist Speech: Considering the Victim's Story," *Michigan Law Review* 87 (1989): 2329–34, 2352.
2. See Richard Delgado, "Words That Wound: A Tort Action for Racial Insults, Epithets and Name-Calling," *Harvard Civil Rights—Civil Liberties Law Review* 17 (1982): 137, 146,
3. Mary Ellen Gale, "Reimagining the First Amendment: Racist Speech and Equal Liberty," *St. John's Law Review* 65 (1991): 179–80.
4. Charles Lawrence, "If He Hollers Let Him Go: Regulating Racist Speech on Campus," *Duke Law Journal* (1990), p. 444.
5. Matsuda, p. 2357.
6. J. L. Austin, *How to Do Things with Words* (New York: Oxford University Press, 1962), pp. 98 ff. The concept of an illocutionary act has been defined and elaborated by John Searle in a series of works starting with "Austin on Locutionary and Illocutionary Acts," *Philosophical Review* 77 (1968): 420–21. Also see his *Speech Acts* (New York: Cambridge University Press, 1969), p. 31, and *Expression and Meaning* (New York: Cambridge University Press, 1979); and John Searle and D. Vanderveken, *Foundations of Illocutionary Logic* (New York: Cambridge University Press, 1985).
7. Both Lawrence and Matsuda describe racist speech as a unique form of speech in its internal relation to subordination.

See Lawrence, p. 440, n. 42; and Matsuda, p. 2356. I do not think that their view is correct. Homophobic and sexist speech, e.g., can also be subordinating. In fact, Lawrence and Matsuda are applying to racist speech essentially the same idea that several feminist writers have applied to pornography. These feminists argue that pornography does not simply depict the subordination of women; it actually subordinates them. See Melinda Vadas, "A First Look at the Pornography/Civil Rights Ordinance: Could Pornography Be the Subordination of Women?" *Journal of Philosophy* 84 (1987): 487–511.

8. See Robert Post, "Racist Speech, Democracy, and the First Amendment," *William and Mary Law Review* 32 (1991): 290–91.

9. See Frederick Schauer, "The Second-Best First Amendment," *William and Mary Law Review* 31(1989): 1–2.

10. Peter Linzer. "White Liberal Looks at Racist Speech," *St. John's Law Review* 65 (1991): 219.

11. Nadine Strossen, "Regulating Racist Speech on Campus: A Modest Proposal?" *Duke Law Journal* (1990), pp. 557–58. Eric Barendt argues that the British criminal law against racist speech "has often been used to convict militant black spokesmen" (Eric Barendt, *Freedom of Speech* [Oxford: Clarendon, 1985], p. 163).

Campus Speech Codes:
Destruction of Free Speech

JONATHAN RAUCH

The war on prejudice is now, in all likelihood, the most uncontroversial social movement in America. Opposition to "hate speech," formerly identified with the liberal left, has become a bipartisan piety. In the past year, groups and factions that agree on nothing else have agreed that the public expression of any and all prejudices must be forbidden. On the left, protesters and editorialists have insisted that Francis L. Lawrence resign as president of Rutgers University for describing blacks as "a disadvantaged population that doesn't have that genetic, hereditary background to have a higher average." On the other side of the ideological divide, Ralph Reed, the executive director of the Christian Coalition, responded to criticism of the religious right by calling a press conference to denounce a supposed outbreak of "namecalling, scapegoating, and religious bigotry." Craig Rogers, an evangelical Christian student at California State University, recently filed a $2.5 million sexual-harassment suit against a lesbian professor of psychology, claiming that anti-male bias in one of her lectures violated campus rules and left him feeling "raped and trapped."

In universities and on Capitol Hill, in workplaces and newsrooms, authorities are declaring that there is no place for racism, sexism, homophobia, Christian-bashing, and other forms of prejudice in public debate or even in private thought. "Only when racism and other forms of prejudice are expunged," say the crusaders for sweetness and light, "can minorities be safe and society be fair." So sweet, this

dream of a world without prejudice. But the very last thing society should do is seek to utterly eradicate racism and other forms of prejudice.

I suppose I should say, in the customary I-hope-I-don't-sound-too-defensive tone, that I am not a racist and that this is not an article favoring racism or any other particular prejudice. It is an article favoring intellectual pluralism, which permits the expression of various forms of bigotry and always will. Although we like to hope that a time will come when no one will believe that people come in types and that each type belongs with its own kind, I doubt such a day will ever arrive. By all indications, *Homo sapiens* is a tribal species for whom "us versus them" comes naturally and must be continually pushed back. Where there is genuine freedom of expression, there will be racist expression. There will also be people who believe that homosexuals are sick or threaten children or—especially among teenagers—are rightful targets of manly savagery. Homosexuality will always be incomprehensible to most people, and what is incomprehensible is feared. As for anti-Semitism, it appears to be a hardier virus than influenza. If you want pluralism, then you get racism and sexism and homophobia, and communism and fascism and xenophobia and tribalism, and that is just for a start. If you want to believe in intellectual freedom and the progress of knowledge and the advancement of science and all those other good things, then you must swallow hard and accept this: for as thickheaded and wayward an animal as us, the realistic question is how to make the best of prejudice, not how to eradicate it.

Indeed, "eradicating prejudice" is so vague a proposition as to be meaningless. Distinguishing prejudice reliably and non-politically from non-prejudice, or even defining it crisply, is quite hopeless. We all feel we know prejudice when we see it. But do we? At the University of Michigan, a student said in a classroom discussion that he considered homosexuality a disease treatable with therapy. He was summoned to a formal disciplinary hearing for violating the school's policy against speech that "victimizes" people based on "sexual orientation." Now, the evidence is abundant that this particular hypothesis is wrong, and any American homosexual can attest to the harm that the student's hypothesis has inflicted on many real people. But was it a statement of prejudice or of misguided belief? Hate speech or hypothesis? Many Americans who do not regard themselves as bigots or haters believe that homosexuality is a treatable disease. They may be wrong, but are they all bigots? I am unwilling to say so, and if you are willing, beware. The line between a prejudiced belief and a merely controversial one is elusive, and the harder you look the more elusive it becomes. "God hates homosexuals" is a statement of fact, not of bias, to those who believe it; "American criminals are disproportionately black" is a statement of bias, not of fact, to those who disbelieve it.

Who is right? You may decide, and so may others, and there is no need to agree. That is the great innovation of intellectual pluralism (which is to say, of post-Enlightenment science, broadly defined). We cannot know in advance or for sure which belief is prejudice and which is truth, but to advance knowledge we don't need to know. The genius of intellectual pluralism lies not in doing away with

prejudices and dogmas but in channeling them—making them socially productive by pitting prejudice against prejudice and dogma against dogma, exposing all to withering public criticism. What survives at the end of the day is our base of knowledge.

What they told us in high school about this process is very largely a lie. The Enlightenment tradition taught us that science is orderly, antiseptic, rational, the province of detached experimenters and high-minded logicians. In the popular view, science stands for reason against prejudice, open-mindedness against dogma, calm consideration against passionate attachment—all personified by pop-science icons like the magisterially deductive Sherlock Holmes, the coolly analytic Mr. Spock, the genially authoritative Mr. Science (from our junior-high science films). Yet one of science's dirty secrets is that although science as a whole is as unbiased as anything human can be, scientists are just as biased as anyone else, sometimes more so. "One of the strengths of science," writes the philosopher of science David L. Hull, "is that it does not require that scientists be unbiased, only that different scientists have different biases." Another dirty secret is that, no less than the rest of us, scientists can be dogmatic and pigheaded. "Although this pigheadedness often damages the careers of individual scientists," says Hull, "it is beneficial for the manifest goal of science," which relies on people to invest years in their ideas and defend them passionately. And the dirtiest secret of all, if you believe in the antiseptic popular view of science, is that this most ostensibly rational of enterprises depends on the most irrational of motives—ambition, narcissism, animus, even revenge. "Scientists acknowledge that among their motivations are natural curiosity, the love of truth, and the desire to help humanity, but other inducements exist as well, and one of them is to 'get that son of a bitch,'" says Hull. "Time and again, scientists whom I interviewed described the powerful spur that 'showing that son of a bitch' supplied to their own research."

Many people, I think, are bewildered by this unvarnished and all too human view of science. They believe that for a system to be unprejudiced, the people in it must also be unprejudiced. In fact, the opposite is true. Far from eradicating ugly or stupid ideas and coarse or unpleasant motives, intellectual pluralism relies upon them to excite intellectual passion and redouble scientific effort. I know of no modern idea more ugly and stupid than that the Holocaust never happened, nor any idea more viciously motivated. Yet the deniers' claims that the Auschwitz gas chambers could not have worked led to closer study and, in 1993, research showing, at last, how they actually did work. Thanks to prejudice and stupidity, another opening for doubt has been shut.

An enlightened and efficient intellectual regime lets a million prejudices bloom, including many that you or I may regard as hateful or grotesque. It avoids any attempt to stamp out prejudice, because stamping out prejudice really means forcing everyone to share the same prejudice, namely that of whoever is in authority. The great American philosopher Charles Sanders Peirce wrote in 1877: "when complete agreement could not otherwise be reached, a general massacre of all who have not thought in a certain way has proved a very effective means of settling opinion in a country." In speaking of "settling opinion," Peirce was writing about one of the two or three most fundamental problems that any human society must confront and solve. For most societies

down through the centuries, this problem was dealt with in the manner he described: errors were identified by the authorities—priests, politburos, dictators—or by mass opinion, and then the error-makers were eliminated along with their putative mistakes. "Let all men who reject the established belief be terrified into silence," wrote Peirce, describing this system. "This method has, from the earliest times, been one of the chief means of upholding correct theological and political doctrines."

Intellectual pluralism substitutes a radically different doctrine: we kill our mistakes rather than each other. Here I draw on another great philosopher, the late Karl Popper, who pointed out that the critical method of science "consists in letting our hypotheses die in our stead." Those who are in error are not (or are not supposed to be) banished or excommunicated or forced to sign a renunciation or required to submit to "rehabilitation" or sent for psychological counseling. It is the error we punish, not the errant. By letting people make errors—even mischievous, spiteful errors (as, for instance, Galileo's insistence on Copernicanism was taken to be in 1633)—pluralism creates room to challenge orthodoxy, think imaginatively, experiment boldly. Brilliance and bigotry are empowered in the same stroke.

Pluralism is the principle that protects and makes a place in human company for that loneliest and most vulnerable of all minorities, the minority who is hounded and despised among blacks and whites, gays and straights, who is suspect or criminal among every tribe and in every nation of the world, and yet on whom progress depends: the dissident. I am not saying that dissent is always or even usually enlightened. Most of the time it is foolish and self-serving. No dissident has the right to be taken seriously, and the fact that Aryan Nation racists or Nation of Islam anti-Semites are unorthodox does not entitle them to respect. But what goes around comes around. As a supporter of gay marriage, for example, I reject the majority's view of family, and as a Jew I reject its view of God. I try to be civil, but the fact is that most Americans regard my views on marriage as a reckless assault on the most fundamental of all institutions, and many people are more than a little discomfited by the statement "Jesus Christ was no more divine than anybody else" (which is why so few people ever say it). Trap the racists and anti-Semites, and you lay a trap for me too. Hunt for them with eradication in your mind, and you have brought dissent itself within your sights.

The new crusade against prejudice waves aside such warnings. Like earlier crusades against antisocial ideas, the mission is fueled by good (if cocksure) intentions and a genuine sense of urgency. Some kinds of error are held to be intolerable, like pollutants that even in small traces poison the water for a whole town. Some errors are so pernicious as to damage real people's lives, so wrongheaded that no person of right mind or goodwill could support them. Like their forebears of other stripe—the Church in its campaigns against heretics, the McCarthyites in their campaigns against Communists— the modern anti-racist and anti-sexist and anti-homophobic campaigners are totalists, demanding not that misguided ideas and ugly expressions be corrected or criticized but that they be eradicated. They make war not on errors but on error, and like other totalists they act in the name of public safety—the safety, especially, of minorities.

The sweeping implications of this challenge to pluralism are not, I think,

well enough understood by the public at large. Indeed, the new brand of totalism has yet even to be properly named. "Multiculturalism," for instance, is much too broad. "Political correctness" comes closer but is too trendy and snide. For lack of anything else, I will call the new antipluralism "purism," since its major tenet is that society cannot be just until the last traces of invidious prejudice have been scrubbed away. Whatever you call it, the purists' way of seeing things has spread through American intellectual life with remarkable speed, so much so that many people will blink at you uncomprehendingly or even call you a racist (or sexist or homophobe, etc.) if you suggest that expressions of racism should be tolerated or that prejudice has its part to play.

The new purism sets out, to begin with, on a campaign against words, for words are the currency of prejudice, and if prejudice is hurtful then so must be prejudiced words. "We are not safe when these violent words are among us," wrote Mari Matsuda, then a UCLA law professor. Here one imagines gangs of racist words swinging chains and smashing heads in back alleys. To suppress bigoted language seems, at first blush, reasonable, but it quickly leads to a curious result. A peculiar kind of verbal shamanism takes root, as though certain expressions, like curses or magical incantations, carry in themselves the power to hurt or heal—as though words were bigoted rather than people. "Context is everything," people have always said. The use of the word "nigger" in *Huckleberry Finn* does not make the book an "act" of hate speech—or does it? In the new view, this is no longer so clear. The very utterance of the word "nigger" (at least by a non-black) is a racist act. When a *Sacramento Bee* cartoonist put the word "nigger" mockingly in the mouth of a white supremacist, there were howls of protest and 1,400 canceled subscriptions and an editorial apology, even though the word was plainly being invoked against racists, not against blacks.

Faced with escalating demands of verbal absolutism, newspapers issue lists of forbidden words. The expressions "gyp" (derived from "Gypsy") and "Dutch treat" were among the dozens of terms stricken as "offensive" in a much-ridiculed (and later withdrawn) *Los Angeles Times* speech code. The University of Missouri journalism school issued a *Dictionary of Cautionary Words and Phrases*, which included "*Buxom*: Offensive reference to a woman's chest. Do not use. See 'Woman.' *Codger*: Offensive reference to a senior citizen."

As was bound to happen, purists soon discovered that chasing around after words like "gyp" or "buxom" hardly goes to the roots of the problem. As long as they remain bigoted, bigots will simply find other words. If they can't call you a kike then they will say Jewboy, Judas, or Hebe, and when all those are banned they will press words like "oven" and "lampshade" into their service. The vocabulary of hate is potentially as rich as your dictionary, and all you do by banning language used by cretins is to let them decide what the rest of us may say. The problem, some purists have concluded, must therefore go much deeper than laws: it must go to the deeper level of ideas. Racism, sexism, homophobia, and the rest must be built into the very structure of American society and American patterns of thought, so pervasive yet so insidious that, like water to a fish, they are both omnipresent and unseen. The mere existence of prejudice constructs a society whose very nature is prejudiced.

This line of thinking was pioneered by feminists, who argued that pornography, more than just being expressive, is an act by which men construct an oppressive society. Racial activists quickly picked up the argument. Racist expressions are themselves acts of oppression, they said. "All racist speech constructs the social reality that constrains the liberty of nonwhites because of their race," wrote Charles R. Lawrence III, then a law professor at Stanford. From the purist point of view, a society with even one racist is a racist society, because the idea itself threatens and demeans its targets. They cannot feel wholly safe or wholly welcome as long as racism is present. Pluralism says: There will always be some racists. Marginalize them, ignore them, exploit them, ridicule them, take pains to make their policies illegal, but otherwise leave them alone. Purists say: That's not enough. Society cannot be just until these pervasive and oppressive ideas are searched out and eradicated.

And so what is now under way is a growing drive to eliminate prejudice from every corner of society. I doubt that many people have noticed how far-reaching this anti-pluralist movement is becoming.

In universities: Dozens of universities have adopted codes proscribing speech or other expression that (this is from Stanford's policy, which is more or less representative) "is intended to insult or stigmatize an individual or a small number of individuals on the basis of their sex, race, color, handicap, religion, sexual orientation or national and ethnic origin." Some codes punish only persistent harassment of a targeted individual, but many, following the purist doctrine that even one racist is too many, go much further. At Penn, an administrator declared: "We at the University of Pennsylvania have guaranteed students and the community that they can live in a community free of sexism, racism, and homophobia." Here is the purism that gives "political correctness" its distinctive combination of puffy high-mindedness and authoritarian zeal.

In school curricula: "More fundamental than eliminating racial segregation has to be the removal of racist thinking, assumptions, symbols, and materials in the curriculum," writes theorist Molefi Kete Asante. In practice, the effort to "remove racist thinking" goes well beyond striking egregious references from textbooks. In many cases it becomes a kind of mental engineering in which students are encouraged to see prejudice everywhere; it includes teaching identity politics as an antidote to internalized racism; it rejects mainstream science as "white male" thinking; and it tampers with history, installing such dubious notions as that the ancient Greeks stole their culture from Africa or that an ancient carving of a bird is an example of "African experimental aeronautics."

In criminal law: Consider two crimes. In each, I am beaten brutally; in each, my jaw is smashed and my skull is split in just the same way. However, in the first crime my assailant calls me an "asshole"; in the second he calls me a "queer." In most states, in many localities, and, as of September 1994, in federal cases, these two crimes are treated differently: the crime motivated by bias—or deemed to be so motivated by prosecutors and juries—gets a stiffer punishment. "Longer prison terms for bigots," shrilled Brooklyn Democratic Congressman Charles Schumer, who introduced the federal hate-crimes legislation, and those are what the law now provides. Evidence that the assailant holds prejudiced beliefs, even if he doesn't actually express them while committing an offense, can serve to elevate the crime. Defendants in hate-crimes cases may be grilled on how many black friends they have and whether they have told racist jokes. To increase a prison sentence only because of the defendant's "prejudice" (as gauged by prosecutor and jury) is, of course, to try minds and punish beliefs.

Purists say, Well, they are dangerous minds and poisonous beliefs.

In the workplace: Though government cannot constitutionally suppress bigotry directly, it is now busy doing so indirectly by requiring employers to eliminate prejudice. Since the early 1980s, courts and the Equal Employment Opportunity Commission have moved to bar workplace speech deemed to create a hostile or abusive working environment for minorities. The law, held a federal court in 1988, "does require that an employer take prompt action to prevent... bigots from expressing their opinions in a way that abuses or offends their co-workers," so as to achieve "the goal of eliminating prejudices and biases from our society." So it was, as UCLA law professor Eugene Volokh notes, that the EEOC charged that a manufacturer's ads using admittedly accurate depictions of samurai, kabuki, and sumo were "racist" and "offensive to people of Japanese origin"; that a Pennsylvania court found that an employer's printing Bible verses on paychecks was religious harassment of Jewish employees; that an employer had to desist using gender-based job titles like "foreman" and "draftsman" after a female employee sued.

On and on the campaign goes, darting from one outbreak of prejudice to another like a cat chasing flies. In the American Bar Association, activists demand that lawyers who express "bias or prejudice" be penalized. In the Education Department, the civil-rights office presses for a ban on computer bulletin board comments that "show hostility toward a person or group based on sex, race or color, including slurs, negative stereotypes, jokes or pranks." In its security checks for government jobs, the FBI takes to asking whether applicants are "free of biases against any class of citizens," whether, for instance, they have told racist jokes or indicated other "prejudices." Joke police! George Orwell, grasping the close relationship of jokes to dissent, said that every joke is a tiny revolution. The purists will have no such rebellions.

The purist campaign reaches, in the end, into the mind itself. In a lecture at the University of New Hampshire, a professor compared writing to sex ("You and the subject become one"); he was suspended and required to apologize, but what was most insidious was the order to undergo university-approved counseling to have his mind straightened out. At the University of Pennsylvania, a law lecturer said, "We have ex-slaves here who should know about the Thirteenth Amendment"; he was banished from campus for a year and required to make a public apology, and he, too, was compelled to attend a "sensitivity and racial awareness" session. Mandatory re-education of alleged bigots is the natural consequence of intellectual purism. Prejudice must be eliminated!

Ah, but the task of scouring minds clean is Augean. "Nobody escapes," said a Rutgers University report on campus prejudice. Bias and prejudice, it found, cross every conceivable line, from sex to race to politics: "No matter who you are, no matter what the color of your skin, no matter what your gender or sexual orientation, no matter what you believe, no matter how you behave, there is somebody out there who doesn't like people of your kind." Charles Lawrence writes: "Racism is ubiquitous. We are all racists." If he means that most of us think racist thoughts of some sort at one time or another, he is right. If we are going to "eliminate prejudices and biases from our society," then the work of the prejudice police is unending. They are doomed to hunt and hunt and hunt, scour and scour and scour.

What is especially dismaying is that the purists pursue prejudice in the name of protecting minorities. In order to protect people like me (homosexual), they must pursue people like me (dissident). In order to bolster minority self-esteem, they suppress minority opinion. There are, of course, all kinds of practical and legal problems with the purists' campaign: the incursions against the First Amendment; the inevitable abuses by prosecutors and activists who define as "hateful" or "violent" whatever speech they dislike or can score points off of; the lack of any evidence that repressing prejudice eliminates rather than inflames it. But minorities, of all people, ought to remember that by definition we cannot prevail by numbers, and we generally cannot prevail by force. Against the power of ignorant mass opinion and group prejudice and superstition, we have only our voices. If you doubt that minorities' voices are powerful weapons, think of the lengths to which Southern officials went to silence the Reverend Martin Luther King Jr. (recall that the city commissioner of Montgomery, Alabama, won a $500,000 libel suit, later overturned in *New York Times v. Sullivan* [1964], regarding an advertisement in the *Times* placed by civil-rights leaders who denounced the Montgomery police). Think of how much gay people have improved their lot over twenty-five years simply by refusing to remain silent. Recall the Michigan student who was prosecuted for saying that homosexuality is a treatable disease, and notice that he was black. Under that Michigan speech code, more than twenty blacks were charged with racist speech, while no instance of racist speech by whites was punished. In Florida, the hate-speech law was invoked against a black man who called a policeman a "white cracker"; not so surprisingly, in the first hate-crimes case to reach the Supreme Court, the victim was white and the defendant black.

In the escalating war against "prejudice," the right is already learning to play by the rules that were pioneered by the purist activists of the left. Last year leading Democrats, including the President, criticized the Republican Party for being increasingly in the thrall of the Christian right. Some of the rhetoric was harsh ("fire-breathing Christian radical right"), but it wasn't vicious or even clearly wrong. Never mind: when Democratic Representative Vic Fazio said Republicans were "being forced to the fringes by the aggressive political tactics of the religious right," the chairman of the Republican National Committee, Haley Barbour, said, "Christian-bashing" was "the left's preferred form of religious bigotry." Bigotry! Prejudice! "Christians active in politics are now on the receiving end of an extraordinary campaign of bias and prejudice," said the conservative leader William J. Bennett. One discerns, here, where the new purism leads. Eventually, any criticism of any group will be "prejudice."

Here is the ultimate irony of the new purism: words, which pluralists hope can be substituted for violence, are redefined by purists *as* violence. "The experience of being called 'nigger,' 'spic,' 'Jap,' or 'kike' is like receiving a slap in the face," Charles Lawrence wrote in 1990. "Psychic injury is no less an injury than being struck in the face, and it often is far more severe." This kind of talk is commonplace today. Epithets, insults, often even polite expressions of what's taken to be prejudice are called by purists "assaultive speech," "words that wound," "verbal violence." "To me, racial epithets are not speech," one University of Michigan law professor said. "They are bullets." In her speech accepting the 1993 Nobel Prize for Literature in Stockholm, Sweden, the author Toni Morrison said this: "Oppressive language does more than represent violence; it is violence."

It is not violence. I am thinking back to a moment on the subway in Washington, a little thing. I was riding home late one night and a squad of noisy kids, maybe seventeen or eighteen years old, noisily piled into the car. They yelled across the car and a girl said, "Where do we get off?"

A boy said, "Farragut North."

The girl: "*Faggot* North!"

The boy: "Yeah! Faggot North!"

General hilarity.

First, before the intellect resumes control, there is a moment of fear, an animal moment. Who are they? How many of them? How dangerous? Where is the way out? All of these things are noted preverbally and assessed by the gut. Then the brain begins an assessment: they are sober, this is probably too public a place for them to do it, there are more girls than boys, they were just talking, it is probably nothing.

They didn't notice me and there was no incident. The teenage babble flowed on, leaving me to think. I became interested in my own reaction: the jump of fear out of nowhere like an alert animal, the sense for a brief time that one is naked and alone and should hide or run away. For a time, one ceases to be a human being and becomes instead a faggot.

The fear engendered by these words is real. The remedy is as clear and as imperfect as ever: protect citizens against violence. This, I grant, is something that American society has never done very well and now does quite poorly. It is no solution to define words as violence or prejudice as oppression, and then by cracking down on words or thoughts pretend that we are doing something about violence and oppression. No doubt it is easier to pass a speech code or hate-crimes law and proclaim the streets safer than actually to make the streets safer, but the one must never be confused with the other. Every cop or prosecutor chasing words is one fewer chasing criminals. In a world rife with real violence and oppression, full of Rwandas and Bosnias and eleven-year-olds spraying bullets at children in Chicago and in turn being executed by gang lords, it is odious of Toni Morrison to say that words are violence.

Indeed, equating "verbal violence" with physical violence is a treacherous, mischievous business. Not long ago a writer was charged with viciously and gratuitously wounding the feelings and dignity of millions of people. He was charged, in effect, with exhibiting flagrant prejudice against Muslims and outrageously slandering their beliefs. "What is freedom of expression?" mused Salman Rushdie a year after the ayatollahs sentenced him to death and put a price on his head. "Without the freedom to offend, it ceases to exist." I can think of nothing sadder than that minority activists, in their haste to make the world better, should be the ones to forget the lesson of Rushdie's plight: for minorities, pluralism, not purism, is the answer. The campaigns to eradicate prejudice—all of them, the speech codes and workplace restrictions and mandatory therapy for accused bigots and all the rest—should stop, now. The whole objective of eradicating prejudice, as opposed to correcting and criticizing it, should be repudiated as a fool's errand. Salman Rushdie is right, Toni Morrison wrong, and minorities belong at his side, not hers.

THE CONTINUING DEBATE:
Speech Codes

What Is New

The general debate over campus hate speech codes often pits those who emphasize the value of unfettered free speech against those who wish to protect the rights of minority groups and to promote campus diversity. In the courts, this conflict often plays out as a tension between the First Amendment right of free speech and the Fourteenth Amendment right of equal protection under the law. The U.S. Supreme Court has consistently ruled that no speech should be restricted for its ideological content (including hate speech and hate posters or banners or songs); however, the Court does allow some restrictions on "fighting words" and on speech aimed at threatening or intimidating: In *Virginia v. Black* (2003) a majority of the Court ruled that the state of Virginia could legitimately prohibit cross-burning because of its notorious history as a "particularly virulent form of intimidation." Outside the U.S., most Western countries have much stronger hate speech laws than those in the U.S. In the United Kingdom, the Public Order Act of 1986 made incitement to racial hatred an offense punishable by up to seven years imprisonment. The Council of Europe recently adopted a measure (rejected by the U.S.) criminalizing Internet hate speech; it prohibits "any written material, any image or any other representation of ideas or theories, which advocates, promotes or incites hatred, discrimination or violence, against any individual or group of individuals, based on race, colour, descent or national or ethnic origin, as well as religion if used as pretext for any of these factors."

Where to Find More

An excellent book on the subject, which includes examination of key court cases as well as essays from a variety of perspectives, is edited by Milton Heumann and Thomas W. Church, *Hate Speech on Campus: Cases, Case Studies, and Commentary* (Boston: Northeastern University Press, 1997). Judith Wagner DeCew, "Free Speech and Offensive Expression," *Social Philosophy and Policy*, volume 21, no. 2 (July 2004): 81–100, addresses both legal and ethical issues.

The American Civil Liberties Union (ACLU) has consistently opposed restrictions on speech, even when the speaker is advocating positions that most regard as vile. An excellent statement of their position can be found in an ACLU briefing paper, "Hate Speech on Campus," at *archive.aclu.org/library/pbp16.html*; see also their home site at *www.aclu.org*.

Speaking of Race, Speaking of Sex: Hate Speech, Civil Rights, and Civil Liberties (New York: New York University Press,) is an excellent collection of essays in defense of free speech and opposing speech codes. The introduction, by Ira Glasser, is a clear overview of the general argument for free speech and against speech codes.

Some of the most eloquent defenders of codes banning hate speech have been advocates of a legal perspective called "Critical Race Theory." For an excellent collection of papers within this viewpoint, see Mari J. Matsuda, Charles R. Lawrence III, Richard Delgado, and Kimberlé Williams Crenshaw, *Words that Wound: Critical Race Theory, Assaultive Speech, and the First Amendment* (Boulder, Colorado: Westview Press, 1993). Mari J. Matsuda's "Public Response to Racist Speech: Considering the

Victim's Story" is reprinted in the collection, and is particularly strong in bringing to life the experience of victims of hate speech.

W. Bradley Wendel, in "'Certain Fundamental Truths': A Dialectic on Negative and Positive Liberty in Hate-Speech Cases," *Law and Contemporary Problems* vol. 65, Spring 2002: 33–85, offers a very interesting and readable dialogue on both legal and ethical issues related to hate-speech. An interesting recent essay by Andrew Altman is "Equality and Expression: The Radical Paradox," *Social Philosophy and Policy*, volume 21, no. 2 (July 2004): 1–22. See also Martin P. Golding, *Free Speech on Campus* (Lanham, MD.: Rowman & Littlefield, 2000).

2   PORNOGRAPHY

Public Harm That Should Be Censored *or* Private Choice That Must Be Tolerated?

PUBLIC HARM THAT SHOULD BE CENSORED

ADVOCATE: Andrea Dworkin, a writer and lecturer, has been very active in passing ordinances that categorize pornography as sex discrimination, thus increasing opportunities for legal action against pornography

SOURCE: *Letters From a War Zone* (New York: Lawrence Hill Books, 1993)

PRIVATE CHOICE THAT MUST BE TOLERATED

ADVOCATE: Mark R. Wicclair, Professor of Philosophy and Adjunct Professor of Community Medicine, West Virginia University; Adjunct Professor of Medicine, University of Pittsburgh

SOURCE: "Feminism, Pornography, and Censorship," © 1985 by Wicclair. Originally published in Thomas A. Mappes and Jane S. Zembaty, *Social Ethics*, 3rd ed. (New York: McGraw-Hill, 1985)

When debating or adjudicating issues concerning pornography the first problem is how to define it. Often the law has made appeal to "community standards," or works that have "no redeeming social value," but such standards are vague. When interpreted broadly, such vague standards lead the censors to ban significant works of art and literature; when the same standards are interpreted narrowly, almost nothing is trapped in the censor's net.

Pornography is a controversial topic, with arguments starting over the definition of pornography and continuing through empirical debates concerning its psychological and social effects. The classic case against censorship of pornography is based on free speech and freedom of adults to make their own choices: While pornography may be repulsive, and may corrupt the user's moral fiber, use of pornography does not harm others and thus a free society should not ban it.

Lines of opposition form in several ways. First, some deny that the freedom of pornographers is a freedom worth protecting: It is not a freedom to present political views or challenge beliefs or develop theories, and thus it is not the sort of speech that warrants protection. Opponents answer that freedom of speech is an indivisible whole: If freedom is worth protecting, we must protect the bad with the good, particularly because it is often so difficult and controversial to distinguish worthless pornography from provocative art.

Second, some argue that indulging in pornography is *not* harmless to others, because those who use pornography may be led to act out their pornographic fantasies in acts of rape and sexual assault. But the evidence for such a causal link between pornography and sexual assault is very weak; after all, even if it should be established that those who use pornography are more likely to commit acts of sexual assault, it would be just as plausible to suppose that their inclination toward sexual violence led them to enjoy pornography, rather than the reverse. Recently, some feminists (such as Andrea Dworkin) have developed a much more sophisticated variation of the harm argument: Pornography does not lead to future harms to others; rather, pornography is in itself a harm to women, reducing them to the status of objects, promoting their subordination, and silencing their voices.

POINTS TO PONDER

➤ One problem that might emerge for Dworkin's view is in the form of a dilemma. She argues that pornography is used to subjugate and silence women, and thus is harmful to women. If it does not deliver such a message, then of course it is not harmful, and should not be censored. But if it does offer such a message, then it expresses an opinion, and should thus be protected under the first amendment. (If it expresses the opinion that women are worthless and deserve to be subjugated and silenced, then surely that is an opinion that most of us will find abominable; but freedom of speech is designed to protect the expression of even abominable opinions, including those of racists and Nazis and misogynists). How might Dworkin deal with that dilemma?

➤ Lorenne M. G. Clark states that "pornography has very little to do with sex, certainly with any conception of egalitarian sexual relations between the sexes, but it has everything to do with showing how to use sexuality as an instrument of active oppression, and that is why it is wrong." Thus the problem is not merely that pornography advocates a certain view, but that it teaches behavior that causes harm to others. By analogy, we might allow people to advocate the enslavement of all persons of Italian descent, but then draw the line at programs of instruction for enslaving Italians. What is your response to that argument? Is the analogy a good one? Is the factual premise behind the analogy (pornography teaches methods of oppression) accurate?

➤ Some of the most vocal opponents of censorship laws have been feminists, who argue that censorship laws invariably cast too wide a net, and will wind up banning erotica that women might use to explore alternatives to sexual practices that stem from a tradition of male domination. How serious is that danger? Could censorship laws be formulated precisely enough to avoid such dangers?

Pornography:
Public Harm That Should Be Censored

ANDREA DWORKIN

Most of them [pornographers] are small-time pimps or big-time pimps. They sell women: the real flesh-and-blood women in the pictures. They like the excitement of domination; they are greedy for profit; they are sadistic in their exploitation of women; they hate women, and the pornography they make is the distillation of that hate. The photographs are what they have created live, for themselves, for their own enjoyment. The exchanges of women among them are part of the fun, too: so that the fictional creature "Linda Lovelace," who was the real woman Linda Marchiano, was forced to "deep-throat" every pornographer her owner-pornographer wanted to impress. Of course, it was the woman, not the fiction, who had to be hypnotized so that the men could penetrate to the bottom of her throat, and who had to be beaten and terrorized to get her compliance at all. The finding of new and terrible things to do to women is part of the challenge of the vocation: so the inventor of "Linda Lovelace" and "deep-throating" is a genius in the field, a pioneer. Or, as Al Goldstein, a colleague, referred to him in an interview with him in *Screw* several years ago: a pimp's pimp.

Even with written pornography, there has never been the distinction between making pornography and the sexual abuse of live women that is taken as a truism by those who approach pornography as if it were an intellectual phenomenon. The Marquis de Sade, as the world's foremost literary pornographer, is archetypal. His sexual practice was the persistent sexual abuse of women and girls, with occasional excursions into the abuse of boys. As an aristocrat in a feudal society, he preyed with near impunity on prostitutes and servants. The pornography he wrote was an urgent part of the sexual abuse he practiced: not only because he did what he wrote, but also because the intense hatred of women that fuelled the one also fuelled the other: not two separate engines, but one engine running on the same tank. The acts of pornography and the acts of rape were waves on the same sea: that sea becoming for its victims, however it reached them, a tidal wave of destruction. Pornographers who use words know that what they are doing is both aggressive and destructive: sometimes they philosophize about how sex inevitably ends in death, the death of a woman being a thing of sexual beauty as well as excitement. Pornography, even when written, is sex because of the dynamism of the sexual hatred in it; and for pornographers, the sexual abuse of women as commonly understood and pornography are both acts of sexual predation, which is how they live.

One reason that stopping pornographers and pornography is not censorship is that pornographers are more like the police in police states than they are like the writers in police states. They are the instruments of terror, not its victims. What police do to the powerless in police states is what pornographers do to women, except that it is entertainment for the masses, not dignified as political. Writers do not do what pornographers do. Secret police do. Torturers do. What pornographers do to women is more like what police do to political prisoners than it is like anything else: except for the fact that it is watched with so much pleasure by so many. Intervening in a system of terror where it is vulnerable to public scrutiny to stop it is not censorship; it is the system of terror that stops speech and creates abuse and despair. The pornographers are the secret police of male supremacy: keeping women subordinate through intimidation and assault.

In the amendment to the Human Rights Ordinance of the City of Minneapolis written by Catharine A. MacKinnon and myself, pornography is defined as the graphic, sexually explicit subordination of women whether in pictures or in words that also includes one or more of the following: women are presented dehumanized as sexual objects, things, or commodities; or women are presented as sexual objects who enjoy pain or humiliation; or women are presented as sexual objects who experience sexual pleasure in being raped; or women are presented as sexual objects tied up or cut up or mutilated or bruised or physically hurt; or women are presented in postures of sexual submission; or women's body parts are exhibited, such that women are reduced to those parts; or women are presented being penetrated by objects or animals; or women are presented in scenarios of degradation, injury, abasement, torture, shown as filthy or inferior, bleeding, bruised, or hurt in a context that makes these conditions sexual.

This statutory definition is an objectively accurate definition of what pornography is, based on an analysis of the material produced by the $8-billion-a-year industry, and also on extensive study of the whole range of pornography extant from other eras and other cultures. Given the fact that women's oppression has an ahistorical character—a sameness across time and cultures expressed in rape, bat-

tery, incest, and prostitution—it is no surprise that pornography, a central phenomenon in that oppression, has precisely that quality of sameness. It does not significantly change in what it is, what it does, what is in it, or how it works, whether it is, for instance, classical or feudal or modern, Western or Asian; whether the method of manufacture is words, photographs, or video. What has changed is the public availability of pornography and the numbers of live women used in it because of new technologies: not its nature. Many people note what seems to them a qualitative change in pornography—that it has gotten more violent, even grotesquely violent, over the last two decades. The change is only in what is publicly visible: not in the range or preponderance of violent pornography (e.g., the place of rape in pornography stays constant and central, no matter where, when, or how the pornography is produced); not in the character, quality, or content of what the pornographers actually produce; not in the harm caused; not in the valuation of women in it, or the metaphysical definition of what women are; not in the sexual abuse promoted, including rape, battery, and incest; not in the centrality of its role in subordinating women. Until recently, pornography operated in private, where most abuse of women takes place.

The oppression of women occurs through sexual subordination. It is the use of sex as the medium of oppression that makes the subordination of women so distinct from racism or prejudice against a group based on religion or national origin. Social inequality is created in many different ways. In my view, the radical responsibility is to isolate the material means of creating the inequality so that material remedies can be found for it.

This is particularly difficult with respect to women's inequality because that inequality is achieved through sex. Sex as desired by the class that dominates women is held by that class to be elemental, urgent, necessary, even if or even though it appears to *require* the repudiation of any claim women might have to full human standing. In the subordination of women, inequality itself is sexualized: made into the experience of sexual pleasure, essential to sexual desire. Pornography is the material means of sexualizing inequality; and that is why pornography is a central practice in the subordination of women.

Subordination itself is a broad, deep, systematic dynamic discernible in any persecution based on race or sex. Social subordination has four main parts. First, there is *hierarchy*, a group on top and a group on the bottom. For women, this hierarchy is experienced both socially and sexually, publicly and privately. Women are physically integrated into the society in which we are held to be inferior, and our low status is both put in place and maintained by the sexual usage of us by men; and so women's experience of hierarchy is incredibly intimate and wounding.

Second, subordination is *objectification*. Objectification occurs when a human being, through social means, is made less than human, turned into a thing or commodity, bought and sold. When objectification occurs, a person is de-personalized, so that no individuality or integrity is available socially or in what is an extremely circumscribed privacy (because those who dominate determine its boundaries). Objectification is an injury right at the heart of discrimination: those who can be used as if they are not fully human are no longer fully human in social terms; their humanity is hurt by being diminished.

Third, subordination is *submission*. A person is at the bottom of a hierarchy because of a condition of birth; a person on the bottom is dehumanized, an object or commodity; inevitably, the situation of that person requires obedience and compliance. That diminished person is expected to be submissive; there is no longer any right to self-determination, because there is no basis in equality for any such right to exist. In a condition of inferiority and objectification, submission is usually essential for survival. Oppressed groups are known for their abilities to anticipate the orders and desires of those who have power over them, to comply with an obsequiousness that is then used by the dominant group to justify its own dominance: the master, not able to imagine a human like himself in such degrading servility, thinks the servility is proof that the hierarchy is natural and that objectification simply amounts to seeing these lesser creatures for what they are. The submission forced on inferior, objectified groups precisely by hierarchy and objectification is taken to be the proof of inherent inferiority and subhuman capacities.

Fourth, subordination is *violence*. The violence is systematic, endemic enough to be unremarkable and normative, usually taken as an implicit right of the one committing the violence. In my view, hierarchy, objectification, and submission are the preconditions for systematic social violence against any group targeted because of a condition of birth. If violence against a group is both socially pervasive and socially normal, then hierarchy, objectification, and submission are already solidly in place.

The role of violence in subordinating women has one special characteristic congruent with sex as the instrumentality of subordination: the violence is supposed to be sex for the woman too—what women want and like as part of our sexual nature; it is supposed to give women pleasure (as in rape); it is supposed to mean love to a woman from her point of view (as in battery). The violence against women is seen to be done not just in accord with something compliant in women, but in response to something active in and basic to women's nature.

Pornography uses each component of social subordination. Its particular medium is sex. Hierarchy, objectification, submission, and violence all become alive with sexual energy and sexual meaning. A hierarchy, for instance, can have a static quality; but pornography, by sexualizing it, makes it dynamic, almost carnivorous, so that men keep imposing it for the sake of their own sexual pleasure—for the sexual pleasure it gives them to impose it. In pornography, each element of subordination is conveyed through the sexually explicit usage of women: pornography in fact is what women are and what women are for and how women are used in a society premised on the inferiority of women. It is a metaphysics of women's subjugation: our existence delineated in a definition of our nature; our status in society predetermined by the uses to which we are put. The woman's body is what is materially subordinated. Sex is the material means through which the subordination is accomplished. Pornography is the institution of male dominance that sexualizes hierarchy, objectification, submission, and violence. As such, pornography creates inequality, not as artifact but as a system of social reality; it creates the necessity for and the actual behaviors that constitute sex inequality.

Subordination can be so deep that those who are hurt by it are utterly silent. Subordination can create a silence quieter than death. The women flattened out on the page are deathly still, except for *hurt me*. *Hurt me* is not women's speech. It is the speech imposed on women by pimps to cover the awful, condemning silence.

The Three Marias of Portugal went to jail for writing this: "Let no one tell me that silence gives consent, because whoever is silent dissents." The women say the pimp's words: the language is another element of the rape; the language is part of the humiliation; the language is part of the forced sex. Real silence might signify dissent, for those reared to understand its sad discourse. The pimps cannot tolerate literal silence—it is too eloquent as testimony—so they force the words out of the woman's mouth. The women say pimp's words: which is worse than silence. The silence of the women not in the picture, outside the pages, hurt but silent, used but silent, is staggering in how deep and wide it goes. It is a silence over centuries: an exile into speechlessness. One is shut up by the inferiority and the abuse. One is shut up by the threat and the injury. In her memoir of the Stalin period, *Hope Against Hope*, Nadezhda Mandeistam wrote that screaming "is a man's way of leaving a trace, of telling people how he lived and died. By his screams he asserts his right to live, sends a message to the outside world demanding help and calling for resistance. If nothing else is left, one must scream. Silence is the real crime against humanity." Screaming is a man's way of leaving a trace. The scream of a man is never misunderstood as a scream of pleasure by passers-by or politicians or historians, nor by the tormentor. A man's scream is a call for resistance. A man's scream asserts his right to live, sends a message; he leaves a trace. A woman's scream is the sound of her female will and her female pleasure in doing what the pornographers say she is for. Her scream is a sound of celebration to those who overhear. Women's way of leaving a trace is the silence, centuries' worth: the entirely inhuman silence that surely one day will be noticed, someone will say that something is wrong, some sound is missing, some voice is lost; the entirely inhuman silence that will be a clue to human hope denied, a shard of evidence that a crime has occurred, the crime that created the silence; the entirely inhuman silence that is a cold, cold condemnation of what those who speak have done to those who do not.

But there is more than the *hurt me* forced out of us, and the silence in which it lies. The pornographers actually use our bodies as their language. We are their speech. Our bodies are the building blocks of their sentences. What they do to us, called speech, is not unlike what Kafka's Harrow machine—"The needles are set in like the teeth of a harrow and the whole thing works something like a harrow, although its action is limited to one place and contrived with much more artistic skill"—did to the condemned in "In the Penal Colony":

"Our sentence does not sound severe. Whatever commandment the prisoner has disobeyed is written upon his body by the Harrow. This prisoner, for instance"—the officer indicated the man—"will have written on his body: HONOR THY SUPERIORS!"

"...The Harrow is beginning to write; when it finishes the first draft of the inscription on the man's back, the layer of cotton wool begins to roll and slowly turns the body over, to give the Harrow fresh space for writing.... So it keeps on writing deeper and deeper..."

Asked if the prisoner knows his sentence, the officer replies: " 'There would be no point in telling him. He'll learn it on his body.' "

This is the so-called speech of the pornographers, protected now by law.

Protecting what they "say" means protecting what they do to us, how they do it. It means protecting their sadism on our bodies, because that is how they write: not like a writer at all; like a torturer. Protecting what they "say" means protecting sexual exploitation, because they cannot "say" anything without diminishing, hurting, or destroying us. Their rights of speech express their rights over us. Their rights of speech require our inferiority: and that we be powerless in relation to them. Their rights of speech mean that *hurt me* is accepted as the real speech of women, not speech forced on us as part of the sex forced on us but originating with us because we are what the pornographers "say" we are.

If what we want to say is not *hurt me*, we have the real social power only to use silence as eloquent dissent. Silence is what women have instead of speech. Silence is our dissent during rape unless the rapist, like the pornographer, prefers *hurt me*, in which case we have no dissent. Silence is our moving, persuasive dissent during battery unless the batterer, like the pornographer, prefers hurt me. Silence is a fine dissent during incest and for all the long years after.

Silence is not speech. We have silence, not speech. We fight rape, battery, incest, and prostitution with it. We lose. But someday someone will notice: that people called women were buried in a long silence that meant dissent and that the pornographers—with needles set in like the teeth of a harrow—chattered on....

Equality for women requires material remedies for pornography, whether pornography is central to the inequality of women or only one cause of it. Pornography's antagonism to civil equality, integrity, and self-determination for women is absolute; and it is effective in making that antagonism socially real and socially determining.

The law that Catharine A. MacKinnon and I wrote making pornography a violation of women's civil rights recognizes the injury that pornography does: how it hurts women's rights of citizenship through sexual exploitation and sexual torture both.

The civil rights law empowers women by allowing women to civilly sue those who hurt us through pornography by trafficking in it, coercing people into it, forcing it on people, and assaulting people directly because of a specific piece of it.

The civil rights law does not force the pornography back underground. There is no prior restraint or police power to make arrests, which would then result in a revivified black market. This respects the reach of the First Amendment, but it also keeps the pornography from getting sexier— hidden, forbidden, dirty, happily back in the land of the obscene, sexy slime oozing on great books. Wanting to cover pornography up, hide it, is the first response of those who need pornography to the civil rights law. If pornography is hidden, it is still accessible to men as a male right of access to women; its injuries to the status of women are safe and secure in those hidden rooms, behind those opaque covers; the abuses of women are sustained as a private right supported by public policy. The civil rights law puts a flood of light on the pornography, what it is, how it is used, what it does, those who are hurt by it.

The civil rights law changes the power relationship between the pornographers and women: it stops the pornographers from producing discrimination with the total impunity they now enjoy, and gives women a legal standing resembling equality from which to repudiate the subordination itself. The secret-police power of the pornographers suddenly has to confront a modest amount of due process.

The civil rights law undermines the subordination of women in society by confronting the pornography, which is the systematic sexualization of that subordination. Pornography is inequality. The civil rights law would allow women to advance equality by removing this concrete discrimination and hurting economically those who make, sell, distribute, or exhibit it. The pornography, being power, has a right to exist that we are not allowed to challenge under this system of law. After it hurts us by being what it is and doing what it does, the civil rights law would allow us to hurt it back. Women, not being power, do not have a right to exist equal to the right the pornography has. If we did, the pornographers would be precluded from exercising their rights at the expense of ours, and since they cannot exercise them any other way, they would be precluded period. We come to the legal system beggars: though in the public dialogue around the passage of this civil rights law we have the satisfaction of being regarded as thieves.

The civil rights law is women's speech. It defines an injury to us from our point of view. It is premised on a repudiation of sexual subordination which is born of our experience of it. It breaks the silence. It is a sentence that can hold its own against the male flood. It is a sentence on which we can build a paragraph, then a page.

It is my view, learned largely from Catharine MacKinnon, that women have a right to be effective. The pornographers, of course, do not think so, nor do other male supremacists; and it is hard for women to think so. We have been told to educate people on the evils of pornography: before the development of this civil rights law, we were told just to keep quiet about pornography altogether; but now that we have a law we want to use, we are encouraged to educate and stop there.

Law educates. This law educates. It also allows women to *do* something. In hurting the pornography back, we gain ground in making equality more likely, more possible—someday it will be real. We have a means to fight the pornographers' trade in women. We have a means to get at the torture and the terror. We have a means with which to challenge the pornography's efficacy in making exploitation and inferiority the bedrock of women's social status. The civil rights law introduces into the public consciousness an analysis: of what pornography is, what sexual subordination is, what equality might be. The civil rights law introduces a new legal standard: these things are not done to citizens of this country. The civil rights law introduces a new political standard: these things are not done to human beings. The civil rights law provides a new mode of action for women through which we can pursue equality and because of which our speech will have social meaning. The civil rights law gives us back what the pornographers have taken from us: hope rooted in real possibility.

Pornography:
Private Choice That Must Be Tolerated

MARK R. WICCLAIR

It is sometimes claimed that pornography is objectionable because it violates conventional standards of sexual morality. Although feminists tend to agree that pornography is objectionable, they reject this particular argument against it. This argument is unacceptable to feminists because it is associated with an oppressive Puritanical sexual ethic that inhibits the sexual fulfillment of all people, but especially women. In order to understand why feminists find pornography objectionable. one has to keep in mind that they do not equate the terms "pornographic" and "sexually explicit." Rather, sexually explicit material is said to be "pornographic" only if it depicts and condones the exploitation, dehumanization, subordination, abuse, or denigration of women. By definition, then, all pornography is sexist and misogynistic. Some pornographic material has the additional feature of depicting and condoning acts of *violence* against women (e.g., rape, brutality, torture, sadism). Thus there is a world of difference between harmless "erotica" and pornography. Whereas erotica depicts sexual activity in a manner which is designed to produce sexual arousal and is therefore likely to he objectionable only to those who subscribe to a Puritanical sexual ethic, pornography is "material that explicitly represents or describes degrading and abusive sexual behavior so as to endorse and/or recommend the behavior as described."

Despite the general agreement among feminists that pornography, understood in the way just described, is objectionable, they are sharply divided over the question of its *censorship*. Whereas some feminists find pornography to be so objectionable that they call for its censorship, others oppose this proposal. I will argue that anyone who supports the aims of feminism and who seeks the liberation of all people should reject the censorship of pornography.

When discussing censorship, it is important to keep in mind that there are very strong reasons to be wary of its use. In our society, the importance of the principle of freedom of expression—an anticensorship principle—is widely recognized. The ability to speak one's mind and to express ideas and feelings without the threat of legal penalties or government control is rightly perceived as an essential feature of a truly free society. Moreover, an environment that tolerates the expression of differing views about politics, art, lifestyles, etc., encourages progress and aids in the search for truth and justice. In addition to the many important values associated with the principle of freedom of expression, it is also necessary to consider likely negative side effects of censorship. There is a serious risk that once any censorship is allowed, the power to censor will, over time, expand in unintended and undesirable directions (the "slippery slope"). This is not mere speculation, for such an expansion of the power to censor is to he expected in view of the fact that it is extremely difficult, if not impossible, to formulate unequivocal and unambiguous criteria of censorship. Then, too, the power to censor can all too easily be abused or misused. Even though it may arise in a genuine effort to promote the general welfare and to protect certain rights, officials and groups might use the power to censor as a means to advance their own interests and values and to suppress the rights, interests, and values of others. Thus, given the value of freedom of expression and the many dangers associated with censorship, there is a strong *prima facie* case against censorship. In other words, advocates of censorship have the burden of showing that there are sufficiently strong overriding reasons which would justify it in a specific area.

Like racist and antisemitic material, sexist and misogynistic films, books, and magazines surely deserve condemnation. But censorship is another matter. In view of the strength of the case against censorship in general, it is unwise to advocate it merely to prevent depicting morally objectionable practices in a favorable light. Fortunately, proponents of the censorship of pornography tend to recognize this, for they usually base their call for censorship on a claim about the *effects* of pornography. Pornography, it is held, is *injurious* or *harmful* to women because it fosters the objectionable practices that it depicts. Pornography generally is said to promote the exploitation, humiliation, denigration, subordination, etc., of women; and pornography that depicts acts of violence against women is said to cause murder, rape, assault, and other acts of violence. On the basis of the "harm principle"—a widely accepted principle that allows us to restrict someone's freedom in order to prevent harm to others—it would appear to be justified to override the principle of freedom of expression and to restrict the freedom of would-be producers, distributors, sellers, exhibitors, and consumers of pornography. In short it seems that censorship of pornography is a legitimate means of preventing harm to women.

However, there are a number of problems associated with this attempt to justify censorship. To begin with, it is essential to recognize the important difference between words and images, on the one hand, and actions, on the other hand. A would-be rapist poses a *direct* threat to his intended victim, and by stopping him, we prevent an act of violence. But if there is a connection between the depiction of a rape—even one which appears to condone it—and someone's committing an act of violence against a woman, the connection is relatively *indirect*; and stopping the production, distribution, sale, and exhibition of depictions of rape does not directly restrict the freedom of would-be rapists to commit acts of violence against women. In recognition of the important difference between restricting words and images and preventing harmful behavior, exceptions to the principle of freedom of expression are generally thought to be justified only if words or images present a "clear and present danger" of harm or injury. Thus, to cite a standard example, it is justified to stop someone from falsely shouting "Fire!" in a crowded theater, for this exclamation is likely to cause a panic that would result in serious injury and even death.

It is doubtful that pornography satisfies the "clear and present danger" condition. For there does not seem to be conclusive evidence that establishes its *causal* significance. Most studies are limited to violent pornography. And even though sonic of these studies do suggest a *temporary* impact on *attitudes* (e.g., those who view violent pornography may be more likely to express the view that women seek and "enjoy" violence), this does not show that viewing violent pornography causes violent *behavior*. Moreover, there is some evidence suggesting that the effect on attitudes is only temporary and that it can be effectively counteracted by additional information.

But even if there is no conclusive evidence that pornography causes harm, is it not reasonable to "play it safe." and does this not require censorship? Unfortunately, the situation is not as simple as this question appears to suggest. For one thing, it is sometimes claimed that exposure to pornography has a "cathartic" effect and that it therefore produces a net *reduction* in harm to women. This claim is based upon two assumptions, neither of which has been proven to be false: (1) Men who are not already violence-prone are more likely to he "turned off" than to be "turned on" by depictions of rape, brutality, dismemberment, etc. (2) For men in the latter category, exposure to pornography can function as a substitute for actually causing harm. It is also necessary to recall that there are significant values associated with the principle of freedom of expression, and that a failure to observe it involves a number of serious dangers. Since censorship has costs which are substantial and not merely speculative, the more speculative the connection between pornography and harm to women, the less basis there is for incurring the costs associated with censorship.

Just as it is easy to overlook the negative side of censorship, it is also common to overplay its positive effects. Surely it would be foolish to think that outlawing anti-semitism in sexually explicit material would have halted the slaughter of Jews in Hitler Germany or that prohibiting racism in sexually explicit material would reduce the suffering of Blacks in South Africa. Similarly, in view of the violent nature of American society generally and the degree to which sexism persists to this day, it is unlikely that censorship of pornography by itself would produce any significant improvement in the condition of women in the United States. Fortunately, there are other, more effective and direct means of eliminating sexism than by censoring pornography. Passage and strict enforcement of the Equal Rights Amendment, electing feminists to local, state, and national political office, achieving genuine economic justice for women, and securing their reproductive freedom will do considerably more to foster the genuine liberation of women in the United States than will the censorship of pornography. With respect to rape and other acts of violence, it has often been noted that American society is extremely violent, and, sadly, there are no magic solutions to the problems of rape and violence. But the magnitude of the problem suggests that censoring pornography only addresses a symptom and not the underlying disease. Although there is still much dispute about the causes of violence generally and rape in particular, it is unlikely that there will be a serious reduction in acts of violence against women until there are rather drastic changes in the socioeconomic environment and in the criminal justice system.

Those who remain concerned about the possible contribution of pornography to violence and sexism should keep in mind that it can be "neutralized" in ways that avoid the dangers of censorship. One important alternative to government censorship is to help people understand why pornography is objectionable and why it and its message should be rejected. This can be accomplished by means of educational campaigns, discussions of pornography on radio and television and at public forums, letter writing, and educational picketing. In addition, attempts might be made to prevent or restrict the production, distribution, display, sale, and consumption of pornographic material by means of organized pickets, boycotts, and the like. Such direct measures by private citizens raise some troubling questions, but the dangers and risks which they pose are considerably less than those associated with government censorship....

I have tried to show that censorship of pornography is neither the most effective nor a legitimate means to achieve the aims of feminism. Much pornographic material is morally repugnant, but there are less costly ways to express one's moral outrage and to attempt to "neutralize" pornography than by censorship. Moreover, pornography is only a relatively minor manifestation of the sexist practices and institutions that still pervade our society. Hence, the genuine liberation of women—and men—is best served by directly attacking those oppressive practices and institutions. It may be easier to identify and attack pornography—and to win some battles—but the payoff would be slight, and the negative side effects would be substantial.

THE CONTINUING DEBATE:
Pornography

What Is New

The FCC has recently become very active in enforcing "decency" on the air waves, levying financial penalties against "shock jock" Howard Stern for his language and against the notorious Super Bowl half time show and one bared breast.

The courts have long struggled with the issue of obscenity: in particular, how obscenity should be defined, and whether obscene materials should enjoy the First Amendment protection of freedom of speech. Current U.S. Supreme Court guidelines were developed in *Miller v. California*. States can regulate obscenity when it meets all the following criteria: first, "the average person, applying contemporary community standards, would find that the work, taken as a whole, appeals to the prurient interest"; second, "the work depicts or describes, in a patently offensive way, sexual conduct specifically defined by the applicable state law;" and third, that "the work, taken as a whole, lacks serious literary, artistic, political, or scientific value." Regarding the third requirement, it's obvious that a jury would have a tough time making that judgment. Add the first requirement—What are the contemporary community standards? What community is in question?—and decisions on obscenity become very difficult.

The Internet has made pornography widely and easily available. The amount of extremely violent and degrading pornography has increased. Child pornography, including difficult-to-regulate pornography originating in third world countries and exploiting impoverished children, is a sad illustration of the problem. The danger of adolescents having their psychosexual inclinations shaped by violent pornography adds a new dimension to the pornography debate. Congress has passed laws prohibiting the Internet transmission of pornography to those below a certain age but the courts have ruled these laws are too broad and interfere with First Amendment rights. Even if new U.S. laws can pass constitutional muster, the worldwide Internet will be difficult to regulate.

Where to Find More

An excellent anthology on the question of pornography is edited by Drucilla Cornell, *Feminism and Pornography* (New York: Oxford University Press, 2000). For controversies among feminists concerning the nature and status of pornography, see Alison M. Jaggar, *Living with Contradictions: Controversies in Feminist Social Ethics* (Boulder, CO: Westview Press, 1994). Robert M. Baird and Stuart E. Rosenbaum, editors, *Pornography: Private Right or Public Menace* (Buffalo, NY: Prometheus, 1991) contains a good collection of opposing views on pornography. *Pornography and Censorship*, edited by David Copp and Susan Wendell (Buffalo, NY: Prometheus, 1983) contains a number of good essays (including David Copp's valuable introduction) and concludes with an excellent collection of judicial writings on the issue. Gloria Steinem attempts to establish a clear distinction between erotica and pornography in her essay, "Erotica and Pornography: A Clear and Present Difference," in *Ms.* magazine, November 1978. A strong statement of the case against pornography, based on the harm it causes to women, can be found in Helen E. Longino, "Pornography, Oppression, and Freedom: A Closer Look," in Laura Lederer, ed., *Take Back the Night: Women on Pornography* (New York: William Morrow, 1980).

3 AFFIRMATIVE ACTION PROGRAMS

Unfair Discrimination *or* Basic Justice?

UNFAIR DISCRIMINATION

ADVOCATE: Carl Cohen, Professor of Philosophy at the University of Michigan, author of many works in ethics, political philosophy, and logic

SOURCE: "Why Race Preference is Wrong and Bad," from *Affirmative Action and Racial Preference: A Debate*, by Carl Cohen and James P. Sterba (New York: Oxford University Press, 2003)

BASIC JUSTICE

ADVOCATE: Luke Charles Harris, Associate Professor of Political Science, Vassar College, and Co-founder of the African American Policy Forum; and Uma Narayan, Associate Professor of Philosophy, Vassar College

SOURCE: "Affirmative Action as Equalizing Opportunity: Challenging the Myth of 'Preferential Treatment,'" *National Black Law Journal* volume 16, issue 2; 1999/2000

When considering the controversies swirling around affirmative action (sometimes characterized by opponents as "reverse discrimination"), we can start with some facts that are not in controversy. For many years in the United States, there was massive and systematic discrimination against "minority groups"—including Blacks, American Indians, Jews, Orientals, and those of Spanish descent—as well as against women. They were excluded from most colleges, and later excluded from graduate schools and professional schools; excluded from many jobs (particularly any jobs that would involve the supervision of a white male); and when finally hired, were passed over for promotions. Though most overt discrimination has been eliminated or at least substantially reduced, subtle forms of discrimination continue: The "glass ceiling" admits only white males to the highest level positions. The "old boy" network that takes special care of those who have traditionally held positions of privilege. Programs such as "legacy admissions" at prestigious universities—whereby children of alumni are given special consideration when they apply—obviously confer special preference to the white children whose parents were admitted during the time when minority groups were systematically excluded.

More controversial is the question of what such a history of discrimination implies for current social programs. There are at least three main lines of argument in favor of affirmative action programs. The first is the argument that affirmative action is justified in order to right past wrongs: Since blacks and women were discriminated against before, they should be given special preference now in order to right that wrong. Opponents reply that two wrongs don't make a right: The fact that Bill's white father gained special benefits when Joe's father suffered racial discrimination is no reason to repeat the wrong on behalf of Joe to the detriment of Bill. Bill, after all, is blameless: The sins of the fathers do not accrue to their children. Besides, those who are benefited by such programs are not the ones who were harmed by the earlier discrimination.

A second line of argument for affirmative action policies—sometimes confused with the first argument—is that discrimination is ongoing, and has not been eliminated from our society; and that affirmative action policies are required in order to combat the subtle prejudices that would otherwise deny well-qualified persons legitimate and equal opportunities.

The third line of argument is that diversity is valuable for fostering a richer educational process, offering role models from minority groups, and helping organizations to function more successfully and sensitively in our multiethnic society and world market place. The diversity argument has received favorable attention from the U.S. Supreme Court in its recent rulings.

"Quota systems" have sometime proved useful in combating the most entrenched forms of discrimination. Some southern states refused for years to hire African-Americans as members of the state police, insisting that despite their best efforts they were simply unable to find any qualified applicants. Not surprisingly, when required to hire a certain number or quota of African-Americans, it turned out that there was no shortage of well-qualified persons to fill the positions. But whatever the virtues or vices of quotas, the courts have ruled that they cannot be adopted. Thus the contemporary debate concerning affirmative action is not a debate about quotas; that is not a real issue, though it sometimes appears in debates as a strawman distortion.

POINTS TO PONDER

➤ Cohen, Harris, and Narayan all agree that discrimination is wrong, whether the discrimination is racist, sexist, or reverse. But Harris and Narayan favor affirmative action programs, while Cohen opposes them. Exactly where do their views split, leading in such different directions?

➤ Cohen states that "Race preference is morally defective also in being *under*inclusive, in that it fails to reward many who deserve compensation." How would Harris and Narayan reply? How would they respond to Cohen's use of the phrase "race preference"?

➤ Harris and Narayan state: "Our position is that affirmative action is best understood as an attempt to promote equality of opportunity in a social context marked by pervasive inequalities—one in which many institutional practices work to impede a fair assessment of the capabilities of those who are working-class, women, or people of color." How does that compare to Cohen's view of affirmative action?

Affirmative Action Programs: Unfair Discrimination

CARL COHEN

THE PRINCIPLE OF EQUALITY

That *equals should he treated equally* is a fundamental principal of morality. Race preference is morally wrong because it violates this principle.

But who are equals? Identical treatment for everyone in all matters is certainly not just. Citizens have privileges and duties that aliens do not have; employers have opportunities and responsibilities that employees do not have; higher taxes may be rightly imposed upon those with higher incomes; the right to vote is withheld from the very young. Groups of persons may deserve different treatment because they *are* different in critical respects. But what respects are critical? Surely the poor or the elderly or the disabled may have special needs that justify community concern.

The principle of equality does not require that all be treated identically; but this much is clear: if some receive a public benefit that others do not receive, that preference will be unfair unless the advantages given can be justified by some feature of the group preferred. Unequal treatment by the state requires defense.

As a justification for unequal treatment some group characteristics are simply not relevant and not acceptable, all agree. Ancestry we reject. Better treatment for Americans of Irish decent than for those of Polish decent is wrong; we haven't any doubt about that. Sex we reject. Privileges to which men are entitled cannot be denied to women. Religion we reject. Opportunities open to Methodists must be open to Baptists. Color we reject. When the state favors white skins over black skins—a common practice for centuries—we are now properly outraged. Such categories cannot determine desert. This matter is morally settled: in dealings with the state, persons *may not* be preferred because of their race, or color, or religion, or sex, or national origin.

Bigots, of course, will draw distinctions by race (or nationality, etc.) in their private lives. But private opinions, however detestable, are not public business. Under rules to be enforced by our body politic, bigotry is forbidden. Persons of all colors, religions, and origins are equals with respect to their rights, equals in the eyes of the law. And equals must be treated equally. Race and nationality simply cannot serve, in our country, as the justification for unequal treatment.

This we do not learn from any book or document. These principles are not true because expressed in the Declaration of Independence, or laid down in the Constitution of the United States. The principles are found in those great documents because they are true. That "all men are created equal" is one way, perhaps the most famous way, of expressing the fundamental moral principle involved. A guarantee that the "equal protection of the laws" is not to be denied to any person by any state (as the Fourteenth Amendment to our Constitution provides) is one way of giving that moral principle political teeth. Our great documents *recognize* and *realize* moral truths grasped by persons everywhere: All the members of humankind are equally ends in themselves, all have equal *dignity*—and therefore all are entitled to equal respect from the community and its laws....

This recognition of the ultimate equality and fellowship of humans with one another is taught by great thinkers in every culture—by Buddha, and St. Francis, and Walt Whitman. At bottom all recognize, as Walter Lippmann wrote, a "spiritual reality behind and independent of the visible character and behavior of a man.... [W]e know, each of us, in a way too certain for doubting, that, after all the weighing and comparing and judging of us is done, there is something left over which is the heart of the matter."

This is the moral standard against which race preference must be judged. The principle of equality certainly entails at least this: It is wrong, always and everywhere, to give special advantages to any group simply on the basis of physical characteristics that have no relevance to the award given or to the burden imposed. To give or to take on the basis of skin color is manifestly unfair.

The most gruesome chapters in human history—the abomination of black slavery, the wholesale slaughter of the Jews—remind us that *racial* categories must never be allowed to serve as the foundation for official differentiation. Nations in which racial distinctions were once embedded in public law are forever shamed. Our own history is by such racism ineradicably stained. The lesson is this: Never again. Never, *ever* again.

What is today loosely called "affirmative action" sticks in our craw because it fails to respect that plain lesson. It uses categories that *must not* be used to distinguish among persons with respect to their entitlements in the community. Blacks and whites are equals, as blondes and brunettes are equals, as Catholics and Jews are equals, as Americans of every ancestry are equal. No matter who the beneficiaries

may be or who the victims, preference on the basis of race is morally wrong. It was wrong in the distant past and in the recent past; it is wrong now; and it will always be wrong. Race preference violates the principle of human equality.

RACE PREFERENCE IS NOT JUSTIFIED AS COMPENSATION

What about people who have been hurt because of their race, damaged or deprived because they were black or brown? Do they not deserve some redress? Of course they do. But it is the *injury* for which compensation is given in such cases, not the skin color.

But (some will respond) it is precisely the *injuries* so long done to minorities that justify special consideration for minorities now. Bearing the past in mind, deliberate preference for groups formerly oppressed reverses historical injustice, and thereby makes fair what would otherwise seem to be unfair. They argue that blacks, Native Americans, Hispanics, and other minorities have for many generations been the victims of outrageous discrimination, the sum of it almost too cruel to contemplate. Explicit preference to these minorities now makes up, in part, for past deprivation. Historical wrongs cannot be undone, but we can take some steps toward the restoration of moral balance. At this point in our history, advocates continue, equal treatment only appears to be just. Minorities have been so long shackled by discriminatory laws and economic deprivation that it is not fair to oblige them to compete now against a majority never burdened in that way. The visible shackles may be gone, but not the residual impact of their long imposition. We must *level the playing field* in the competition for employment and other goods. Only explicit race preference can do this, they contend; therefore, explicit race preference is just.

This is the essence of the argument in support of race preference upon which most of its advocates chiefly rely. It is an argument grounded in the demand for *compensation*, for redress. It seeks to turn the tables in the interests of justice. White males, so long the beneficiaries of preference, are now obliged to give preference to others. Past oppression must be paid for. Is turnabout not fair play?

No, it is not—not when the instrument turned about is essentially unjust. The compensatory argument is appealing but mistaken, because preference *by race* cannot serve as just compensation for earlier wrongs. It cannot do so because race, as a standard, is crude and morally blind. Color, national origin, and other accidents of birth have no moral weight. Historical injustices we now seek to redress were themselves a product of moral stupidity; they were inflicted because burdens and benefits were awarded on grounds entirely irrelevant to what was deserved. Blacks and other minorities were not injured by *being* black or brown. They were injured by treatment unfairly *based* on their being black or brown. Redress deserved is redress that goes to *them*, to persons injured, in the light of the injuries they suffered. Many are long dead and can never be compensated. Those ancient injuries are not remedied by bestowing benefits now upon other persons who happen to belong to the ethnic group of those injured.

Using race to award benefits now does injustice in precisely the way injustice was done originally, by giving moral weight to skin color in itself. The discriminatory use of racial classifications is no less unfair when directed at whites now than it was when directed at blacks then. A wrong is not redressed by inflicting that same wrong on others. By devising new varieties of race preference, moreover, we give legitimacy to the consideration of race, rein-

forcing the very injustice we seek to eradicate. We compound injustice with injustice, further embedding racial categories in public policy and law.

The moral blindness of race preference is exhibited from both sides: *the wrong people benefit, and the wrong people pay the price of that benefit.*

Consider first who benefits. Race preference gives rewards to some persons who deserve no rewards at all, and this is *over*inclusive. Preferential systems are designed to give special consideration to *all* those having some physical or genetic feature, all those who are black, or female, or of some specified national origin. Hispanics, for example, receive the advantage because they have parents or grandparents (is one enough?) of certain national origins. But have all those of Hispanic origin been wrongly injured? Do all those of that single national origin deserve compensation now for earlier injuries? No one seriously believes that. Discrimination against Hispanics in our country has been (and remains) common, to be sure. But it is also true that many of Hispanic ancestry now enjoy here, and have long enjoyed. circumstances as decent amid as well protected as those enjoyed by Americans of all other ethnicities. The same is true of African Americans, some of whom are impoverished and some of whom are rich and powerful. Rewards distributed on the basis of ethnic membership assume that the damage suffered by some were suffered by all—an assumption that we know to be false....

Race preference is morally defective also in being *under*inclusive, in that it fails to reward many who deserve compensation. If redress is at times in order, for what injuries might it be deserved? Inadequate education perhaps: teachers poorly qualified, books out of date or in short supply, buildings vermin-infested and deteriorating, schools rotten all around. High school graduates who come to the verge of college admission in spite of handicaps like these may indeed be thought worthy of special consideration— but that would be a consideration given them not because of the color of their skins, but because of what they have accomplished in spite of handicap. *Everyone* whose accomplishments are like those, whose determination has overcome great barriers, is entitled to whatever compensatory relief we think graduation from such inferior schools deserves. Everyone, no matter the color of her skin.

So race preference is morally faulty in what it does not do, as well as in what it does. Seeing only race we cannot see what may truly justify special regard. Blacks and Hispanics are not the only ones to have been burdened by bad schools, or undermined by poverty or neglect, or wounded by absent or malfunctioning families. But those with skins of other colors, however much they too may have been unfairly injured or deprived, get no support from race-based "affirmative action." They are simply left out.

Also left out are most of those blacks and Native Americans who really were seriously damaged by educational deprivation, but who fell so far behind in consequence that they cannot possibly compete for slots in professional schools, or for prestigious training programs, and therefore cannot benefit from the race preferences commonly given. So those most in need of help usually get none, and those equally entitled to help whose skins are the wrong color get absolutely none.

Whatever the community response to adversity ought to be, this much is clear: what is given must be given without regard to the race or sex or national origin of the recipients. It is the injury and not the ethnicity for which relief may be in order,

and therefore relief cannot be justly restricted to some minorities only. If some injury or deprivation does justify compensatory redress, whites and blacks who have suffered that injury should be entitled to the same redress. Racial lenses obscure this truth.

A just apportionment of remedies should be designed to compensate most those who were injured most, and to compensate least, or not at all, those who were injured least, or not at all. Therefore a keen regard for the nature of the injury suffered, and the degree of suffering, is critical in giving redress. Remedy for injury is a complicated matter; naked race preference must fail as the instrument in providing remedy because by hypothesis it has no regard for variety or degree. How gravely injured are they who complete undergraduate studies and compete for admission to law school, or medical school? The daughter of a black physician who graduates from a fine college has been done no injury entitling her to preferential consideration in competitive admissions simply because she is black—but she will surely receive it. The principal beneficiaries of "affirmative action" in law schools and medical schools are the children of upper middle-class minority families, for the simple reason that they are the minority applicants most likely to be in a position to apply to such schools. Those whose personal histories of deprivation may in truth entitle them to some special consideration are rarely in a position even to hope for preference in such contexts. It is one of the great ironies of "affirmative action" that those among minority groups receiving its preferences are precisely those least likely to deserve them....

In sum, race preference gives to those who don't deserve, and doesn't give to those who do. It gives more to those who deserve less, and less to those who deserve more. These failings are inescapable because the preferences in question are grounded not in earlier injury but in physical characteristics that cannot justly serve as grounds for advantage or disadvantage. Whatever is owed persons because of injuries they suffered is owed them without any regard to their ethnicity. Many who may now deserve remedy for past abuse are not minority group members: many who are minority group members deserve no remedy. Preference awarded only to persons in certain racial categories, and to all in those categories whatever their actual desert, invariably overrides the moral considerations that are genuinely relevant, and cannot be rightly defended as compensatory.

RACE PREFERENCE IMPOSES UNFAIR PENALTIES UPON THOSE NOT PREFERRED

Not only the benefits. but also the *burdens* imposed by race-based preferences are distributed unfairly. By attending to skin color rather than to what should truly count, racial instruments invariably impose penalties upon those who deserve no penalty at all, persons entirely innocent of the earlier wrong for which is the preference is allegedly given, but whose skin is of the wrong color.

Even if those receiving race preference now had been injured earlier because of their race, it is plainly false to suppose that those over whom they are now preferred were in any way responsible for the earlier injuries. A race-based system of penalty and reward is morally cockeyed.

In a competitive setting, advantages given must be paid for by disadvantages borne. If the goods are in short supply—as jobs and promotions and seats in a law school and the like are certainly in short supply—whatever is given to some by race is necessarily taken from others by race. If

some are advantaged because of their color or sex, others must be disadvantaged because of their color or sex. This is a truth of logic that cannot be escaped. *There is no ethnic preference that can be "benign."*

Advocates of preference scoff at the alleged burden of race preferences, contending that their impact upon the majority is insignificant. The body of white job applicants, or white contractors, or white university applicants is large, while the number of minority applicants given preference is small. So if those preferences impose a burden, the advocates contend, it is at worst a trivial burden because of the great number over whom that burden is distributed. The complaint about unfairness, the advocates conclude, thus makes a mountain of a molehill. Preferences given to minority applicants are so greatly *diluted* by the size of the majority that their consequences are barely detectable.

This argument is deceptive and its conclusion is false. True it is that only some in the majority are directly affected, and true also that after such preferences are given we often cannot know precisely who among the majority would have been appointed or admitted if that preferential system had not been in place. But it is not true that, because the group from whom the benefits are taken is large, the burden of preference is diluted or rendered insignificant. The price must be paid, and some among that larger group must pay it. Some individual members of the majority must have been displaced, and upon them the burden is as heavy as it is unfair. Injustice is not made trivial because the names of its victims of not known....

In many contexts that penalty, inevitably imposed by preference, is very heavy. Getting a job, or keeping one, is no minor matter. Some folks lose out in their quest for employment *because of their race.*

Some employees who might have been promoted in their workplace are passed over. Some who might have been admitted to fine colleges, or law schools, or medical schools, are not admitted because of their race, and must go elsewhere, or perhaps go nowhere. The white applicants squeezed out in this process are, ironically, often the children of first generation Americans, the first members of their families pulling their way into universities and professional life. They, not the established rich, are the ones hit hardest by race preference.

Persons who have been displaced in this way usually do not know, cannot know, that they are the ones who are paying this price. That first list constructed hypothetically in our thought experiment never gets constructed in fact. The names on it are never specified, so we cannot know which among them have been deleted when the second list takes its place. But there *is* such a first list; that is, there is a list of persons who would have been accepted had race not been weighed, and the second list (constructed with race as a factor) *does* take the place of that one. The fact that we cannot name the persons squeezed out of the first list does not make the squeezing any less unfair.

Because the names of those actually displaced cannot be identified, each of these many applicants who thought his chances of admission excellent or at least good is likely to think, when rejected, that *he* is one of those whose race cost him his place. Most rejected white applicants may reasonably suppose that if only their skin color had been darker they would have been accepted. Ugly and awful are the consequences of what is now commonly done with good intentions: some deserving applicants do not get, simply because of their race, what they would have gotten if their color had not been held against

them. This outcome is morally unacceptable, but it is an ineluctable consequence of every system of race preference.

The underlying problem is everywhere the same: in deciding upon what is to be given by way of redress for injury the properly critical moral consideration is the injury itself, its nature and its degree—not the race or national origin of the persons compensated. When preference is given to persons because of their race alone, many who are in fact owed redress do not receive it (either because they had been too greatly damaged, or because they happen not to be members of the favored categories), while many who are members of the favored categories receive benefits although owed nothing in the way of redress. And those who bear the burden of the preferential award are totally innocent of wrong doing, bearing no responsibility whatever for injuries that may have been done to persons of the race preferred. Because both benefits and burdens are a function of race, and are not determined by considerations having genuine moral weight, race preference is perfectly incapable of achieving the compensatory objective offered in its defense; such preference is inevitably unfair and morally wrong....

[I]ts worst consequences... are the injuries it inflicts upon the racial minorities preferred, *creating widespread resentment, reinforcing stereotypes*, and *humiliating its purported beneficiaries* in the eyes of their classmates, colleagues, workmates, teachers—and even in their own eyes. Race preference has been an utter catastrophe for the ethnic minorities it was intended to benefit.

Some individual members of the favored minorities are advantaged by preference, of course. But the minority as a whole is undermined. Preference puts distinguished minority achievement under a cloud. It imposes upon every member of the preferred minority the demeaning burden of presumed inferiority. Preference *creates* that burden; it *makes* a stigma of the race of those who are preferred by race. An ethnic group given special favor by the community is *marked* as needing special favor—and the mark is borne prominently by every one of its members. Nasty racial stereotypes are reinforced, and the malicious imputation of inferiority is inescapable because it is tied to the color of skin....

Racial oppression and racial discrimination have plagued our nation from its earliest days. Americans created these hostilities; it is our moral obligation to do, in our lifetimes, the very best we can to heal racial wounds, and to eliminate racism root and branch. Fulfilling this duty is greatly hindered by race preference.

Injustice is only part of the problem. Race preference does indeed violate our laws and our deepest moral principles of which none is more important than equality before the law. But preference does damage to our society that goes beyond injustice. Mutual respect among the races is undermined. Racial divisions are intensified. Distrust is engendered. Disharmony, even anger, is provoked.

Ethnic preferences presuppose some generally understood sorting of the community into ethnic categories, necessary for the award of advantages to this group or to that one. Each person must be *iden-*

tifiable—by others and by himself—as a member of one ethnic group or another. To receive the benefits reserved for any minority, the beneficiaries must be seen, *and see themselves*, as members of that minority. Without identifiable memberships, preferences make no sense. But the pervasive application of racial classifications is malignant in a civil society. What obliges individuals to identify themselves by group divides the groups, builds barriers between them.

"Black" and "white," "Hispanic" and "Asian," and all the now-common names for ethnic groups are attended by confusion and many absurdities. Preferences didn't create those ethnic labels, but by preferences they are made more sensitive, and their importance is magnified. Of course, we want a society in which cultural attachments are protected and heritage preserved, but also one in which no citizen is by birth inferior to any another. We honor our origins, but no one's origins are second class. We strive for a community in which ethnic membership is a source of satisfaction, yet cannot impinge on any individual's rights or opportunities. The American ideal is that of a society in which neither race nor national origin are given *official* function.

The ideal is subverted by formally awarded ethnic preferences. When corporations, universities, and government agencies first classify and then reward and penalize their employees or applicants by race, the categories of race are hardened, entrenched. This hardening has very bad consequences for society at large....

Affirmative Action Programs: Basic Justice

Luke Charles Harris and Uma Narayan

INTRODUCTION

Affirmative action is an issue about which there has been considerable public debate. We think, however, that it is a policy that has often been misunderstood and mischaracterized, not only by those opposed to it, but even by its defenders. In this essay, we intend to describe these misconceptions, explain why we consider them to be misconceptions, and put forward a much stronger defense of affirmative action policies than that which is usually offered. In the first section, we examine and challenge prevalent misrepresentations of the scope of affirmative action policies—both misconceptions about the groups of people these policies are designed to benefit and about the benefits they are intended to achieve. In the second section, we address misunderstandings about the rationales for affirmative action policies and take issues with those who regard affirmative action as bestowing "preferential treatment" on its beneficiaries. We argue that affirmative action policies should he understood as attempts to equalize opportunity for groups of people who confront ongoing forms of institutional discrimination and a lack of equal opportunity....

We also take issue with (1) those who defend affirmative action on the grounds that it is nothing more than a form of compensation and (2) those who defend it merely on the grounds that it promotes diversity and a range of other long-term goals. We argue that such rationales mischaracterize affirmative action as providing justifiable "preferences" to its beneficiaries. In the last section, we contend that

the "stigma argument" against affirmative action dissolves when these programs are understood to equalize opportunities rather than as initiatives that merely bestow preferences on their beneficiaries.

CLARIFYING THE SCOPE OF AFFIRMATIVE ACTION POLICIES

Debates surrounding affirmative action often misrepresent the scope of these policies in several important ways. The most perturbing of these misrepresentations is the widespread tendency to construe affirmative action policies as race-based policies alone, and further, to talk about African Americans as the only racial group they are intended to benefit. This picture of affirmative action policies is, to put it bluntly, false. When these policies were first initiated, they were designed to benefit members of other disadvantaged racial minority groups besides African Americans. For example, almost two-thirds of the students admitted under the affirmative action program of the Davis Medical School that was challenged in the 1978 landmark *Bakke* case were Latino or Asian American. Yet, most of the public debate surrounding the *Bakke* decision discussed it strictly in terms of Blacks and whites only. Even more oddly, the opinions of the Supreme Court justices that considered this case—the plurality opinions as well as the dissenting opinion—discussed affirmative action as though African Americans were chief beneficiaries. This misrepresentation was unfortunate. Why? Because in the context of the racial history of the United States, such a misrepresentation of the scope of these policies is not only false, but also dangerous, since it is easier to create negative stereotypes about these programs when African Americans are viewed as their principle beneficiaries.

As a result, it is important that we recognize that, even at their inception, when affirmative action policies were predominantly race-based, they were designed to remedy the institutional exclusion of a number of racially-disadvantaged groups. In many institutional contexts, affirmative action policies have long since been expanded to cover other areas of discrimination and unequal opportunity. Many educational institutions, professions and trades have opened their doors to women as a result of affirmative action, promoting the entry of women into a range of areas that were largely male dominated, ranging from law schools to corporations to police departments. These new opportunities have benefitted not only women of color, but also many middle class White women. Affirmative action policies in some institutions, such as professional schools, have also promoted the entry of working class applicants, including working class White men, a fact that is seldom discussed and little known. Derrick Bell points out that "special admissions criteria have been expanded to encompass disadvantaged but promising White applicants." For example, the open admissions program of New York's City University system, which was initiated by minority pressure, has benefitted even greater numbers of lower, middle, and working class Whites than Blacks.

We need to remember that the world in which affirmative action policies were initiated was a world where a great many prestigious institutions and professions were almost exclusively enclaves of upper class White men; and where many of the blue collar trades were predominantly the preserve of White working class men. Af-

firmative action has been crucial in opening up the former to women, members of racial minorities, and working class Whites; and in opening up the latter to women and members of racial minorities. This is not to say, however, that each and every instance of affirmative action does or should consider each category of class, race and gender. Which factors should be considered depends on the patterns of exclusion within a particular occupation and institution. For example, affirmative action policies in the blue collar trades and police and fire departments should work affirmatively to promote the entry of women of all races and of minority men, since they were the groups that faced obstacles to entry,. not White working class men. Student admissions policies at historically elite women's colleges attended predominantly by White upper-class women, such as Vassar College, where we teach, on the other hand, should affirmatively seek not only to recruit students of color and women from working class backgrounds and white working-class men once they adopt co-ed policies. Taken as a whole, affirmative action policies in many institutional contexts have long operated on multiple criteria of inclusion, even though they continue to be portrayed as policies that either solely or principally benefit Blacks.

The prevalent failure to consider the range of people that affirmative action policies have benefitted breeds a number of misplaced objections to these policies. For example, many people argue that affirmative action policies should be class-based instead of race-based, since they believe that middle class African Americans do not need or "deserve" affirmative action. This view is problematic in a number of ways. First, many proponents of this view pose the issue as a choice between race and class, ignoring the fact that affirmative action policies have been both class and race based. Second, proponents of this view believe that middle class Blacks do not suffer from the effects of discrimination despite substantial evidence to the contrary.

In the mid-1980s, independent studies by the Grier Partnership and the Urban League revealed striking disparities in the employment levels of Blacks and Whites in Washington, D.C.—an area of the country deemed to be one of the "best markets" for Blacks. Both studies cite racial discrimination as the major factor that accounts for this difference. In the early 1990s, a study by the Urban Institute examined employment practices in the Chicago and Washington, D.C. areas by sending equally qualified and identically dressed White and Black applicants to newspaper-advertised positions. These testers were also matched for speech patterns, age, work experience, physical build and personal characteristics. The study found repeated discrimination that increased with the level of the advertised position, and revealed that Whites received job offers three times more often than equally qualified Blacks.

Finally, the limitations of the view that middle class Blacks do not suffer racial discrimination becomes clear when we attend to gender-based affirmative action policies. No one has seriously suggested that the sexism and gender-based discrimination women face in a variety of institutions is merely a product of their class status, or that middle class status shields White women from these effects. Just as affirmative action policies that only address class disadvantages are unlikely to remedy the gender based institutional exclusions faced by women, they would surely fail to remedy race-based exclusions faced by members of several racial minority groups. In short, the effects of gender and race bias would be only partially curtailed by purely class-based policies. Indeed, purely class-based policies would primarily benefit working class White men, whose race and gender are not the sources of invidious discrimination. As some recent feminist works teach us, we must, therefore, pay particular attention to the interconnected ways in which factors such as class, race, gender and sexual orientation work together to sustain disparities between different groups of Americans in a variety of institutional and social contexts.

There is, then, no need to pit class against race—or against gender—and frame it as the only valid basis for affirmative action. An array of factors that contribute to institutional discrimination—such as class, race, gender and sexual orientation—should be taken into account. When several factors intersect and jointly contribute to a process of discrimination, as in the case of a working class Black woman, each factor should be considered. When only one aspect of a person's identity adversely affects his or her opportunities in a given setting—for instance, class status in the case of working class White men, or race in the case of middle class Black men—then only that factor should be taken into account.

Another prevalent objection to affirmative action policies that seems connected to the misunderstanding of its actual scope is the argument that truly disadvantaged poor Blacks have not benefitted from these policies. The impression that affirmative action benefits only the Black middle class and that few working class or poor Blacks benefit from these programs is mistaken. The vast majority of Blacks were working class prior to the Civil Rights Era and the promulgation of civil rights laws and affirmative action initiatives. These efforts have combined to play a major role in the creation of the Black middle class that exists today. Bob Blauner points out that due to occupational mobility that is in part a product of affirmative action, nearly 25 percent of Black families had incomes of more than $25,000 (in constant dollars) in 1982, compared with 8.7 percent in 1960. Moreover, the proportion of employed Blacks who hold middle class jobs rose from 13.4 percent in 1960 to 37.8 percent in 1981. The number of Black college students rose from 340,000 in 1966 to more than one million in 1982. From sanitation departments to university departments, from the construction industry to corporate America, these programs have helped to open doors that were once tightly sealed.

An empirically accurate assessment of affirmative action policies shows that they have not only benefitted poor and working class Blacks, but poor and working class people of all races, including some White working class men and women. Thus, White working class opposition to these policies is mistakenly based on the belief that they are by definition "victims" of such programs, a mistake facilitated by discussions that portray these policies as only benefitting Blacks.

Finally, some people also argue against affirmative action on the grounds that it has not solved a host of problems pertaining to poverty, the inner city and the "underclass." It is true that affirmative action has not solved these problems—nor has it solved problems such as rape, domestic violence and sexual harassment. However, we do not think that these are legitimate objections, since they more obviously over-inflate the scope of what these policies were intended to accomplish. Affirmative action policies cannot be, nor were they ever intended to be, a magic solution to all of our social problems; indeed, no

single set of policies can solve every social problem that we confront. Their purpose is limited in scope—for they are designed only to partially counter the ways in which factors such as class, race, gender and sexual orientation function in our society to impede equal access and opportunity in a range of American institutions and occupations. In this respect, they have clearly succeeded.

RE-ENVISIONING THE RATIONALE FOR AFFIRMATIVE ACTION: FROM "PREFERENTIAL TREATMENT" TO "EQUAL OPPORTUNITY"

We believe that many mistaken views about affirmative action result from misunderstandings about the justifications or rationales for such policies. Unfortunately, the debate about affirmative action has largely been a dialogue between two broadly characterized positions. On the one hand, its critics describe it as a form of "reverse discrimination" that bestows "undeserved preferences" on its beneficiaries. On the other hand, its defenders continue to characterize these policies as "preferential treatment," but argue that these preferences are justified, either as forms of "compensation" or on grounds of "social utility." Few question the assumption that affirmative action involves the "bestowal of preferences," or challenge the premise that it marks a sudden deviation from a system that, until its advent, operated strictly and clearly on the basis of merit. Setting out a view of affirmative action that rejects these ideas is our central task here.

In our view, affirmative action is not a matter of affording "preferential treatment" to its beneficiaries. Our position is that affirmative action is best understood as an attempt to promote equality of opportunity in a social context marked by pervasive inequalities—one in which many institutional practices work to impede a fair assessment of the capabilities of those who are working-class, women or people of color. In this regard, affirmative action is an attempt to equalize opportunity for people who continue to face institutional obstacles to equal consideration and equal treatment. These obstacles include not only continuing forms of blatant discrimination, but more importantly, they include a variety of subtle institutional criteria and practices that unwarrantedly circumscribe mobility in contemporary America. These criteria and practices are often not deliberately designed to discriminate and exclude: the fact remains, however, that they nevertheless function to do so, as our subsequent examples demonstrate. In countering such forms of discrimination, affirmative action policies attempt only to "level the playing field." They do not "bestow preferences" on their beneficiaries: rather, they attempt to undo the effects of institutional practices and criteria that, however unintentionally, amount in effect to "preferential treatment" for Whites and men, among others.

Those who believe that affirmative action constitutes "preferential treatment" often assume (a) that the criteria and procedures generally used for admissions and hiring are neutral indicators of "merit," unaffected by factors such as class, race, or gender; and (b) that such criteria are fairly and impartially applied to all individuals at each stage of the selection process. In this section, we will try to show why these two assumptions are seriously open to question.

Although standardized tests are often "taken as absolute by both the public and the institutions that use the scores in decision making," there is ample evidence that they do not predict equally well for men and women. A study of three college admissions tests (the SAT, the PSAT/NM-SQT, and the ACT) reveals that although women consistently earn better high school and college grades, they receive lower scores on all three tests. Rosser argued that "if the SAT predicted equally well for both sexes, girls would score about 20 points higher than the boys, not 61 points lower". Standardized test scores adversely affect women's chances for admission to colleges and universities, their chances for scholarships, and entry into "gifted" programs, as well as their academic self-perceptions. Similarly, James Crouse and Dale Trusheim argue, on the basis of statistical evidence, that the test scores are not very useful indicators for helping to "admit black applicants who would succeed and to reject black applicants who would fail".

The literature on such standardized tests demonstrates that they are often inaccurate indicators even with respect to their limited stated objective of predicting students' first-year grades in college and professional schools. Yet, they are often used as if they measured a person's overall intelligence and foretold long-term success in educational institutions and professional life. As a result of these unsupported beliefs, affirmative action policies that depart from strict considerations of these test scores are often taken to constitute the strongest evidence for institutional deviation from standards of merit. Such policies are also thought to represent the type of "preferences" somehow reserved only for women and minority applicants.

There are also many other examples of established institutional rules, practices and policies that, no matter how benign their intention, have the effect of discriminating against the members of relatively marginalized groups. For instance, word-of-mouth recruitment—where the existing labor pool consists of predominantly White men—reduces the opportunity for women and people of color to apply for the jobs in question. Other examples include unions that influence or control hiring in well-paid jobs in the construction, transportation and printing industries when recruiting is solely accomplished through personal contacts. A 1990 study reports that over eighty percent of executives find their jobs through networking, and that about eighty-six percent of available jobs do not appear in the classifieds. "Last hired, first fired" rules make more recently hired women and minorities more susceptible to lay-offs. The "old boy network" that results from years of social and business contacts among White men, as well as racially or sexually segregated country clubs or social organizations—which are often paid for by employers—also bear a disparate impact on women and minorities. Furthermore, stereotyped beliefs about women and minorities often justify hiring them for low-level, low-paying jobs, regardless of their qualifications for higher-level jobs.

Indeed, some empirical studies show that many Black candidates for jobs are rated more negatively than White candidates with identical credentials. Other studies demonstrate that the same resume with a woman's name on it receives a significantly lower rating than when it has a man's name on it, showing that gender-bias operates even when there is no direct contact with the persons evaluated. Still other problematic practices include evaluations where subjective assessments of factors such as "fitting in," "personality," and "self-confidence" work to accomodate class, race and gender prejudice.

Personal interviews, job evaluations, and recommendations all have an inescapable subjective element which often works in the favor of better-off White men. As Lawrence A. Blum writes:

> Persons can fail to be judged purely on ability because they have not gone to certain colleges or professional schools, because they do not know the right people, because they do not present themselves in a certain way. And, again, sometimes this sort of discrimination takes place without either those doing the discriminating or those being discriminated against realizing it... Often these denials of equal opportunity have a lot to do with class background, as well as race or sex, or with a combination of these.

Interview processes that precede being selected or hired are often not as "neutral" as assumed. A two-step experiment done at Princeton University began with White undergraduates interviewing both White and Black job applicants. Unknown to the interviewers, the applicants in the first stage of the experiment were all confederates of the experimenters and were trained to behave consistently from interview to interview. This study reported that interviewers spent less time with Black applicants and were less friendly and outgoing than with the White applicants. In the second stage of the experiment, confederates of the experimenters were trained to approximate the two styles of interviewing observed during the first stage of the study when they interviewed two groups of White applicants. A panel of judges who reviewed the tapes of these interviews reported that White applicants subjected to the style previously accorded Blacks performed noticeably worse in the interviews than other White applicants. In this respect, there is also substantial evidence that women are asked inappropriate questions and subject to discrimination in interviews.

None of the discriminatory institutional structures and practices we have detailed above necessarily involve conscious antipathy toward women and minorities or the operation of conscious sexist or racist stereotypes. Some discriminatory structures and practices involve unconscious stereotypes at work, from which women and people of color are hardly immune in their own evaluations of other women and minorities. Many of the examples we discussed above involve practices central to hiring and promotion that work to disadvantage many marginalized Americans, even when all persons involved sincerely believe themselves to be fair and impartial. Because the process of getting through an educational program, or being hired, retained or promoted in a job involves the possibility of women and minority applicants being subject to a variety of such practices, it seems likely that few, if any, women or people of color are apt to escape the cumulative adverse effects of these practices. In the context of these structures and practices that systematically disadvantage some Americans, it would be naïve, at best, to believe that our society is a well-functioning meritocracy.

The problem is far more complicated than is captured by the common perspective that working class people, women and the members of some racial minorities have generally not had equal advantages and opportunities to acquire the relevant qualifications, and therefore, they should be compensated by being awarded preferences even though they are not as qualified as their White male peers. The qualifications of members of marginalized groups, in fact, tend to be under-valued and under-appraised in many institutional contexts. Moreover, many of the criteria that are seen as important impartial indicators of their competencies, merit and potential (such as test scores) not only fail to be precise measurements of these qualities, but systematically stigmatize these individuals within institutions in which these tests unwarrantedly function as important criteria of admission.

We do not, however, wish to deny that factors such as class, race and gender often impede people from acquiring qualifications. Black school districts often receive less funding and inferior educational resources compared to similar White districts, often as a result of decision making by Whites. There is also increasing evidence of disadvantaging practices in the pre-college advising offered to minority students. Teachers often interpret linguistic and cultural differences as indications of low potential or a lack of academic interests on the part of minority students. Guidance counselors often steer female and minority students away from "hard" subjects, such as mathematics and science, which are often paths to high-paying jobs.

In such contexts, even if the criteria used to determine admission and hiring were otherwise unproblematic. it is not at all clear that taking them simply "at face value" would fairly or accurately gauge the talents and potential of individuals from distinctly different backgrounds. When some candidates have to overcome certain educational and social obstacles that others do not, similarity of credentials may well amount to a significant difference in talent and potential. Thus, treating identical credentials as signs of identical capabilities and effort may, under prevailing conditions of inequality, significantly devalue the worth of credentials obtained in the teeth of such obstacles. We argue that individuals who obtained their credentials in the face of severe obstacles are likely to perform better than those who have similar or even somewhat better credentials obtained without coping with such obstacles. This is especially true over a period of years, where they have had opportunities to remedy the handicaps that they face. Affirmative action policies, with respect to admissions and hiring, recruit individuals for positions where "success" depends on the nature of one's performance over several years. Such recruitment policies should rightly concern themselves with a person's evidenced potential for success rather than simply assess what a person's capabilities appear to be based on the comparison of credentials acquired by individuals under distinctly different circumstances.

Still, we are not arguing that affirmative action policies are, or can be, magical formulas that help us determine with perfect precision in every ease the exact weights that must be accorded to a person's class background, gender, or minority status so as to afford him or her perfect equality of opportunity. Particular institutions must use practical wisdom and good-faith efforts to determine the exact measures that they will undertake to promote equality within their frameworks, as well as monitor and periodically reassess the parameters and scope of their institutional policies. Nor do we wish to deny that some persons recruited as a result of affirmative action policies might turn out to be incompetent or demonstrate significant limitations in their ability to meet requirements. After all, the same incompetencies are manifested by some who are recruited through "regular" channels. No recruitment policies are immune to these problems. What we argue is that in situations where issues of class, race, and gender operate to impede equality of opportunity, affirmative action policies have enabled many talented and promising individuals to have their talent and promise more fairly evaluated by the institutions in

question than would otherwise have been the case....

CHALLENGING THE "STIGMA" OF AFFIRMATIVE ACTION

Affirmative action has been criticized on the grounds that it "stigmatizes" its participants because both they themselves as well as others regard the beneficiaries of affirmative action as "less qualified" than non-beneficiaries....

There are a number of... troublesome assumptions that underlie the stigma arguments. For example, for decades, almost all of our elite institutions and professions, as well as many non-elite career paths, were domains that permitted entry to a very small, and extremely privileged segment of the population. Yet there were millions of equally talented individuals who, because they were either working class, or women, or members of racial minority groups were denied the same chance to develop their talents and capabilities in these spheres—talents and capabilities that may well have exceeded those of many of their privileged White male counterparts. Rarely, if ever, have the privileged White men who benefitted from such "undeserved preferences" ever castigated themselves or publicly expressed the feeling that they were not "really talented" or "really deserving of their positions," even though they acquired them under circumstances that eliminated most of their fellow citizens, including the female members of their own families, from the competitive pool. We are unaware of a body of literature from these individuals filled with anxiety and self-doubt about their capabilities and merit. Indeed, one of the unnerving effects of privilege is that it permits the privileged to feel so entitled to their privileges that they often fail to see them as privileges at all. In such a setting, it is more than a little ironic that the beneficiaries of affirmative action programs, designed to counteract the effects of institutional discrimination, are now viewed by many Americans as stigmatized by the very programs that eliminate the unwarranted obstacles faced by affirmative action's beneficiaries.

Many who complain about the preferential treatment they believe affirmative action accords to women and minorities in academia assume that everyone other than its beneficiaries is admitted purely as a result of merit. Yet, paradoxically, policies that favor relatives of alumni, and children of faculty members or donors to the university have not created a storm of legal or social controversy. Perhaps this is because such policies tend to benefit predominantly White middle class individuals. Our point is not simply to claim, however, that people who accept preferential policies that benefit middle class Whites are often outraged by "preferences" rooted in affirmative action policies. Our point is a much stronger one that hinges on the profound differences between affirmative action and these other policies. Policies that favor children of alumni or donors to the university are policies that may serve some useful goals. But they are genuinely "favors" or "preferences" with respect to the individuals admitted in that such policies are in no way intended to equalize the opportunities of those thus admitted. Thus, we insist on a conceptual distinction between affirmative action and policies that are genuinely tantamount to bestowing preferences.

In this respect, our point is not to endorse a "purely meritocractic society" as the ideal society. Rather we seek to highlight the reality that many existing institutional structures not only fail to function as pure meritocracies, but also serve systematically to disadvantage whole groups of people, including working class people,

women and people of color. To those strongly committed to traditional meritocratic ideals, we suggest that when close attention is paid to the systematically disadvantaging effects of many institutional procedures, they may actually have reason to see affirmative action as conducive to their meritocratic ideals rather than as serious deviations from them.

CONCLUSION

The intellectual confusion surrounding affirmative action transcends ideological categories. Critics and supporters of all political stripes have underestimated the significance of these policies, collaborated in equating affirmative action with "preferential treatment," and permitted important assumptions about how institutions function to lie unchallenged. As a result, the issues raised in the context of the current major affirmative action law suits pending against the Universities of Michigan and Washington which challenge race-based admissions programs and the terms of the debate that informs the referendum initiatives to amend state law to bar race-based affirmative action in California and Washington have served only to obscure our understanding of what is at stake in the affirmative action debate. We argue that these policies do not automatically involve preferential treatment, and that instead they should be understood as attempts to promote fairness and equal citizenship by affording the members of marginalized groups a fair chance to enter significant societal institutions.

The fact that formal legal equality seems commonplace and obviously justified to many today should not obscure how recently formal equality has been a reality for many, nor the struggles it took to make it a reality. More importantly, we should not imagine that the achievement of formal legal equality erased the consequences of centuries of inequality, making the promise of equality and full citizenship an immediate reality for those previously excluded. The institutional consequences of such historically group-based exclusions in significant domains of occupational and social life still remain. Class, race and gender, for example, continue to deprive people of the opportunities to participate in numerous forms of association and work that are crucial to the development of talents and capabilities that enable people to contribute meaningfully to, and benefit from, the collective possibilities of national life.

Only since the latter part of the nineteenth century and the early decades of the twentieth century have some democratic political communities, such as the United States, sought to embrace the members of marginalized groups they had once excluded from the rights and privileges of citizenship. Only in the latter part of the twentieth century has there dawned the recognition that laws and policies that promote formal equality do not necessarily ensure substantive equality or genuine equal opportunity for all Americans. In this respect, affirmative action policies are a significant and historic achievement, for they constitute an attempt to transform our legacy of unequal treatment with respect to certain marginalized groups of Americans. They symbolize our political commitment to ensuring substantive participation in all domains of life for various groups of our diverse citizenry. Thus, we believe that affirmative action programs warrant a more favorable evaluation, both as an historic achievement and in terms of their positive effects within contemporary American institutions, than they are usually accorded.

THE CONTINUING DEBATE:
Affirmative Action Programs

What Is New

For contrasting legal views on affirmative action, see *City of Richmond v. J. A. Croson and Company*, Justice Sandra Day O'Connor writing in opposition to affirmative action and Justice Thurgood Marshall writing in support. A more recent case is *Grutter v. Bollinger* (2003), in which the Court ruled that the University of Michigan Law School was justified in seeking diverse students because of:

> the substantial, important, and laudable educational benefits that diversity is designed to produce, including cross-racial understanding and the breaking down of racial stereotypes. The Law School's claim is further bolstered by numerous expert studies and reports showing that such diversity promotes learning outcomes and better prepares students for an increasingly diverse workforce, for society, and for the legal profession. Major American businesses have made clear that the skills needed in today's increasingly global marketplace can only be developed through exposure to widely diverse people, cultures, ideas, and viewpoints.

Where to Find More

An excellent article in support of the majority decision in *Grutter v. Bollinger* is James P. Sterba's "The Michigan Cases and Furthering the Justification for Affirmative Action," in *International Journal of Applied Philosophy*, volume 18, no. 1, 2004, pp. 1-12. Sterba's paper is followed by Terence J. Pell's "The Nature of Claims about Race and the Debate Over Racial Preferences," which opposes affirmative action for diversity; and following Pell's paper, Sterba offers a critique of Pell's arguments, followed by Pell's criticisms of Sterba's position. Ronald Dworkin devotes chapters 11 and 12 of his excellent *Sovereign Virtue* (Cambridge, MA: Harvard University Press, 2000) to the question of affirmative action, with very insightful discussion of recent U. S. Supreme Court decisions on the subject. A very good affirmative action debate is Carl Cohen and James P. Sterba, *Affirmative Action and Racial Preference: A Debate* (New York: Oxford University Press, 2003).

Daniel Sabbagh's excellent 2004 background paper, "Affirmative Action Policies: An International Perspective," is available online from Human Development Reports at *http://hdr.undp.org/publications/papers.cfm*. The online Stanford Encyclopedia of Philosophy has an excellent introduction to the issues at *http://plato.stanford.edu/entries/affirmative-action*. A good online resource (including detailed descriptions of the relevant literature, links to other sites, and a comprehensive review of all the important Supreme Court affirmative action cases) is at *www.personal.umich.edu/~eandersn/biblio.htm*.

Arguments in favor of affirmative action can be found in Bernard Boxill, *Blacks and Social Justice* (Totowa, NJ: Rowman and Littlefield, 1984); Barbara R. Bergmann, *In Defense of Affirmative Action* (New York: BasicBooks, 1996), who explains (supported with extensive psychological research) how subtle patterns of discrimination disadvantage well-qualified women and minority candidates; Elizabeth Anderson, "Integration, Affirmative Action, and Strict Scrutiny," *NYU Law Review*,

77, 2002: 1195-1271; Gertrude Ezorsky, *Racism and Justice: The Case for Affirmative Action* (Ithaca, NY: Cornell University Press, 1991); Stanley Fish, "Reverse Racism, or How the Pot Got to Call the Kettle Black," *The Atlantic*, November 1993; Cornel West, *Race Matters* (Boston: Beacon Press, 1993); Charles R. Lawrence III and Mari J. Matsuda, *We Won't Go Back: Making the Case for Affirmative Action* (Boston: Houghton Mifflin, 1997); and a very creative article by Susan Sturm and Lani Guinier, "The Future of Affirmative Action: Reclaiming the Innovative Ideal," in *California Law Review*, 1996, volume 84, pp. 953-1037.

Opposing views are found in George Sher, "Reverse Discrimination, the Future, and the Past," *Ethics*, vol. 90, 1979; Shelby Steele, who argues that affirmative action programs stigmatize those who are supposed to be benefitted, in *The Content of Our Character: A New Vision of Race in America* (New York: HarperPerennial, 1991); and Carl Cohen, *Naked Racial Preference* (Boston: Madison Books, 1995).

Some anthologies on the subject include Robert K. Fullinwider and Claudia Mills, editors, *The Moral Foundations of Civil Rights* (Totowa, NJ: Rowman & Littlefield, 1986); Russell Nieli, editor, *Racial Preference and Racial Justice: The New Affirmative Action Controversy* (Washington, D.C.: Ethics and Public Policy Center, 1991), which contains many of the key opposing legal arguments by U.S. Supreme Court Justices and others; Steven M. Cahn, editor, *The Affirmative Action Debate* (New York: Routledge, 1995); also by Steven Cahn, ed., *Affirmative Action and the University* (Philadelphia: Temple University Press, 1993), which starts from three major papers taking distinctly different views, and follows with comments on those essays by two dozen writers; and the excellent collection edited by M. Cohen, T. Nagel, and T. Scanlon, *Equality and Preferential Treatment* (Princeton: Princeton University Press, 1977).

NONHUMAN ANIMAL RIGHTS

Sorely Neglected *or* Nonexistent?

SORELY NEGLECTED

ADVOCATE: Tom Regan, Professor of Philosophy at North Carolina State University, leader in the animal rights movement, and author of *The Case for Animal Rights* (Berkeley: The University of California Press, 1983)

SOURCE: "The Case for Animal Rights," from Peter Singer, editor, *In Defense of Animals* (Oxford: Basil Blackwell, Inc., 1985): 13–26

NONEXISTENT

ADVOCATE: Carl Cohen, Professor of Philosophy at the University of Michigan, Ann Arbor

SOURCE: "The Case for the Use of Animals in Biomedical Research," *The New England Journal of Medicine*, volume 315 (October 2, 1986): 865–870

The question of our moral obligations toward nonhuman animals is an ethical issue we confront daily when deciding what food to eat, what clothes to wear, and what laboratory experiments to pursue. Our religious views, our deepest beliefs about ourselves and our place in the world, and many of our most mundane daily practices involve our beliefs about animals and their appropriate treatment. It is hardly surprising, then, that questions about our treatment of animals provoke strong reactions on both sides of the issue.

Wearing fur has been a focal point of many protests, since the practice is obvious and very public, and the killing of animals in order to provide the ostentatious luxury of fur coats seems a clear example of cruelty to animals for frivolous purposes. But obviously the major place where animals are killed for human use is in agriculture and scientific experimentation. Though scientists have often argued that the sacrifice of animals is vital for advances in the treatment of terrible diseases, animal rights activists point to the widespread testing of such things as cosmetics, oven cleaners, and shampoos on animals—for example, dropping concentrated forms of cosmetics into the eyes of restrained rabbits to test for harm—that are for purposes not quite so serious. Animal rights activists also argue that non-animal alternatives are available for legitimate scientific studies.

The most obvious basis for extending ethical consideration to animals is utilitarian ethics. According to utilitarian ethics, the right act is the act that produces the greatest balance of pleasure over suffering for all involved. In the utilitarian view, suffering is suffering, whether the suffering is experienced by a human or a dog. While many advocates for animals (such as Peter Singer) have been utilitarians, Tom Regan favors a *rights* view of ethics. In Regan's view, the most plausible grounds for claiming that humans have rights will also apply to nonhuman animals. When considering

Regan's position, it is important to note that Regan is not claiming that animals can act morally. While some writers have argued that animals are moral actors in their own right, most who have been concerned with the issue have denied that nonhuman animals are moral actors, but instead insist that—like human infants and humans who are severely demented—nonhuman animals are due our moral consideration (and may have a *right* to such moral consideration), even though they are not themselves moral actors.

POINTS TO PONDER

➤ Some animal researchers—especially at universities—have made an effort to treat their animal research subjects more humanely: providing larger cages, imposing less isolation on social species, reducing suffering during experiments. Some who support animal rights see this as a valuable step in the right direction, while others deride such measures as part of the "clean cage movement": an effort to gain positive publicity without addressing the fundamental abuses of animals in experimentation. What is your view of programs to ameliorate the suffering of laboratory animals while continuing to run experiments that harm and ultimately kill the animals?

➤ It is always possible—as a matter of religious doctrine—to insist that only humans have souls, and therefore only humans have rights (though at least some Eastern views, not to mention St. Francis of Assisi in the Christian tradition, would argue that other animals do have souls). But leaving aside such religious doctrines, *is* there any characteristic that would apply to *all* humans whom you would say have rights (including the demented, the severely retarded, small children) but would *not* apply to nonhuman animals (such as chimpanzees or pigs)?

➤ What are Regan's objections to social contract theory as a theory of ethics? Do you agree with his critique?

➤ Cohen insists that if an individual human cannot reason or follow moral principles, that doesn't matter: That individual still has rights, because—being human—it is the right *kind* of being to reason and follow moral principles. Suppose a single brilliant chimpanzee could argue, reason, and follow moral principles (in fact, this brilliant chimpanzee is so good at moral reasoning that she is awarded a position as an ethics professor at Oxford University). In Cohen's view, would that chimpanzee still have no rights, because she is the wrong kind of being to have rights?

NonHuman Animal Rights
Sorely Neglected

TOM REAGAN

I regard myself as an advocate of animal rights—as a part of the animal rights movement. That movement, as I conceive it, is committed to a number of goals, including:

- the total abolition of the use of animals in science;
- the total dissolution of commercial animal agriculture;
- the total elimination of commercial and sport hunting and trapping.

There are, I know, people who profess to believe in animal rights but do not avow these goals. Factory farming, they say, is wrong—it violates animals' rights—but traditional animal agriculture is all right. Toxicity tests of cosmetics on animals violates their rights, but important medical research—cancer research, for example—does not. The clubbing of baby seals is abhorrent, but not the harvesting of adult seals. I used to think I understood this reasoning. Not any more. You don't change unjust institutions by tidying them up.

What's wrong—fundamentally wrong—with the way animals are treated isn't the details that vary from case to case. It's the whole system. The forlornness of the veal calf is pathetic, heart wrenching; the pulsing pain of the chimp with electrodes planted deep in her brain is repulsive; the slow, torturous death of a raccoon caught in the leg-hold trap is agonizing. But what is wrong isn't the pain, isn't the suffering, isn't the deprivation. These compound what's wrong. Sometimes—often—they make it much worse. But they are not the fundamental wrong.

The fundamental wrong is the system that allows us to view animals as *our resources*, here for *us*—to be eaten, or surgically manipulated, or exploited for sport or money. Once we accept this view of animals—as our resources—the rest is as predictable as it is regrettable. Why worry about their loneliness, their pain, their death? Since animals exist for us, to benefit us in one way or another, what harms them really doesn't matter—or matters only if it starts to bother us, makes us feel a trifle uneasy when we eat our veal escalope, for example. So, yes, let us get veal calves out of solitary confinement, give them more space, a little straw, a few companions. But let us keep our veal escalope.

But a little straw, more space and a few companions won't eliminate—won't even touch—the basic wrong that attaches to our viewing and treating these animals as our resources. A veal calf killed to be eaten after living in close confinement is viewed and treated in this way: but so, too, is another who is raised (as they say) "more humanely". To right the wrong of our treatment of farm animals requires more than making rearing methods "more humane"; it requires the total dissolution of commercial animal agriculture....

We begin by asking how the moral status of animals has been understood by thinkers who deny that animals have rights. Then we test the mettle of their ideas by seeing how well they stand up under the heat of fair criticism. If we start our thinking in this way, we soon find that some people believe that we have no direct duties to animals, that we owe nothing to them, that we can do nothing that wrongs them. Rather, we can do wrong acts that involve animals, and so we have duties regarding them, though none to them. Such views may be called indirect duty views. By way of illustration: suppose your neighbour kicks your dog. Then your neighbour has done something wrong. But not to your dog. The wrong that has been done is a wrong to you. After all, it is wrong to upset people, and your neighbour's kicking your dog upsets you. So you are the one who is wronged, not your dog. Or again: by kicking your dog your neighbour damages your property. And since it is wrong to damage another person's property, your neighbour has done something wrong—to you, of course, not to your dog. Your neighbour no more wrongs your dog than your car would be wronged if the windshield were smashed. Your neighbour's duties involving your dog are indirect duties to you. More generally, all of our duties regarding animals are indirect duties to one another—to humanity.

How could someone try to justify such a view? Someone might say that your dog doesn't feel anything and so isn't hurt by your neighbour's kick, doesn't care about the pain because none is felt, is as unaware of anything as is your windshield. Someone might say this, but no rational person will, since, among other considerations, such a view will commit anyone who holds it to the position that no human being feels pain either—that human beings also don't care about what happens to them. A second possibility is that though both humans and your dog are hurt when kicked, it is only human pain that matters. But, again, no rational person can believe this. Pain is pain wherever it occurs. If your neighbour's causing you pain is wrong because of the pain that is caused, we cannot rationally ignore or dismiss the

moral relevance of the pain that your dog feels.

Philosophers who hold indirect duty views—and many still do—have come to understand that they must avoid the two defects just noted: that is, both the view that animals don't feel anything as well as the idea that only human pain can be morally relevant. Among such thinkers the sort of view now favoured is one or other form of what is called *contractarianism*.

Here, very crudely, is the root idea: morality consists of a set of rules that individuals voluntarily agree to abide by, as we do when we sign a contract (hence the name contractarianism). Those who understand and accept the terms of the contract are covered directly; they have rights created and recognized by, and protected in, the contract. And these contractors can also have protection spelled out for others who, though they lack the ability to understand morality and so cannot sign the contract themselves, are loved or cherished by those who can. Thus young children, for example, are unable to sign contracts and lack rights. But they are protected by the contract nonetheless because of the sentimental interests of others, most notably their parents. So we have, then, duties involving these children, duties regarding them, but no duties to them. Our duties in this case are indirect duties to other human beings, usually their parents.

As for animals, since they cannot understand contracts, they obviously cannot sign; and since they cannot sign, they have no rights. Like children, however, some animals are the objects of the sentimental interest of others. You, for example, love your dog or cat. So those animals that enough people care about (companion animals, whales, baby seals, the American bald eagle), though they lack rights themselves, will be protected because of the sentimental interests of people. I have, then, according to contractarianism, no duty directly to your dog or any other animal, not even the duty not to cause them pain or suffering; my duty not to hurt them is a duty I have to those people who care about what happens to them. As for other animals, where no or little sentimental interest is present—in the case of farm animals, for example, or laboratory rats—what duties we have grow weaker and weaker, perhaps to the vanishing point. The pain and death they endure, though real, are not wrong if no one cares about them.

When it comes to the moral status of animals, contractarianism could be a hard view to refute if it were an adequate theoretical approach to the moral status of human beings. It is not adequate in this latter respect, however, which makes the question of its adequacy in the former case, regarding animals, utterly moot. For consider: morality, according to the (crude) contractarian position before us, consists of rules that people agree to abide by. What people? Well, enough to make a difference—enough, that is, *collectively* to have the power to enforce the rules that are drawn up in the contract. That is very well and good for the signatories but not so good for anyone who is not asked to sign. And there is nothing in contractarianism of the sort we are discussing that guarantees or requires that everyone will have a chance to participate equally in framing the rules of morality. The result is that this approach to ethics could sanction the most blatant forms of social, economic, moral and political injustice, ranging from a repressive caste system to systematic racial or sexual discrimination. Might, according to this theory, does make right. Let those who are the victims of injustice suffer as they will. It matters not so long as no one else—no contractor,

or too few of them—cares about it. Such a theory takes one's moral breath away... as if, for example, there would be nothing wrong with apartheid in South Africa if few white South Africans were upset by it. A theory with so little to recommend it at the level of the ethics of our treatment of our fellow humans cannot have anything more to recommend it when it comes to the ethics of how we treat our fellow animals.

The version of contractarianism just examined is, as I have noted, a crude variety, and in fairness to those of a contractarian persuasion it must be noted that much more refined, subtle and ingenious varieties are possible. For example, John Rawls, in his *A Theory of Justice*, sets forth a version of contractarianism that forces contractors to ignore the accidental features of being a human being—for example, whether one is white or black, male or female, a genius or of modest intellect. Only by ignoring such features, Rawls believes, can we ensure that the principles of justice that contractors would agree upon are not based on bias or prejudice. Despite the improvement of such a view over the cruder forms of contractarianism, it remains deficient; it systematically denies that we have direct duties to those human beings who do not have a sense of justice—young children, for instance, and many mentally retarded humans. And yet it seems reasonably certain that, were we to torture a young child or retarded elder, we would be doing something that wronged him or her, not something that would be wrong if (and only if) other humans with a sense of justice were upset. And since this is true in the case of these humans, we cannot rationally deny the same in the case of animals.

Indirect duty views, then, including the best among them, fail to command our rational assent. Whatever ethical theory we should accept rationally, therefore, it must at least recognize that we have some duties directly to animals, just as we have some duties directly to each other....

Some people think that the theory we are looking for is utilitarianism. A utilitarian accepts two moral principles. The first is that of equality: everyone's interests count, and similar interests must be counted as having similar weight or importance. White or black, American or Iranian, human or animal—everyone's pain or frustration matter, and matter just as much as the equivalent pain or frustration of anyone else. The second principle a utilitarian accepts is that of utility: do the act that will bring about the best balance between satisfaction and frustration for everyone affected by the outcome.

As a utilitarian, then, here is how I am to approach the task of deciding what I morally ought to do: I must ask who will be affected if I choose to do one thing rather than another, how much each individual will be affected, and where the best results are most likely to lie—which option, in other words, is most likely to bring about the best results, the best balance between satisfaction and frustration. That option, whatever it may be, is the one I ought to choose. That is where my moral duty lies.

The great appeal of utilitarianism rests with its uncompromising *egalitarianism*: everyone's interests count and count as much as the like interests of everyone else. The kind of odious discrimination that some forms of contractarianism can justify—discrimination based on race or sex, for example—seems disallowed in principle by utilitarianism, as is speciesism, systematic discrimination based on species membership.

The equality we find in utilitarianism, however, is not the sort an advocate of animal or human rights should have in mind. Utilitarianism has no room for the equal moral rights of different individuals because it has no room for their equal inherent value or worth. What has value for the utilitarian is the satisfaction of an individual's interests, not the individual whose interests they are. A universe in which you satisfy your desire for water, food and warmth is, other things being equal, better than a universe in which these desires are frustrated. And the same is true in the case of an animal with similar desires. But neither you nor the animal have any value in your own right. Only your feelings do.

Here is an analogy to make the philosophical point clearer: a cup contains different liquids, sometimes sweet, sometimes bitter, sometimes a mix of the two. What has value are the liquids: the sweeter the better, the bitterer the worse. The cup, the container, has no value. It is what goes into it, not what they go into, that has value. For the utilitarian you and I are like the cup; we have no value as individuals and thus no equal value. What has value is what goes into us, what we serve as receptacles for; our feelings of satisfaction have positive value, our feelings of frustration negative value.

Serious problems arise for utilitarianism when we remind ourselves that it enjoins us to bring about the best consequences. What does this mean? It doesn't mean the best consequences for me alone, or for my family or friends, or any other person taken individually. No, what we must do is, roughly, as follows: we must add up (somehow!) the separate satisfactions and frustrations of everyone likely to be affected by our choice, the satisfactions in one column, the frustrations in the other. We must total each column for each of the options before us. That is what it means to say the theory is aggregative. And then we must choose that option which is most likely to bring about the best balance of totaled satisfactions over totaled frustrations. Whatever act would lead to this outcome is the one we ought morally to perform—it is where our moral duty lies. And that act quite clearly might not be the same one that would bring about the best results for me personally, or for my family or friends, or for a lab animal. The best aggregated consequences for everyone concerned are not necessarily the best for each individual.

That utilitarianism is an aggregative theory—different individuals' satisfactions or frustrations are added, or summed, or totaled—is the key objection to this theory. My Aunt Bea is old, inactive, a cranky, sour person, though not physically ill. She prefers to go on living. She is also rather rich. I could make a fortune if I could get my hands on her money, money she intends to give me in any event, after she dies, but which she refuses to give me now. In order to avoid a huge tax bite, I plan to donate a handsome sum of my profits to the local children's hospital. Many, many children will benefit from my generosity, and much joy will be brought to their parents, relatives and friends. If I don't get the money rather soon, all these ambitions will come to naught. The once-in-a-lifetime opportunity to make a real killing will be gone. Why, then, not kill my Aunt Bea? Of course, I *might* get caught. But I'm no fool and, besides, her doctor can be counted on to cooperate (he has an eye for the same investment and I happen to know a good deal about his shady past). The deed can be done... professionally, shall we say. There is *very* little chance of getting caught. And as for my conscience being guilt-ridden, I am a resourceful sort of fellow and will take more than sufficient comfort—as I lie on the beach at Acapulco—in contemplating the joy and health I have brought to so many others.

Suppose Aunt Bea is killed and the rest of the story comes out as told. Would I have done anything wrong? Anything immoral? One would have thought that I had. Not according to utilitarianism. Since what I have done has brought about the best balance between totaled satisfaction and frustration for all those affected by the outcome, my action is not wrong. Indeed, in killing Aunt Bea the physician and I did what duty required.

This same kind of argument can be repeated in all sorts of cases, illustrating, time after time, how the utilitarian's position leads to results that impartial people find morally callous. It *is* wrong to kill my Aunt Bea in the name of bringing about the best results for others. A good end does not justify an evil means. Any adequate moral theory will have to explain why this is so. Utilitarianism fails in this respect and so cannot be the theory we seek.

What to do? Where to begin anew? The place to begin, I think, is with the utilitarian's view of the value of the individual—or, rather, lack of value. In its place, suppose we consider that you and I, for example, do have value as individuals—what we'll call *inherent value*. To say we have such value is to say that we are something more than, something different from, mere receptacles. Moreover, to ensure that we do not pave the way for such injustices as slavery or sexual discrimination, we must believe that all who have inherent value have it equally, regardless of their sex, race, religion, birthplace and so on. Similarly to be discarded as irrelevant are one's talents or skills, intelligence and wealth, personality or pathology, whether one is loved and admired or despised and loathed. The genius and the retarded child, the prince and the pauper, the brain surgeon and the fruit vendor, Mother Teresa and the most unscrupulous used-car salesman—all have inherent value, all possess it equally, and all have an equal right to be treated with respect, to be treated in ways that do not reduce them to the status of things, as if they existed as resources for others. My value as an individual is independent of my usefulness to you. Yours is not dependent on your usefulness to me. For either of us to treat the other in ways that fail to show respect for the other's independent value is to act immorally, to violate the individual's rights.

Some of the rational virtues of this view—what I call the rights view—should be evident. Unlike (crude) contractarianism, for example, the rights view *in principle* denies the moral tolerability of any and all forms of racial, sexual or social discrimination; and unlike utilitarianism, this view *in principle* denies that we can justify good results by using evil means that violate an individual's rights—denies, for example, that it could be moral to kill my Aunt Bea to harvest beneficial consequences for others. That would be to sanction the disrespectful treatment of the individual in the name of the social good, something the rights view will not—categorically will not—ever allow.

The rights view, I believe, is rationally the most satisfactory moral theory. It surpasses all other theories in the degree to which it illuminates and explains the foundations of our duties to one another—the domain of human morality. On this score it has the best reasons, the best arguments, on its side. Of course, if it were possible to show that only human beings are included within its scope, then a person like myself, who believes in animal rights, would be obliged to look elsewhere.

But attempts to limit its scope to humans only can be shown to be rationally defective. Animals, it is true, lack many of the abilities humans possess. They can't

read, do higher mathematics, build a bookcase or make *baba ghanoush*. Neither can many human beings, however, and yet we don't (and shouldn't) say that they (these humans) therefore have less inherent value, less of a right to be treated with respect, than do others. It is the *similarities* between those human beings who most clearly, most non-controversially have such value (the people reading this, for example), not our differences, that matter most. And the real crucial, the basic similarity is simply this: we are each of us the experiencing subject of a life, a conscious creature having an individual welfare that has importance to us whatever our usefulness to others. We want and prefer things, believe and feel things, recall and expect things. And all these dimensions of our life, including our pleasure and pain, our enjoyment and suffering, our satisfaction and frustration, our continued existence or our untimely death—all make a difference to the quality of our life as lived, as experienced, by us as individuals. As the same is true of those animals that concern us (the ones that are eaten and trapped, for example), they too must be viewed as the experiencing subjects of a life, with inherent value of their own.

Some there are who resist the idea that animals have inherent value. "Only humans have such value", they profess. How might this narrow view be defended? Shall we say that only humans have the requisite intelligence, or autonomy, or reason? But there are many, many humans who fail to meet these standards and yet are reasonably viewed as having value above and beyond their usefulness to others. Shall we claim that only humans belong to the right species, the species *Homo sapiens*? But this is blatant speciesism. Will it be said, then, that all—and only—humans have immortal souls? Then our opponents have their work cut out for them. I am myself not ill-disposed to the proposition that there are immortal souls. Personally, I profoundly hope I have one. But I would not want to rest my position on a controversial ethical issue on the even more controversial question about who or what has an immortal soul. That is to dig one's hole deeper, not to climb out. Rationally, it is better to resolve moral issues without making more controversial assumptions than are needed. The question of who has inherent value is such a question, one that is resolved more rationally without the introduction of the idea of immortal souls than by its use.

Well, perhaps some will say that animals have some inherent value, only less than we have. Once again, however, attempts to defend this view can be shown to lack rational justification. What could be the basis of our having more inherent value than animals? Their lack of reason, or autonomy, or intellect? Only if we are willing to make the same judgement in the case of humans who are similarly deficient. But it is not true that such humans—the retarded child, for example, or the mentally deranged—have less inherent value than you or I. Neither, then, can we rationally sustain the view that animals like them in being the experiencing subjects of a life have less inherent value. *All* who have inherent value have it *equally*, whether they be human animals or not.

Inherent value, then, belongs equally to those who are the experiencing subjects of a life. Whether it belongs to others—to rocks and rivers, trees and glaciers, for example—we do not know and may never know. But neither do we need to know, if we are to make the case for animal rights. We do not need to know, for example, how many people are eligible to vote in the next presidential election before we can know whether I am. Similarly, we do

not need to know how many individuals have inherent value before we can know that some do. When it comes to the case for animal rights, then, what we need to know is whether the animals that, in our culture, are routinely eaten, hunted and used in our laboratories, for example, are like us in being subjects of a life. And we do know this. We do know that many— literally, billions and billions—of these animals are the subjects of a life in the sense explained and so have inherent value if we do. And since, in order to arrive at the best theory of our duties to one another, we must recognize our equal inherent value as individuals, reason—not sentiment, not emotion—reason compels us to recognize the equal inherent value of these animals and, with this, their equal right to be treated with respect.

That, *very* roughly, is the shape and feel of the case for animal rights....

[T]he theory that underlies the case for animal rights shows that the animal rights movement is a part of, not antagonistic to, the human rights movement. The theory that rationally grounds the rights of animals also grounds the rights of humans. Thus those involved in the animal rights movement are partners in the struggle to secure respect for human rights—the rights of women, for example, or minorities, or workers. The animal rights movement is cut from the same moral cloth as these.

[H]aving set out the broad outlines of the rights view, I can now say why its implications for farming and science, among other fields, are both clear and uncompromising. In the case of the use of animals in science, the rights view is categorically abolitionist. Lab animals are not our tasters; we are not their kings. Because these animals are treated routinely, systematically as if their value were reducible to their usefulness to others, they are routinely, systematically treated with a lack of respect, and thus are their rights routinely, systematically violated. This is just as true when they are used in trivial, duplicative, unnecessary or unwise research as it is when they are used in studies that hold out real promise of human benefits. We can't justify harming or killing a human being (my Aunt Bea, for example) just for these sorts of reason. Neither can we do so even in the case of so lowly a creature as a laboratory rat. It is not just refinement or reduction that is called for, not just larger, cleaner cages, not just more generous use of anaesthetic or the elimination of multiple surgery, not just tidying up the system. It is complete replacement. The best we can do when it comes to using animals in science is—not to use them. That is where our duty lies, according to the rights view.

As for commercial animal agriculture, the rights view takes a similar abolitionist position. The fundamental moral wrong here is not that animals are kept in stress-ful close confinement or in isolation, or that their pain and suffering, their needs and preferences are ignored or discounted. All these *are* wrong, of course, but they are not the fundamental wrong. They are symptoms and effects of the deeper, systematic wrong that allows these animals to be viewed as lacking independent value, as resources for us—as, indeed, a renewable resource. Giving farm animals more space, more natural environments, more companions does not right the fundamental wrong, any more than giving lab animals more anaesthesia or bigger, cleaner cages would right the fundamental wrong in their case. Nothing less than the total dissolution of commercial animal agriculture will do this, just as, for similar reasons I won't develop at length here, morality requires nothing less than the total elimination of hunting and trapping for commercial and sporting ends. The rights view's implications, then, as I have said, are clear and uncompromising....

NonHuman Animal Rights:
Nonexistent?

TOM REGAN

Using animals as research subjects in medical investigations is widely condemned on two grounds: first, because it wrongly violates the *rights* of animals, and second, because it wrongly imposes on sentient creatures much avoidable *suffering*. Neither of these arguments is sound. The first relies on a mistaken understanding of rights; the second relies on a mistaken calculation of consequences. Both deserve definitive dismissal.

WHY ANIMALS HAVE NO RIGHTS

A right, properly understood, is a claim, or potential claim, that one party may exercise against another. The target against whom such a claim may be registered can be a single person, a group, a community, or (perhaps) all humankind. The content of rights claims also varies greatly: repayment of loans, nondiscrimination by employers, noninterference by the state, and so on. To comprehend any genuine right fully, therefore, we must know *who* holds the right, *against whom* it is held, and to *what* it is a right.

Alternative sources of rights add complexity. Some rights are grounded in constitution and law (e.g., the right of an accused to trial by jury); some rights are moral but give no legal claims (e.g., my right to your keeping the promise you gave me); and some rights (e.g., against theft or assault) are rooted both in morals and in law.

The differing targets, contents, and sources of rights, and their inevitable conflict, together weave a tangled web. Notwithstanding all such complications, this much is clear about rights in general: they are in every case claims, or potential claims, within a community of moral agents. Rights arise, and can be intelligibly defended, only among beings who actually do, or can, make moral claims against one another. Whatever else rights may be, therefore, they are necessarily human; their possessors are persons, human beings.

The attributes of human beings from which this moral capability arises have been described variously by philosophers, both ancient and modern: the inner consciousness of a free will (Saint Augustine); the grasp, by human reason, of the binding character of moral law (Saint Thomas); the self-conscious participation of human beings in an objective ethical order (Hegel); human membership in an organic moral community (Bradley); the development of the human self through the consciousness of other moral selves (Mead); and the underivative, intuitive cognition of the rightness of an action (Prichard). Most influential has been Immanuel Kant's emphasis on the universal human possession of a uniquely moral will and the autonomy its use entails. Humans confront choices that are purely moral; humans—but certainly not dogs or mice—lay down moral laws, for others and for themselves. Human beings are self-legislative, morally *auto-nomous*.

Animals (that is, nonhuman animals, the ordinary sense of that word) lack this capacity for free moral judgment. They are not beings of a kind capable of exercising or responding to moral claims. Animals therefore have no rights, and they can have none. This is the core of the argument about the alleged rights of animals. The holders of rights must have the capacity to comprehend rules of duty, governing all including themselves. In applying such rules, the holders of rights must recognize possible conflicts between what is in their own interest and what is just. Only in a community of beings capable of self-restricting moral judgments can the concept of a right be correctly invoked.

Humans have such moral capacities. They are in this sense self-legislative, are members of communities governed by moral rules, and do possess rights. Animals do not have such moral capacities. They are not morally self-legislative, cannot possibly be members of a truly moral community, and therefore cannot possess rights. In conducting research on animal subjects, therefore, we do not violate their rights, because they have none to violate.

To animate life, even in its simplest forms, we give a certain natural reverence. But the possession of rights presupposes a moral status not attained by the vast majority of living things. We must not infer, therefore, that a live being has, simply in being alive, a "right" to its life. The assertion that all animals, only because they are alive and have interests, also possess the "right to life" is an abuse of that phrase, and wholly without warrant.

It does not follow from this, however, that we are morally free to do anything we please to animals. Certainly not. In our dealings with animals, as in our dealings with other human beings, we have obligations that do not arise from claims against us based on rights. Rights entail obligations, but many of the things one ought to do are in no way tied to another's entitlement. Rights and obligations are not reciprocals of one another, and it is a serious mistake to suppose that they are.

Illustrations are helpful. Obligations may arise from internal commitments made: physicians have obligations to their patients not grounded merely in their patients' rights. Teachers have such obligations to their students, shepherds to their dogs, and cowboys to their horses. Obligations may arise from differences of status: adults owe special care when playing with young children, and children owe special care when playing with young pets. Obligations may arise from special relationships: the payment of my son's college tuition is something to which he may have no right, although it may be my obligation to bear the burden if I reasonably can; my dog has no right to daily exercise and veterinary care, but I do have the obligation to provide these things for her. Obligations may arise from particular acts or circumstances: one may be obliged to another for a special kindness done, or obliged to put an animal out of its misery in view of its condition—although neither the human benefactor nor the dying animal may have had a claim of right.

Plainly, the grounds of our obligations to humans and to animals are manifold and cannot be formulated simply. Some hold that there is a general obligation to do no gratuitous harm to sentient creatures (the principle of nonmaleficence); some hold that there is a general obligation to do good to sentient creatures when that is reasonably within one's power (the principle of beneficence). In our dealings with animals, few will deny that we are at least obliged to act humanely—that is, to treat them with the decency and concern that we owe, as sensitive human beings, to other sentient creatures. To treat animals humanely, however, is not to treat them as humans or as the holders of rights.

A common objection, which deserves a response, may be paraphrased as follows:

> If having rights requires being able to make moral claims, to grasp and apply moral laws, then many humans—the brain-damaged, the comatose, the senile—who plainly lack those capacities must be without rights. But that is absurd. This proves [the critic concludes] that rights do not depend on the presence of moral capacities.

This objection fails; it mistakenly treats an essential feature of humanity as though it were a screen for sorting humans. The capacity for moral judgment that distinguishes humans from animals is not a test to be administered to human beings one by one. Persons who are unable, because of some disability, to perform the full moral functions natural to human beings are certainly not for that reason ejected from the moral community. The issue is one of kind. Humans are of such a kind that they may be the subject of experiments only with their voluntary consent. The choices they make freely must be respected. Animals are of such a kind that it is impossible for them, in principle, to give or withhold voluntary consent or to make a moral choice. What humans retain when disabled, animals have never had.

A second objection, also often made, may be paraphrased as follows:

> Capacities will not succeed in distinguishing humans from the other animals. Animals also reason; animals also communicate with one another; animals also care passionately for their young; animals also exhibit desires and preferences. Features of moral relevance—rationality, interdependence, and love—are not exhibited uniquely by human beings. Therefore [this critic concludes], there can be no solid moral distinction between humans and other animals.

This criticism misses the central point. It is not the ability to communicate or to reason, or dependence on one another, or care for the young, or the exhibition of preference, or any such behavior that marks the critical divide. Analogies between human families and those of monkeys, or between human communities and those of wolves, and the like, are entirely beside the point. Patterns of conduct are not at issue. Animals do indeed exhibit remarkable behavior at times. Conditioning, fear, instinct, and intelligence all contribute to species survival. Membership in a community of moral agents nevertheless remains impossible for them. Actors subject to moral judgment must be capable of grasping the generality of an ethical premise in a practical syllogism. Humans act immorally often enough, but only they—never wolves or monkeys—can discern, by applying some moral rule to the facts of a case, that a given act ought or ought not to be performed. The moral restraints imposed by humans on themselves are thus highly abstract and are often in conflict with the self-interest of the agent. Communal behavior among animals, even when most intelligent and most endearing, does not approach autonomous morality in this fundamental sense.

Genuinely moral acts have an internal as well as an external dimension. Thus, in law, an act can be criminal only when the guilty deed, the actus reus, is done with a guilty mind, mens rea. No animal can ever commit a crime; bringing animals to criminal trial is the mark of primitive ignorance. The claims of moral right are similarly inapplicable to them. Does a lion have a right to eat a baby zebra? Does a baby zebra have a right not to be eaten? Such questions, mistakenly invoking the concept of right where it does not belong, do not make good sense. Those who condemn biomedical research because it violates "animal rights" commit the same blunder....

Consistency

Finally, inconsistency between the profession and the practice of many who oppose research using animals deserves comment. This frankly ad hominem observation aims chiefly to show that a coherent position rejecting the use of animals in medical research imposes costs so high as to be intolerable even to the critics themselves.

One cannot coherently object to the killing of animals in biomedical investigations while continuing to eat them. Anesthetics and thoughtful animal husbandry render the level of actual animal distress in the laboratory generally lower than that in the abattoir. So long as death and discomfort do not substantially differ in the two contexts, the consistent objector must not only refrain from all eating of animals but also protest as vehemently against others eating them as against others experimenting on them. No less vigorously must the critic object to the wearing of animal hides in coats and shoes, to employment in any industrial enterprise that uses animal parts, and to any commercial development that will cause death or distress to animals.

Killing animals to meet human needs for food, clothing, and shelter is judged entirely reasonable by most persons. The ubiquity of these uses and the virtual universality of moral support for them confront the opponent of research using animals with an inescapable difficulty. How can the many common uses of animals be judged morally worthy, while their use in scientific investigation is judged unworthy?

The number of animals used in research is but the tiniest fraction of the total used to satisfy assorted human appetites. That these appetites, often base and satisfiable in other ways. morally justify the far larger consumption of animals, whereas the quest for improved human health and understanding cannot justify the far smaller, is wholly implausible. Aside from the numbers of animals involved, the distinction in terms of worthiness of use, drawn with regard to any single animal, is not defensible. A given sheep is surely not more justifiably used to put lamb chops on the supermarket counter than to serve in testing a new contraceptive or a new prosthetic device. The needless killing of animals is wrong; if the common killing of them for our food or convenience is right, the less common but more humane uses of animals in the service of medical science are certainly not less right.

Scrupulous vegetarianism, in matters of food, clothing, shelter, commerce, and recreation, and in all other spheres. is the only fully coherent position the critic may adopt. At great human cost, the lives of fish and crustaceans must also be protected, with equal vigor, if speciesism has been forsworn. A very few consistent critics adopt this position. It is the reduction ad absurdum of the rejection of moral distinctions between animals and human beings.

Opposition to the use of animals in research is based on arguments of two different kinds—those relying on the alleged rights of animals and those relying on the consequences for animals. I have argued that arguments of both kinds must fail. We surely do have obligations to animals, but they have, and can have, no rights against us on which research can infringe. In calculating the consequences of animal research, we must weigh all the long-term benefits of the results achieved—to animals and to humans—and in that calculation we must not assume the moral equality of all animate species.

THE CONTINUING DEBATE:
Nonhuman Animal Rights

What Is New

For supporters of animal rights, the most significant abuses of animals occur in factory farming and in laboratory research. Hunting is also regarded as wrong, but on a much smaller scale than the massive use of animals in agriculture and research. Still, battles over hunting often gain disproportionate publicity, and the opposing positions can become quite heated and polarized. This is most obvious in the current fierce debate over foxhunting in England, recently banned by Parliament.

Where to Find More

For an interesting debate on animal rights, see *The Animal Rights Debate*, by Carl Cohen and Tom Regan (Lanham, Maryland: Rowman & Littlefield, 2001). *Animal Rights and Human Obligations* (2nd ed.), edited by Tom Regan and Peter Singer (Englewood Cliffs, N.J.: Prentice-Hall, 1989), is a good collection of essays, both pro and con, on the rights of animals. The collection of historical views, ranging from ancient Greece and Medieval thought up through the modern period, is a strong point of this anthology. Another good collection of pro and con articles, covering a wide range of subjects in the area of animal rights and the treatment of animals, is by Andrew Harnack, *Animal Rights: Opposing Viewpoints* (San Diego, Cal.: Greenhaven Press, 1996). Harlan B. Miller and William H. Williams, eds., *Ethics and Animals* (Clifton, N.J.: Humana Press, 1983), contains a very good collection of philosophical articles by leading philosophers. *The Animal Rights Reader*, edited by Susan J. Armstrong and Richard G. Botzler (London: Routledge, 2003), is a broad ranging collection of excellent essays from a variety of perspectives.

Peter Singer's *Animal Liberation* first appeared in 1976, and is now in a second edition (New York: Avon Books, 1990); it is probably the most famous book in the campaign for animal rights. Tom Regan's *The Case for Animal Rights* (Berkeley: The University of California Press, 1983) is another modern classic; his more recent essays are collected in *Defending Animal Rights* (Urbana: University of Illinois Press, 2001). Paola Cavalieri's *The Animal Question: Why Nonhuman Animals Deserve Human Rights*, trans. Catherine Woollard (Oxford: Oxford University Press, 2001) is a brief but creative and well-argued case for animal rights. Another excellent defense of animal rights is Bernard E. Rollin, *Animal Rights and Human Morality*, revised edition (Buffalo, N.Y.: Prometheus Books, 1992). Stephen R. L. Clark, in *The Moral Status of Animals* (Oxford: Clarendon Press, 1977), offers a detailed, powerful, and philosophically complex argument for a radical revision of our view of animals (as well as ourselves) . See also Clark's fascinating book, *The Nature of the Beast: Are Animals Moral?* (Oxford: Oxford University Press, 1982), for his argument that the study of animal behavior can enhance our understanding of ethics. Two very good books, whose authors emphasize the close biological links between humans and other animals, are Mary Midgley, *Animals and Why They Matter* (Athens, Georgia: University of Georgia Press, 1983); and James Rachels, *Created From Animals: The Moral Implications of Darwinism* (Oxford: Oxford University Press, 1991). A remarkable and very readable book, that examines both recent research on teaching chimpanzees

American Sign Language and recent attempts to stop the mistreatment of chimpanzees in research settings, is Roger Fouts, *Next of Kin: What Chimpanzees Have Taught Me About Who We Are* (New York: William Morrow, 1997); Fouts also has an interesting website at *www.cwu.edu/~cwuchi/*.

Books opposing animal rights arguments, written from a variety of perspectives, are R. G. Frey, *Interests and Rights: The Case Against Animals* (Oxford: Clarendon Press, 1980); Michael P. T. Leahy, *Against Liberation: Putting Animals in Perspective* (London and New York: Routledge, 1991); and Peter Carruthers, *The Animals Issue* (Cambridge: Cambridge University Press, 1992).

On a subject in which the debate has raged for decades, even centuries, it is difficult to find a new perspective; but novelist J. M. Coetzee manages it brilliantly, in *The Lives of Animals* (Princeton, N.J., 1999).

The Great Ape Project, an organization dedicated to securing basic moral and legal protection for nonhuman great apes, has a website that is well worth a visit, at *www.greatapeproject.org*. Lawrence Hinman's Ethics Updates Website has a superb collection of material on the moral status of animals, including many links to other sites; go to *ethics.sandiego.edu/Applied/Animals*.

ILLEGAL DRUGS

Should They Remain Illegal or Should We Decriminalize Drugs?

ILLEGAL DRUGS SHOULD REMAIN ILLEGAL

ADVOCATE: Theodore Dalrymple, a physician and psychiatrist, works in a British prison. A contributing editor of *City Journal*, he recently wrote *Life at the Bottom: The Worldview that Makes the Underclass* (Chicago: Ivan R. Dee, 2001)

SOURCE: "Don't Legalize Drugs," *City Journal*, Volume 7, No. 2 (Spring 1997)

ILLEGAL DRUGS SHOULD BE DECRIMINALIZED

ADVOCATE: Ethan A. Nadelmann, Professor of Politics and Public Affairs at the Woodrow Wilson School of Public and International Affairs at Princeton University

SOURCE: "The Case for Legalization," *The Public Interest*, Summer 1998

The debate over whether marijuana (and perhaps other illegal drugs) should be decriminalized is not a debate over whether elementary school children should be able to buy marijuana at the candy store, or smoke a joint in the school cafeteria after lunch. The question is whether to decriminalize drugs that are currently illegal (such as marijuana, cocaine, and opium) and the possession or sale of which are punishable by criminal sanctions. Instead their sale and use would be regulated, much as we now regulate alcohol and tobacco. Perhaps the regulation would be more strict than with alcohol or tobacco, but that is a point of detail, and not the fundamental issue.

This is an issue that divides people along interesting lines. Though most conservatives are vehemently against drug decriminalization, there are many leading conservatives—Ethan Nadelmann, for example, but also Nobel prize laureate and conservative economist Milton Friedman, conservative columnist William Buckley, and others—who view the U.S. drug policy as not only a disastrous and expensive failure but also as a fundamental infringement on our rights as adult citizens to make our own decisions about things that affect only ourselves and do not harm others. That includes, of course, the right to make stupid decisions that cause us harm, as the decision to use cocaine or smoke tobacco might well be. While those who favor decriminalization are more likely to fall on the liberal side, many liberals adamantly oppose the decriminalization of drugs. So this is a particularly good issue on which to forget about labels and attend to arguments.

While currently the United States' "war on drugs" is being pursued fervently, complete with a "drug czar" and an enormous prison population, other countries—The Netherlands is a noteworthy example—take a very different approach to the problem of drugs. In the Netherlands, marijuana is legally available on a "coffee shop" model, in which shops selling small quantities of marijuana are regulated by local ordinance, and those that prove troublesome are shut down, analo-

gously to the shutting down of U.S. taverns that lose their liquor licenses. While there is dispute concerning the level of drug addiction in the Netherlands, most studies indicate that the rate of adult addiction and teenage drug use is lower than in the U.S., and there is no dispute that the violent crime rate there is only a fraction of ours. While other European countries do not have as liberal a policy as the Netherlands, neither do they have policies as harsh as those of the United States, particularly toward the use of marijuana.

There are two major lines of argument concerning drug decriminalization. One is that the current criminal policy is and will remain a costly failure, both in terms of financial and human costs; that there is no way of making criminal policies work, so we are better off trying a new policy to deal with this ineradicable problem. In this argument, the sociological question of what effect decriminalization would have—on drug addiction, violence, law enforcement—looms large. The other argument for decriminalization is that even if the current criminal program worked, it should still be rejected as a paternalistic program that violates our right of free choice. In the second argument for lifting criminal penalties, we find a recurring question: What are the rights of individuals to make their own decisions (including harmful ones) as opposed to the right of the community or state to regulate behavior that might be harmful to the individual and thus potentially lead to indirect damage to the state?

POINTS TO PONDER

➤ Dalrymple acknowledges the importance of freedom, but he opposes the "freedom" of butterflies and children. What concept of freedom does Dalrymple favor?
➤ Dalrymple rejects the "pragmatic" argument for legalization: the argument that legalizing drugs would have good practical effects in reducing crime. He claims that legalizing drugs would *possibly* produce another effect, which would possibly lead to *increased* crime. What is the possible effect on which his argument hinges, and how plausible is his supposition?
➤ Dalrymple characterizes his major argument as a "slippery slope" argument. Does it meet the conditions for a legitimate slippery slope argument?
➤ If you favor the decriminalization of drugs, and letting each citizen make his or her own decision concerning drug use, then in order to be consistent would you also have to allow athletes to use performance-enhancing drugs in competitive sports? That is, could you consistently favor decriminalization and also favor a ban on performance-enhancing drugs for competitive athletes?

Illegal Drugs:
Illegal Drugs Should Remain Illegal

Theodore Dalrymple

There is a progression in the minds of men: first the unthinkable becomes thinkable, and then it becomes an orthodoxy whose truth seems so obvious that no one remembers that anyone ever thought differently. This is just what is happening with the idea of legalizing drugs: it has reached the stage when millions of thinking men are agreed that allowing people to take whatever they like is the obvious, indeed only, solution to the social problems that arise from the consumption of drugs.

Man's desire to take mind-altering substances is as old as society itself—as are attempts to regulate their consumption. If intoxication in one form or another is inevitable, then so is customary or legal restraint upon that intoxication. But no society until our own has had to contend with the ready availability of so many different mind-altering drugs, combined with a citizenry jealous of its right to pursue its own pleasures in its own way.

The arguments in favor of legalizing the use of all narcotic and stimulant drugs are twofold: philosophical and pragmatic. Neither argument is negligible, but both are mistaken, I believe, and both miss the point.

The philosophic argument is that, in a free society, adults should be permitted to do whatever they please, always provided that they are prepared to take the consequences of their own choices and that they cause no direct harm to others. The locus classicus for this point of view is John Stuart Mill's famous essay On Liberty: "The only purpose for which power can be rightfully exercised over any member of the community, against his will, is to prevent harm to others," Mill wrote. "His own good, either physical or moral, is not a sufficient warrant." This radical individualism allows society no part whatever in shaping, determining, or enforcing a moral code: in short, we have nothing in common but our contractual agreement not to interfere with one another as we go about seeking our private pleasures.

In practice, of course, it is exceedingly difficult to make people take all the consequences of their own actions—as they must, if Mill's great principle is to serve as a philosophical guide to policy. Addiction to, or regular use of, most currently prohibited drugs cannot affect only the person who takes them—and not his spouse, children, neighbors, or employers. No man, except possibly a hermit, is an island; and so it is virtually impossible for Mill's principle to apply to any human action whatever, let alone shooting up heroin or smoking crack. Such a principle is virtually useless in determining what should or should not be permitted.

Perhaps we ought not be too harsh on Mill's principle: it's not clear that anyone has ever thought of a better one. But that is precisely the point. Human affairs cannot be decided by an appeal to an infallible rule, expressible in a few words, whose simple application can decide all cases, including whether drugs should be freely available to the entire adult population. Philosophical fundamentalism is not preferable to the religious variety; and because the desiderata of human life are many, and often in conflict with one another,

mere philosophical inconsistency in policy—such as permitting the consumption
of alcohol while outlawing cocaine—is
not a sufficient argument against that policy. We all value freedom, and we all value
order; sometimes we sacrifice freedom for
order, and sometimes order for freedom.
But once a prohibition has been removed,
it is hard to restore, even when the new-
found freedom proves to have been ill-
conceived and socially disastrous.

Even Mill came to see the limitations
of his own principle as a guide for policy
and to deny that all pleasures were of
equal significance for human existence. It
was better, he said, to be Socrates discon-
tented than a fool satisfied. Mill acknowledged that some goals were intrinsically
worthier of pursuit than others.

This being the case, not all freedoms
are equal, and neither are all limitations of
freedom: some are serious and some trivial. The freedom we cherish—or should
cherish—is not merely that of satisfying
our appetites, whatever they happen to be.
We are not Dickensian Harold Skimpoles,
exclaiming in protest that "Even the butterflies are free!" We are not children who
chafe at restrictions because they are restrictions. And we even recognize the apparent paradox that some limitations to
our freedoms have the consequence of
making us freer overall. The freest man is
not the one who slavishly follows his appetites and desires throughout his life—as
all too many of my patients have discovered to their cost.

We are prepared to accept limitations
to our freedoms for many reasons, not just
that of public order. Take an extreme hypothetical case: public exhibitions of
necrophilia are quite rightly not permitted, though on Mill's principle they
should be. A corpse has no interests and
cannot be harmed, because it is no longer
a person; and no member of the public is

harmed if he has agreed to attend such an
exhibition.

Our resolve to prohibit such exhibitions would not be altered if we discovered
that millions of people wished to attend
them or even if we discovered that millions already were attending them illicitly.
Our objection is not based upon pragmatic considerations or upon a head
count: it is based upon the wrongness of
the would-be exhibitions themselves. The
fact that the prohibition represents a genuine restriction of our freedom is of no
account.

It might be argued that the freedom to
choose among a variety of intoxicating
substances is a much more important freedom and that millions of people have derived innocent fun from taking stimulants
and narcotics. But the consumption of
drugs has the effect of reducing men's freedom by circumscribing the range of their
interests. It impairs their ability to pursue
more important human aims, such as raising a family and fulfilling civic obligations. Very often it impairs their ability to
pursue gainful employment and promotes
parasitism. Moreover, far from being ex-
panders of consciousness, most drugs severely limit it. One of the most striking
characteristics of drug takers is their intense and tedious self-absorption; and
their journeys into inner space are generally forays into inner vacuums. Drug
taking is a lazy man's way of pursuing happiness and wisdom, and the shortcut turns
out to be the deadest of dead ends. We
lose remarkably little by not being permitted to take drugs.

The idea that freedom is merely the
ability to act upon one's whims is surely
very thin and hardly begins to capture the
complexities of human existence; a man
whose appetite is his law strikes us not as
liberated but enslaved. And when such a
narrowly conceived freedom is made the

touchstone of public policy, a dissolution of society is bound to follow. No culture that makes publicly sanctioned self-indulgence its highest good can long survive: a radical egotism is bound to ensue, in which any limitations upon personal behavior are experienced as infringements of basic rights. Distinctions between the important and the trivial, between the freedom to criticize received ideas and the freedom to take LSD, are precisely the standards that keep societies from barbarism.

So the legalization of drugs cannot be supported by philosophical principle. But if the pragmatic argument in favor of legalization were strong enough, it might overwhelm other objections. It is upon this argument that proponents of legalization rest the larger part of their case.

The argument is that the overwhelming majority of the harm done to society by the consumption of currently illicit drugs is caused not by their pharmacological properties but by their prohibition and the resultant criminal activity that prohibition always calls into being. Simple reflection tells us that a supply invariably grows up to meet a demand; and when the demand is widespread, suppression is useless. Indeed, it is harmful, since—by raising the price of the commodity in question—it raises the profits of middlemen, which gives them an even more powerful incentive to stimulate demand further. The vast profits to be made from cocaine and heroin—which, were it not for their illegality, would be cheap and easily affordable even by the poorest in affluent societies—exert a deeply corrupting effect on producers, distributors, consumers, and law enforcers alike. Besides, it is well known that illegality in itself has attractions for youth already inclined to disaffection. Even many of the harmful physical effects of illicit drugs stem from their illegal status: for example, fluctuations in the purity

of heroin bought on the street are responsible for many of the deaths by overdose. If the sale and consumption of such drugs were legalized, consumers would know how much they were taking and thus avoid overdoses.

Moreover, since society already permits the use of some mind-altering substances known to be both addictive and harmful, such as alcohol and nicotine, in prohibiting others it appears hypocritical, arbitrary, and dictatorial. Its hypocrisy, as well as its patent failure to enforce its prohibitions successfully, leads inevitably to a decline in respect for the law as a whole. Thus things fall apart, and the center cannot hold.

It stands to reason, therefore, that all these problems would be resolved at a stroke if everyone were permitted to smoke, swallow, or inject anything he chose. The corruption of the police, the luring of children of 11 and 12 into illegal activities, the making of such vast sums of money by drug dealing that legitimate work seems pointless and silly by comparison, and the turf wars that make poor neighborhoods so exceedingly violent and dangerous, would all cease at once were drug taking to be decriminalized and the supply regulated in the same way as alcohol.

But a certain modesty in the face of an inherently unknowable future is surely advisable. That is why prudence is a political virtue: what stands to reason should happen does not necessarily happen in practice. As Goethe said, all theory (even of the monetarist or free-market variety) is gray, but green springs the golden tree of life. If drugs were legalized, I suspect that the golden tree of life might spring some unpleasant surprises.

It is of course true, but only trivially so, that the present illegality of drugs is the cause of the criminality surrounding their distribution. Likewise, it is the illegality of stealing cars that creates car thieves. In fact, the ultimate cause of all criminality is law. As far as I am aware, no one has ever suggested that law should therefore be abandoned. Moreover, the impossibility of winning the "war" against theft, burglary, robbery, and fraud has never been used as an argument that these categories of crime should be abandoned. And so long as the demand for material goods outstrips supply, people will be tempted to commit criminal acts against the owners of property. This is not an argument, in my view, against private property or in favor of the common ownership of all goods. It does suggest, however, that we shall need a police force for a long time to come.

In any case, there are reasons to doubt whether the crime rate would fall quite as dramatically as advocates of legalization have suggested. Amsterdam, where access to drugs is relatively unproblematic, is among the most violent and squalid cities in Europe. The idea behind crime—of getting rich, or at least richer, quickly and without much effort—is unlikely to disappear once drugs are freely available to all who want them. And it may be that officially sanctioned antisocial behavior—the official lifting of taboos—breeds yet more antisocial behavior, as the "broken windows" theory would suggest.

Having met large numbers of drug dealers in prison, I doubt that they would return to respectable life if the principal article of their commerce were to be legalized. Far from evincing a desire to be reincorporated into the world of regular work, they express a deep contempt for it and regard those who accept the bargain of a fair day's work for a fair day's pay as cowards and fools. A life of crime has its attractions for many who would otherwise lead a mundane existence. So long as there is the possibility of a lucrative racket or illegal traffic, such people will find it and extend its scope. Therefore, since even legalizers would hesitate to allow children to take drugs, decriminalization might easily result in dealers turning their attentions to younger and younger children, who—in the permissive atmosphere that even now prevails—have already been inducted into the drug subculture in alarmingly high numbers.

Those who do not deal in drugs but commit crimes to fund their consumption of them are, of course, more numerous than large-scale dealers. And it is true that once opiate addicts, for example, enter a treatment program, which often includes maintenance doses of methadone, the rate at which they commit crimes falls markedly. The drug clinic in my hospital claims an 80 percent reduction in criminal convictions among heroin addicts once they have been stabilized on methadone.

This is impressive, but it is not certain that the results should be generalized. First, the patients are self-selected: they have some motivation to change, otherwise they would not have attended the clinic in the first place. Only a minority of addicts attend, and therefore it is not safe to conclude that, if other addicts were to receive methadone, their criminal activity would similarly diminish.

Second, a decline in convictions is not necessarily the same as a decline in criminal acts. If methadone stabilizes an addict's life, he may become a more efficient, harder-to-catch criminal. Moreover, when the police in our city do catch an addict, they are less likely to prosecute him if he can prove that he is undergoing anything remotely resembling psychiatric treatment. They return him directly to his doctor. Having once had a psychiatric consultation is an all-purpose alibi for a robber or a burglar; the police, who do not want to fill in the 40-plus forms it now takes to charge anyone with anything in England, consider a single contact with a psychiatrist sufficient to deprive anyone of legal responsibility for crime forever.

Third, the rate of criminal activity among those drug addicts who receive methadone from the clinic, though reduced, remains very high. The deputy director of the clinic estimates that the number of criminal acts committed by his average patient (as judged by self-report) was 250 per year before entering treatment and 50 afterward. It may well be that the real difference is considerably less than this, because the patients have an incentive to exaggerate it to secure the continuation of their methadone. But clearly, opiate addicts who receive their drugs legally and free of charge continue to commit large numbers of crimes. In my clinics in prison, I see numerous prisoners who were on methadone when they committed the crime for which they are incarcerated.

Why do addicts given their drug free of charge continue to commit crimes? Some addicts, of course, continue to take drugs other than those prescribed and have to fund their consumption of them. So long as any restriction whatever regulates the consumption of drugs, many addicts will seek them illicitly, regardless of what they receive legally. In addition, the drugs themselves exert a long-term effect on a person's ability to earn a living and severely limit rather than expand his horizons and mental repertoire. They sap the will or the ability of an addict to make long-term plans. While drugs are the focus of an addict's life, they are not all he needs to live, and many addicts thus continue to procure the rest of what they need by criminal means.

For the proposed legalization of drugs to have its much vaunted beneficial effect on the rate of criminality, such drugs would have to be both cheap and readily available. The legalizers assume that there is a natural limit to the demand for these drugs, and that if their consumption were legalized, the demand would not increase substantially. Those psychologically unstable persons currently taking drugs would continue to do so, with the necessity to commit crimes removed, while psychologically stabler people (such as you and I and our children) would not be enticed to take drugs by their new legal status and cheapness. But price and availability, I need hardly say, exert a profound effect on consumption: the cheaper alcohol becomes, for example, the more of it is consumed, at least within quite wide limits.

I have personal experience of this effect. I once worked as a doctor on a British government aid project to Africa. We were building a road through remote African bush. The contract stipulated that the construction company could import, free of all taxes, alcoholic drinks from the United Kingdom. These drinks the company then sold to its British workers at cost, in the local currency at the official exchange rate, which was approximately one-sixth the black-market rate. A liter bottle of gin thus cost less than a dollar and could be sold on the open market for almost ten dollars. So it was theoretically possible to remain dead drunk for several years for an initial outlay of less than a dollar.

Of course, the necessity to go to work somewhat limited the workers' consumption of alcohol. Nevertheless, drunkenness among them far outstripped anything I have ever seen, before or since. I discovered that, when alcohol is effectively free of charge, a fifth of British construction workers will regularly go to bed so drunk that they are incontinent both of urine and feces. I remember one man who very rarely got as far as his bed at night: he fell asleep in the lavatory, where he was usually found the next morning. Half the men shook in the mornings and resorted to the hair of the dog to steady their hands before they drove their bulldozers and other heavy machines (which they frequently wrecked, at enormous expense to the British taxpayer); hangovers were universal. The men were either drunk or hung over for months on end.

Sure, construction workers are notoriously liable to drink heavily, but in these circumstances even formerly moderate drinkers turned alcoholic and eventually suffered from delirium tremens. The heavy drinking occurred not because of the isolation of the African bush: not only did the company provide sports facilities for its workers, but there were many other ways to occupy oneself there. Other groups of workers in the bush whom I visited, who did not have the same rights of importation of alcoholic drink but had to purchase it at normal prices, were not nearly as drunk. And when the company asked its workers what it could do to improve their conditions, they unanimously asked for a further reduction in the price of alcohol, because they could think of nothing else to ask for.

The conclusion was inescapable: that a susceptible population had responded to the low price of alcohol, and the lack of other effective restraints upon its consumption, by drinking destructively large quantities of it. The health of many men suffered as a consequence, as did their capacity for work; and they gained a well-deserved local reputation for reprehensible, violent, antisocial behavior.

It is therefore perfectly possible that the demand for drugs, including opiates, would rise dramatically were their price to fall and their availability to increase. And if it is true that the consumption of these drugs in itself predisposes to criminal behavior (as data from our clinic suggest), it is also possible that the effect on the rate of criminality of this rise in consumption would swamp the decrease that resulted from decriminalization. We would have just as much crime in aggregate as before, but many more addicts.

The intermediate position on drug legalization, such as that espoused by Ethan Nadelmann, director of the Lindesmith Center, a drug policy research institute sponsored by financier George Soros, is emphatically not the answer to drug-related crime. This view holds that it should be easy for addicts to receive opiate drugs from doctors, either free or at cost, and that they should receive them in municipal injecting rooms, such as now exist in Zurich. But just look at Liverpool, where 2,000 people of a population of 600,000 receive official prescriptions for methadone: this once proud and prosperous city is still the world capital of drug-motivated burglary, according to the police and independent researchers.

Of course, many addicts in Liverpool are not yet on methadone, because the clinics are insufficient in number to deal with the demand. If the city expended more money on clinics, perhaps the number of addicts in treatment could be increased five- or tenfold. But would that solve the problem of burglary in Liverpool? No, because the profits to be made from selling illicit opiates would still be large: dealers would therefore make efforts to expand into parts of the population hitherto relatively untouched, in order to protect their profits. The new addicts would still burgle to feed their habits. Yet more clinics dispensing yet more methadone would then be needed. In fact Britain, which has had a relatively liberal approach to the prescribing of opiate drugs to addicts since 1928 (I myself have prescribed heroin to addicts), has seen an explosive increase in addiction to opiates and all the evils associated with it since the

1960s, despite that liberal policy. A few hundred have become more than a hundred thousand.

At the heart of Nadelmann's position, then, is an evasion. The legal and liberal provision of drugs for people who are already addicted to them will not reduce the economic benefits to dealers of pushing these drugs, at least until the entire susceptible population is addicted and in a treatment program. So long as there are addicts who have to resort to the black market for their drugs, there will be drug-associated crime. Nadelmann assumes that the number of potential addicts wouldn't soar under considerably more liberal drug laws. I can't muster such Panglossian optimism.

The problem of reducing the amount of crime committed by individual addicts is emphatically not the same as the problem of reducing the amount of crime committed by addicts as a whole. I can illustrate what I mean by an analogy: it is often claimed that prison does not work because many prisoners are recidivists who, by definition, failed to be deterred from further wrongdoing by their last prison sentence. But does any sensible person believe that the abolition of prisons in their entirety would not reduce the numbers of the law-abiding? The murder rate in New York and the rate of drunken driving in Britain have not been reduced by a sudden upsurge in the love of humanity, but by the effective threat of punishment. An institution such as prison can work for society even if it does not work for an individual.

The situation could be very much worse than I have suggested hitherto, however, if we legalized the consumption of drugs other than opiates. So far, I have considered only opiates, which exert a generally tranquilizing effect. If opiate addicts commit crimes even when they re-

ceive their drugs free of charge, it is because they are unable to meet their other needs any other way; but there are, unfortunately, drugs whose consumption directly leads to violence because of their psychopharmacological properties and not merely because of the criminality associated with their distribution. Stimulant drugs such as crack cocaine provoke paranoia, increase aggression, and promote violence. Much of this violence takes place in the home, as the relatives of crack takers will testify. It is something I know from personal acquaintance by working in the emergency room and in the wards of our hospital. Only someone who has not been assaulted by drug takers rendered psychotic by their drug could view with equanimity the prospect of the further spread of the abuse of stimulants.

And no one should underestimate the possibility that the use of stimulant drugs could spread very much wider, and become far more general, than it is now, if restraints on their use were relaxed. The importation of the mildly stimulant khat is legal in Britain, and a large proportion of the community of Somali refugees there devotes its entire life to chewing the leaves that contain the stimulant, miring these refugees in far worse poverty than they would otherwise experience. The reason that the khat habit has not spread to the rest of the population is that it takes an entire day's chewing of disgustingly bitter leaves to gain the comparatively mild pharmacological effect. The point is, however, that once the use of a stimulant becomes culturally acceptable and normal, it can easily become so general as to exert devastating social effects. And the kinds of stimulants on offer in Western cities—cocaine, crack, amphetamines—are vastly more attractive than khat.

In claiming that prohibition, not the drugs themselves, is the problem, Nadelmann and many others—even police-men—have said that "the war on drugs is lost." But to demand a yes or no answer to the question "Is the war against drugs being won?" is like demanding a yes or no answer to the question "Have you stopped beating your wife yet?" Never can an unimaginative and fundamentally stupid metaphor have exerted a more baleful effect upon proper thought.

Let us ask whether medicine is winning the war against death. The answer is obviously no, it isn't winning: the one fundamental rule of human existence remains, unfortunately, one man one death. And this is despite the fact that 14 percent of the gross domestic product of the United States (to say nothing of the efforts of other countries) goes into the fight against death. Was ever a war more expensively lost? Let us then abolish medical schools, hospitals, and departments of public health. If every man has to die, it doesn't matter very much when he does so.

If the war against drugs is lost, then so are the wars against theft, speeding, incest, fraud, rape, murder, arson, and illegal parking. Few, if any, such wars are winnable. So let us all do anything we choose.

Even the legalizers' argument that permitting the purchase and use of drugs as freely as Milton Friedman suggests will necessarily result in less governmental and other official interference in our lives doesn't stand up. To the contrary, if the use of narcotics and stimulants were to become virtually universal, as is by no means impossible, the number of situations in which compulsory checks upon people would have to be carried out, for reasons of public safety, would increase enormously. Pharmacies, banks, schools, hospitals—indeed, all organizations dealing with the public—might feel obliged to check regularly and randomly on the drug consumption of their employees. The general use of such drugs would increase the locus standi of innumerable agencies, public and private, to interfere in our lives; and freedom from interference, far from having increased, would have drastically shrunk.

The present situation is bad, undoubtedly; but few are the situations so bad that they cannot be made worse by a wrong policy decision.

The extreme intellectual elegance of the proposal to legalize the distribution and consumption of drugs, touted as the solution to so many problems at once (AIDS, crime, overcrowding in the prisons, and even the attractiveness of drugs to foolish young people) should give rise to skepticism. Social problems are not usually like that. Analogies with the Prohibition era, often drawn by those who would legalize drugs, are false and inexact: it is one thing to attempt to ban a substance that has been in customary use for centuries by at least nine-tenths of the adult population, and quite another to retain a ban on substances that are still not in customary use, in an attempt to ensure that they never do become customary. Surely we have already slid down enough slippery slopes in the last 30 years without looking for more such slopes to slide down.

Illegal Drugs:
Illegal Drugs Should Be Decriminalized

ETHAN A. NADELMANN

THE COSTS OF PROHIBITION

The fact that drug-prohibition laws and policies cannot eradicate or even significantly reduce drug abuse is not necessarily a reason to repeal them. They do, after all, succeed in deterring many people from trying drugs, and they clearly reduce the availability and significantly increase the price of illegal drugs. These accomplishments alone might warrant retaining the drug laws, were it not for the fact that these same laws are also responsible for much of what Americans identify as the "drug problem." Here the analogies to alcohol and tobacco are worth noting. There is little question that we could reduce the health costs associated with use and abuse of alcohol and tobacco if we were to criminalize their production, sale, and possession. But no one believes that we could eliminate their use and abuse, that we could create an "alcohol-free" or "tobacco-free" country. Nor do most Americans believe that criminalizing the alcohol and tobacco markets would be a good idea. Their opposition stems largely from two beliefs: that adult Americans have the right to choose what substances they will consume and what risks they will take; and that the costs of trying to coerce so many Americans to abstain from those substances would be enormous. It was the strength of these two beliefs that ultimately led to the repeal of Prohibition, and it is partly due to memories of that experience that criminalizing either alcohol or tobacco has little support today.

Consider the potential consequences of criminalizing the production, sale, and possession of all tobacco products. On the positive side, the number of people smoking tobacco would almost certainly decline, as would the health costs associated with tobacco consumption. Although the "forbidden fruit" syndrome would attract some people to cigarette smoking who would otherwise have smoked, many more would likely be deterred by the criminal sanction, the moral standing of the law, the higher cost and unreliable quality of the illicit tobacco, and the difficulties involved in acquiring it. Nonsmokers would rarely if ever be bothered by the irritating habits of their fellow citizens. The anti-tobacco laws would discourage some people from ever starting to smoke, and would induce others to quit.

On the negative side, however, millions of Americans, including both tobacco addicts and recreational users, would no doubt defy the law, generating a massive underground market and billions in profits for organized criminals. Although some tobacco farmers would find other work, thousands more would become outlaws and continue to produce their crops covertly. Throughout Latin America, farmers and gangsters would rejoice at the opportunity to earn untold sums of gringo greenbacks, even as U.S. diplomats pressured foreign governments to cooperate with U.S. laws. Within the United States, government helicopters would spray herbicides on illicit tobacco fields; people would be rewarded by the government for informing on their tobacco-growing, -selling, and

-smoking neighbors; urine tests would be employed to identify violators of the anti-tobacco laws; and a Tobacco Enforcement Administration (the T.E.A.) would employ undercover agents, informants, and wiretaps to uncover tobacco-law violators. Municipal, state, and federal judicial systems would be clogged with tobacco traffickers and "abusers." "Tobacco-related murders" would increase dramatically as criminal organizations competed with one another for turf and markets. Smoking would become an act of youthful rebellion, and no doubt some users would begin to experiment with more concentrated, potent, and dangerous forms of tobacco. Tobacco-related corruption would infect all levels of government, and respect for the law would decline noticeably. Government expenditures on tobacco-law enforcement would climb rapidly into the billions of dollars, even as budget balancers longingly recalled the almost ten billion dollars per year in tobacco taxes earned by the federal and state governments prior to prohibition. Finally, the State of North Carolina might even secede again from the Union.

This seemingly far-fetched tobacco-prohibition scenario is little more than an extrapolation based on the current situation with respect to marijuana, cocaine, and heroin. In many ways, our predicament resembles what actually happened during Prohibition. Prior to Prohibition, most Americans hoped that alcohol could be effectively banned by passing laws against its production and supply. During the early years of Prohibition, when drinking declined but millions of Americans nonetheless continued to drink, Prohibition's supporters placed their faith in tougher laws and more police and jails. After a few more years, however, increasing numbers of Americans began to realize that laws and policemen were unable to

eliminate the smugglers, bootleggers, and illicit producers, as long as tens of millions of Americans continued to want to buy alcohol. At the same time, they saw that more laws and policemen seemed to generate more violence and corruption, more crowded courts and jails, wider disrespect for government and the law, and more power and profits for the gangsters. Repeal of Prohibition came to be seen not as a capitulation to Al Capone and his ilk, but as a means of both putting the bootleggers out of business and eliminating most of the costs associated with the prohibition laws.

Today, Americans are faced with a dilemma similar to that confronted by our forebears sixty years ago. Demand for illicit drugs shows some signs of abating, but no signs of declining significantly. Moreover, there are substantial reasons to doubt that tougher laws and policing have played an important role in reducing consumption. Supply, meanwhile, has not abated at all. Availability of illicit drugs, except for marijuana in some locales, remains high. Prices are dropping, even as potency increases. And the number of drug producers, smugglers, and dealers remains sizable, even as jails and prisons fill to overflowing. As was the case during Prohibition, the principal beneficiaries of current drug policies are the new and old organized-crime gangs. The principal victims, on the other hand, are not the drug dealers, but the tens of millions of Americans who are worse off in one way or another as a consequence of the existence and failure of the drug-prohibition laws.

All public policies create beneficiaries and victims, both intended and unintended. When a public policy results in a disproportionate magnitude of unintended victims, there is good reason to reevaluate the assumptions and design of the policy. In the case of drug prohibition policies, the intended beneficiaries are those individuals who would become drug abusers but for the existence and enforcement of the drug laws. The intended victims are those who traffic in drugs and suffer the legal consequences. The unintended beneficiaries' conversely, are the drug producers and traffickers who profit handsomely from the illegality of the market, while avoiding arrest by the authorities and the violence perpetrated by criminals. The unintended victims of drug prohibition policies are rarely recognized as such, however. Viewed narrowly, they are the 30 million Americans who use illegal drugs, thereby risking loss of their jobs, imprisonment, and the damage done to health by ingesting illegally produced drugs; viewed broadly, they are all Americans, who pay the substantial costs of our present ill-considered policies, both as taxpayers and as the potential victims of crime. These unintended victims are generally thought to be victimized by the unintended beneficiaries (i.e., the drug dealers), when in fact it is the drug-prohibition policies themselves that are primarily responsible for their plight.

If law-enforcement efforts could succeed in significantly reducing either the supply of illicit drugs or the demand for them, we would probably have little need to seek alternative drug-control policies. But since those efforts have repeatedly failed to make much of a difference and show little indication of working better in the future, at this point we must focus greater attention on their costs. Unlike the demand and supply of illicit drugs, which have remained relatively indifferent to legislative initiatives, the costs of drug-enforcement measures can be affected— quite dramatically—by legislative measures. What tougher criminal sanctions and more police have failed to accomplish, in terms of reducing drug-related violence,

corruption, death, and social decay, may well be better accomplished by legislative repeal of the drug laws, and adoption of less punitive but more effective measures to prevent and treat substance abuse....

Drug laws typically have two effects on the market in illicit drugs. The first is to restrict the general availability and accessibility of illicit drugs, especially in locales where underground drug markets are small and isolated from the community. The second is increase, often significantly, the price of illicit drugs to consumers. Since the costs of producing most illicit drugs are not much different from the costs of alcohol, tobacco, and coffee, most of the price paid for illicit substances is in effect a value-added tax created by their criminalization, which is enforced and supplemented by the law-enforcement establishment, but collected by the drug traffickers. A report by Wharton Econometrics for the President's Commission on Organized Crime identified the sale of illicit drugs as the source of more than half of all organized crime revenues in 1986, with the marijuana and heroin business each providing over seven billion, and the cocaine business over thirteen billion. By contrast, revenues from cigarette bootlegging, which persists principally because of differences among states in their cigarette-tax rates, were estimated at 290 million dollars. If the marijuana, cocaine, and heroin markets were legal, state and federal governments would collect billions of dollars annually in tax revenues. Instead, they expend billions on what amounts to a subsidy of organized crime and unorganized criminals.

DRUGS AND CRIME

The drug/crime connection is one that continues to resist coherent analysis, both because cause and effect are so difficult to distinguish and because the role of the drug-prohibition laws in causing and labeling "drug-related crime" is so often ignored. There are four possible connections between drugs and crime, at least three of which would be much diminished if the drug-prohibition laws were repealed. First, producing, selling, buying, and consuming strictly controlled and banned substances is itself a crime that occurs billions of times each year in the United States alone. In the absence of drug-prohibition laws, these activities would obviously cease to be crimes. Selling drugs to children would, of course, continue to be criminal, and other evasions of government regulation of a legal market would continue to be prosecuted; but by and large the drug/crime connection that now accounts for all of the criminal-justice costs noted above would be severed.

Second, many illicit-drug users commit crimes such as robbery and burglary, as well as drug dealing, prostitution, and numbers running, to earn enough money to purchase the relatively high-priced illicit drugs. Unlike the millions of alcoholics who can support their habits for relatively modest amounts, many cocaine and heroin addicts spend hundreds and even thousands of dollars a week. If the drugs to which they are addicted were significantly cheaper—which would be the case if they were legalized—the number of crimes committed by drug addicts to pay for their habits would, in all likelihood, decline dramatically. Even if a legal-drug policy included the imposition of relatively high consumption taxes in order to discourage consumption, drug prices would probably still be lower than they are today.

The third drug/crime connection is the commission of crimes—violent crimes in particular—by people under the influence of illicit drugs. This connection seems to have the greatest impact upon the popular imagination. Clearly, some drugs do "cause" some people to commit crimes by reducing normal inhibitions, unleashing aggressive and other antisocial tendencies, and lessening the sense of responsibility. Cocaine, particularly in the form of crack, has gained such a reputation in recent years, just as heroin did in the 1960s and 1970s, and marijuana did in the years before that. Crack's reputation for inspiring violent behavior may or may not be more deserved than those of marijuana and heroin; reliable evidence is not yet available. No illicit drug, however, is as widely associated with violent behavior as alcohol. According to Justice Department statistics, 54 percent of all jail inmates convicted of violent crimes in 1983 reported having used alcohol just prior to committing their offense. The impact of drug legalization on this drug/crime connection is the most difficult to predict. Much would depend on overall rates of drug abuse and changes in the nature of consumption, both of which are impossible to predict. It is worth noting, however, that a shift in consumption from alcohol to marijuana would almost certainly contribute to a decline in violent behavior.

The fourth drug/crime link is the violent, intimidating, and corrupting behavior of the drug traffickers. Illegal markets tend to breed violence not only because they attract criminally-minded individuals, but also because participants in the market have no resort to legal institutions to resolve their disputes. During Prohibition, violent struggles between bootlegging gangs and hijackings of booze-laden trucks and sea vessels were frequent and notorious occurrences. Today's equivalents are the booby traps that surround some marijuana fields, the pirates of the Caribbean looking to rip off drug-laden vessels en route to the shores of the United States, and the machine-gun battles and executions carried out by drug lords—all of which occasionally kill innocent people. Most law-enforcement officials agree that the dramatic increases in urban murder rates during the past few years can be explained almost entirely by the rise in drug-dealer killings.

Perhaps the most unfortunate victims of the drug-prohibition policies have been the law-abiding residents of America's ghettos. These policies have largely proven futile in deterring large numbers of ghetto dwellers from becoming drug abusers, but they do account for much of what ghetto residents identify as the drug problem. In many neighborhoods, it often seems to be the aggressive gun-toting drug dealers who upset law-abiding residents far more than the addicts nodding out in doorways. Other residents, however, perceive the drug dealers as heroes and successful role models. In impoverished neighborhoods, they often stand out as symbols of success to children who see no other options. At the same time, the increasingly harsh criminal penalties imposed on adult drug dealers have led to the widespread recruitment of juveniles by drug traffickers. Formerly, children started dealing drugs only after they had been using them for a while; today the sequence is often reversed: many children start using illegal drugs now only after working for drug dealers. And the juvenile-justice system offers no realistic options for dealing with this growing problem.

The conspicuous failure of law-enforcement agencies to deal with this drug/crime connection is probably most responsible for the demoralization of neighborhoods and police departments alike. Intensive police crackdowns in urban neighborhoods do little more than chase the menace a short distance away to infect new areas. By contrast, legalization of the drug market would drive the drug-dealing business off the streets and out of the apartment buildings, and into legal, government-regulated, taxpaying stores. It would also force many of the gun-toting dealers out of business, and would convert others into legitimate businessmen. Some, of course, would turn to other types of criminal activities, just as some of the bootleggers did following Prohibition's repeal. Gone, however, would be the unparalleled financial temptations that lure so many people from all sectors of society into the drug-dealing business.

THE COSTS OF CORRUPTION

All vice-control efforts are particularly susceptible to corruption, but none so much as drug enforcement. When police accept bribes from drug dealers, no victim exists to complain to the authorities. Even when police extort money and drugs from traffickers and dealers, the latter are in no position to report the corrupt officers. What makes drug enforcement especially vulnerable to corruption are the tremendous amounts of money involved in the business. Today many law-enforcement officials believe that police corruption is more pervasive than at any time since Prohibition. In Miami, dozens of law-enforcement officials have been charged with accepting bribes, stealing from drug dealers, and even dealing drugs themselves. Throughout many small towns and rural communities in Georgia, where drug smugglers en route from Mexico, the Caribbean, and Latin America drop their loads of cocaine and marijuana, dozens of sheriffs have been implicated in drug-related corruption. In New York, drug-related corruption in one Brooklyn police precinct has generated the city s most far-reaching police corruption scandal since the 1960s. More than a hundred cases of drug-related corruption are now prosecuted each year in state and federal courts.

Every one of the federal law-enforcement agencies charged with drug-enforcement responsibilities has seen an agent implicated in drug-related corruption.

It is not difficult to explain the growing pervasiveness of drug-related corruption. The financial temptations are enormous relative to other opportunities, legitimate or illegitimate little effort is required. Many police officers are demoralized by the scope of the drug traffic, their sense that maybe citizens are indifferent, and the fact that many sectors of society do not even appreciate their efforts—as well as the fact that many drug dealers who are arrested do not remain in prison. Some police also recognize that enforcing the drug laws does not protect the victims from predators so much as it regulates an illicit market that cannot be suppressed, but can be kept underground. In every respect, the analogy to prohibition is apt. Repealing the drug-prohibition laws would dramatically reduce police corruption. By contrast the measures being proposed to deal with the growing problem, including better funding and more aggressive internal investigations, offer relatively little promise.

Among the most difficult costs to evaluate are those that relate to the widespread defiance of the drug-prohibition laws: the effects of labeling as criminals the tens of millions of people who use drugs illicitly, subjecting them to the risks of criminal sanction, and obliging many of these same people to enter into relationships with drug dealers (who may be criminals in many more senses of the word) in order to purchase their drugs; the cynicism that such laws generate toward other laws and the law in general; and the sense of hostility and suspicion that many otherwise law-abiding individuals feel toward law-enforcement officials. It was costs such as these that strongly influenced many of Prohibition's more conservative opponents.

PHYSICAL AND MORAL COSTS

Perhaps the most paradoxical consequence of the drug laws is the tremendous harm they cause to the millions of drug users who have not been deterred from using illicit drugs in the first place. Nothing resembling an underground Food and Drug Administration has arisen to impose quality control on the illegal-drug market and provide users with accurate information on the drugs they consume. Imagine that Americans could not tell whether a bottle of wine contained 6 percent, 30 percent, or 90 percent alcohol, or whether an aspirin tablet contained 5 or 500 grams of aspirin. Imagine, too, that no controls existed to prevent winemakers from selling their product with methanol and other dangerous impurities, and that vineyards and tobacco fields were fertilized with harmful substances by ignorant growers and sprayed with poisonous herbicides by government agents. Fewer people would use such substances, but more of those who did would get sick. Some would die.

The above scenario describes, of course, the current state of the illicit drug market. Many marijuana smokers are worse off for having smoked cannabis that was grown with dangerous fertilizers, sprayed with the herbicide paraquat, or mixed with more dangerous substances. Consumers of heroin and the various synthetic substances sold on the street face even severer consequences, including fatal overdoses and poisonings from unexpectedly potent or impure drug supplies. More often than not, the quality of a drug addict's life depends greatly upon his or her access to reliable supplies. Drug-enforcement operations that succeed in temporarily disrupting supply networks are thus a double-edged sword: they encourage some addicts to seek admission into drug-treatment programs, but they oblige others to seek out new and hence less reliable suppliers; the result is that more, not fewer, drug-related emergencies and deaths occur.

Today, over 50 percent of all people with AIDS in New York City, New Jersey, and many other parts of the country, as well as the vast majority of AIDS-infected heterosexuals throughout the country, have contracted the disease directly or indirectly through illegal intravenous drug use. Reports have emerged of drug dealers beginning to provide clean syringes together with their illegal drugs. But even as other governments around the world actively attempt to limit the spread of AIDS by and among drug users by instituting free syringe-exchange programs, state and municipal governments in the United States resist following suit, arguing that to do so would "encourage" or "condone" the use of illegal drugs. Only in January 1988 did New York City approve such a program on a very limited and experimental basis. At the same time, drug-treatment programs remain notoriously underfunded, turning away tens of thousands of addicts seeking help, even as billions of dollars more are spent to arrest, prosecute, and imprison illegal drug sellers and users. In what may represent a sign of shifting priorities, the President's Commission on AIDS, in its March 1988 report, emphasized the importance of making drug-treatment programs available to all in need of them. In all likelihood, however, the criminal-justice agencies will continue to receive the greatest share of drug control funds.

Most Americans perceive the drug problem as a moral issue and draw a moral distinction between use of the illicit drugs and use of alcohol and tobacco. Yet when one subjects this distinction to reasonable analysis, it quickly disintegrates. The most consistent moral perspective of those who favor drug laws is that of the Mormons and Puritans, who regard as immoral any intake of substances to alter one's state of consciousness or otherwise cause pleasure: they forbid not only the illicit drugs and alcohol, but also tobacco, caffeine, even chocolate. The vast majority of Americans are hardly so consistent with respect to the propriety of their pleasures. Yet once one acknowledges that there is nothing immoral about drinking alcohol or smoking tobacco for non-medicinal purposes, it is difficult to condemn the consumption of marijuana, cocaine, and other substances on moral grounds. The "moral" condemnation of some substances and not others proves to be little more than a prejudice in favor of some drugs and against others.

The same false distinction is drawn with respect to those who provide the psychoactive substances to users and abusers alike. If degrees of immorality were measured by the levels of harm caused by one's products, the "traffickers" in tobacco and alcohol would be vilified as the most evil of all substance purveyors. That they are perceived instead as respected members of our community, while providers of the no more dangerous illicit substances are punished with long prison sentences, says much about the prejudices of most Americans with respect to psychoactive substances, but little about the morality or immorality of their activities.

Much the same is true of gun salesmen. Most of the consumers of their products use them safely; a minority, however, end up shooting themselves or someone else. Can we hold the gun salesman morally culpable for the harm that probably would not have occurred but for his existence? Most people say no, except perhaps where the salesman clearly knew that his product would be used to commit a crime. Yet in the case of those who sell illicit substances to willing customers, the providers are deemed not only legally guilty but also morally reprehensible. The law does not require any demonstration that the dealer knew of a specific harm to follow; indeed, it does not require any evidence at all of harm having resulted from the sale. Rather, the law is predicated on the assumption that harm will inevitably follow. Despite the patent falsity of that assumption, it persists as the underlying justification for the drug laws.

Although a valid moral distinction cannot be drawn between the licit and the illicit psychoactive substances, one can point to a different kind of moral justification for the drug laws: they arguably reflect a paternalistic obligation to protect those in danger of succumbing to their own weaknesses. If drugs were legally available, most people would either abstain from using them or would use them responsibly and in moderation. A minority without self-restraint, however, would end up harming themselves if the substances were more readily available. Therefore, the majority has a moral obligation to deny itself legal access to certain substances because of the plight of the minority. This obligation is presumably greatest when children are included among the minority.

At least in principle, this argument seems to provide the strongest moral justification for the drug laws. But ultimately the moral quality of laws must be judged not by how those laws are intended to work in principle, but by how they function in practice. When laws intended to serve a moral end inflict great damage on innocent parties, we must rethink our moral position.

Because drug-law violations do not create victims with an interest in notifying the police, drug-enforcement agents rely heavily on undercover operations, electronic surveillance, and information provided by informants. These techniques are indispensable to effective law enforcement, but they are also among the least palatable investigative methods employed by the police. The same is true of drug testing: it may be useful and even necessary for determining liability in accidents, but it also threatens and undermines the right of privacy to which many Americans believe they are entitled. There are good reasons for requiring that such measures be used sparingly.

Equally disturbing are the increasingly vocal calls for people to inform not only on drug dealers but also on neighbors, friends, and even family members who use illicit drugs. Government calls on people not only to "just say no," but also to report those who have not heeded the message. Intolerance of illicit-drug use and users is heralded not only as an indispensable ingredient in the war against drugs, but also as a mark of good citizenship. Certainly every society requires citizens to assist in the enforcement of criminal laws. But societies—particularly democratic and pluralistic ones—also rely strongly on an ethic of tolerance toward those who are different but do no harm to others. Overzealous enforcement of the drug laws risks undermining that ethic, and encouraging the creation of a society of informants. This results in an immorality that is far more dangerous in its own way than that associated with the use of illicit drugs.

THE BENEFITS OF LEGALIZATION

Repealing the drug-prohibition laws promises tremendous advantages. Between reduced government expenditures on enforcing drug laws and new tax revenue from legal drug production and sales, public treasuries would enjoy a net benefit of at least ten billion dollars a year, and possibly much more. The quality of urban life would rise significantly. Homicide rates would decline. So would robbery and burglary rates. Organized criminal groups, particularly the newer ones that have yet to diversify out of drugs, would be dealt a devastating setback. The police, prosecutors, and courts would focus their resources on combating the types of crimes that we cannot walk away from. More ghetto residents would turn their backs on criminal careers and seek out legitimate opportunities instead. And the health and quality of life of many drug users—and drug abusers—would improve significantly.

All the benefits of legalization would be for naught, however, if millions more Americans were to become drug abusers. Our experience with alcohol and tobacco provides ample warnings. Today, alcohol is consumed by 140 million Americans and tobacco by 50 million. All of the health costs associated with abuse of the illicit drugs pale in comparison with those resulting from tobacco and alcohol abuse. In 1986, for example, alcohol was identified as a contributing factor in 10 percent of work-related injuries, 40 percent of the suicide attempts, and about 40 percent of the approximately 46,000 annual traffic deaths in 1983. An estimated eighteen million Americans are reported to be either alcoholics or alcohol abusers. The cost of alcohol abuse to American society is estimated at over 100 billion dollars annually. Alcohol has been identified as the direct cause of 80,000 to 100,000 deaths annually, and as a contributing factor in an additional 100,000 deaths. The health costs of tobacco use are of similar magnitude. In the United States alone, an estimated 320,000 people die prematurely each year as a consequence of their consumption of tobacco. By comparison, the National Council on Alcoholism reported that only 3,562 people were known to have died in 1985 from use of all illegal drugs combined. Even if we assume that thousands more deaths were related in one way or another to illicit drug abuse but not reported as such, we are still left with the conclusion that all of the health costs of marijuana, cocaine, and heroin combined amount to only a small fraction of those caused by tobacco and alcohol....

CAN LEGALIZATION WORK?

It is thus impossible to predict whether legalization would lead to greater levels of drug abuse, and exact costs comparable to that of alcohol and tobacco abuse. The lessons that can be drawn from other societies are mixed. China's experience with the British opium pushers of the nineteenth century, when millions became addicted to the drug, offers one worst-case scenario. The devastation of many native American tribes by alcohol presents another. On the other hand, the legal availability of opium and cannabis in Asian societies did not result in large addict populations until recently. Indeed, in many countries U.S.-inspired opium bans imposed during the past few decades have paradoxically contributed to dramatic increases in heroin consumption among Asian youth. Within the United States, the decriminalization of marijuana by about a dozen states during the 1970s did not lead to increases in marijuana consumption. In the Netherlands, which went even further in decriminalizing cannabis during the 1970s, consumption has actually declined significantly. The policy has succeeded, as the government intended, in making drug use boring. Finally, late nineteenth-century America was a society in which there were almost no drug laws or even drug regulations— but levels of drug use then were about what they are today. Drug abuse was considered a serious problem, but the criminal-justice system was not regarded as part of the solution.

There are, however, reasons to believe that none of the currently illicit substances would become as popular as alcohol or tobacco, even if they were legalized. Alcohol has long been the principal intoxicant in most societies, including many in which other substances have been legally available. Presumably, its diverse properties account for its popularity—it quenches thirst, goes well with food, and promotes appetite as well as sociability. The popularity of tobacco probably stems not just from its powerful addictive qualities, but from the fact that its psychoactive effects are sufficiently subtle that cigarettes can be integrated with most other human activities. The illicit substances do not share these qualities to the same extent, nor is it likely that they would acquire them if they were legalized. Moreover, none of the illicit substances can compete with alcohol's special place in American culture and history.

An additional advantage of the illicit drugs is that none of them appears to be as insidious as either alcohol or tobacco. Consumed in their more benign forms, few of the illicit substances are as damaging to the human body over the long term as alcohol and tobacco, and none is as strongly linked with violent behavior as alcohol. On the other hand, much of the damage caused today by illegal drugs stems from their consumption in particularly dangerous ways. There is good reason to doubt that many Americans would inject cocaine or heroin into their veins even if given the chance to do so legally. And just as the dramatic growth in the heroin-consuming population during the 1960s leveled off for reasons apparently having little to do with law enforcement, so we

can expect a leveling-off—which may already have begun—in the number of people smoking crack. The logic of legalization thus depends upon two assumptions: that most illegal drugs are not so dangerous as is commonly believed; and that the drugs and methods of consumption that are most risky are unlikely to prove appealing to many people, precisely because they are so obviously dangerous.

Perhaps the most reassuring reason for believing that repeal of the drug-prohibition laws will not lead to tremendous increases in drug-abuse levels is the fact that we have learned something from our past experiences with alcohol and tobacco abuse. We now know, for instance, that consumption taxes are an effective method of limiting consumption rates. We also know that restrictions and bans on advertising, as well as a campaign of negative advertising, can make a difference. The same is true of other government measures including restrictions on time and place of sale, prohibition of consumption in public places, packaging requirements, mandated adjustments in insurance policies, crackdowns on driving while under the influence, and laws holding bartenders and hosts responsible for the drinking of customers and guests. There is even some evidence that government-sponsored education programs about the dangers of cigarette smoking have deterred many children from beginning to smoke.

Clearly it is possible to avoid repeating the mistakes of the past in designing an effective plan for legalization. We know more about the illegal drugs now than we knew about alcohol when Prohibition was repealed, or about tobacco when the anti-tobacco laws were repealed by many states in the early years of this century. Moreover, we can and must avoid having effective drug-control policies undermined by powerful lobbies like those that now protect the interests of alcohol and tobacco producers. We are also in a far better position than we were sixty years ago to prevent organized criminals from finding and creating new opportunities when their most lucrative source of income dries up.

It is important to stress what legalization is not. It is not a capitulation to the drug dealers—but rather a means to put them out of business. It is not an endorsement of drug use—but rather a recognition of the rights of adult Americans to make their own choices free of the fear of criminal sanctions. It is not a repudiation of the "just say no" approach—but rather an appeal to government to provide assistance and positive inducements, not criminal penalties and more repressive measures, in support of that approach. It is not even a call for the elimination of the criminal-justice system from drug regulation—but rather a proposal for the redirection of its efforts and attention.

There is no question that legalization is a risky policy, since it may lead to an increase in the number of people who abuse drugs. But that is a risk—not a certainty. At the same time, current drug control policies are failing and new proposals promise only to be more costly and more repressive. We know that repealing the drug prohibition laws would eliminate or greatly reduce many of the ills that people commonly identify as part and parcel of the "drug problem." Yet legalization is repeatedly and vociferously dismissed, without any attempt to evaluate it openly and objectively. The past twenty years have demonstrated that a drug policy shaped by exaggerated rhetoric designed to arouse fear has only led to our current disaster. Unless we are willing to honestly evaluate our options, including various legalization strategies, we will run a still greater risk: we may never find the best solution for our drug problems.

THE CONTINUING DEBATE:
Illegal Drugs

What Is New

The debate over U.S. drug policy has been long and loud. It was raised to a new level at the U. S. Conference of Mayors in 1988, when Baltimore mayor, Kurt L. Schmoke, proposed legalizing drugs. Since then, Canada has decriminalized marijuana, several states have passed laws making drug penalties less severe, and a number of states have passed medicinal marijuana laws. The U.S. federal government, however, continues to pursue a stern policy toward drugs: The federal Higher Education Act prohibits student loans to students convicted of any drug offense (including marijuana posses-sion), while murderers and armed robbers remain eligible; and federal authorities vig-orously prosecute those who seek to supply and use medicinal marijuana.

The issue of medicinal marijuana has pitted several states against the federal gov-ernment. Under the 1996 Federal Controlled Substances Act, no patients are allowed to use marijuana, though many physicians have affirmed its value in relieving the nausea and suffering of patients undergoing severe cancer and AIDS treatments, and some states, such as California, have approved the use of medicinal marijuana. Re-cently the 9th U.S. Circuit Court of Appeals ruled that medicinal marijuana usage is noncommercial and therefore is exclusively up to the states, and that the federal gov-ernment and Congress have no authority on the subject. The case will be decided by the Supreme Court in 2005, but it is not likely to be the last marijuana case adjudi-cated by the Supreme Court.

Where to Find More

Searching for Alternatives: Drug-Control Policy in the United States, edited by Melvyn B. Krauss and Edward P. Lazear (Stanford, CA.: Hoover Institution Press, 1991) con-tains articles exploring competing views on drug policies. Another collection, arranged as opposing positions on different aspects of the controversy is Rod L. Evans and Irwin M. Berent, editors, *Drug Legalization: For and Against* (La Salle, IL: Open Court, 1992). Another good collection of essays, containing both pro and con views, is James A. Inciardi, *The Drug Legalization Debate* (Newbury Park, CA.: Sage Publications, 1991).

The Cato Institute think tank focusing on political issues, generally supports minimizing the role of government, and thus opposes government interference in adults' choices concerning what drugs they take, and so favors drug legalization. A major paper by James Ostrowski, "Thinking about Drug Legalization," argues in favor of drug legalization, and can be found at *www.cato.org/pubs/pas/pa121.html*. Ostrowski's paper, along with papers by Kurt L. Schmoke and several others, are followed by a number of brief essays that criticize drug prohibition, in David Boaz, editor, *The Crisis in Drug Prohibition* (Washington, D.C.: The Cato Institute, 1991).

The Netherlands has adopted very liberal drug laws concerning marijuana, and is often regarded as an interesting test of marijuana decriminalization. Studies indicate that drug problems in The Netherlands are significantly less than in the U.S. For a more detailed examination, see Craig Reinarman, "The Dutch Example Shows that

Liberal Drug Laws Can Be Beneficial," at *www.cedri-uva.org/lib/reinarman. dutch.pdf*, or in Scott Barbour, ed., *Drug Legalization: Current Controversies* (San Diego: Greenhaven Press, 1999, 2000), pp. 102–108.

On June 16, 1999, the United States Congress' Criminal Justice, Drug Policy, and Human Resources Subcommittee held a hearing on "Drug Legalization, Criminalization, and Harm Reduction." A number of papers were read into the record, both pro and con, and there was considerable discussion. A transcript of the hearing and the papers can be found at the Federal News Service. The conservative journal, *National Review*, favors drug legalization; their editorial statement, along with the views of several other writers, can be found at *www.nationalreview.com/ 12feb96/drug.html*.

6 PERFORMANCE ENHANCING DRUGS

Should They Be Banned from Athletics *or* Should Athletes Be Allowed to Use Them?

THEY SHOULD BE BANNED FROM ATHLETICS

ADVOCATE: Robert L. Simon, Professor of Philosophy at Hamilton College, Coach of the Hamilton College varsity golf team from 1986–2000. He is a past president of the Philosophic Society for the Study of Sport and a member of the editorial board for the *Journal of the Philosophy of Sport.*

SOURCE: "Good Competition and Drug-Enhanced Competition," *Journal of the Philosophy of Sport,* volume 11 (1984), pages 6–13

ATHLETES SHOULD BE ALLOWED TO USE THEM

ADVOCATE: W. M. Brown, a philosophy professor at Trinity College, Hartford, Connecticut, and dean of the faculty. He has written extensively in philosophy of science and the philosophy of sport

SOURCE: "As American as Gatorade and Apple Pie: Performance Drugs and Sports," in Joram Graf Haber, editor, *Ethics for Today and Tomorrow* (Sudbury, Mass.: Jones and Bartlett, 1997), pp. 324–341

The most common argument for banning performance-enhancing drugs is that they are too dangerous and harmful to athletes. Whether such paternalism is ever justified, and whether it is justified in special limited cases, are long debated questions, but paternalism is not a special issue for athletics. If you think paternalism is legitimate, there is no problem extending such paternalism to athletes. If you reject paternalism but still wish to ban the athletic use of performance enhancing drugs, then you will need nonpaternalistic grounds for such a ban.

One line of nonpaternalistic argument against performance-enhancing drugs is based on the essential elements of human athletic competition. In athletic competition we are not interested in how fast a mile can be traversed, but in how fast a human athlete can do it. There is nothing wrong with competitions in which giant mechanical contraptions hurl pumpkins a mile or more, and nothing wrong with seeing how far such a mechanical marvel might throw a discus or javelin. Likewise, we might find a bionic man competition entertaining: how well can clever scientists engineer a human form that is designed to run very fast, lift enormous weights and leap tall buildings in a single bound, all within the confines of a human skin? It might well become a great favorite on cable television, but it would not be human athletic competition.

Another argument is based on fairness: the wealthy nations hire great trainers and contrive optimum diets and their best athletes are still outrun by the swift Kenyans, who have gloried in long distance racing since childhood. And that is an element that most people want in sport: the outcome ultimately depending on athletic skill and training, and perhaps a lucky bounce, rather than by which side has hired the most creative drug designer or the most ambitious genetic enhancer. The "integrity of sport" aside, much of the joy and satisfaction that people take in sports would be lost if sporting ability could be produced in a laboratory and injected into athletes. Robert L. Simon develops his argument for restrictions on performance-enhancing drugs along these lines.

There is another fairness line of argument: If drug enhancement becomes common in a sport, then persons who prefer not to use the drugs will be forced out of the highest level of competition. If steroid use becomes commonplace among football linemen, then those who do not use steroids will be placed at a great disadvantage and be unable to compete at the top levels. Many people find that unfair, but others challenge that conclusion.

POINTS TO PONDER

➤ Genetic scientists have discovered that injecting specific genetic materials causes mice to increase muscle density by an average of 25%, and the mice don't have to lift weights to achieve the increase. Leaving aside the very substantial health risks, suppose that we gave such injections to all NFL players, who by next season had added an extra 25% muscle density (the 240 pound running back end is now about 300 pounds of super dense muscle). Suppose that this innovation were used by *everyone* in the league. From the perspective of the fan watching the game: Would that make NFL football better, or worse, or would it have no effect?

➤ I have a special drug, and it will turn you into a brilliant musician (or novelist, physicist, philosopher, or gymnast—take your choice). Your candle will burn very bright but briefly: the drug will cut your life expectancy in half. The question is not whether you would choose to take the drug; rather, should you have the *choice* to take such a drug, or should it be banned?

➤ Following up on the previous question: Suppose that this new drug enhances musical performance to such a degree that those not taking the drug cannot compete, and all opportunities for professional musical performance are monopolized by those taking the drug. Would those who desire a career in musical performance but do not wish to take this dangerous drug have grounds for complaint?

➤ One key point on which Robert Simon and W. M. Brown disagree is whether drug-enhanced athletic performance is a threat to the athlete's "personhood": as Simon puts it, if athletic performance is drug-enhanced, the result may be that "athletes are no longer reacting to each other as persons but rather become more like competing bodies." How strong is this objection? Is it possible to formulate this objection more precisely than Simon does? Does Brown have an adequate response?

Performance Enhancing Drugs:
They Should Be Banned from Athletics

ROBERT L. SIMON

Competition in sport frequently has been defended in terms of the search for excellence in performance. Top athletes, whether their motivation arises from adherence to the internal values of competition or desire for external reward, are willing to pay a heavy price in time and effort in order to achieve competitive success. When this price consists of time spent in hard practice, we are prepared to praise the athlete as a worker and true competitor. But when athletes attempt to achieve excellence through the use of performance-enhancing drugs, there is widespread condemnation. Is such condemnation justified? What is wrong with the use of drugs to achieve excellence in sport? Is prohibiting the use of performance-enhancing drugs in athletic competition justified?

The relatively widespread use of such drugs as anabolic steroids to enhance performance dates back at least to the Olympics of the 1960s, although broad public awareness of such drug use seems relatively recent. Anabolic steroids are drugs, synthetic derivatives of the male hormone testosterone, which are claimed to stimulate muscle growth and tissue repair. While claims about possible bad consequences of steroid use are controversial, the American College of Sports Medicine warns against serious side effects. These are believed to include liver damage, artherosclerosis, hypertension, personality changes, a lowered sperm count in males, and masculinization in females. Particularly frightening is that world-class athletes are reportedly taking steroids at many times the recommended medical

dosage—at levels so high that, as Thomas Murray has pointed out, under "current federal regulations governing human subjects... no institutional review board would approve a research design that entailed giving subjects anywhere near the levels... used by the athletes."

The use of such high levels of a drug raises complex empirical as well as ethical issues. For example, even if steroid use at a low level does not actually enhance athletic performance, as some authorities claim, it is far from clear whether heavy use produces any positive effects on performance. At the very least, athletes who believe in the positive effects of heavy doses of steroids are not likely to be convinced by data based on more moderate intake.

As interesting as these issues are, it will be assumed in what follows that the use of certain drugs does enhance athletic performance and does carry with it some significant risk to the athlete. Although each of these assumptions may be controversial, by granting them, the discussion can concentrate on the ethical issues raised by use of performance-enhancing drugs.

I. WHAT IS A PERFORMANCE-ENHANCING DRUG?

If we are to discuss the ethics of using drugs to enhance athletic performance, we should begin with a clear account of what counts as such a drug. Unfortunately, a formal definition is exceedingly hard to come by, precisely because it is unclear to what substances such a definition ought to apply.

If it is held to be impermissible to take steroids or amphetamines to enhance performance, what about special diets, the use of coffee to promote alertness, or the bizarre practice of "blood doping," by which runners store their own blood in a frozen state and then return it to their body before a major meet in order to increase the oxygen sent to the muscles?

It is clear that the concept of an "unnatural" or "artificial" substance will not take us very far here, since testosterone hardly is unnatural. Similarly, it is difficult to see how one's own blood can be considered artificial. In addition, we should not include on any list of forbidden substances the use of medication for legitimate reasons of health.

Moreover, what counts as a performance-enhancing drug will vary from sport to sport. For example, drinking alcohol normally will hurt performance. However, in some sports, such as riflery, it can help. This is because as a depressant, alcohol will slow down one's heart rate and allow for a steadier stance and aim.

Rather than spend considerable time and effort in what is likely to be a fruitless search for necessary conditions, we would do better to ignore borderline cases and focus on such clear drugs of concern as amphetamines and steroids. If we can understand the ethical issues that apply to use of such drugs, we might then be in a better position to handle borderline cases as well. However, it does seem that paradigm cases of the drugs that are of concern satisfy at least some of the following criteria.

1. If the user did not believe that use of the substance in the amount ingested would increase the chances of enhanced athletic performance, that substance would not be taken.
2. The substance, in the amount ingested, is believed to carry significant risk to the user.

3. The substance, in the amount ingested, is not prescribed medication taken to relieve an illness or injury.

These criteria raise no concern about the normal ingestion of such drugs as caffeine in coffee or tea, or about medication since drugs used for medicinal purposes would not fall under them. The use of amphetamines and steroids, on the other hand, do fall under the criteria....

Why should the use of possibly harmful drugs solely for the purpose of enhancing athletic performance be regarded as impermissible? In particular, why shouldn't individual athletes be left at liberty to pursue excellence by any means they freely choose?

II. PERFORMANCE-ENHANCING DRUGS, COERCION, AND THE HARM PRINCIPLE

One argument frequently advanced against the use of such performance-enhancing drugs as steroids is based on our second criterion of harm to the user. Since use of such drugs is harmful to the user, it ought to be prohibited.

However, if we accept the "harm principle," which is defended by such writers as J. S. Mill, paternalistic interference with the freedom of others is ruled out. According to the harm principle, we are entitled to interfere with the behavior of competent, consenting adults only to prevent harm to others. After all, if athletes prefer the gains that the use of drugs provide along with possible side effects to the alternative of less risk but worse performance, external interference with their freedom of choice seems unwarranted.

However, at least two possible justifications of paternalistic interference are compatible with the harm principle. First, we can argue that athletes do not give informed consent to the use of performance-enhancing drugs. Second, we can argue that the use of drugs by some athletes does harm other competitors. Let us consider each response in turn.

Informed Consent

Do athletes freely choose to use such performance-enhancing drugs as anabolic steroids? Consider, for example, professional athletes whose livelihood may depend on the quality of their performance. Athletes whose performance does not remain at peak levels may not be employed for very long. As Carolyn Thomas maintains, "the onus is on the athlete to… consent to things that he or she would not otherwise consent to…. Coercion, however, makes the athlete vulnerable. It also takes away the athlete's ability to act and choose freely with regard to informed consent." Since pressures on top amateur athletes in national and world-class competition may be at least as great as pressures on professionals, a comparable argument can be extended to cover them as well.

However, while this point is not without some force, we need to be careful about applying the notion of coercion too loosely. After all, no one is forced to try to become a top athlete. The reason for saying top athletes are "coerced" is that if they don't use performance-enhancing drugs, they may not get what they want. But they still have the choice of settling for less. Indeed, to take another position is to virtually deny the competence of top athletes to give consent in a variety of sports related areas including adoption of training regimens and scheduling. Are we to say, for example, that coaches coerce athletes into training and professors coerce students into doing work for their courses? Just as students can choose not to take a college degree, so too can athletes revise their goals. It is also to suggest that *any* individual who strives for great reward is not competent to give consent, since the

fear of losing such a reward amounts to a coercive pressure.

While the issue of coercion and the distinction between threats and offers is highly complex, I would suggest that talk of coercion is problematic as long as the athlete has an acceptable alternative to continued participation in highly competitive sport. While coercion may indeed be a real problem in special cases, the burden of proof would seem to be on those who deny that top athletes *generally* are in a position to consent to practices affecting performance.

Harm to Others

This rejoinder might be satisfactory, critics will object, if athletes made their choices in total isolation. The competitive realities are different, however. If some athletes use drugs, others—who on their own might refrain from becoming users—are "forced" to indulge just to remain competitive. As Manhattan track coach Fred Dwyer points out, "The result is that athletes—none of whom understandingly, are willing to settle for second place—feel that "if my opponent is going to get for himself that little extra, then I'm a fool not to." Athletes may feel trapped into using drugs in order to stay competitive. According to this argument, then, the user of performance-enhancing drugs is harming others by coercing them into becoming users as well.

While the competitive pressures to use performance-enhancing drugs undoubtedly are real, it is far from clear that they are unfair or improperly imposed. Suppose, for example, that some athletes embark on an especially heavy program of weight training. Are they coercing other athletes into training just as hard in order to compete? If not, why are those athletes who use steroids "coercing" others into going along? Thus, if performance-enhancing drugs were available to all, no one would cheat by using them; for all would have the same opportunity and, so it would be argued, no one would be forced into drug use any more than top athletes are forced to embark on rigorous training programs.

Perhaps what bothers us about the use of drugs is that the user may be endangering his or her health. But why isn't the choice about whether the risk is worth the gain left to the individual athlete to make? After all, we don't always prohibit new training techniques just because they carry along with them some-risk to health. Perhaps the stress generated by a particularly arduous training routine is more dangerous to some athletes than the possible side effects of drugs are to others?

Arguably, the charge that drug users create unfair pressures on other competitors begs the very question at issue. That is, it presupposes that such pressures are morally suspect in ways that other competitive pressures are not, when the very point at issue is whether that is the case. What is needed is some principled basis for asserting that certain competitive pressures—those generated by the use of performance enhancing drugs—are illegitimately imposed while other competitive pressures—such as those generated by hard training—are legitimate and proper. It will not do to point out that the former pressures are generated by drug use. What is needed is an explanation of why the use of performance enhancing drugs should be prohibited in the first place.

While such arguments, which describe a position we might call a libertarianism of sports, raise important issues, they may seem to be open to clear counter-example when applied in nonathletic contexts. Suppose for example that your co-workers choose to put in many extra hours on the job. That may put pressure on you to

work overtime as well, if only to show your employer that you are just as dedicated as your colleagues. But now, suppose your fellow workers start taking dangerous stimulants to enable them to put even more hours into their jobs. Your employer then asks why you are working less than they are. You reply that you can keep up the pace only by taking dangerous drugs. Is the employer's reply, "Well, no one is forcing you to stay on the job, but if you do you had better put in as many hours as the others" really acceptable?

However, even here, intuitions are not a particularly reliable guide to principle. Suppose you have other less stressful alternatives for employment and that the extra hours the others originally work without aid of drugs generate far more harmful stress than the risk generated by the use of the stimulant? Perhaps in that case your employer is not speaking impermissibly in telling you to work harder. If not, just why does the situation change when the harmful effects are generated by drugs rather than stress? Alternatively, if we think there should be limits both on the stress generated by pressures from overtime *and* the risks created by drug use, why not treat similar risks alike, regardless of source? Similarly, in the context of sport, if our goal is to lower risk, it is far from clear that the risks imposed by performance-enhancing drugs are so great as to warrant total prohibition, while the sometimes equal risks imposed by severe training regimens are left untouched.

Harm and the Protection of the Young
Even if athletes at top levels of competition can give informed consent to the use of performance-enhancing drugs, and even if users do not place unfair or coercive competitive pressures on others, the harm principle may still support prohibition.

Consider, for example, the influence of the behavior of star athletes on youngsters. Might not impressionable boys and girls below the age of consent be driven to use performance-enhancing drugs in an effort to emulate top stars? Might not high school athletes turn to performance-enhancing drugs to please coaches, parents, and fans?

Unfortunately, consideration of such remote effects of drug use is far from conclusive. After all, other training techniques such as strict weight programs also may be dangerous if adopted by young athletes who are too physically immature to take the stress such programs generate. Again, what is needed is not simply a statement that a practice imposes some risk on others. Also needed is a justification for saying the risk is improperly imposed. Why restrict the freedom of top athletes rather than increase the responsibility for supervision of youngsters assigned to coaches, teachers, and parents? After all, we don't restrict the freedom of adults in numerous other areas where they may set bad examples for the young.

III. DRUGS AND THE IDEAL OF COMPETITIVE SPORT

Our discussion so far suggests that although the charges that use of performance-enhancing drugs by some athletes harms others do warrant further examination, they amount to less than a determinative case against such drug use. However, they may have additional force when supported by an account of competitive sport which implies a distinction between appropriate and inappropriate competitive pressures. What we need, then, is an account of when risk is improperly imposed on others in sport. While I am unable to provide a full theory here, I do want to suggest a principled basis, grounded on an ethic of athletic competition, for prohibition of paradigm performance-enhancing drugs.

My suggestion, which I can only outline here, is that competition in athletics is best thought of as a mutual quest for excellence through challenge. Competitors are obliged to do their best so as to bring out the best in their opponents. Competitors are to present challenges to one another within the constitutive rules of the sport being played. Such an account may avoid the charges, often directed against competitive sports, that they are zero-sum games which encourage the selfish and egotistical desire to promote oneself by imposing losses on others.

In addition, the ideal of sport as a *mutual* quest for excellence brings out the crucial point that a sports contest is a competition between *persons*. Within the competitive framework, each participant must respond to the choices, acts, and abilities of others—which in turn manifest past decisions about what one's priorities should be and how one's skills are to be developed. The good competitor, then, does not see opponents as things to be overcome and beaten down but rather sees them as persons whose acts call for appropriate, mutually acceptable responses. On this view, athletic competition, rather than being incompatible with respect for our opponents as persons, actually presupposes it.

However, when use of drugs leads to improved play, it is natural to say that it is not athletic ability that determines outcome but rather the efficiency with which the athlete's body reacts to the performance enhancer. But the whole point of athletic competition is to test the athletic ability of persons, not the way bodies react to drugs. In the latter case, it is not the athlete who is responsible for the gain. Enhanced performance does not result from the qualities of the athlete *qua* person, such as dedication, motivation, or courage. It does not result from innate or developed ability, of which it is the point of competition to test. Rather, it results from an external factor, the ability of one's body to efficiently utilize a drug, a factor which has only a contingent and fortuitous relationship to athletic ability.

Critics may react to this approach in at least two different ways. First, they may deny that drug use radically changes the point of athletic competition, which presumably is to test the physical and mental qualities of athletes in their sport. Second, they may assert that by allowing the use of performance-enhancing drugs, we expand the point of athletic competition in desirable ways. That is, they may question whether the paradigm of athletic competition to which I have appealed has any privileged moral standing. It may well be an accepted paradigm, but what makes it acceptable?

Drugs and Tests of Ability

Clearly, drugs such as steroids are not magic pills that guarantee success regardless of the qualities of the users. Athletes using steroids must practice just as hard as others to attain what may be only marginal benefits from use. If performance enhancers were available to all competitors, it would still be the qualities of athletes that determined the results.

While this point is not without force, neither is it decisive. Even if all athletes used drugs, they might not react to them equally. The difference in reaction might determine the difference between competitive success and failure. Hence, outcomes would be determined not by the relevant qualities of the athletes themselves but rather by the natural capacity of their bodies to react to the drug of choice.

Is this any different, the critic may reply, from other innate differences in athletes which might enable them to benefit more than others from weight training or to run faster or swing harder than others? Isn't it inconsistent to allow some kinds of innate differences to affect outcomes but not the others?

Such an objection, however, seems to ignore the point of athletic competition. The point of such competition is to select those who do run the fastest, swing the hardest, or jump the farthest. The idea is not for all to come out equally, but for differences in outcome to correlate with differences in ability and motivation. Likewise, while some athletes may be predisposed to benefit more from a given amount of weight training than others, this trait seems relevant to selection of the best athlete. Capacity to benefit from training techniques seems part of what makes one a superior athlete in a way that capacity to benefit from a drug does not.

Competition and Respect for Persons

At this point, a proponent of the use of performance-enhancing drugs might acknowledge that use of such drugs falls outside the prevailing paradigm of athletic competition. However, such a proponent might ask, "What is the *moral* force of such a conclusion?" Unless we assume that the accepted paradigm not only is acceptable, but in addition that deviance from it should be prohibited, nothing follows about the ethics of the use of performance-enhancing drugs.

Indeed, some writers seem to suggest that we consider new paradigms compatible with greater freedom for athletes, including freedom to experiment with performance-enhancing drugs. W. M. Brown seems to advocate such a view when he writes,

> Won't it [drug use] change the nature of our sports and ourselves? Yes…. But then people can choose, as they always have, to compete with

those similar to themselves or those different.... I can still make my actions an "adventure in freedom" and "explore the limits of my strength" however I choose to develop it.

I believe Brown has raised a point of fundamental significance here. I wish I had a fully satisfactory response to it. Since I don't, perhaps the best I can do is indicate the lines of a reply I think is worth considering, in the hope that it will stimulate further discussion and evaluation.

Where athletic competition is concerned, if all we are interested in is better and better performance, we could design robots to "run" the hundred yards in 3 seconds or hit a golf ball 500 hundred yards when necessary. But at isn't just enhanced performance that we are after. In addition, we want athletic competition to be a test of *persons*. It is not only raw ability we are testing for; it is what people do with their ability that counts at least as much. In competition itself, each competitor is reacting to the choices, strategies, and valued abilities of the other, which in turn are affected by past decisions and commitments. Arguably, athletic competition is a paradigm example of an area in which each individual competitor respects the other competitors as persons. That is, each reacts to the intelligent choices and valued characteristics of the other. These characteristics include motivation, courage, intelligence, and what might be called the metachoice of which

talents and capacities are to assume priority over others for a given stage of the individual's life.

However, if outcomes are significantly affected not by such features but instead by the capacity of the body to benefit physiologically from drugs, athletes are no longer reacting to each other as persons but rather become more like competing bodies. It becomes more and more appropriate to see the opposition as things to be overcome—as mere means to be overcome in the name of victory—rather than as persons posing valuable challenges. So, insofar as the requirement that we respect each other as persons is ethically fundamental, the prevailing paradigm does enjoy a privileged perspective from the moral point of view.

It is of course true that the choice to develop one's capacity through drugs is a choice a person might make. Doesn't respect for persons require that we respect the choice to use performance enhancers as much as any other? The difficulty, I suggest, is the effect that such a choice has on the process of athletic competition itself. The use of performance-enhancing drugs in sports restricts the area in which we can be respected as persons. Although individual athletes certainly can make such a choice, there is a justification inherent in the nature of good competition for prohibiting participation by those who make such a decision. Accordingly, the use of performance-enhancing drugs should be prohibited in the name of the value of respect for persons itself.

Performance Enhancing Drugs:
Athletes Should Be Allowed to Use Them

W. M. BROWN

As long as people have played at sports they have tried to develop their skills and capacities with all the means at their disposal. In recent years, public discussion of such efforts has focused on the use of performance-enhancing drugs, in part because we are caught up in a quagmire of issues relating to illegal drug use, and in part because we are perplexed by ethical and practical issues relating to developments in biotechnology. Our sports have changed and our attitudes toward them and the athletes who perform in them are undergoing similar changes. By and large, the controversies over professionalism and race in sport are over, those over sex and gender are passing, but the controversy over performance drugs is unresolved.

This paper is a critique of a number of arguments that are frequently made to resolve that controversy by showing why performance drugs should be forbidden to all athletes participating in organized sports such as amateur and professional leagues and international competitions like the Olympic Games. The arguments have moral as well as practical aspects, focusing as they do on athletes' rights and principles of liberty or of avoiding harm. Surprisingly, perhaps, one of the most curious aspects of the controversy is what people mean when they argue about drugs in sports.

One reason for this is that much of the notoriety of drug use in sports is related to athletes' use of recreational drugs: cocaine, alcohol, and tobacco, for example. Few of these drugs are thought by anyone to enhance athletic performance. Indeed, aside from the illegality of some of them, they are deplored because they diminish one's skills and produce aberrant behavior on and off the playing fields. Another reason is that many of the substances used to enhance athletic performance are not usually thought of as drugs at all, for example an athlete's own blood, or hormones, or widely used food products like caffeine or sugar. And finally, there is puzzlement over the availability of synthetically produced substances that naturally occur in the human body such as testosterone, human growth hormone, and erythropoietin which have widespread therapeutic uses and even uses for otherwise healthy individuals coping with the processes of aging.

But having mentioned a few, I will not catalogue the list of substances that are used to enhance athletic performance or seek to define them. The issues I will discuss cut across such lists and concern more general views about fairness, health, consensus, autonomy, and the nature of sports as they are brought to bear on the practice of enhancing athletic performance. Nor will the arguments I will consider hinge on the effectiveness of such substances. No one really knows whether many of these products are effective at all or in what ways or with what risks. Virtually no serious major studies of their use by athletes have been made, and most of our evidence is speculative and anecdotal, extrapolated from very different contexts or reported by journalists. So I will assume that some performance drugs are effective and some are not, that some are risky and some are safe, and proceed to explore what conclusions we can reach about their use by athletes.

FAIRNESS

Perhaps the most frequently cited issue concerning drugs and sports is that of fairness. The claim is that taking "performance drugs" is a form of cheating, that it is therefore fundamentally unfair. After all, if some athletes are using something that gives them a decisive advantage, it is argued, it is unfair to the basic premise of competition in sports (whether competition against present opponents or competition for records). Competition in sports (as opposed to competition in love and war) assumes some basic similarities among all participants so that contests are close and, therefore, both bring out the best in the competitors and are exciting to watch. Such a situation also, it is claimed (rightly, it seems to me), makes it more likely that the contest will be won in the margin where various factors come into play that are dear to our traditions: effort, will, determination, fortitude, and courage, among others.

And it is true: when an athlete breaks the rules, such as those banning the use of performance drugs, that is clearly a form of cheating, and its practice introduces an aspect of unfairness into the sport. But in an important way this argument misses the point. The ethical issue we are addressing is precisely that of the value of such rules, of the wisdom or justification of prohibiting the use of performance drugs. It therefore begs the question to stress that such drugs are forbidden and so it is wrong to use them.

There is a version of this argument that seems to acknowledge this point, but goes on to claim that when some athletes use drugs and others do not (for whatever reason other than that they are banned), an inequality is introduced that renders competition unfair, not because of any cheating, but because of the discrepancy in performance that drug use may introduce. The short answer to this argument is that there are always likely to be differences among athletes (even if they are clones) and that these differences are (to mention a particular sport) what makes for horse racing. Without them, sports competition would surely hold little interest for us. Competition would resemble the predicament of Buridan's ass with unresolveable stalemates or contests won by random chance.

A more persuasive version of this argument is to note that in highly competitive sports where there are many pressures from family, coaches, teammates, managers, and owners, there can be no free choice to use performance drugs. At best it is a subtle form of coercion, a "forced choice," that produces for some athletes an unhappy dilemma: don't compete or take drugs. We can acknowledge the crucial premise that individual autonomy is a central value. (Indeed, it is one I will employ frequently.) The additional factual premise that no one can be expected to withstand such pressures is more problematic. For one thing, it is clear that although many athletes now use performance drugs, many do not, and the latter are among the finest and most successful athletes now performing. But for another, every innovation or change in training, techniques, and equipment places similar pressure on athletes to adopt the changes or lose a competitive edge (assuming also that the changes are really effective in enhancing performance). The charge of coercion hinges on the prior assumption that the choice to use performance drugs is deeply objectionable and therefore many people would not want to use them. Of course, if their use is illegal or harmful, many athletes will be reluctant to use them. So athletes who choose not to use drugs are at an unfair advantage only if there is a good reason not to use them. And that, of course, is just the issue at stake. But these reasons need to be assessed. Someone might complain that he can be a boxer only if competitors are allowed to punch the head, and since that is very dangerous, he is unfairly forced to choose between boxing and getting his head punched (and punching others in the head) or not competing at all. The wise choice may be to switch to swimming, but the choice is not in any interesting sense coerced....

In the discussion to follow, various additional arguments concerning the use of performance drugs are examined to assess their cogency and persuasiveness.

HEALTH

Performance drugs are dangerous, so this argument goes, and banning their use is a way of protecting athletes from their own ill-conceived acts. The danger lies in the injuries that the use of performance drugs may cause. Recently, this case has been made most vociferously in regard to anabolic steroids, the drug of choice for athletes seeking to increase muscle mass useful for various sports ranging from football to track to gymnastics. But many other drugs are also available, including beta-blockers, growth hormones, and food ingredients such as caffeine; presumably the argument can be made in regard to them as well.

There are, however, two issues that need to be separated in this regard. One is an empirical issue concerning the actual harms likely to he caused by performance drug use. The other is the ethical issue of paternalism, the justification of restricting the actions of others ostensibly for their own good. A byproduct of this argument is what appears to be a remarkable case of hypocrisy.

As for the first issue, there is some evidence that the use of some performance drugs carries risks of injury to the users. But the evidence is remarkably sparse and, of course, differs for different drugs. Much of it is anecdotal—the lore of boxing and weight-lifting aficionados, the stuff of locker room banter. Such research-based evidence as is available is often inconclusive. Some studies suggest that steroids are effective in enhancing performance; others claim that is no significant enhancing effect. Athletes tend to discount the extreme claims of risk of injury because their own experience has not confirmed them; and much of the research evidence has been based not on studies of efforts to enhance athletic performance but rather on cases of medical therapy and extrapolation to nonmedical circumstances. What this suggests is that the factual claims concerning performance drugs remain significantly unsubstantiated both in regard to drug risks and in regard to performance enhancement. The sensible thing to do would surely be to find out who is right by encouraging careful and competent research into both kinds of claims.

But this would not be the end of it. It seems likely that some substances or procedures would be relatively dangerous and others relatively risk-free; some would be relatively effective, others ineffective. In this case, it could be argued that dangerous ones especially should be carefully used, if effective, to eliminate or minimize their side effects, but that all performance drugs should be studied and the results be widely and publicly available to athletes and their coaches and physicians. The goal should be to eliminate or reduce the likelihood of harm to athletes, as it is for other risks in sport.

A brief comment is in order about relative risk. In many sports, the activities of the sports themselves are far more dangerous than the use of any of the performance drugs that have even a bare chance of being effective. Deaths and injuries due to the use of performance drugs are rare. Scarcely more than a dozen deaths are noted by some authorities, and most of these can be attributed not to performance drugs, but to recreational drugs like cocaine and alcohol used off the playing fields and unconnected to competitive efforts. But deaths and serious injuries due to the sports themselves number in the hundreds in sports like football, boxing, mountain climbing, hockey, cycling, and skiing. Where the sports themselves are far more dangerous than anything risked by using performance drugs, one can only wonder at the hypocrisy that prompts the extraordinary tirades directed at the latter but seldom at the former. The most vociferous criticism of performance drugs seems far more closely linked to our national hysteria about illicit drugs in general than to the health of our athletes.

Still, if we assume that there are dangers in using performance drugs, and clearly there are some even if their use is monitored by knowledgeable physicians, should we prohibit them on the grounds that athletes cannot be expected to make rational choices about their use and hence are at risk of excessive injury to their health? I have argued elsewhere that child athletes should be prohibited on paternalistic grounds from using such drugs. But the issue is not so clear with adult athletes. Unlike airline pilots or subway train drivers, for example, athletes who use performance drugs pose no obvious dangers to others. Nor are the drugs in question related to diminished performance, but rather to enhanced and improved performance. So concerns about athletes' health are paternalistic in the strong sense of being directed not toward preventing

harm to others, but to the drug users themselves. There often seems to be a discrepancy between concerns about athletes' health and safety in general and concerns about risks of using performance drugs. In any case, one could equally well argue that making their use safer while preserving the autonomy and freedom of choice of the athletes is a far preferable approach. If there are effective performance-enhancing drugs (and there seem to be some), and if they are or could be relatively safe to use (and some are), then the health argument, as I have called it, seems ineffective as a general argument against their use.

One final note. Hormonal supplements for healthy adults are not a new item in the pharmacopoeia. More recently men and women are being given sex hormones and growth hormone supplements to offset the effects of aging, apparently with favorable results. Women have taken estrogen for years to offset the effects of menopause. The World Health Organization is currently administering steroids as a male contraceptive in doses greater than those said to have been used by Ben Johnson when he was disqualified after his victory at the Seoul Olympics. It is hard to argue in light of such practices that the use of performance drugs, even the most risky kinds, including steroids, should have no place in the training or performance of athletes.

NATURALNESS AND NORMALITY

The argument shifts at this point, therefore, to the claim that performance drugs are unnatural additives to the athlete's training or performance regimen. Even if their careful use is relatively harmless, the argument goes, they are objectionable because they are artificial and unnatural additives to sporting activities. There are two versions of this argument. One is that it is the drugs that are unnatural; the other is that it is the athletes who use them who are unnatural or abnormal.

The first version is the less plausible. The reason is that many of the drugs used to enhance performance are as natural as testosterone, caffeine, or an athlete's own blood. True, some drugs are the product of manufacturing processes or are administered using medical technologies. But, of course, so are many of our foods, vitamins, and medicines, all routine parts of the athlete's regimen. If by *natural* one means not artificially synthesized or processed, or known to occur in nature independent of human intervention, few of the nutritional and medical resources available to athletes today would be allowed. Performance drugs, therefore, cannot be identified or forbidden under this rubric without taking many things we find indispensable down the drain with them.

The claim for abnormality may be a bit stronger. After all, to the extent that performance drugs work effectively at all, they are designed to render their users superior in ability and rates of success beyond what we would expect otherwise. And this, the argument concludes, renders them abnormal. Of course, this is in one sense true. If normality is defined in terms of statistical frequencies, then highly effective athletes are abnormal by definition. Such people are already abnormal if compared with the rest of us; their reflexes, coordination, neuromuscular development, and fitness levels already place them far to the right on the bell-shaped curves showing the range of human capacities and performance. Performance drugs are scarcely needed to place them among the abnormal, that is, the statistically rare individuals who can run a mile under 3:50, accomplish a gymnastic routine, slam dunk a basketball, or climb Mt. Everest without canisters of extra oxygen. Looked

at another way, however, athletes are probably the most natural components of their sports; their efforts reveal to all of us various ranges of human abilities as currently manifested under the very artificial and unnatural constraints of our present-day sports and their assortment of bats, balls, rules, shoes, training techniques, and ideologies.

Surely, however, those who make this argument know this. Perhaps they are using the word *abnormal* in its other sense of connoting what is bad or undesirable, and since they can't quite articulate what is so bad about performance drugs, they rely on the claim of abnormality or unnaturalness to carry the weight of their condemnation. Here again, then, we need to move on to other arguments that may make the case more substantively and effectively, or at least make clearer what it is about the use of performance drugs that seems to some critics so deplorable....

THE NATURE OF SPORT

Some claim that there are central characteristics of sports that mitigate against the use of performance drugs. I want to consider one such claim, formulated by Alasdair MacIntyre, and developed by others. The claim is that sports are practices, coherent forms of organized social activity that create certain goods and values intrinsic to them and which are attained by performing in accordance with the standards of excellence integral to the practices. This characterization of practices gives rise to a distinction between those goods that are internal to the practices and those that are external to it. Internal goods arise out of the exercise of skills developed to fulfill the defining goals of the activities; external goods are rewards typically offered by institutions that support the practices but also tend to exploit them for reasons of their own that are unconnected with the practices' own immediate activities. Thus a well-thrown pitch, a stolen base, and a perfect bunt are exercises of skill within the practice of baseball and offer their own rewards. The fame, salaries, and trophies that are also rewarded are external to the game and provided by institutions not directly involved in the practice itself.

There is much to be said for this conception of sports. It highlights some of the features of a favorite view of them: the virtuous and innocent player motivated by the love of the game; the power and skill of the practitioner, a thing of beauty and grace; the corrupt and venal exploiters of youth and innocence for worldly gain. But it divides motives and satisfactions too neatly, borrowing the metaphor of inside and outside to suggest that practices are like the bodies of the players themselves, inwardly pure and driven by their own dynamics, confronted by external forces of corruption and greed. The idea is that performance drugs, like an invading microorganism, infiltrate from the outside to foul the internal workings of sports, the athletes themselves, distorting their skills, depriving them of the internal goods of the sports, and motivating them toward the external rewards of larger social institutions. The argument then goes something like this. Performance drugs are not relevant to the internal goods of sports which derive from "achieving those standards of excellence" characteristic of the practice. Their use tends rather to be driven by external goals of winning and victory and the fame or riches attendant on them.

But this argument is unpersuasive for several reasons. The first is that the basic distinction between internal and external goods, though serviceable for some purposes, blurs at crucial places. For example, there are clearly satisfactions to be gained from the exercise of the skills one develops in sport. Such skills are largely specific to given sports: taking a turn on a 400m track and other tactical skills in a foot race, for example, are not easily carried over to golf or basketball. This is due by and large to the arbitrary character of sports, their curious separateness from the skills of the workplace and home. Nevertheless, such skills are sometimes carried over to other sports. And in sports where many diverse skills are called for—in the biathlon, triathlon, and decathlon—for example, skills developed in one sport are transferable to others. No matter that the combination often limits performance to less than that of the specialist; the satisfaction of each skill's development, not just in their combination, is still present. But now such skills and their attendant satisfactions must be both internal and external to specific sports, and if transferable to practices other than the sports themselves—as are the skills, many argue, of teamwork, cooperativeness, and planning—are doubly external.

Or take the good of winning. Winning it is said is an external good of sports and as such would seem to cut across various sports. But winning in one sport is surely not the same as winning in another, and winning at one level of competition is surely different from winning at another. Indeed winning surely emerges as the final, overall configuration of the game itself, internal to the dynamics of the play, its culmination, not an externally imposed determination by those external to the activity. Even in those rare cases where controversial results lead to reviews by others, they are decided by the internal constraints of the sport, not by external institutional needs. And the rewards of winning may be internal or external. True, fortune is usually introduced from outside sports these days, but fame and admiration run deep within the sports themselves and are not just the province of institutional or social renown.

Health and fitness would seem to be external goods imposed on sports, as we have seen in our earlier discussion of the effects of performance drugs. But both are elusive. Fitness is to sports as intelligence is to tests: both seem specific to the ways in which they are measured, by essentially arbitrary cultural norms. Just as there seems no clear way to measure a general intelligence or IQ, so there seems no way to measure general fitness beyond capabilities developed in specific sports or other activities. (Questions like, "Are musicians smarter than lawyers?" give place to "Are basketball players more fit than swimmers?") Health is a notoriously slippery concept. Indeed, it is an uneasy companion of sports like boxing, mountain climbing, football, and many others, which carry with them inherent risks of injury that may be reduced but not eliminated: those risks are integral to the sports themselves and help define the excitement and challenge that are among their internal goods.

So little is to be gained for our purposes from the distinction between internal and external goods. And this is brought out by the second reason, that performance drugs are intended to enhance performance, as measured by the sports' own activities and standards, their own internal goods. Schneider and Butcher have argued that such enhancement is tantamount to changing the skills required by a sport and thus "changes the sport." But this claim is implausible. Training at high altitude greatly enhances the oxygen transport capacity of long-distance runners, but few would argue that it changes the skills required to run a marathon or changes the sport itself. The jump shot, a basketball skill first performed in the late 1940s, changed the sport only in the sense that it added excitement and challenge to the game. In-

deed, Schneider and Butcher emphasize this point themselves. And to the extent that performance drugs could enhance performance, they would contribute to the exercise of skills at a higher level where the challenges and satisfactions might be all the greater.

Surely this is the reason why athletes have always tried to better their opponents, to find ways to excel, in spite of the fact that no one doubts that their secrets to success will soon be out. No one would seek to ignore a new training technique, equipment modification, or diet on the grounds that since one's opponents will soon catch on, the discovery will just escalate the competition, soon making it harder than ever to win. To this extent, sports recapitulate life and reflect a constant striving to win and enjoy, to compete and share in the competition of the game. In this sense, performance drugs may be as relevant to sports and their internal goods as any other way of enhancing one's performance....

SLIPPERY SLOPES

... Another way, I think, of expressing worries that some have about performance drugs is by seeing their claims as slippery slope arguments. I have considerable sympathy for such arguments because they force us to consider longer-range consequences of proposals and to factor in both the past history of human folly and the broad outlines of human behavior as telling evidence for prospects of the future. I have touched on this kind of argument by noting that we might imagine that performance drugs were highly significant factors in athletic achievements rather than marginal or sometimes even negative ones as they now in fact seem to be. In such imaginary circumstances, it is probable that our sports would change. Certainly high-performance sports or professional sports might well come to seem far different for us as spectators from the everyday variety of sports that most of us participate in as amateurs. But in many ways, this is already true. Few of us play basketball or tennis or swim in ways that even our fantasies can liken to professional or even collegiate athletics. So such changes are not necessarily ones we need deplore. The range of abilities and achievements in sports is already enormous and provides niches for us all to enjoy our various skills and interests.

Furthermore, performances in sports have changed in astonishing ways over the last century independently of what we now think of as performance drugs. Training methods, diet, equipment, and above all the selection of the most gifted potential athletes from larger pools have all contributed to these changes that are, I suspect, far greater than any we might expect by the use of performance drugs even in the distant future....

But if performance drugs are allowed, what's next? Aren't there further ways in which athletic performance could be enhanced? And are we to tolerate these, too, in the name of personal choice and autonomy on the part of athletes? For example, some years ago someone invented a mechanical device for moving one's legs fast enough to enable one to run at record-breaking speed. We need only recall the fictional "bionic man" of television to imagine more sophisticated aids to physical activity. Such cases seem to challenge our very conception of athletic endeavor. As Robert Simon noted, "If all we are interested in is better and better performance, we could design robots" to do it for us. But, of course, what we are interested in is human performance, our own and that of those we watch as spectators, though we can easily imagine interest in android or robot performance, too, just as

we acknowledge our interest in competition among other animals in dog and horse racing, for example. But the issue here is the limits of human performance, even the limits of what is to count as human for purposes of sport. So let's consider whether there are some reasonable stopping places on the slippery slope.

One place is the body's own basic boundary, the skin (though it is a porous and partial boundary at best). The differences between sports that are most evident are the differences in equipment and technical aids: the balls, bats, padding, skates, skis, cars, spikes, and other paraphernalia that define different sports, even the other animals who are used sometimes to augment human efforts. Changing the type of equipment in effect changes the identity of the sport. Changing the quality of the equipment also changes the sport, but not its identity, though it complicates efforts to compare performances across such equipment changes and sometimes requires minor changes in the rules. So where the slippery slope involves modifications of equipment, we can easily accept the new technologies as changing the sport.

The problem with performance drugs is that they are integrated into the body's own biosynthetic and metabolic pathways and so are intended to change the performance quality of the athlete, not the circumstances of the sport as defined by its goals, equipment, and rules. Here the slippery slope may yield the more difficult case where the last two possibilities come together, integration into the body of nonbiological technologies. If we condone the use of performance drugs, why not also the use of bionic implants, of artificial bones or organs? Most of the surgery available today for athletes is restorative, repairing the ravages of sports injuries. But not all. Some surgery may enhance performance, allowing greater muscle development or range of movement. And if this were possible on a wider scale, would we consider it, like performance drugs, to be liable to control? Should tissue implants to increase metabolic activity be forbidden? Should surgically improved visual acuity be outlawed? These are the stuff of science fiction for the most part, but we can begin to see the possibility of such procedures.

To some extent, we are at a loss to answer these questions, and not just for sports. Our fears about such changes run deep. Would such procedures be fraught with severe side effects that would make their transient benefits pale by adverse comparison? Do they finally threaten our sense of human identity to a degree that we would find intolerable? Do they hold out the prospects of further divisions among us, not only by wealth, race, and belief, but also by health, talent, and access to biotechnology? I do not have adequate answers to these questions. Even after we satisfy ourselves of the reasonable safety of performance drugs or other performance enhancers (assuming that we could do that), many of these other questions would remain. But they are not limited to the case of sports. These fundamental issues are the spawn of biological technology in general and its possible future impact on our society. It is probably impossible to decide them in advance of the actual development of our knowledge and technology.

PERSONHOOD

I want now to look at an argument that… performance drugs, by stressing the physical competence of athletes, detract from their qualities as persons and hence corrupt the ideal of sport as competition among persons. The gist of the argument seems to be that performance drugs somehow provide a physical boost to athletic

ability that is totally separate from the personal qualities we often cherish in athletes, such as perseverance, good judgment, sportsmanship, grace under pressure, and a striving for excellence. Sometimes, the argument goes further in stressing that when some athletes use performance drugs, they force others to use them, contrary to their desires and hence can corrupt their autonomy and freedom as persons.

These are serious claims, but are they cogent? Two considerations suggest that they are not. One is that the use of performance drugs is no different in these effects than are other ways that athletes develop their skills and capacities or enhance their competitive performance. The other is that none of these approaches to developing their excellence need undermine the athletes' qualities as persons. Consider the first of these two points. Athletes use a variety of means to improve their skills and extend their capacities to perform in their chosen sports. Training methods and diets are obvious ones, but many other techniques are common including psychological counseling and, above all, practice and competition which can develop mental toughness and tactical acuity. Performance drugs can also be used to promote training and the development of athletic skills. They are never a substitute for the hard work of general athletic preparation, and, if they are useful at all, are helpful in enhancing the effects of that work, not in substituting for it. Living at high altitude promotes the body's production of red blood cells, but it is worth little if training is absent. The same is true in actual performance. Performance drugs do not provide skill, stamina, and knowledge; at most, they give a boost to those already developed.

So far, then, performance drugs seem no more a threat to an athlete's "personhood" than any other technique of training or performance. Little is to be gained by stressing that performance drugs have effects on one's body: that's the point of them, as it is of most athletic training and practice. But it is worth noting that there are few other experiences in life outside of sports where we feel so unified in mind and body, where the distinction between being persons and having bodies seems so fatuous. And nothing, so far as I can see, in the use of performance drugs need threaten the development of those personal qualities that we often value in athletes. If it is true that some performance drugs can alter mood and outlook, then careful study is needed to determine how these can affect one's personality. But pep talks, rivalries, and counseling can also affect mood and attitude, as can the sports themselves and are indeed relied on to do so as teams and individuals gear up for tough competition. If we are worried about performance drugs affecting moods, then we must also consider other tried and true methods for doing the same thing. Presumably it is only some moods, perhaps aggressive ones, that are said to be objectionable. If so, then much in the way certain sports are played and their players are developed must be changed as well. Performance drugs, like other athletic techniques, work primarily to enhance what is already there.

Again, it is said that athletes are coerced into choosing to use performance drugs, a curious contradictory claim in itself, by the fact that if some competitors use them, others must use them as well in order to compete successfully. But this is surely true of all changes in technique or training or tactics that athletes develop, as I have already noted. No one can introduce a successful change without others adopting it if they wish to compete suc-cessfully. We do not usually suggest that this denies athletes their autonomy. If you can't develop a good jump shot, or move to Colorado to train in the mountains, or develop a new tactical ploy, it is not your autonomy or free choice that is threatened. There may be an element of unfairness when the adoption of new techniques depends on wealth or special knowledge. But this may be the case for many features of dynamic and changing sports, not just for the use of performance drugs. The remedy would seem to be openness and research, not banning and secrecy....

Our sports have changed over the years. The days of the leisured amateur performing with elegant insouciance seem quaint and puzzling in an age of professionalism and "high-performance" skills driven by commerce and nationalism. There is much to deplore in these changes, but much also to commend. We have seen the end to racism in American sport and positive efforts to resolve the problems of full participation in sports for women. Amateur and school sports flourish as never before. But because sports present so visibly to us a view of what it is to be human (though to be sure in only one of the many ways we understand ourselves), they are a focus of the concerns we have about the impact on human life of modern technologies, especially biomedical technologies. We should not, I believe, either reject or embrace these technologies uncritically, but study and reflect on the way they are changing our lives and our conceptions of who we are. They will continue to change us and our sports. I have argued not so much for the use of performance drugs as for the flourishing in sports of a critical exploration of their use and its impact on how we understand our skills and achievements.

THE CONTINUING DEBATE:
Performance Enhancing Drugs

What Is New

Major League Baseball now tests for performance enhancing drugs, following revelations of steroid use by players. Olympic athletes are banned from competition. Football players get bigger and stronger; and some seem to die younger. Drug testing is a step behind drug design, and new ways are constantly found to avoid being caught. What the sports fans think about all this is unclear. Appearing before a San Francisco grand jury investigating drug use in baseball, Gary Roberts—a Tulane University expert in sports law—testified, "For all we know, the American public may not give a damn. They may be happy if all their gladiators were stoked up on steroids and hitting 500 home runs."

While drug or steroid enhanced athletic performance have received lots of attention (cases from the Olympics, Major League Baseball and NFL Football spring to mind), many scientists believe we are only at the earliest stages of artificially enhancing athletic performance. In the future they suggest, there will be genetic enhancement techniques that will produce much more dramatic effects, with perhaps considerably greater dangers to the athletes, and they believe that such enhancements will be remarkably expensive. Still, with the stakes so high—and sports *is* a multibillion dollar business—the temptations will be great. Questions concerning artificial enhancement of athletic performance will not go away; to the contrary, we may have seen only the opening crack of this Pandora's Box.

Where to Find More

John Hoberman, "Listening to Steroids," offers an interesting history of the issue, with attention to the tension between the desire for drugs that enhance, restore, and rejuvenate and, on the other side, the widespread distrust of pharmacological solutions to our problems. Hoberman also examines the contrast between our negative attitude toward using drugs for athletic enhancement and our tacit approval of drug use for enhancement of musical performances. The article, along with many others, can be found in an excellent anthology edited by William J. Morgan, Klaus V. Meier, and Angela J. Schneider, *Ethics in Sport* (Champaign, IL.: Human Kinetics, 1991).

Dr. Robert Voy, former Chief Medical Officer for the United States Olympic Committee, is opposed to the use of drugs to enhance athletic performance and disturbed by the extent to which drugs are currently involved in sports. His book, *Drugs, Sport, and Politics* (Champaign, IL: Leisure Press, 1991), gives an inside view of the problems, and his proposals for reform.

A discussion of some of the changes in sport driven by professionalism and commercialism can be found in William Morgan, *Leftist Theories of Sport: A Critique and Reconstruction* (Urbana and Chicago: University of Illinois Press, 1994). A general collection on ethics and sports is Jan Boxill, editor, *Sports Ethics* (Oxford: Blackwell Publishing, 2003). Another anthology, with an excellent collection of articles on athletics and drugs, is William J. Morgan and Klaus V. Meier, Editors, *Philosophic Inquiry in Sport*, 2nd Edition (Champaign, IL: Human Kinetics, 1995). Still another is William J. Morgan, Klaus V. Meier, and Angela J. Schneider, editors, *Ethics in Sport* (Champaign, IL: Human Kinetics, 2001).

HOMOSEXUAL SEX

Immoral or Moral?

IMMORAL

ADVOCATE: John Finnis, Professor of law and legal philosophy at Oxford and Biolchini Professor of Law at the University of Notre Dame, is a leader of the new "natural lawyers."

SOURCE: "Law, Morality, and 'Sexual Orientation,'" *Notre Dame Journal of Law, Ethics, and Public Policy*, volume 9, 1995

MORAL

ADVOCATE: John Corvino, Philosophy Professor at Wayne State University, specializes in ethical theory and applied ethics, and is a well-known lecturer on topics related to homosexuality

SOURCE: "Why Shouldn't Tommy and Jim Have Sex? A Defense of Homosexuality," from *Same Sex: Debating the Ethics, Science, and Culture of Homosexuality* (Rowman & Littlefield, 1997).

Homosexual rights, gay marriage, gays in the military: these issues evoke strong feelings. Though some societies have been quite tolerant or even positive toward homosexual relations (the ancient Greeks and Romans, for example), there is no doubt that homosexuals have suffered severe persecution. Homosexuals face imprisonment and even capital punishment in many cultures; and social ostracism, abuse, and violent assaults are far from uncommon. The U. S. military policy under which homosexuals are allowed to serve in the military so long as they keep their sexual activities and identities hidden was perhaps well-intentioned, but ultimately it satisfies no one. "You can join us, so long as you constantly pretend to be someone else" is not a very welcoming invitation. If you are heterosexual, imagine that one condition for enrolling in your university is that you must constantly hide your sexual orientation and always pretend to be homosexual. Conservative icon and decorated Air Force pilot Senator Barry Goldwater was a strong advocate for open admission of homosexuals into the armed forces, and he stated his view with characteristic bluntness: "Everyone knows that gays have served honorably in the military since at least the time of Julius Caesar. They'll still be serving long after we're all dead and buried. That should not surprise anyone.... You don't need to be 'straight' to fight and die for your country. You just need to shoot straight." (*Washington Post*, June 10, 1993)

In order to examine the question fairly it is necessary to set aside some of the hot button controversies and concentrate coolly and precisely on the specific issue: Is homosexuality immoral? Many other issues are too easily conflated with that one. First, this is not a question of whether child sexual abuse is immoral. Almost everyone agrees that it is, whether the abuser is heterosexual or homosexual; and after all, most cases of child sexual abuse are committed by heterosexuals, which does not suggest that heterosexuality itself is morally wrong. Second, this is not a question of sexual promiscuity. Both heterosexual and homosexual relationships can be monogamous, and both homosexuals and heterosexuals are sometimes promiscuous (as anyone who lives in a college community is well aware). Third, this is not a question of whether some religion approves or condemns homosexuality. That some religious traditions have condemned homosexuality is clear. Although there is considerable dispute about whether Judeo-Christian doctrines should be interpreted as condemning homosexuality. And fourth, this is not a debate about the legal status of homosexual acts: One might believe that homosexual acts are wrong, but that in a free society people's private lives should not be under the control of law—just as one might believe that heterosexual oral sex is wrong, or that drinking alcohol is wrong, but still believe that they should not be legally prohibited. Or one might believe that the moral status of homosexuality is irrelevant to the question of legality, since the government should not legislate morality: Again, Barry Goldwater:

> The conservative movement, to which I subscribe, has as one of its basic tenets the belief that government should stay out of people's private lives. Government governs best when it governs least—and stays out of the impossible task of legislating morality. But legislating someone's version of morality is exactly what we do by perpetuating discrimination against gays. (*Washington Post*, June 10, 1993)

The question at issue here is whether homosexual acts between consenting adults are morally wrong. In that controversy, one of the contested issues is the question of what is "natural." That question leads to two more: First, how do we define "natural"? And second, what reasons are there for considering what is "natural" as good and anything "unnatural" bad?

POINTS TO PONDER

➤ Why does Finnis regard heterosexual relations within marriage as a special good?
➤ In what way does Finnis regard his argument as based on natural facts?
➤ Of the various accounts of "unnatural" that Corvino gives, which is closest to the way that Finnis thinks of homosexuality as unnatural?
➤ Corvino states that for homosexuals, the choice is not between homosexual relations and heterosexual relations but between homosexual relations and celibacy; and he suggests that no matter what one thinks about whether heterosexual relations are more fulfilling than homosexual relations, clearly homosexual relations are more fulfilling than celibacy, and thus homosexual relations should not be condemned. Could Finnis agree with that conclusion?

Homosexual Sex:
Immoral

JOHN FINNIS

I.

During the past thirty years there has emerged in Europe a standard form of legal regulation of sexual conduct. This standard form or scheme, which I shall call the "standard modern [European] position," is accepted by the European Court of Human Rights and the European Commission of Human Rights (the two supra-national judicial and quasi-judicial institutions of the European Convention for the Protection of Human Rights and Fundamental Freedoms (1950), to which almost all European states are party, whether or not they are also party to the European [Economic] Community now known as the European Union). The standard modern European position has two limbs. On the one hand, the state is not authorized to, and does not, make it a punishable offence for adult consenting persons to engage, in private, in immoral sexual acts (for example, homosexual acts). On the other hand, states do have the authority to discourage, say, homosexual conduct and "orientation" (i.e. overtly manifested active willingness to engage in homosexual conduct). And typically, though not universally, they do so. That is to say, they maintain various criminal and administrative laws and policies which have as part of their purpose the discouraging of such conduct. Many of these laws, regulations, and policies discriminate (i.e. distinguish) between heterosexual and homosexual conduct adversely to the latter....

II.

The standard modern [European] position is consistent with the view that (apart perhaps from special cases and contexts) it is unjust for A to impose any kind of disadvantage on B simply because A believes (perhaps correctly) that B has sexual inclinations (which he may or may not act on) towards persons of the same sex. The position does not give B the widest conceivable legal protection against such unjust discrimination (just as it generally does not give wide protection against needless acts of adverse private discrimination in housing or employment to people with unpopular or eccentric political views). But the position does not itself encourage, sponsor or impose any such unjust burden. (And it is accompanied by many legal protections for homosexual persons with respect to assaults, threats, unreasonable discrimination by public bodies and officials, etc.)

The concern of the standard modern position itself is not with inclinations but entirely with certain *decisions* to *express* or *manifest* deliberate promotion of, or readiness to engage in, homosexual *activity* or *conduct*, including promotion of forms of life (e.g. purportedly marital cohabitation) which both encourage such activity and present it as a valid or acceptable alternative to the committed heterosexual union which the state recognizes as marriage. Subject only to the written or unwritten constitutional requirement of freedom of discussion of ideas, the state laws and state policies which I have outlined are intended to discourage decisions which are thus deliberately oriented towards homosexual conduct and are manifested in public ways.

The standard modern position differs from the position which it replaced, which made adult consensual sodomy and like acts crimes per se. States which adhere to the standard modern position make it clear by laws and policies such as I have referred to that the state has by no means renounced its legitimate concern with public morality and the education of children and young people towards truly worthwhile and against alluring but bad forms of conduct and life. Nor have such states renounced the judgment that a life involving homosexual conduct is bad even for anyone unfortunate enough to have innate or quasi-innate homosexual inclinations.

The difference between the standard modern position and the position it has replaced can be expressed as follows. The standard modern position considers that the state's proper responsibility for upholding true worth (morality) is a responsibility *subsidiary* (auxiliary) to the *primary* responsibility of parents and non-political voluntary associations. The subsidiary character of government is widely emphasized and increasingly accepted, at least in principle, in contemporary European politics. (It was, for example, a cornerstone of the Treaty of Maastricht of 1992.) This conception of the proper role of government has been taken to exclude the state from assuming a directly parental disciplinary role in relation to consenting *adults*. That role was one which political theory and practice formerly ascribed to the state on the assumption that the role followed by logical necessity from the truth that the state should encourage true worth and discourage immorality. That assumption is now judged to be mistaken.

So the modern theory and practice draws a distinction not drawn in the former legal arrangements—a distinction between (a) supervising the truly private conduct of adults and (b) supervising the *public realm or environment*. The importance of the latter includes the following considerations: (1) this is the environment or public realm in which young people (of whatever sexual inclination) are educated; (2) it is the context in which and by which everyone with responsibility for the well being of young people is helped or hindered in assisting them to avoid bad forms of life; (3) it is the milieu in which and by which all citizens are encouraged and helped, or discouraged and undermined, in their own resistance to being lured by temptation into falling away from their own aspirations to be people of integrated good character, and to be autonomous, self-controlled persons rather than slaves to impulse and sensual gratification.

While the type (a) supervision of truly private adult consensual conduct is now considered to be outside the state's normally proper role (with exceptions such as sadomasochistic bodily damage, and assistance in suicide), type (b) supervision of the moral-cultural-educational environment is maintained as a very important part of the state's justification for claiming legitimately the loyalty of its decent citizens....

IV.

The standard modern position involves a number of explicit or implicit judgments about the proper role of law and the compelling interests of political communities, and about the evil of homosexual conduct. Can these be defended by reflective, critical, publicly intelligible and rational arguments? I believe they can. Since even the advocates of "gay rights" do not seriously assert that the state can never have any compelling interests in public morality or the moral formation of its young people or the moral environment in which parents, other educators, and young people themselves must undertake this formation, I shall in this lecture focus rather on the underlying issue which receives far too little public discussion: What is wrong with homosexual conduct? Is the judgment that it is morally wrong inevitably a manifestation either of mere hostility to a hated minority, or of purely religious, theological, and sectarian belief which can ground no constitutionally valid determination disadvantaging those who do not conform to it?

I have been using and shall continue to use the terms "homosexual activity," "homosexual acts" and "homosexual conduct" synonymously, to refer to bodily acts, on the body of a person of the same sex, which are engaged in with a view to securing orgasmic sexual satisfaction for one or more of the parties....

At the heart of the Platonic-Aristotelian and later ancient philosophical rejections of all homosexual conduct, and thus of the modern "gay" ideology, are three fundamental theses: (1) The commitment of a man and woman to each other in the sexual union of marriage is intrinsically good and reasonable, and is incompatible with sexual relations outside marriage. (2) Homosexual acts are radically and peculiarly non-marital, and for that reason intrinsically unreasonable and unnatural. (3) Furthermore, according to Plato, if not Aristotle, homosexual acts have a special similarity to solitary masturbation, and both types of radically non-marital act are manifestly unworthy of the human being and immoral.

V.

I want now to offer an interpretation of these three theses which articulates them more clearly.... My account also articulates thoughts which have historically been implicit in the judgments of many non-philosophical people, and which have been held to justify the laws adopted in many nations and states both before and after the period when Christian beliefs as such were politically and socially dominant. And it is an application of the theory of morality and natural law developed over the past thirty years by Germain Grisez and others....

Plato's mature concern, in the *Laws*, for familiarity, affection and love between spouses in a chastely exclusive marriage, Aristotle's representation of marriage as an intrinsically desirable friendship between quasi-equals, and as a state of life even more natural to human beings than political life, and Musonius Rufus's conception of the inseparable double goods of marriage, all find expression in Plutarch's celebration of marriage—as a union not of mere instinct but of reasonable love, and not merely for procreation but for mutual help, goodwill and cooperation for their own sake. Plutarch's severe critiques of homosexual conduct (and of the disparagement of women implicit in homosexual ideology), develop Plato's critique of homosexual and all other extra-marital sexual conduct. Like Musonius Rufus, Plutarch does so by bringing much closer to explicit articulation the following thought. Genital intercourse between spouses enables them to actualize and experience (and in that sense express) their marriage itself, as a single reality with two blessings (children and mutual affection). Non-marital intercourse, especially but not only homosexual, has no such point and therefore is unacceptable.

The core of this argument can be clarified by comparing it with Saint Augustine's treatment of marriage in his *De Bono Coniugali*. The good of marital communion is here an instrumental good, in the service of the procreation and education of children so that the intrinsic, non-instrumental good of friendship will be promoted and realized by the propagation of the human race, and the intrinsic good of inner integration be promoted and realized by the "remedying" of the disordered desires of concupiscence. Now, when considering sterile marriages, Augustine had identified a further good of marriage, the natural *societas* (companionship) of the two sexes. Had he truly integrated this into his synthesis, he would have recognized that in sterile and fertile marriages alike, the communion, companionship, *societas* and *amicitia* of the spouses—their being married—*is* the very good of marriage, and is an intrinsic, basic human good, not merely instrumental to any other good. And this communion of married life, this integral amalgamation of the lives of the two persons (as Plutarch put it before John Paul II), has as its intrinsic elements, as essential *parts* of one and the same good, the goods and ends to which the theological tradition, following Augustine, for a long time subordinated that communion. It took a long and gradual process of development of doctrine, through the Catechism of the Council of Trent, the teachings of Pius XI and Pius XII, and eventually those of Vatican II—a process brilliantly illuminated by Germain Grisez—to bring the tradition to the position that procreation and children are neither the *end* (whether primary or secondary) to which marriage is instrumental (as Augustine taught), nor instrumental to the good of the spouses (as much secular and "liberal Christian" thought supposes), but rather: Parenthood and children and family are the intrinsic fulfillment of a communion which, because it is not merely instrumental, can exist and fulfill the spouses even if procreation happens to be impossible for them.

Now if, as the recent encyclical on the foundations of morality, *Veritatis Splendor*,

teaches, "the communion of persons in marriage" which is violated by every act of adultery is itself a "fundamental human good," there fall into place not only the elements of the classic philosophical judgments on non-marital sexual conduct but also the similar judgments reached about such conduct by decent people who cannot articulate explanatory premises for those judgments, which they reach rather by an insight into what is and is not *consistent with* realities whose goodness they experience and understand at least sufficiently to will and choose. In particular, there fall into place the elements of an answer to the question: Why cannot non-marital friendship be promoted and expressed by sexual acts? Why is the attempt to express affection by orgasmic non-marital sex the pursuit of an illusion? Why did Plato and Socrates, Xenophon, Aristotle, Musonius Rufus, and Plutarch, right at the heart of their reflections on the homoerotic culture around them, make the very deliberate and careful judgment that homosexual *conduct* (and indeed all extramarital sexual gratification) is radically incapable of participating in, actualizing, the common good of friendship?

Implicit in the philosophical and commonsense rejection of extra-marital sex is the answer: The union of the reproductive organs of husband and wife really unites them biologically (and their biological reality is part of, not merely an instrument of, their *personal* reality); reproduction is one function and so, in respect of that function, the spouses are indeed one reality, and their sexual union therefore can *actualize* and allow them to *experience* their *real common good—their marriage* with the two goods, parenthood and friendship, which (leaving aside the order of grace) are the parts of its wholeness as an intelligible common good even if, independently of what the spouses will, their capacity for biological parenthood will not be fulfilled by that act of genital union. But the common good of friends who are not and cannot be married (for example, man and man, man and boy, woman and woman) has nothing to do with their having children by each other, and their reproductive organs cannot make them a biological (and therefore personal) unit. So their sexual acts together cannot do what they may hope and imagine. Because their activation of one or even each of their reproductive organs cannot be an actualizing and experiencing of the *marital* good—as marital intercourse (intercourse between spouses in a marital way) can, even between spouses who *happen* to be sterile—it can do no more than provide each partner with an individual gratification. For want of a *common good* that could be actualized and experienced *by and in this bodily union*, that conduct involves the partners in treating their bodies as instruments to be used in the service of their consciously experiencing selves; their choice to engage in such conduct thus dis-integrates each of them precisely as acting persons.

Reality is known in judgment, not in emotion, and *in reality*, whatever the generous hopes and dreams and thoughts of *giving* with which some same-sex partners may surround their sexual acts, those acts cannot express or do more than is expressed or done if two strangers engage in such activity to give each other pleasure, or a prostitute pleasures a client to give him pleasure in return for money, or (say) a man masturbates to give himself pleasure and a fantasy of more human relationships after a gruelling day on the assembly line. This is, I believe, the substance of Plato's judgment—at that moment in the *Gorgias* which is also decisive for the moral and political philosophical critique of hedonism—that there is no important

distinction in essential moral worthlessness between solitary masturbation, being sodomized as a prostitute, and being sodomized for the pleasure of it. Sexual acts cannot *in reality* be self-giving unless they are acts by which a man and a woman actualize and experience sexually the real giving of themselves to each other—in biological, affective and volitional union in mutual commitment, both open-ended and exclusive—which like Plato and Aristotle and most peoples we call marriage.

In short, sexual acts are not unitive in their significance unless they are marital (actualizing the all-level unity of marriage) and (since the common good of marriage has two aspects) they are not marital unless they have not only the generosity of acts of friendship but also the procreative significance, not necessarily of being intended to generate or capable in the circumstances of generating but at least of being, as human conduct, acts of the reproductive kind—actualizations, so far as the spouses then and there can, of the reproductive function in which they are biologically and thus personally one.

The ancient philosophers do not much discuss the case of sterile marriages, or the fact (well known to them) that for long periods of time (e.g. throughout pregnancy) the sexual acts of a married couple are naturally incapable of resulting in reproduction. They appear to take for granted what the subsequent Christian tradition certainly did, that such sterility does not render the conjugal sexual acts of the spouses non-marital. (Plutarch indicates that intercourse with a sterile spouse is a desirable mark of marital esteem and affection.) For: A husband and wife who unite their reproductive organs in an act of sexual intercourse which, so far as they then can make it, is of a kind suitable for generation, do function as a biological (and thus personal) unit and thus can be actualizing and experiencing the two-in-one-flesh common good and reality of marriage, even when some biological condition happens to prevent that unity resulting in generation of a child. Their conduct thus differs radically from the acts of a husband and wife whose intercourse is masturbatory, for example sodomitic or by fellatio or coitus interruptus. In law such acts do not consummate a marriage, because in reality (whatever the couple's illusions of intimacy and self-giving in such acts) they do not actualize the one-flesh, two-part marital good.

Does this account seek to "make moral judgments based on natural facts"? Yes and no. No, in the sense that it does not seek to infer normative conclusions or theses from non-normative (natural-fact) premises. Nor does it appeal to any norm of the form "Respect natural facts or natural functions." But yes, it does apply the relevant practical reasons (especially that marriage and inner integrity are basic human goods) and moral principles (especially that one may never *intend* to destroy, damage, impede, or violate any basic human good, or prefer an illusory instantiation of a basic human good to a real instantiation of that or some other human good) to facts about the human personal organism.

VI.

Societies such as classical Athens and contemporary England (and virtually every other) draw a distinction between behavior found merely (perhaps extremely) offensive (such as eating excrement), and behavior to be repudiated as destructive of human character and relationships. Copulation of humans with animals is repudiated because it treats human sexual activity and satisfaction as something appropriately sought in a manner as divorced from the actualizing of an intelligible common good as is the instinctive coupling of beasts—and so treats human bodily life, in one of its most intense activities, as appropriately lived as merely animal. The deliberate genital coupling of persons of the same sex is repudiated for a very similar reason. It is not simply that it is sterile and disposes the participants to an abdication of responsibility for the future of humankind. Nor is it simply that it cannot *really* actualize the mutual devotion which some homosexual persons hope to manifest and experience by it, and that it harms the personalities of its participants by its dis-integrative manipulation of different parts of their one personal reality. It is also that it treats human sexual capacities in a way which is deeply hostile to the self-understanding of those members of the community who are willing to commit themselves to real marriage in the understanding that its sexual joys are not mere instruments or accompaniments to, or mere compensations for, the accomplishment of marriage's responsibilities, but rather enable the spouses to *actualize and experience* their intelligent commitment to share in those responsibilities, in that genuine self-giving.

Now, as I have said before, "homosexual orientation," in one of the two main senses of that highly equivocal term, is precisely the deliberate willingness to promote and engage in homosexual acts—the state of mind, will, and character whose self-interpretation came to be expressed in the deplorable but helpfully revealing name "gay." So this willingness, and the whole "gay" ideology, treats human sexual capacities in a way which is deeply hostile to the self-understanding of those members of the community who are willing to commit themselves to real marriage.

Homosexual orientation in this sense is, in fact, a standing denial of the intrinsic aptness of sexual intercourse to actualize and in that sense give expression to the exclusiveness and open-ended commitment of marriage as something good in itself. All who accept that homosexual acts can be a humanly appropriate use of sexual capacities must, if consistent, regard sexual capacities, organs and acts as instruments for gratifying the individual "selves" who have them. Such an acceptance is commonly (and in my opinion rightly) judged to be an active threat to the stability of existing and future marriages; it makes nonsense, for example, of the view that adultery is per se (and not merely because

it may involve deception), and in an important way, inconsistent with conjugal love. A political community which judges that the stability and protective and educative generosity of family life is of fundamental importance to that community's present and future can rightly judge that it has a compelling interest in denying that homosexual conduct—a "gay lifestyle"—is a valid, humanly acceptable choice and form of life, and in doing whatever it *properly* can, as a community with uniquely wide but still subsidiary functions, to discourage such conduct....

Homosexual Sex:
Moral

John Corvino

Tommy and Jim are a homosexual couple I know. Tommy is an accountant; Jim is a botany professor. They are in their forties and have been together fourteen years, the last five of which they've lived in a Victorian house that they've lovingly restored. Although their relationship has had its challenges, each has made sacrifices for the sake of the other's happiness and the relationship's long-term success.

I assume that Tommy and Jim have sex with each other (although I've never bothered to ask). Furthermore, I contend that they probably *should* have sex with each other. For one thing, sex is pleasurable. But it is also much more than that: a sexual relationship can unite two people in a way that virtually nothing else can. It can be an avenue of growth, of communication, and of lasting interpersonal fulfillment. These are reasons why most heterosexual couples have sex even if they don't want children, don't want children yet, or don't want additional children. And if these reasons are good enough for most heterosexual couples, then they should be good enough for Tommy and Jim.

Of course, having a reason to do something does not preclude there being an even better reason for not doing it. Tommy might have a good reason for drinking orange juice (it's tasty and nutritious) but an even better reason for not doing so (he's allergic). The point is that one would need a pretty good reason for denying a sexual relationship to Tommy and Jim, given the intense benefits widely associated with such relationships. The question I shall consider in this paper is

thus quite simple: Why shouldn't Tommy and Jim have sex?

HOMOSEXUAL SEX IS "UNNATURAL"

Many contend that homosexual sex is "unnatural." But what does that mean? Many things that people value—clothing, houses, medicine, and government, for example—are unnatural in some sense. On the other hand, many things that people detest—disease, suffering, and death, for example—are "natural" in the sense that they occur "in nature." If the unnaturalness charge is to be more than empty rhetorical flourish, those who levy it must specify what they mean. Borrowing from Burton Leiser, I will examine several possible meanings of "unnatural."

What Is Unusual or Abnormal Is Unnatural

One meaning of "unnatural" refers to that which deviates from the norm, that is, from what most people do. Obviously, most people engage in heterosexual relationships. But does it follow that it is wrong to engage in homosexual relationships? Relatively few people read Sanskrit, pilot ships, play the mandolin, breed goats, or write with both hands, yet none of these activities is immoral simply because it is unusual. As the Ramsey Colloquium, a group of Jewish and Christian scholars who oppose homosexuality, writes, "The statistical frequency of an act does not determine its moral status." So while homosexuality might be unnatural in the sense of being unusual, that fact is morally irrelevant.

What Is Not Practiced by Other Animals Is Unnatural

Some people argue, "Even animals know better than to behave homosexually; homosexuality must be wrong." This argument is doubly flawed. First, it rests on a false premise. Numerous studies—including Anne Perkins's study of "gay" sheep and George and Molly Hunt's study of "lesbian" seagulls—have shown that some animals do form homosexual pair-bonds. Second, even if animals did not behave homosexually, that fact would not prove that homosexuality is immoral. After all, animals don't cook their food, brush their teeth, participate in religious worship, or attend college; human beings do all of these without moral censure. Indeed, the idea that animals could provide us with our standards—especially our sexual standards—is simply amusing.

What Does Not Proceed from Innate Desires Is Unnatural

Recent studies suggesting a biological basis for homosexuality have resulted in two popular positions. One side proposes that homosexual people are "born that way" and that it is therefore natural (and thus good) for them to form homosexual relationships. The other side maintains that homosexuality is a lifestyle choice, which is therefore unnatural (and thus wrong). Both sides assume a connection between the origin of homosexual orientation, on the one hand, and the moral value of homosexual activity, on the other. And insofar as they share that assumption, both sides are wrong.

Consider first the pro-homosexual side: "They are born that way; therefore it's natural and good." This inference assumes that all innate desires are good ones (i.e., that they should be acted upon). But that assumption is clearly false. Research suggests that some people are born with a predisposition toward violence, but such people have no more right to strangle their neighbors than anyone else. So while people like Tommy and Jim may he born with homosexual tendencies, it doesn't follow that they ought to act on them. Nor does it follow that they ought *not* to act on them, even if the tendencies are not innate I probably do not have any innate tendency to write with my left hand (since I, like everyone else in my family, have always been right-handed), but it doesn't follow that it would be immoral for me to do so. So simply asserting that homosexuality is a lifestyle choice will not show that it is an immoral lifestyle choice.

Do people "choose" to be homosexual? People certainly don't seem to choose their sexual *feelings*, at least not in any direct or obvious way. (Do you? Think about it.) Rather, they find certain people attractive and certain activities arousing, whether they "decide" to or not. Indeed, most people at some point in their lives wish that they could control their feelings more—for example, in situations of unrequited love—and find it frustrating that they cannot. What they *can* control to a considerable degree is how and when they act upon those feelings. In that sense, both homosexuality and heterosexuality involve lifestyle choices. But in either case, determining the origin of the feelings will not determine whether it is moral to act on them.

What Violates an Organ's Principal Purpose Is Unnatural

Perhaps when people claim that homosexual sex is unnatural they mean that it cannot result in procreation. The idea behind the argument is that human organs have various natural purposes: eyes are for seeing, ears are for hearing, genitals are for procreating. According to this argument, it is immoral to use an organ in a way that violates its particular purpose.

Many of our organs, however, have multiple purposes. Tommy can use his mouth for talking, eating, breathing, licking stamps, chewing guns, kissing women, or kissing Jim; and it seems rather arbitrary to claim that all but the last use are "natural." (And if we say that some of the other uses are "unnatural, but not immoral," we have failed to specify a morally relevant sense of the term "natural.")

Just because people can and do use their sexual organs to procreate, it does not follow that they should not use them for other purposes. Sexual organs seem very well suited for expressing love, for giving and receiving pleasure, and for celebrating, replenishing, and enhancing a relationship—even when procreation is not a factor. Unless opponents of homosexuality are prepared to condemn heterosexual couples who use contraception or individuals who masturbate, they must abandon this version of the unnaturalness argument. Indeed, even the Roman Catholic Church, which forbids contraception and masturbation, approves of sex for sterile couples and of sex during pregnancy, neither of which can lead to procreation. The Church concedes here that intimacy and pleasure are morally legitimate purposes for sex, even in cases where procreation is impossible. But since homosexual sex can achieve these purposes as well, it is inconsistent for the Church to condemn it on the grounds that it is not procreative.

One might object that sterile heterosexual couples do not *intentionally* turn away from procreation, whereas homosexual couples do. But this distinction doesn't hold. It is no more possible for Tommy to procreate with a woman whose uterus has been removed than it is for him to procreate with Jim. By having sex with either one, he is intentionally engaging in a nonprocreative sexual act.

Yet one might press the objection further and insist that Tommy and the woman *could* produce children if the woman were fertile: whereas homosexual relationships are essentially infertile, heterosexual relationships are only incidentally so. But what does that prove? Granted, it might require less of a miracle for a woman without a uterus to become pregnant than for Jim to become pregnant, but it would require a miracle nonetheless. Thus it seems that the real difference here is not that one couple is fertile and the other not, nor that one couple "could" be fertile (with the help of a miracle) and the other not, but rather that one couple is male-female and the other male-male. In other words, sex between Tommy and Jim is wrong because it's male-male—i.e., because it's homosexual. But that, of course, is no argument at all.

What Is Disgusting or Offensive Is Unnatural

It often seems that when people call homosexuality "unnatural" they really just mean that it's disgusting. But plenty of morally neutral activities—handling snakes, eating snails, performing autopsies, cleaning toilets, and so on—disgust people. Indeed, for centuries, most people found interracial relationships disgusting, yet that feeling—which has by no means disappeared—hardly proves that such relationships are wrong. In sum, the charge that homosexuality is unnatural, at least in its most common forms, is longer on rhetorical flourish than on philosophical cogency. At best it expresses an aesthetic judgment, not a moral judgment.

HOMOSEXUAL SEX IS HARMFUL

One might instead argue that homosexuality is harmful. The Ramsey Colloquium, for instance, argues that homosexuality leads to the breakdown of the family and, ultimately, of human society, and it points to the "alarming rates of sexual promiscuity, depression, and suicide and the ominous presence of AIDS within the homosexual subculture." Thomas Schmidt marshals copious statistics to show that homosexual activity undermines physical and psychological health. Such charges, if correct, would seem to provide strong evidence against homosexuality. But are the charges correct? And do they prove what they purport to prove?

One obvious (and obviously problematic) way to answer the first question is to ask people like Tommy and Jim. It would appear that no one is in a better position to judge the homosexual lifestyle than those who know it firsthand. Yet it is unlikely that critics would trust their testimony. Indeed, the more homosexual people try to explain their lives, the more critics accuse them of deceitfully promoting an agenda. (It's like trying to prove that you're not crazy. The more you object, the more people think, "That's exactly what a crazy person would say.")

One might instead turn to statistics. An obvious problem with this tack is that both sides of the debate bring forth extensive statistics and "expert" testimony, leaving the average observer confused. There is a more subtle problem as well. Because of widespread antigay sentiment, many homosexual people won't acknowledge their romantic feelings to themselves, much less to researchers. I have known a number of gay men who did not "come out" until their forties and fifties, and no amount of professional competence on the part of interviewers would have been likely to open their closets sooner. Such problems compound the usual difficulties of finding representative population samples for statistical study.

Yet even if the statistical claims of gay rights opponents were true, they would not prove what they purport to prove, for several reasons. First, as any good statistician realizes, correlation does not equal cause. Even if homosexual people were more likely to commit suicide, be promiscuous, or contract AIDS than the general population, it would not follow that their homosexuality causes them to do these things. An alternative—and very plausible—explanation is that these phenomena, like the disproportionately high crime rates among African Americans, are at least partly a function of society's treatment of the group in question. Suppose you were told from a very early age that the romantic feelings that you experienced were sick, unnatural, and disgusting. Suppose further that expressing these feelings put you at risk of social ostracism or, worse yet, physical violence. Is it not plausible that you would, for instance, be more inclined to depression than you would be without such obstacles? And that such depression could, in its extreme forms, lead to suicide or other self-destructive behaviors? (It is indeed remarkable that couples like Tommy and Jim continue to flourish in the face of such obstacles.)

A similar explanation can be given for the alleged promiscuity of homosexuals. The denial of legal marriage, the pressure to remain in the closet, and the overt hostility toward homosexual relationships are all more conducive to transient, clandestine encounters than they are to long-term unions. As a result, that which is challenging enough for heterosexual couples—settling down and building a life together—becomes far more challenging for homosexual couples.

Indeed, there is an interesting tension in the critics' position here. Opponents of homosexuality commonly claim that "marriage and the family... are fragile institutions in need of careful and continuing support." And they point to the increasing prevalence of divorce and pre-marital sex among heterosexuals as evidence that such support is declining. Yet they refuse to concede that the complete absence of similar support for homosexual relationships might explain many of the alleged problems of homosexuals. The critics can't have it both ways: if heterosexual marriages are in trouble despite the various social, economic, and legal incentives for keeping them together, society should be little surprised that homosexual relationships—which not only lack such supports, but face overt hostility—are difficult to maintain....

Of course, there's more to a flourishing life than avoiding harm. One might argue that even if Tommy and Jim are not harming each other by their relationship, they are still failing to achieve the higher level of fulfillment possible in a heterosexual relationship, which is rooted in the complementarity of male and female. But this argument just ignores the facts: Tommy and Jim are homosexual *precisely because* they find relationships with men (and, in particular, with each other) more fulfilling than relationships with women. Even evangelicals (who have long advocated "faith healing" for homosexuals) are beginning to acknowledge that the choice for most homosexual people is not between homosexual relationships and heterosexual relationships, but rather between homosexual relationships and celibacy. What the critics need to show, therefore. is that no matter how loving, committed, mutual, generous, and fulfilling the relationship may be, Tommy and Jim would flourish more if they were celibate. Given the evidence of their lives (and of others like them), this is a formidable task indeed....

But doesn't homosexuality threaten society? A Roman Catholic priest once put the argument to me as follows: "Of course homosexuality is bad for society. If everyone were homosexual, there would be no society." Perhaps it is true that if everyone were homosexual, there would be no society. But if everyone were a celibate priest, society would collapse just as surely, and my friend the priest didn't seem to think that he was doing anything wrong simply by failing to procreate. Jeremy Bentham made the point somewhat more acerbically roughly 200 years ago: "If then merely out of regard to population it were right that [homosexuals] should be burnt alive, monks ought to be roasted alive by a slow fire."

From the fact that the continuation of society requires procreation, it does not follow that *everyone* must procreate. Moreover, even if such an obligation existed, it would not preclude homosexuality. At best, it would preclude *exclusive* homosexuality: homosexual people who occasionally have heterosexual sex can procreate just fine. And given artificial insemination, even those who are exclusively homosexual can procreate. In short, the priest's claim—if everyone were homosexual, there would be no society—is false; and even if it were true, it would not establish that homosexuality is immoral.

The Ramsey Colloquium commits a similar fallacy. Noting (correctly) that heterosexual marriage promotes the continuation of human life, it then infers that homosexuality is immoral because it fails to accomplish the same. But from the fact that procreation is good, it does not follow that childlessness is bad—a point that the members of the colloquium, several of whom are Roman Catholic priests, should readily concede.

I have argued that Tommy and Jim's sexual relationship harms neither them nor society. On the contrary, it benefits both. It benefits them because it makes them happier—not merely in a short-term, hedonistic sense, but in a long-term, "big picture" sort of way. And, in turn, it benefits society, since it makes Tommy and Jim more stable, more productive, and more generous than they would otherwise be. In short, their relationship—including its sexual component—provides the same kinds of benefits that infertile heterosexual relationships provide (and perhaps other benefits as well). Nor should we fear that accepting their relationship and others like it will cause people to flee in droves from the institution of heterosexual marriage. After all, as Thomas Williams points out, the usual response to a gay person is not "How come *he* gets to be gay and I don't?"

HOMOSEXUALITY VIOLATES BIBLICAL TEACHING

At this point in the discussion, many people turn to religion. "If the secular arguments fail to prove that homosexuality is wrong," they say, "so much the worse for secular ethics. This failure only proves that we need God for morality." Since people often justify their moral beliefs by appeal to religion, I will briefly consider the biblical position.

At first glance, the Bible's condemnation of homosexual activity seems unequivocal. Consider, for example, the following two passages, one from the "Old" Testament and one from the "New":

You shall not lie with a male as with a woman; it is an abomination. (Lev. 18:22)

For this reason God gave them up to degrading passions. Their women exchanged natural intercourse for unnatural, and in the same way also the men, giving up natural intercourse with women, were consumed with passion for one another. Men committed shameless acts with men

and received in their own persons the due penalty for their error. (Rom. 1:26-27)

Note, however, that these passages are surrounded by other passages that relatively few people consider binding. For example, Leviticus also declares,

The pig... is unclean for you. Of their flesh you shall not eat, and their carcasses you shall not touch; they are unclean for you. (11:7–8)

Taken literally, this passage not only prohibits eating pork, but also playing football, since footballs are made of pigskin. (Can you believe that the University of Notre Dame so flagrantly violates Levitical teaching?)

Similarly, St. Paul, author of the Romans passage, also writes, "Slaves, obey your earthly masters with fear and trembling, in singleness of heart, as you obey Christ" (Eph. 6:5)—morally problematic advice if there ever were any. Should we interpret this passage (as Southern plantation owners once did) as implying that it is immoral for slaves to escape? After all, God himself says in Leviticus,

[Y]ou may acquire male and female slaves... from among the aliens residing with you, and from their families that are with you, who have been born in your land; and they may be your property. You may keep them as a possession for your children after you, for them to inherit as property. (25:44–46)

How can people maintain the inerrancy of the Bible in light of such passages? The answer, I think, is that they learn to interpret the passages *in their historical context.*

Consider the Bible's position on usury, the lending of money for interest (for *any* interest, not just excessive interest). The

Bible condemns this practice in no uncertain terms. In Exodus God says that "if you lend money to my people, to the poor among you, you shall not exact interest from them" (22:25). Psalm 15 says that those who lend at interest may not abide in the Lord's tent or dwell on his holy hill (1–5). Ezekiel calls usury "abominable"; compares it to adultery, robbery, idolatry, and bribery; and states that anyone who "takes advanced or accrued interest… shall surely die; his blood shall be upon himself" (18:13).

Should believers therefore close their savings accounts? Not necessarily. According to orthodox Christian teaching, the biblical prohibition against usury no longer applies. The reason is that economic conditions have changed substantially since biblical times, such that usury no longer has the same negative consequences it had when the prohibitions were issued. Thus, the practice that was condemned by the Bible differs from contemporary interest banking in morally relevant ways.

Yet are we not in a similar position regarding homosexuality? Virtually all scholars agree that homosexual relations during biblical times were vastly different from relationships like Tommy and Jim's. Often such relationships were integral to pagan practices. In Greek society, they typically involved older men and younger boys. If those are the kinds of features that the biblical authors had in mind when they issued their condemnations, and such features are no longer typical, then the biblical condemnations no longer apply. As with usury, substantial changes in cultural context have altered the meaning and consequences—and thus the moral value—of the practice in question. Put another way, using the Bible's condemnations of homosexuality against contemporary homosexuality is like using its

condemnations of usury against contemporary banking.

Let me be clear about what I am not claiming here. First, I am *not* claiming that the Bible has been wrong before and therefore may be wrong this time. The Bible may indeed be wrong on some matters, but for the purpose of this argument I am assuming its infallibility. Nor am I claiming that the Bible's age renders it entirely inapplicable to today's issues. Rather, I am claiming that when we do apply it, *we must pay attention to morally relevant cultural differences between biblical times and today*. Such attention will help us distinguish between specific time-bound prohibitions (for example, laws against usury or homosexual relations) and the enduring moral values they represent (for example, generosity or respect for persons). And as the above argument shows, my claim is not very controversial. Indeed, to deny it is to commit oneself to some rather strange views on slavery, usury, women's roles, astronomy, evolution, and the like.

Here, one might also make an appeal to religious pluralism. Given the wide variety of religious beliefs (e.g., the Muslim belief that women should cover their faces, the Orthodox Jewish belief against working on Saturday, the Hindu belief that cows are sacred and should not be eaten), each of us inevitably violates the religious beliefs of others. But we normally don't view such violations as occasions for moral censure, since we distinguish between beliefs that depend on particular revelations and beliefs that can be justified independently (e.g., that stealing is wrong). Without an independent justification for condemning homosexuality, the best one can say is, "My religion says so." But in a society that cherishes religious freedom, that reason alone does not normally provide grounds for moral or legal sanctions. That people still fall back on that reason in discussions of homosexuality suggests that they may not have much of a case otherwise.

CONCLUSION

As a last resort, opponents of homosexuality typically change the subject: "But what about incest, polygamy, and bestiality? If we accept Tommy and Jim's sexual relationship, why shouldn't we accept those as well?" Opponents of interracial marriage used a similar slippery-slope argument in the 1960s when the Supreme Court struck down antimiscegenation laws. It was a bad argument then, and it is a bad argument now.

Just because there are no good reasons to oppose interracial or homosexual relationships, it does not follow that there are no good reasons to oppose incestuous, polygamous, or bestial relationships. One might argue, for instance, that incestuous relationships threaten delicate familial bonds, or that polygamous relationships result in unhealthy jealousies (and sexism), or that bestial relationships—do I need to say it?—aren't really "relationships" at all, at least not in the sense we've been discussing. Perhaps even better arguments could be offered (given much more space than I have here). The point is that there is no logical connection between homosexuality, on the one hand, and incest, polygamy, and bestiality, on the other.

Why, then, do critics continue to push this objection? Perhaps it's because accepting homosexuality requires them to give up one of their favorite arguments: "It's wrong because we've always been taught that it's wrong." This argument—call it the argument from tradition—has an obvious appeal: people reasonably favor tried-and-true ideas over unfamiliar ones, and they recognize the foolishness of trying to invent morality from scratch. But the argument from tradition is also a dangerous argument, as any honest look at history will reveal.

I conclude that Tommy and Jim's relationship, far from being a moral abomination, is exactly what it appears to be to those who know them: a morally positive influence on their lives and on others. Accepting this conclusion takes courage, since it entails that our moral traditions are fallible. But when these traditions interfere with people's happiness for no sound reason, they defeat what is arguably the very point of morality: promoting individual and communal well-being. To put the argument simply, Tommy and Jim's relationship makes them better people. And that's not just good for Tommy and Jim: that's good for everyone.

THE CONTINUING DEBATE:
Homosexual Sex

What Is New

In the last decade, the U.S. Supreme Court has ruled on three significant cases involving homosexuality. The first was *Boy Scouts of America et al. v. Dale*. Dale was dismissed from his position as assistant scoutmaster when the Scouts learned he was a gay rights activist and homosexual. Dale sued for reinstatement, and the Court decided against him, on very narrow grounds. The Court ruled that the Boy Scouts promotes certain views, including the view that homosexual conduct is immoral. The Court said, they have the right to promote that view, and retaining Dale would make promoting that view more difficult. A second case is *Romer et al. v. Evans et al.* Colorado passed an amendment to the state constitution which blocked any state or local law to protect homosexuals. The Court ruled that the U.S. Constitution requires equal protection of all citizens, and does not allow treating some citizens as belonging to a different class and enjoying less than equal protection of their rights; and that the Colorado law violated the equal protection requirement, and thus was unconstitutional. The Court said the amendment withheld "Protections taken for granted by most people either because they already have them or do not need them; these are protections against exclusion from an almost limitless number of transactions and endeavors that constitute ordinary civic life in a free society." The third Supreme Court ruling was *Lawrence et al. v. Texas*, which started when Houston police mistakenly entered the apartment of John Lawrence and observed him engaged in a sex act with another man. The police arrested the men and charged them with violating a state law against homosexual acts. The Court ruled that the Texas law is unconstitutional because it violates the Constitution's due process clause, which states that no one can be deprived of life, liberty, or property without due process of law. The Court held that the Texas law touched upon "the most private human conduct, sexual behavior, and in the most private of places, the home. They seek to control a personal relationship that,... is within the liberty of persons to choose without being punished as criminals. The liberty protected by the Constitution allows homosexual persons the right to choose to enter relationships in the confines of their homes and their own private lives and still retain their dignity as free persons."

Where to Find More

John Corvino is the editor of an anthology, *Same Sex: Debating the Ethics, Science, and Culture of Homosexuality* (Lanham, MD: Rowman & Littlefield, 1997). Another anthology is Robert M. Baird & M. Katherine Baird, *Homosexuality: Debating the Issues* (Amherst, NY: Prometheus, 1995). For a sympathetic approach to homosexual rights, see Richard D. Mohr's *Gays/Justice: A Study of Ethics, Society, and Law* (NY: Columbia University Press, 1988). For the opposing view, see Roger Scruton, *Sexual Desire* (London: Weidenfeld and Nicolson, 1985). Michael Ruse offers a critique of the claim that homosexuality is "unnatural," in "The Morality of Homosexuality," in *Philosophy and Sex*, rev. ed., Robert Baker and Frederick Elliston, eds. (Buffalo, NY: Prometheus, 1984). Linda J. Tessier, *Dancing After the Whirlwind: Feminist Reflections on Sex, Denial, and Spiritual Transformation* (Boston: Beacon Press, 1997) combines philosophy, religion, psychology, and poetry in a unique exploration of the lesbian relations.

THE QUESTION OF ABORTION

Immoral or Morally Acceptable?

IMMORAL

Advocate: Don Marquis, Professor of Philosophy, University of Kansas

Source: "Why Abortion is Immoral," *Journal of Philosophy*, vol. 86 (April 1989)

MORALLY ACCEPTABLE

Advocate: Bonnie Steinbock, Professor of Philosophy, University at Albany, SUNY

Source: "Why Most Abortions Are Not Wrong," *Advances in Bioethics*, volume 5, 1999, pp. 245–267

"Pro-life" and "pro-choice" positions are often presented as absolute and monolithic forces, with each side arrayed under a single banner and no shades of grey. In fact some people favor an absolute prohibition on abortion, but others oppose abortion *except* in cases of rape, incest, or to save the life of the mother. Still others would expand the list of exceptions to include cases where the pregnancy poses a risk to the health of the mother or when tests indicate significant health problems for the fetus. Among those who count themselves as pro-choice, there are many who would restrict abortions to the first trimester and some who would deny only "partial-birth" abortions. Some see abortion as a great tragedy, but believe that the woman's right to make her own choices about what happens inside her own body trump such concerns, or that at least that such rights should not be blocked by law.

In this sea of controversy, it is worth noting one point of general agreement: No one is in favor of abortion. That is, no one thinks that abortion is great, and that every woman should plan to have a couple. Many believe that—in at least some circumstances—women should have the right to choose an abortion, and others think women should not have such a right; but everyone agrees that abortion is something best avoided.

Arguments concerning abortion are concentrated around three distinct issues: First, what is the status of the fetus (or as pro-life forces prefer, the "unborn child")? This issue is formulated in many different ways: At what point does the fetus gain consciousness? At what point is the fetus "viable" (at what point could it survive outside the womb)? When—if ever—does the fetus become a person; when is the fetus a living being? And (an issue that traditional Catholic theology found important) when does the fetus gain a soul? Second, what are the rights of the woman who is carrying the fetus, and when—if ever—do they trump the rights of the fetus (if the fetus has rights)? And third, what would be the effects of making abortion illegal? Would we still have abortions, but at greatly increased risk to the life and health of the woman? Would safe abortions be available only to the wealthy and well-connected?

➤ Don Marquis starts from the basic premise that what makes killing wrong is that the individual killed is deprived of the value of his or her future. Based on that premise he concludes that abortion is wrong, but he also draws out some implications that are not usually associated with the pro-life view. What views does Marquis hold that *most* pro-life theorists would not share?

➤ Marquis claims that his argument against abortion is *analogous* (structurally similar) to a strong argument against inflicting suffering on animals; and that since the latter argument is sound, that is good reason for thinking the former argument, against abortion, is also sound. Is the comparison a good one?

➤ Marquis claims that his argument shows that "morally permissible abortions will be rare indeed unless, perhaps, they occur so early in pregnancy that a fetus is not yet definitely an individual." That is certainly an exception that most advocates of the pro-life position would *not* make. Is it an exception required by Marquis' position? Does it provide any possibility of finding common ground between Marquis and Steinbock?

➤ Bonnie Steinbock bases her view of which individuals have moral status (are due moral consideration) on whether the individual is *sentient*; Marquis bases his arguments on whether an individual has a future that will have value for that individual. Arguing from very different starting points, they wind up with very different conclusions. Is there any objective way of deciding which starting point is *better*, or which is *correct*?

➤ We all believe that it is wrong to kill humans who are temporarily unconscious. Marquis believes that his account gives the best explanation of this belief, while Steinbock maintains that the account given by her explanation is better. This is an interesting test case. Which account do you find more plausible?

The Question of Abortion:
Immoral

Don Marquis

The view that abortion is, with rare exceptions, seriously immoral has received little support in the recent philosophical literature. No doubt most philosophers affiliated with secular institutions of higher education believe that the anti-abortion position is either a symptom of irrational religious dogma or a conclusion generated by seriously confused philosophical argument. The purpose of this essay is to undermine this general belief. This essay sets out an argument that purports to show, as well as any argument in ethics can show, that abortion is, except possibly in rare cases, seriously immoral, that it is in the same moral category as killing an innocent adult human being.

The argument is based on a major assumption. Many of the most insightful and careful writers on the ethics of abortion... believe that whether or not abortion is morally permissible stands or falls on whether or not a fetus is the sort of being whose life it is seriously wrong to end. The argument of this essay will assume, but not argue, that they are correct.

Also, this essay will neglect issues of great importance to a complete ethics of abortion. Some anti-abortionists will allow that certain abortions, such as abortion before implantation or abortion when the life of a woman is threatened by a pregnancy or abortion after rape, may be morally permissible. This essay will not explore the casuistry of these hard cases. The purpose of this essay is to develop a general argument for the claim that the overwhelming majority of deliberate abortions are seriously immoral....

If the generalization a partisan in the abortion dispute adopts were derived from the reason why ending the life of a human being is wrong, then there could not be exceptions to that generalization unless some special case obtains in which there are even more powerful countervailing reasons. Such generalizations would not be merely accidental generalizations; they would point to, or be based upon, the essence of the wrongness of killing, what it is that makes killing wrong. All this suggests that a necessary condition of resolving the abortion controversy is a more theoretical account of the wrongness of killing. After all, if we merely believe, but do not understand, why killing adult human beings such as ourselves is wrong, how could we conceivably show that abortion is either immoral or permissible?

In order to develop such an account, we can start from the following unproblematic assumption concerning our own case: it is wrong to kill *us*. Why is it wrong? Some answers can be easily eliminated. It might be said that what makes killing us wrong is that a killing brutalizes the one who kills. But the brutalization consists of being inured to the performance of an act that is hideously immoral; hence, the brutalization does not explain the immorality. It might be said that what makes killing us wrong is the great loss others would experience due to our absence. Although such hubris is understandable, such an explanation does not account for the wrongness of killing hermits, or those whose lives are relatively independent and whose friends find it easy to make new friends.

A more obvious answer is better. What primarily makes killing wrong is neither its effect on the murderer nor its effect on the victim's friends and relatives, but its effect on the victim. The loss of one's life is one of the greatest losses one can suffer. The loss of one's life deprives one of all the experiences, activities, projects, and enjoyments that would otherwise have constituted one's future. Therefore, killing someone is wrong, primarily because the killing inflicts (one of) the greatest possible losses on the victim. To describe this as the loss of life can be misleading, however. The change in my biological state does not by itself make killing me wrong. The effect of the loss of my biological life is the loss to me of all those activities, projects, experiences, and enjoyments which would otherwise have constituted my future personal life. These activities, projects, experiences, and enjoyments are either valuable for their own sakes or are means to something else that is valuable for its own sake. Some parts of my future are not valued by me now, but will come to be valued by me as I grow older and as my values and capacities change. When I am killed, I am deprived both of what I now value which would have been part of my future personal life, but also what I would come to value. Therefore, when I die, I am deprived of all of the value of my future. Inflicting this loss on me is ultimately what makes killing me wrong. This being the case, it would seem that what makes killing any adult human being prima facie seriously wrong is the loss of his or her future.

How should this rudimentary theory of the wrongness of killing be evaluated? It cannot be faulted for deriving an 'ought' from an 'is', for it does not. The analysis assumes that killing me (or you, reader) is prima facie seriously wrong. The point of the analysis is to establish which natural property ultimately explains the wrongness of the killing, given that it is wrong. A natural property will ultimately explain the wrongness of killing, only if (1) the explanation fits with our intuitions about the matter and (2) there is no other natural property that provides the basis for a better explanation of the wrongness of killing. This analysis rests on the intuition that what makes killing a particular human or animal wrong is what it does to that particular human or animal. What makes killing wrong is some natural effect or other of the killing....

The claim that what makes killing wrong is the loss of the victim's future is directly supported by two considerations. In the first place, this theory explains why we regard killing as one of the worst of crimes. Killing is especially wrong, because it deprives the victim of more than perhaps any other crime. In the second place, people with AIDS or cancer who know they are dying believe, of course, that dying is a very bad thing for them. They believe that the loss of a future to them that they would otherwise have experienced is what makes their premature death a very bad thing for them. A better theory of the wrongness of killing would require a different natural property associated with killing which better fits with the attitudes of the dying. What could it be?

The view that what makes killing wrong is the loss to the victim of the value of the victim's future gains additional support when some of its implications are examined. In the first place, it is incompatible with the view that it is wrong to kill only beings who are biologically human. It is possible that there exists a different species from another planet whose members have a future like ours. Since having a future like that is what makes killing someone wrong, this theory entails that it would be wrong to kill members of such a species. Hence, this theory is opposed to the claim that only life that is biologically human has great moral worth, a claim which many anti-abortionists have seemed to adopt. This opposition, which this theory has in common with personhood theories, seems to be a merit of the theory.

In the second place, the claim that the loss of one's future is the wrong-making feature of one's being killed entails the possibility that the futures of some actual nonhuman mammals on our own planet are sufficiently like ours that it is seriously wrong to kill them also. Whether some animals do have the same right to life as human beings depends on adding to the account of the wrongness of killing some additional account of just what it is about my future or the futures of other adult human beings which makes it wrong to kill us. No such additional account will be offered in this essay. Undoubtedly, the provision of such an account would be a very difficult matter. Undoubtedly, any such account would be quite controversial. Hence, it surely should not reflect badly on this sketch of an elementary theory of the wrongness of killing that it is indeterminate with respect to some very difficult issues regarding animal rights.

In the third place, the claim that the loss of one's future is the wrong-making feature of one's being killed does not entail, as sanctity of human life theories do, that active euthanasia is wrong. Persons who are severely and incurably ill, who face a future of pain and despair, and who wish to die will not have suffered a loss if they are killed. It is, strictly speaking, the value of a human's future which makes killing wrong in this theory. This being so, killing does not necessarily wrong some

persons who are sick and dying. Of course, there may be other reasons for a prohibition of active euthanasia, but that is another matter. Sanctity-of-human-life theories seem to hold that active euthanasia is seriously wrong even in an individual case where there seems to be good reason for it independently of public policy considerations. This consequence is most implausible, and it is a plus for the claim that the loss of a future of value is what makes killing wrong that it does not share this consequence.

In the fourth place, the account of the wrongness of killing defended in this essay does straightforwardly entail that it is prima facie seriously wrong to kill children and infants, for we do presume that they have futures of value. Since we do believe that it is wrong to kill defenseless little babies, it is important that a theory of the wrongness of killing easily account for this. Personhood theories of the wrongness of killing, on the other hand, cannot straightforwardly account for the wrongness of killing infants and young children. Hence, such theories must add special ad hoc accounts of the wrongness of killing the young. The plausibility of such ad hoc theories seems to be a function of how desperately one wants such theories to work. The claim that the primary wrong-making feature of a killing is the loss to the victim of the value of its future accounts for the wrongness of killing young children and infants directly; it makes the wrongness of such acts as obvious as we actually think it is. This is a further merit of this theory. Accordingly, it seems that this value of a future-like-ours theory of the wrongness of killing shares strengths of both sanctity-of-life and personhood accounts while avoiding weaknesses of both. In addition, it meshes with a central intuition concerning what makes killing wrong.

The claim that the primary wrong-making feature of a killing is the loss to the victim of the value of its future has obvious consequences for the ethics of abortion. The future of a standard fetus includes a set of experiences, projects, activities, and such which are identical with the futures of adult human beings and are identical with the futures of young children. Since the reason that is sufficient to explain why it is wrong to kill human beings after the time of birth is a reason that also applies to fetuses, it follows that abortion is prima facie seriously morally wrong.

This argument does not rely on the invalid inference that, since it is wrong to kill persons, it is wrong to kill potential persons also. The category that is morally central to this analysis is the category of having a valuable future like ours; it is not the category of personhood. The argument to the conclusion that abortion is prima facie seriously morally wrong proceeded independently of the notion of person or potential person or any equivalent. Someone may wish to start with this analysis in terms of the value of a human future, conclude that abortion is, except perhaps in rare circumstances, seriously morally wrong, infer that fetuses have the right to life, and then call fetuses "persons" as a result of their having the right to life. Clearly, in this case, the category of person is being used to state the *conclusion* of the analysis rather than to generate the *argument* of the analysis.

The structure of this anti-abortion argument can be both illuminated and defended by comparing it to what appears to be the best argument for the wrongness of the wanton infliction of pain on animals. This latter argument is based on the assumption that it is prima facie wrong to inflict pain on me (or you, reader). What is the natural property associated with the

infliction of pain which makes such infliction wrong? The obvious answer seems to be that the infliction of pain causes suffering and that suffering is a misfortune. The suffering caused by the infliction of pain is what makes the wanton infliction of pain on me wrong. The wanton infliction of pain on other adult humans causes suffering. The wanton infliction of pain on animals causes suffering. Since causing suffering is what makes the wanton infliction of pain wrong and since the wanton infliction of pain on animals causes suffering, it follows that the wanton infliction of pain on animals is wrong.

This argument for the wrongness of the wanton infliction of pain on animals shares a number of structural features with the argument for the serious prima facie wrongness of abortion. Both arguments start with an obvious assumption concerning what it is wrong to do to me (or you, reader). Both then look for the characteristic or the consequence of the wrong action which makes the action wrong. Both recognize that the wrong-making feature of these immoral actions is a property of actions sometimes directed at individuals other than postnatal human beings. If the structure of the argument for the wrongness of the wanton infliction of pain on animals is sound, then the structure of the argument for the prima facie serious wrongness of abortion is also sound, for the structure of the two arguments is the same. The structure common to both is the key to the explanation of how the wrongness of abortion can be demonstrated without recourse to the category of person. In neither argument is that category crucial....

Of course, this value of a future-like-ours argument, if sound, shows only that abortion is prima facie wrong, not that it is wrong in any and all circumstances. Since the loss of the future to a standard fetus, if killed, is, however, at least as great a loss as the loss of the future to a standard adult human being who is killed, abortion, like ordinary killing, could be justified only by the most compelling reasons. The loss of one's life is almost the greatest misfortune that can happen to one. Presumably abortion could be justified in some circumstances, only if the loss consequent on failing to abort would be at least as great. Accordingly, morally permissible abortions will be rare indeed unless, perhaps, they occur so early in pregnancy that a fetus is not yet definitely an individual. Hence, this argument should be taken as showing that abortion is presumptively very seriously wrong, where the presumption is very strong—as strong as the presumption that killing another adult human being is wrong.

How complete an account of the wrongness of killing does the value of a future-like-ours account have to be in order that the wrongness of abortion is a consequence? This account does not have to be an account of the necessary conditions for the wrongness of killing. Some persons in nursing homes may lack valuable human futures, yet it may be wrong to kill them for other reasons. Furthermore, this account does not obviously have to be the sole reason killing is wrong where the victim did have a valuable future. This analysis claims only that, for any killing where the victim did have a valuable future like ours, having that future by itself is sufficient to create the strong presumption that the killing is seriously wrong....

In this essay, it has been argued that the correct ethic of the wrongness of killing can be extended to fetal life and used to show that there is a strong presumption that any abortion is morally impermissible. If the ethic of killing adopted here entails, however, that contraception is also seriously immoral, then there would appear to be a difficulty with the analysis of this essay.

But this analysis does not entail that contraception is wrong. Of course, contraception prevents the actualization of a possible future of value. Hence, it follows from the claim that futures of value should be maximized that contraception is prima facie immoral. This obligation to maximize does not exist, however; furthermore, nothing in the ethics of killing in this paper entails that it does. The ethics of killing in this essay would entail that contraception is wrong only if something were denied a human future of value by contraception. Nothing at all is denied such a future by contraception, however.

Candidates for a subject of harm by contraception fall into four categories: (1) some sperm or other, (2) some ovum or other, (3) a sperm and an ovum separately, and (4) a sperm and an ovum together. Assigning the harm to some sperm is utterly arbitrary, for no reason can be given for making a sperm the subject of harm rather than an ovum. Assigning the harm to some ovum is utterly arbitrary, for no reason can be given for making an ovum the subject of harm rather than a sperm. One might attempt to avoid these problems by insisting that contraception deprives both the sperm and the ovum separately of a valuable future like ours. On this alternative, too many futures are lost. Contraception was supposed to be wrong, because it deprived us of one future of value, not two. One might attempt to avoid this problem by holding that contraception deprives the combination of sperm and ovum of a valuable future like ours. But here the definite article misleads.

At the time of contraception, there are hundreds of millions of sperm, one (released) ovum and millions of possible combinations of all of these. There is no actual combination at all. Is the subject of the loss to be a merely possible combination? Which one? This alternative does not yield an actual subject of harm either. Accordingly, the immorality of contraception is not entailed by the loss of a future-like-ours argument simply because there is no nonarbitrarily identifiable subject of the loss in the case of contraception.

The purpose of this essay has been to set out an argument for the serious presumptive wrongness of abortion subject to the assumption that the moral permissibility of abortion stands or falls on the moral status of the fetus. Since a fetus possesses a property, the possession of which in adult human beings is sufficient to make killing an adult human being wrong, abortion is wrong. This way of dealing with the problem of abortion seems superior to other approaches to the ethics of abortion, because it rests on an ethics of killing which is close to self-evident, because the crucial morally relevant property clearly applies to fetuses, and because the argument avoids the usual equivocations on 'human life', 'human being', or 'person'. The argument rests neither on religious claims nor on Papal dogma. It is not subject to the objection of "speciesism." Its soundness is compatible with the moral permissibility of euthanasia and contraception. It deals with our intuitions concerning young children.

Finally, this analysis can be viewed as resolving a standard problem—indeed, *the* standard problem—concerning the ethics of abortion. Clearly, it is wrong to kill adult human beings. Clearly, it is not wrong to end the life of some arbitrarily chosen single human cell. Fetuses seem to be like arbitrarily chosen human cells in some respects and like adult humans in other respects. The problem of the ethics of abortion is the problem of determining the fetal property that settles this moral controversy. The thesis of this essay is that the problem of the ethics of abortion, so understood, is solvable.

The Question of Abortion:
Morally Acceptable

BONNIE STEINBOCK

I. INTRODUCTION

… My belief that abortion is not wrong is based on two considerations: the moral status of the embryo and fetus and the burdens imposed by pregnancy and childbirth on women. I begin by presenting briefly the view of moral status that I take to be correct, that is, the interest view. The interest view limits moral status to beings who have interests and restricts the possession of interests to conscious, sentient beings. The implication for abortion is that it is not seriously wrong to kill a nonconscious, nonsentient fetus where there is an adequate reason for doing so, such as not wanting to be pregnant. Next I discuss Don Marquis' challenge to the interest view (Marquis, 1989). According to Marquis, killing is prima facie wrong when it deprives a being of a valuable future like ours. If a being has a valuable future, the fact that it is now nonconscious and nonsentient is irrelevant. Marquis' account of the wrongness of killing implies that abortion is almost always wrong. I try to show that his view has serious problems, in particular, that it applies to gametes as well as fetuses, and it makes contraception as well as abortion seriously wrong.…

II. THE MORAL STATUS OF THE FETUS

I use the term "fetus" to refer to the unborn at all stages of pregnancy, even though this is not, strictly speaking, correct. Between conception and 8 weeks, the correct term is "embryo;" the term "fetus" is correctly used between 8 weeks gestation age and birth. I will use the term "fetus" throughout, both in order to avoid the inconvenience of the phrase "embryo or fetus" and because using the term "embryo", which refers to the earliest weeks of pregnancy, might convey an unfair advantage to my argument. Everything I have to say about abortion in this essay applies as much to a 12-week-old fetus as it does to a newly fertilized egg.

I will not discuss the morality of abortion beyond the first trimester of pregnancy (approximately 12 weeks long) since the vast majority of abortions (approximately 90 percent) take place by then. I am quite willing to accept that late abortions, especially those that occur after 24 weeks, are morally problematic; but since these are quite rare (about one percent of all abortions) and almost always done for very serious moral reasons such as to preserve the life or health of the mother or to prevent the birth of an infant with a serious disability, I will not discuss these abortions. Instead, I will focus on so-called elective abortions, those chosen to avoid the burdens of pregnancy, childbearing, and childrearing.

Most opponents of abortion say that abortion is wrong because it is the killing of an innocent human being. They see no morally relevant difference between an early gestation fetus and a newborn baby. If it would be wrong to kill a newborn because it is unwanted (something on which there is virtually unanimous agreement), then, according to this thinking, it is equally wrong to perform an abortion, which deliberately kills the fetus.

The question, then, is whether an early gestation fetus (or simply "fetus" as I will say from now on) is morally equivalent to a newborn baby. This seems to me completely implausible. A newborn can feel, react, and perceive. It cries when it is hungry or stuck with needles. Very soon after birth it cries from boredom or loneliness as well and can be soothed by being rocked and held. By contrast, the first-trimester fetus cannot think, feel, or perceive anything. It is certainly alive and human, but it feels and is aware of nothing; it is more like a gamete (a sperm or an ovum), which is also alive and human, than a baby. While early abortion is not the psychological equivalent of contraception, it is morally closer to contraception than to homicide.

My thesis is that killing fetuses is morally different from killing babies because fetuses are not, and babies are, sentient. By sentience, I mean the ability to experience pain and pleasure. But what is the moral significance of sentience? I have argued (Steinbock, 1992) that sentience is important because nonsentient beings, whether mere things (e.g., cars and rocks and works of art) or living things without nervous systems (e.g., plants), lack interests of their own. Therefore, nonsentient beings are not among those beings whose interests we are required to consider. To put it another way, nonsentient beings lack moral status. I refer to this view of moral status as "the interest view."

Critics of the interest view ask why a being has to feel or experience anything to have interests. Leaving a bicycle out in the rain will cause it to rust, affecting adversely both its appearance and its performance. Why can we not say that this is contrary to its interests? Stripping the bark off a tree will cause it to die. Why can't we say that this is against the tree's interest? Limiting interests to sentient beings (namely, animals—human and otherwise) seems to limit unduly the arena of our concern. What about rivers and forests and mountains? What about the environment?

However, this objection misconceives the interest view. The claim is not that we should be concerned to protect and preserve only sentient beings, but rather that only sentient beings can have an interest or a stake in their own existence. It is only sentient beings to whom anything matters, which is quite different from saying that only sentient beings matter. The interest view can acknowledge the value of many nonsentient beings, from works of art to wilderness areas. It recognizes that we have all kinds of reasons—economic, aesthetic, symbolic, even moral reasons— to protect or preserve nonsentient beings. The difference between sentient and nonsentient beings is not that sentient beings have value and nonsentient ones lack value. Rather, it is that since nonsentient beings cannot be hurt or made to suffer, it does not matter *to them* what is done to them. In deciding what we should do, we cannot consider *their* interests since they do not have any. It might be wrong to deface a work of art or to burn a flag, but it is not a wrong *to* the painting or the flag. Put another way "golden rule"-type reasons do not apply to nonsentient beings. That is, no one would explain opposition to burning the flag of the United States of America by saying, "How would you like it if you were a flag and someone burned you?" Instead, such opposition would have to be based on the symbolic importance of the flag and the message that is conveyed when it is burned in a political demonstration. (I am not saying that flag-burning *is* wrong, only contrasting an intelligible reason for opposing flag-burning, based on the symbolic value of the flag, with an absurd reason.)

The interest view is a general theory about moral status, but it has implications for the morality of abortion. During early gestation, fetuses are nonsentient beings and, as such, they do not have interests.

Scientists do not agree on precisely when fetuses become sentient, but most agree that first-trimester fetuses are not sentient. The reason is that, in the first trimester, the fetal nervous system is not sufficiently developed to transmit pain messages to the brain. Since the brain cannot receive pain messages, the first-trimester fetus is not sentient; it cannot feel anything. The synaptic connections necessary for pain perception are established in the fetal brain between 20 and 24 weeks of gestation (Anand and Hickey, 1987). This means not only that premature infants *are* capable of experiencing pain—something that doctors rejected until very recently—but also that, throughout the first and most of the second trimester, fetuses do not experience pain or any other sensation. Despite the claims of propaganda films like *The Silent Scream*, first-trimester fetuses do not suffer when they are aborted.

Prolifers may think that I have missed the point of their opposition to abortion. They need not claim that abortion *hurts* the fetus, or causes it to experience pain, but rather that abortion deprives the fetus of its *life*. I quite agree that this is the important issue, but I maintain that a non-sentient being is not deprived of anything by being killed. In an important sense, it does not have a life to lose.

Now this claim may strike some people as odd. If the fetus is alive, then surely it has a life to lose? But this is just what I am denying. It seems to me that unless there is conscious awareness of some kind, a being does not have a life to lose. Consider all the living cells in our bodies which die or are killed. Surely it would be absurd to speak of all of them as losing their lives or being deprived of their lives. Or consider those in a state of permanent unconsciousness, with no hope of regaining consciousness. I would say that such persons have already lost their lives in any sense

that matters, even though they are still biologically alive. It is not biological life that matters, but rather conscious existence. Killing the fetus before it becomes conscious and aware deprives it of nothing. To put it another way, the first-trimester fetus has a biological life, but its biographical life has not yet begun (Rachels, 1986). The interest view suggests that it is *prima facie* wrong to deprive beings of their biographical lives, but not wrong to end merely biological lives, at least where there are good reasons for doing so, such as not wanting to bear a child.

III. THE ARGUMENT FROM POTENTIAL

Of course, there is one difference between a human fetus and any other living, non-sentient being, namely, that if the fetus is not killed, but allowed to develop and grow, it will become a person, just like you or me. Some opponents of abortion cite the potential of the fetus to become a sentient being, with interests and a welfare of its own, as the reason for ascribing to it the moral status belonging to sentient beings. Equally, on this view, the potential of the fetus to become a person gives it the same rights as other persons, including the right to life.

The potentiality principle has been criticized on several grounds. Firstly, it does not follow from the fact that something is a potential *x* that it should be treated as an actual *x*. This is often called "the logical problem with potentiality." As John Harris (1985) puts it, we're all potentially dead, but that's no reason to treat living people as if they were corpses. Secondly, it is not clear why potential personhood attaches only to the fertilized egg. Why aren't unfertilized eggs and sperm also potential people? If certain things happen to them (like meeting a gamete) and certain other things do not (like meeting a contraceptive), they too will develop into people. Admittedly, the chance of any particular sperm becoming a person is absurdly low, but why should that negate its potential? Isn't every player a potential winner in a state lottery, even though the chances of winning are infinitesmal? We should not confuse potentialities with probabilities. So if abortion is wrong because it kills a potential person, then using a spermicide as a contraceptive is equally wrong because it also kills a potential person. Few opponents of abortion are willing to accept this conclusion, which means either giving up the argument from potential or finding a way to differentiate morally between gametes and embryos.

IV. MARQUIS' ARGUMENT

Don Marquis (1989) argues that traditional arguments on abortion, both those of opponents of abortion and those of proponents of a woman's right to choose, are seriously flawed. His argument against abortion derives from a general principle about the wrongness of killing. Killing adult human beings is is *prima facie* wrong because it deprives them of their worthwhile future. Marquis writes:

> The loss of one's life is one of the greatest losses one can suffer. The loss of one's life deprives one of all the experiences, activities, projects, and enjoyments that would otherwise have constituted one's future. Therefore, killing someone is wrong, primarily because the killing inflicts (one of) the greatest possible losses on the victim.... When I am killed, I am deprived both of what I now value which would have been part of my future personal life, but also what I would come to value. Therefore, when I die, I am deprived of all of the value of my future. Inflicting this loss on me is ultimate-

ly what makes killing me wrong. This being the case, it would seem that what makes killing *any* adult human being *prima facie* seriously wrong is the loss of his or her future (Marquis, 1989, pp. 189–190).

This argument for the wrongness of killing applies only to those who in fact have a future with experiences, activities, projects, and enjoyments. In Marquis' view, it might not be wrong to kill someone in a persistent vegetative state (PVS), for example, who will never regain consciousness, because such a person no longer has a valuable future. (There might be other reasons against killing PVS patients, but these would not refer to the loss inflicted on the patient.) Similarly, persons who are severely and incurably ill and who face a future of pain and despair and who wish to die may not be wronged if they are killed, because the future of which they are deprived is not considered by them to be a valuable one. However, most fetuses (leaving aside those with serious anomalies) do have valuable futures. If they are not aborted, they will come to have lives they will value and enjoy, just as you and I value and enjoy our lives. Therefore, abortion is seriously wrong for the same reason that killing an innocent adult human being is seriously wrong: it deprives the victim of his or her valuable future.

Marquis' argument against abortion is similar to arguments based on the principle of potentiality in that the wrongness of killing is derived from the loss of the valuable future the fetus will have, if allowed to grow and develop, rather than being based on any characteristic, such as genetic humanity, the fetus now has. However, Marquis' view differs from traditional potentiality arguments in two ways. Firstly, most arguments from potential maintain that it is wrong not only to kill persons, but also to kill potential persons.

Though a human fetus is not now a person, it will develop into one if allowed to grow and develop. By contrast, Marquis' argument says nothing about the wrongness of killing persons and therefore nothing about the wrongness of killing potential persons. Marquis is explicit about his argument not necessarily being limited to persons but applying to any beings who have valuable futures like ours. Some nonpersons (e.g., some animals) also might have such futures, and so it might be wrong to kill them in Marquis' account. Admittedly, the concept of a person is not coextensive with the capacity to have a valuable future, and there are heated debates about what it is to be a person. However, if we use the term "person" simply to mean an individual with a valuable future like ours and hence one it would be seriously wrong to kill, we can reword Marquis' account in terms of the wrongness of killing persons.

Another way in which Marquis differs from potentiality theorists is that his argument is not based on the potential of the fetus to become something different from what it is now. Rather, it is wrong to kill a fetus because killing it deprives it of its valuable future—the very same reason why it is wrong to kill you or me. Thus, although Marquis focuses on a certain kind of potential, namely, the fetus's potential to have experiences in the future, this potential is no different from the potential that any born human being has to have future experiences. Thus, he cannot be accused of basing the wrongness of killing born human beings on a feature that we actually possess, while basing the wrongness of abortion' on a (merely) potential feature of the fetus.

Marquis thinks that his view is superior to other accounts of moral status in that it is able to explain what is wrong with killing people who are temporarily unconscious, something the interest view seems incapable of doing. If it is morally permissible to kill nonsentient beings, why is it wrong to kill someone in a reversible coma? Such a person is not now conscious or sentient. And if we appeal to his future conscious states, the same argument seems to apply to the fetus, who will become conscious and sentient if we just leave it alone.

Two responses can be made to this objection to the interest view. The first is to note an important difference between a temporarily unconscious person and a fetus. The difference is that the person who is now unconscious has had experiences, plans, beliefs, desires, etc. in the past. These past experiences are relevant because they form the basis for saying that the comatose person wants not to be killed while unconscious. "He valued his life," we might say. "Of course he would not want to be killed." This desire or preference is the basis for saying that the temporarily unconscious person has an interest in not being killed. But the same cannot be said of a nonsentient fetus. A nonsentient fetus cannot be said to want anything, and so cannot be said to want not to be killed. By contrast, if I am killed while sleeping or temporarily comatose, I am deprived of something I want very much, namely, to go on living. This is not an *occurrent* desire; that is, it is rarely if ever a desire of which I am consciously aware, but it is certainly one of my desires. We have all sorts of desires of which we are not at any particular moment consciously aware, and it would be absurd to limit our desires to what we are actually thinking about. Nor do our desires, plans, and goals, or the interests composing them, vanish when we fall into dreamless sleep.

However, our interests are not limited to what we take an interest in, as Tom Regan (1976) has correctly noted. Our interests also include what is *in* our interest, whether or not we are interested in it. For example, getting enough sleep, eating moderately, and foregoing tobacco might be in the interest of a person who has no interest in following such a regime. Now even if the nonconscious fetus is not interested in continuing to live, could we not say that continued existence is *in* its interest? If the fetus will go on to have a valuable future, is not that future in its interest?

The issue raised here is whether the future the fetus will go on to have is in an important sense *its* future. Marquis considers the existence of past experiences to be entirely irrelevant to the question of whether an entity can be deprived of its future. But this is not at all clear. Killing embryos or early gestation fetuses differs from killing adult human beings because adult human beings have a life that they (ordinarily) value and which they would prefer not to lose: a biographical as opposed to merely biological life. How might the idea of having a biographical life be connected with the possibility of having a personal future, a future of one's own? In an unpublished manuscript, "The Future-Like-Ours Argument Against Abortion and The Problem of Personal Identity," David Boonin-Vail uses a plausible theory of personal identity—the psychological continuity account—to argue that nonsentient fetuses do not have a personal future. According to the psychological continuity account of personal identity, having a certain set of past experiences is what makes me the person I am, and the experiences that I have, *my* experiences. What makes experiences at two different times experiences of the same person is that they are appropriately related by a chain of memories, desires, intentions, and the like. So an individual's past experiences are not, as Marquis claims, otiose to an account of the value of his future; indeed, they are precisely what makes his future *his*.

On this account of personal identity, then, there is an important difference between someone who is temporarily unconscious and a fetus. The difference is this: when the unconscious person regains consciousness, "there will be a relationship of continuity involving memories, intentions, character traits, and so on between his subsequent experiences and those which he had before he lapsed into the coma" (Boonin-Vail, 1996, p. 11).

This is what makes his future experiences (those he will have if he is not killed) *his*. The situation of the preconscious fetus is quite different.

> When he gains (rather than regains) consciousness, there will he no relationship of continuity involving memories, intentions, character traits, and so on between his subsequent experiences and those which he had before he gained consciousness precisely because he *had* no experiences before he gained consciousness. This is what permits us to say of the preconscious fetus that it is not he who will have these later experiences if he is not killed. And this, in turn, is what permits us to deny that *he* will be harmed if we present these experiences from occurring (Boning-Vail, 1996, P. 12).

If we accept the psychological continuity account of personal identity, then past experiences do matter because without past experiences there is no one with a personal future. This is not to say that this provides us with a reason to kill the presentient fetus but rather that we lack the strong reason for not killing it that we have in the case of people like you and me. The justificatory reason for killing the fetus stems from the woman's rights to bodily autonomy and self-determination.

However, perhaps the psychological continuity account is wrong. Perhaps personal identity is better based on physical continuity. In that case, even if the born human being has no memories connecting her to the fetal stage, we can still say that she is the same individual because there is physical continuity between the born human and the fetal human.

There are certain advantages to a physical continuity account of personal identity. It allows us to say of someone who develops total amnesia that he has a history of which he has absolutely no memory, and this seems to be a plain statement of fact. Similarly, most people have very few memories about anything that occurred before the ages of four or five; yet most of us are convinced that we are the same individuals we were when very young. Of course, there could be psychological connections of which we have no memory. For example, providing an infant with secure, loving experiences as opposed to terrifying or traumatic ones is likely to affect the psychological development of the eventual adult, whether or not she remembers what happened. So it may be that a more sophisticated psychological account, one that is not entirely dependent on memory, is the better account of identity, but I will not pursue that issue.

Boonin-Vail argues that the trouble with basing identity on physical continuity is that this implies that contraception is as wrong as abortion, something most people, including Marquis, want to reject. Thus, the claim that contraception prevents a gamete from enjoying a future like ours takes the form of a *reductio ad absurdum*: the argument (allegedly) commits one to an absurd (or at least unacceptable) conclusion. A physical continuity account of personal identity is vulnerable to the objection that it makes contraception as wrong as abortion because there seems to

be no reason why embryos have and gametes do not have valuable futures. For the embryo does not appear *ex nihilo*. Its physical history goes back to the conjoining of the sperm and ovum. Thus, if you prevent the sperm and ovum from conjoining, you deprive each of them of the future they would have had if fertilization had taken place.

Marquis says that his view does not apply to contraception because, prior to fertilization, there is no entity that has a future. It is only after fertilization, when there is a being with a specific genetic code, that there is an individual with a future who can be deprived of that future by being killed. But why should this be so? Admittedly, neither gamete can have a future all by itself, but that is also true of the embryo, which cannot develop all by itself. It needs a uterus and adequate nutrients to develop into a fetus and a baby. Admittedly, the future the sperm will have is not its future alone; it shares its future with the ovum it fertilizes. This makes the situation of gametes unusual, perhaps unique, but does not seem to provide a reason why gametes cannot have futures if the criterion of identity is physical continuity.

Sometimes it is said that a sperm is not a unique individual in the way that a fetus is. For who the sperm turns out to be depends on which ovum it unites with. Why, however, should this lack of uniqueness deprive the sperm of being a potential person, or to use Marquis' language, why should its lack of uniqueness prevent it from having "a future like ours"? Although we cannot specify which future existence the sperm will have, if it is allowed to fertilize an egg, it will become somebody and that *somebody* will have a valuable future.

I think the reason we do not usually think of sperm as having futures is that, in the ordinary reproductive context, literally millions of sperm are released, and only one can fertilize the egg. The rest are doomed. So it seems implausible to say that by killing sperm, we are depriving them of a future. Still, *one* of them might fertilize the egg, even though we cannot say which one it will be, and that one sperm will not get to develop into an embryo and eventual person if it is killed before conception occurs.

Moreover, assisted reproductive technology (ART) facilitates the tracing of an embryo back to its constituent gametes in a way never before possible. In the context of *in vitro* fertilization (IVF), where an egg and sperm are placed in a petri dish for fertilization to occur, we *can* identify the particular gametes who might unite. If dumping out the contents of the petri dish after fertilization has occurred would be immoral because doing that deprives the fertilized egg of "a future like ours," why is it not equally wrong to dump out the contents of the petri dish seconds before fertilization occurs? The ability to identify which gametes make up the embryo is even greater in the micromanipulation technique known as intracytoplasmic sperm injection (ICSI). The ICSI technique enables patients with male factor infertility, where not enough motile sperm can be recovered for ordinary *in vitro* fertilization (IVF), to be considered for assisted reproductive intervention. In ICSI, a single sperm is injected directly into the egg. The isolation of a single sperm makes it possible for us to identify with certainty which sperm conjoined with the egg in the resultant embryo. Thus, the individual who comes to be after fertilization is physically continuous with the sperm in the pipette and the egg in the petri dish. Killing the gametes before fertilization deprives both of them of the future they would have had.

Marquis might respond to the ART examples by maintaining, in his account, that embryos *in vitro* do not have valuable futures like ours. It is only after implantation, when twinning is no longer possible, that we have an individual who can be said to have a personal future. Thus, Marquis need not be backed into claiming a moral difference between dumping out a petri dish just before or just after conception. Equally, his view is compatible with allowing contraceptives and abortifacients that kill the embryo before implantation occurs. These are seen as importantly morally different from terminating a clinical pregnancy. that is, after implantation occurs. Certainly most of us do regard abortion, even in the first trimester, as morally different from contraception or even a morning-after pill. It seems to me, however, that the reason is not that the status of the embryo radically changes with implantation. Rather, it is that most people have very different feelings toward the termination of a pregnancy than they have toward the prevention of pregnancy....

In any event, I do not think Marquis has adequately explained why embryos have valuable futures and gametes do not. For this reason, I consider his account of why abortion is immoral to be vulnerable to the usual objection to potentiality arguments, namely, that they make contraception seriously wrong. The interest view avoids this difficulty. As for its alleged difficulty with explaining why it is wrong to kill sleeping and temporarily comatose people, I maintain that this can be explained in terms of the interests of the nonconscious person, interests that a fetus does not yet have. For these reasons, the interest view seems to me a better account of moral status than the future-like-ours account.

THE CONTINUING DEBATE:
The Question of Abortion

What Is New

Roe v. Wade (1973) is the landmark ruling in the U.S. Supreme Court's consideration of abortion. The decision to legalize abortion was supported by a vote of 7 to 2, based primarily on the woman's right to personal privacy in making decisions concerning her own body. However, the decision of *Roe v. Wade* was supported by the narrowest majority on the current Court, and many believe that the replacement of one retiring Justice could result in the ruling being reversed.

More recent Supreme Court cases have dealt with the regulation of abortion: Can states require a waiting period or special counseling, or limit the stage at which abortion is allowed, or require that minors have parental approval, or require notification of the husband of a married woman who seeks an abortion? The deep divisions on the Court are reflected in the positions taken in *Planned Parenthood of Southeastern Pennsylvania v. Casey*, in which the Court ruled that states cannot impose laws or regulations that place an "undue burden" on women seeking to exercise their right to an abortion—though what counts as an undue burden remains problematic. The most recent controversy concerns what antiabortion groups call "partial birth abortions," a specific procedure sometimes employed in second trimester abortions. Congress passed, and President Bush signed, an act banning such abortions, and attaching severe criminal and civil penalties to anyone performing them. The vagueness of the law's specification of what abortion procedures were banned under the law, the severe penalties involved, and the very narrow range for exceptions to the law (only to prevent a woman's death, and not for protection of health) had the obvious effect of making physicians nervous about performing any abortion, and pro-choice advocates argued that the act placed an unconstitutional burden on a woman's right to an abortion. The United States District Court of Southern New York, the United States District Court of Nebraska, and the United States District Court of Northern California have all ruled the act unconstitutional because it failed to provide an exception when the health of the mother was threatened; the New York Court also concluded that it placed an undue burden on a woman's right to choose. The appeals process is likely to reach the United States Supreme Court.

Where to Find More

Among the anthologies on abortion are Susan Dwyer and Joel Feinberg's *The Problem of Abortion*, 3rd Edition (Belmont, CA: Wadsworth, 1997). An anthology that compares competing views on issues related to abortion is Charles P. Cozic and Stacey L. Tipp, *Abortion: Opposing Viewpoints* (San Diego, CA: Greenhaven Press, 1991). An anthology edited by William B. Bondeson, H. Tristram Engelhardt, Jr., Stuart F. Spicker and Daniel H. Winship, *Abortion and the Status of the Fetus* (Dordrecht, Holland: D. Reidel Publishing, 1984) contains interesting articles concerning the physical and moral status of the fetus, and a fascinating historical introduction by H. Tristram Engelhardt, Jr.

Bryan Hilliard, *The U.S. Supreme Court and Medical Ethics* (St. Paul: Paragon House, 2004) provides a clear analysis of the key Supreme Court cases related to abortion.

Ronald Dworkin's *Life's Dominion: An Argument about Abortion, Euthanasia, and Individual Freedom* (New York: Alfred A. Knopf, 1993) treats the issue very carefully, showing respect for both sides of this deeply contentious issue. Frances Myrna Kamm, *Creation and Abortion: A Study in Moral and Legal Philosophy* (New York: Oxford University Press, 1992) is another excellent and thoughtful book on the subject. Laurence Tribe, *Abortion: The Clash of Absolutes* (New York: W. W. Norton, 1990) is the work of a distinguished legal scholar who seeks some common ground on the question.

For an evenhanded resource on the abortion controversy, including many links to other sites as well as to videos, recorded radio discussions, and a wide variety of full text articles, go to Ethics Updates at *ethics.sandiego.edu/*.

CLONING

Scientific Horror or Potential Benefit?

SCIENTIFIC HORROR

ADVOCATE: Leon Kass, Chairman of the President's Council on Bioethics, Addie Clark Harding Professor in the Committee on Social Thought and the College at the University of Chicago, and Hertog Fellow in Social Thought at the American Enterprise Institute

SOURCE: "Preventing A Brave New World: Why We Should Ban Human Cloning Now," *The New Republic*, May 21, 2001: 30–39

POTENTIAL BENEFIT

ADVOCATE: Dan W. Brock, Charles C. Tillinghast, Jr. University Professor of Philosophy and Biomedical Ethics, and Director, Center for Biomedical Ethics at Brown University

SOURCE: "Cloning Human Beings," Commissioned paper for the National Bioethics Advisory Commission, contained in *Cloning Human Beings, Volume II: Commissioned Papers, Report and Recommendations of the National Bioethics Advisory Commission* (Rockville, Maryland: June 1997): E1-E23

There are two types of cloning: cloning by *fission* involves dividing an embryo, whereas cloning by *fusion* or *nuclear transfer* (the process that produced Dolly as well as most of the controversy) is carried out by removing the nucleus from an unfertilized egg and replacing it with genetic material from a cell of the donor.

Dolly, the cloned sheep, was no doubt the most famous sheep since Mary's little lamb followed her to school. Suddenly the stuff of science fiction became sober scientific reality, and many people envisioned great dangers on the horizon. The InterAcademy Panel on International Issues (IAP), which represents more than 60 scientific academies worldwide, urged the United Nations to adopt a resolution banning human reproductive cloning. Yves Quere, co-chair of the IAP Executive Committee, made the view of the group quite clear: "Human reproductive cloning is unsafe and no responsible scientist would attempt it given the huge health risks that are involved." Thus there appears to be settled consensus that now is not the time to clone a human child. Whether such a time might ever come is a question that is not settled. What is clear is that research on cloning is continuing, that cloning techniques have been extended to many more species, and that while we have not yet reached the point of being able to successfully clone our nearest genetic relatives—such as chimpanzees—that point is likely to be reached in a matter of years rather than decades. The step from cloning chimpanzees to cloning humans will not be a large scientific step. Whether it would be a large ethical step, and a step that should never be taken, is the subject of this debate.

One important issue in deciding whether to allow human reproductive cloning is the potential harm to children produced in this manner, particularly in the earliest uses of this methodology. Leaving aside questions of potential psychological harm (Will the child feel that her future is fixed? Will the child be burdened by set expectations of what she is supposed to accomplish?), there are questions about the risks of producing a child that is so physically malformed that she will live only briefly and painfully. However, this raises questions of whether we should hold those who reproduce by cloning to a higher standard than we currently use for sexually produced children. For example, suppose that we know that a couple are both carriers of a recessive gene for a terrible genetic disease (such as Tay-Sachs), and that their children will have a twenty-five percent chance of having the disease and dying painfully in infancy. While some might favor restricting the procreative rights of such parents, most believe that their decision to have children ultimately must be left up to them. If we are willing to accept a twenty-five percent chance of infant death in such cases, is it fair to hold cloning to a stricter standard?

POINTS TO PONDER

➤ Kass asks us to consider revulsion or deep repugnance as quite possibly "the emotional expression of deep wisdom." But revulsion seems to lead different people along conflicting paths. Some feel profound revulsion toward the eating of pork, others toward the eating of dogs, and still others find one or both of those perfectly acceptable food sources. Not many years ago, white racists expressed deep revulsion toward social contact with blacks; now, fortunately, most people feel deep revulsion toward such racists. Is this a problem for any attempt to draw moral conclusions on the basis of "revulsion"?

➤ Some people (like Kass) want a total ban on human cloning. Others, like Brock, seem to suggest that—at least eventually—human cloning should be permitted. Suppose someone proposed that cloning be allowed only for persons who cannot reproduce in any other manner: Would such a position be acceptable to both sides? To either? To neither? To you?

➤ At one time many people were shocked or horrified by "test tube babies" produced by in vitro fertilization (IVF). That procedure has now become almost commonplace, and in any case no longer seems to raise many objections. What is the likelihood that cloning will follow the same course?

➤ If one of your close friends informed you (truthfully) that she was created by cloning, would that change your attitude toward her? Would you have less respect for her? Would it compromise your friendship?

Cloning:
Scientific Horror

Leon Kass

I.

"To clone or not to clone a human being" is no longer a fanciful question. Success in cloning sheep, and also cows, mice, pigs, and goats, makes it perfectly clear that a fateful decision is now at hand: whether we should welcome or even tolerate the cloning of human beings. If recent newspaper reports are to be believed, reputable scientists and physicians have announced their intention to produce the first human clone in the coming year. Their efforts may already be under way.

The media, gawking and titillating as is their wont, have been softening us up for this possibility by turning the bizarre into the familiar. In the four years since the birth of Dolly the cloned sheep, the tone of discussing the prospect of human cloning has gone from "Yuck" to "Oh?" to "Gee whiz" to "Why not?" The sentimentalizers, aided by leading bioethicists, have downplayed talk about eugenically cloning the beautiful and the brawny or the best and the brightest. They have taken instead to defending clonal reproduction for humanitarian or compassionate reasons: to treat infertility in people who are said to "have no other choice," to avoid the risk of severe genetic disease, to "replace" a child who has died. For the sake of these rare benefits, they would have us countenance the entire practice of human cloning, the consequences be damned.

But we dare not be complacent about what is at issue, for the stakes are very high. Human cloning, though partly continuous with previous reproductive tech-nologies, is also something radically new in itself and in its easily foreseeable consequences—especially when coupled with powers for genetic "enhancement" and germline genetic modification that may soon become available, owing to the recently completed Human Genome Project. I exaggerate somewhat, but in the direction of the truth: we are compelled to decide nothing less than whether human procreation is going to remain human, whether children are going to be made to order rather than begotten, and whether we wish to say yes in principle to the road that leads to the dehumanized hell of *Brave New World*....

II.

What is cloning? Cloning, or asexual reproduction, is the production of individuals who are genetically identical to an already existing individual. The procedure's name is fancy—"somatic cell nuclear transfer"—but its concept is simple. Take a mature but unfertilized egg; remove or deactivate its nucleus; introduce a nucleus obtained from a specialized (somatic) cell of an adult organism. Once the egg begins to divide, transfer the little embryo to a woman's uterus to initiate a pregnancy. Since almost all the hereditary material of a cell is contained within its nucleus, the re-nucleated egg and the individual into which it develops are genetically identical to the organism that was the source of the transferred nucleus.

An unlimited number of genetically identical individuals—the group, as well as each of its members, is called "a clone"—could be produced by nuclear transfer. In principle, any person, male or female, newborn or adult, could be cloned, and in any quantity; and because stored cells can outlive their sources, one may even clone the dead. Since cloning requires no personal involvement on the part of the person whose genetic material is used, it could easily be used to reproduce living or deceased persons without their consent—a threat to reproductive freedom that has received relatively little attention.

Some possible misconceptions need to be avoided. Cloning is not Xeroxing: the clone of Bill Clinton, though his genetic double, would enter the world hairless, toothless, and peeing in his diapers, like any other human infant. But neither is cloning just like natural twinning: the cloned twin will be identical to an older existing adult; and it will arise not by chance but by deliberate design; and its entire genetic makeup will be pre-selected by its parents and/or scientists. Moreover the success rate of cloning, at least at first, will probably not be very high: the Scots transferred two hundred seventy-seven adult nuclei into sheep eggs, implanted twenty-nine clonal embryos, and achieved the birth of only one live lamb clone.

For this reason, among others, it is unlikely that, at least for now, the practice would be very popular; and there is little immediate worry of mass-scale production of multicopies. Still, for the tens of thousands of people who sustain more than three hundred assisted-reproduction clinics in the United States and already avail themselves of in vitro fertilization and other techniques, cloning would be an option with virtually no added fuss. Panos Zavos, the Kentucky reproduction specialist who has announced his plans to clone a child, claims that he has already received thousands of e-mailed requests from people eager to clone, despite the known risks of failure and damaged offspring. Should commercial interests develop in "nucleus-banking," as they have in sperm-banking and egg-harvesting; should famous athletes or other celebrities decide to market their DNA the way they now market their autographs and nearly everything else; should techniques of embryo and germline genetic testing and manipulation arrive as anticipated, increasing the use of laboratory assistance in order to obtain "better" babies—should all this come to pass, cloning, if it is permitted, could become more than a marginal practice simply on the basis of free reproductive choice.

What are we to think about this prospect? Nothing good. Indeed, most people are repelled by nearly all aspects of human cloning: the possibility of mass production of human beings, with large clones of look-alikes, compromised in their individuality; the idea of father-son or mother-daughter "twins"; the bizarre prospect of a woman bearing and rearing a genetic copy of herself, her spouse, or even her deceased father or mother; the grotesqueness of conceiving a child as an exact "replacement" for another who has died; the utilitarian creation of embryonic duplicates of oneself to be frozen away or created when needed to provide homologous tissues or organs for transplantation; the narcissism of those who would clone themselves, and the arrogance of others who think they know who deserves to be cloned; the Frankensteinian hubris to create a human life and increasingly to control its destiny; men playing at being God. Almost no one finds any of the suggested reasons for human cloning compelling, and almost everyone anticipates its possible misuses and abuses. And the popular belief that human cloning cannot be prevented makes the prospect all the more revolting.

Revulsion is not an argument; and some of yesterday's repugnances are today calmly accepted—not always for the better. In some crucial cases, however, repugnance is the emotional expression of deep wisdom, beyond reason's power completely to articulate it. Can anyone really give an argument fully adequate to the horror that is father-daughter incest (even with consent), or bestiality, or the mutilation of a corpse, or the eating of human flesh, or the rape or murder of another human being? Would anybody's failure to give full rational justification for his revulsion at those practices make that revulsion ethically suspect?

I suggest that our repugnance at human cloning belongs in this category. We are repelled by the prospect of cloning human beings not because of the strangeness or the novelty of the undertaking, but because we intuit and we feel, immediately and without argument, the violation of things that we rightfully hold dear. We sense that cloning represents a profound defilement of our given nature as procreative beings, and of the social relations built on this natural ground. We also sense that cloning is a radical form of child abuse. In this age in which everything is held to be permissible so long as it is freely done, and in which our bodies are regarded as mere instruments of our autonomous rational will, repugnance may be the only voice left that speaks up to defend the central core of our humanity. Shallow are the souls that have forgotten how to shudder.

III.

Yet repugnance need not stand naked before the bar of reason. The wisdom of our horror at human cloning can be at least partially articulated, even if this is finally one of those instances about which the heart has its reasons that reason cannot

entirely know. I offer four objections to human cloning: that it constitutes unethical experimentation; that it threatens identity and individuality; that it turns procreation into manufacture (especially when understood as the harbinger of manipulations to come); and that it means despotism over children and perversion of parenthood. Please note: I speak only about so-called reproductive cloning, not about the creation of cloned embryos for research. The objections that may be raised against creating (or using) embryos for research are entirely independent of whether the research embryos are produced by cloning. What is radically distinct and radically new is reproductive cloning.

Any attempt to clone a human being would constitute an unethical experiment upon the resulting child-to-be. In all the animal experiments, fewer than two to three percent of all cloning attempts succeeded. Not only are there fetal deaths and stillborn infants, but many of the so-called "successes" are in fact failures. As has only recently become clear, there is a very high incidence of major disabilities and deformities in cloned animals that attain live birth. Cloned cows often have heart and lung problems; cloned mice later develop pathological obesity; other live-born cloned animals fail to reach normal developmental milestones.

The problem, scientists suggest, may lie in the fact that an egg with a new somatic nucleus must re-program itself in a matter of minutes or hours (whereas the nucleus of an unaltered egg has been prepared over months and years). There is thus a greatly increased likelihood of error in translating the genetic instructions, leading to developmental defects some of which will show themselves only much later. (Note also that these induced abnormalities may also affect the stem cells that scientists hope to harvest from cloned embryos. Lousy embryos, lousy stem cells.) Nearly all scientists now agree that attempts to clone human beings carry massive risks of producing unhealthy, abnormal, and malformed children. What are we to do with them? Shall we just discard the ones that fall short of expectations? Considered opinion is today nearly unanimous, even among scientists: attempts at human cloning are irresponsible and unethical. We cannot ethically even get to know whether or not human cloning is feasible.

If it were successful, cloning would create serious issues of identity and individuality. The clone may experience concerns about his distinctive identity not only because he will be, in genotype and in appearance, identical to another human being, but because he may also be twin to the person who is his "father" or his "mother"—if one can still call them that. Unaccountably, people treat as innocent the homey case of intrafamilial cloning—the cloning of husband or wife (or single mother). They forget about the unique dangers of mixing the twin relation with the parent-child relation. (For this situation, the relation of contemporaneous twins is no precedent; yet even this less problematic situation teaches us how difficult it is to wrest independence from the being for whom one has the most powerful affinity.) Virtually no parent is going to be able to treat a clone of himself or herself as one treats a child generated by the lottery of sex. What will happen when the adolescent clone of Mommy becomes the spitting image of the woman with whom Daddy once fell in love? In case of divorce, will Mommy still love the clone of Daddy, even though she can no longer stand the sight of Daddy himself?

Most people think about cloning from the point of view of adults choosing to clone. Almost nobody thinks about what it would be like to be the cloned child. Surely his or her new life would constantly be scrutinized in relation to that of the older version. Even in the absence of unusual parental expectations for the clone—say, to live the same life, only without its errors—the child is likely to be ever a curiosity, ever a potential source of déjà vu. Unlike "normal" identical twins, a cloned individual—copied from whomever—will be saddled with a genotype that has already lived. He will not be fully a surprise to the world: people are likely always to compare his doings in life with those of his alter ego, especially if he is a clone of someone gifted or famous. True, his nurture and his circumstance will be different; genotype is not exactly destiny. But one must also expect parental efforts to shape this new life after the original—or at least to view the child with the original version always firmly in mind. For why else did they clone from the star basketball player, the mathematician, or the beauty queen—or even dear old Dad—in the first place?

Human cloning would also represent a giant step toward the transformation of begetting into making, of procreation into manufacture (literally "handmade"), a process that has already begun with in vitro fertilization and genetic testing of embryos. With cloning, not only is the process in hand, but the total genetic blueprint of the cloned individual is selected and determined by the human artisans. To be sure, subsequent development is still according to natural processes; and the resulting children will be recognizably human. But we would be taking a major step into making man himself simply another one of the man-made things.

How does begetting differ from making? In natural procreation, human beings come together to give existence to another being that is formed exactly as we were, by what we are—living, hence perishable, hence aspiringly erotic, hence procreative human beings. But in clonal reproduction, and in the more advanced forms of manufacture to which it will lead, we give existence to a being not by what we are but by what we intend and design.

Let me be clear. The problem is not the mere intervention of technique, and the point is not that "nature knows best." The problem is that any child whose being, character, and capacities exist owing to human design does not stand on the same plane as its makers. As with any product of our making, no matter how excellent, the artificer stands above it, not as an equal but as a superior, transcending it by his will and creative prowess. In human cloning, scientists and prospective "parents" adopt a technocratic attitude toward human children: human children become their artifacts. Such an arrangement is profoundly dehumanizing, no matter how good the product.

Procreation dehumanized into manufacture is further degraded by commodification, a virtually inescapable result of allowing baby-making to proceed under the banner of commerce. Genetic and reproductive biotechnology companies are already growth industries, but they will soon go into commercial orbit now that the Human Genome Project has been completed. "Human eggs for sale" is already a big business, masquerading under the pretense of "donation." Newspaper advertisements on elite college campuses offer up to $50,000 for an egg "donor" tall enough to play women's basketball and with SAT scores high enough for admis-

sion to Stanford; and to nobody's surprise, at such prices there are many young coeds eager to help shoppers obtain the finest babies money can buy. (The egg and womb-renting entrepreneurs shamelessly proceed on the ancient, disgusting, misogynist premise that most women will give you access to their bodies, if the price is right.) Even before the capacity for human cloning is perfected, established companies will have invested in the harvesting of eggs from ovaries obtained at autopsy or through ovarian surgery, practiced embryonic genetic alteration, and initiated the stockpiling of prospective donor tissues. Through the rental of surrogate-womb services, and through the buying and selling of tissues and embryos priced according to the merit of the donor, the commodification of nascent human life will be unstoppable.

Finally, the practice of human cloning by nuclear transfer—like other anticipated forms of genetically engineering the next generation—would enshrine and aggravate a profound misunderstanding of the meaning of living children and of the parent-child relationship. When a couple normally chooses to procreate, the partners are saying yes to the emergence of new life in its novelty—are saying yes not only to having a child, but also to having whatever child this child turns out to be. In accepting our finitude, in opening ourselves to our replacement we tacitly confess the limits of our control.

Embracing the future by procreating means precisely that we are relinquishing our grip in the very activity of taking up our own share in what we hope will be the immortality of human life and the human species. This means that our children are not our children: they are not our property, they are not our possessions. Neither are they supposed to live our lives for us, or to live anyone's life but their own. Their genetic distinctiveness and independence are the natural foreshadowing of the deep truth that they have their own, never-before-enacted life to live. Though sprung from a past, they take an uncharted course into the future.

Much mischief is already done by parents who try to live vicariously through their children. Children are sometimes compelled to fulfill the broken dreams of unhappy parents. But whereas most parents normally have hopes for their children, cloning parents will have expectations. In cloning, such overbearing parents will have taken at the start a decisive step that contradicts the entire meaning of the open and forward-looking nature of parent-child relations. The child is given a genotype that has already lived, with full expectation that this blueprint of a past life ought to be controlling the life that is to come. A wanted child now means a child who exists precisely to fulfill parental wants. Like all the more precise eugenic manipulations that will follow in its wake, cloning is thus inherently despotic, for it seeks to make one's children after one's own image (or an image of one's choosing) and their future according to one's will.

Is this hyperbolic? Consider concretely the new realities of responsibility and guilt in the households of the cloned. No longer only the sins of the parents, but also the genetic choices of the parents, will be visited on the children—and beyond the third and fourth generation; and everyone will know who is responsible. No parent will be able to blame nature or the lottery of sex for an unhappy adolescent's big nose, dull wit, musical ineptitude, nervous disposition, or anything else that he hates about himself. Fairly or not, children will hold their cloners responsible for everything, for nature as well as for

nurture. And parents, especially the better ones, will be limitlessly liable to guilt. Only the truly despotic souls will sleep the sleep of the innocent.

IV.

The defenders of cloning are not wittingly friends of despotism. Quite the contrary. Deaf to most other considerations, they regard themselves mainly as friends of freedom: the freedom of individuals to reproduce, the freedom of scientists and inventors to discover and to devise and to foster "progress" in genetic knowledge and technique, the freedom of entrepreneurs to profit in the market. They want large-scale cloning only for animals, but they wish to preserve cloning as a human option for exercising our "right to reproduce"—our right to have children, and children with "desirable genes." As some point out, under our "right to reproduce" we already practice early forms of unnatural, artificial, and extra-marital reproduction, and we already practice early forms of eugenic choice. For that reason, they argue, cloning is no big deal.

We have here a perfect example of the logic of the slippery slope. The principle of reproductive freedom currently enunciated by the proponents of cloning logically embraces the ethical acceptability of sliding all the way down: to producing children wholly in the laboratory from sperm to term (should it become feasible), and to producing children whose entire genetic makeup will be the product of parental eugenic planning and choice. If reproductive freedom means the right to have a child of one's own choosing by whatever means, then reproductive freedom knows and accepts no limits.

Proponents want us to believe that there are legitimate uses of cloning that can be distinguished from illegitimate uses, but by their own principles no such limits can be found. (Nor could any such limits be enforced in practice: once cloning is permitted, no one ever need discover whom one is cloning and why.) Reproductive freedom, as they understand it, is governed solely by the subjective wishes of the parents-to-be. The sentimentally appealing case of the childless married couple is, on these grounds, indistinguishable from the case of an individual (married or not) who would like to clone someone famous or talented, living or dead. And the principle here endorsed justifies not only cloning but also all future artificial attempts to create (manufacture) "better" or "perfect" babies.

The "perfect baby," of course, is the project not of the infertility doctors, but of the eugenic scientists and their supporters, who, for the time being, are content to hide behind the skirts of the partisans of reproductive freedom and compassion for the infertile. For them, the paramount right is not the so-called right to reproduce, it is what the biologist Bentley Glass called, a quarter of a century ago, "the right of every child to be born with a sound physical and mental constitution, based on a sound genotype... the inalienable right to a sound heritage." But to secure this right, and to achieve the requisite quality control over new human life, human conception and gestation will need to be brought fully into the bright light of the laboratory, beneath which the child-to-be can be fertilized, nourished, pruned, weeded, watched, inspected, prodded, pinched, cajoled, injected, tested, rated, graded, approved, stamped, wrapped, sealed, and delivered. There is no other way to produce the perfect baby.

If you think that such scenarios require outside coercion or governmental tyranny, you are mistaken. Once it becomes possible, with the aid of human genomics, to produce or to select for what some regard as "better babies"—smarter, prettier, healthier, more athletic—parents will leap at the opportunity to "improve" their offspring. Indeed, not to do so will be socially regarded as a form of child neglect. Those who would ordinarily be opposed to such tinkering will be under enormous pressure to compete on behalf of their as yet unborn children—just as some now plan almost from their children's birth how to get them into Harvard. Never mind that, lacking a standard of "good" or "better," no one can really know whether any such changes will truly be improvements.

Proponents of cloning urge us to forget about the science-fiction scenarios of laboratory manufacture or multiple-copy clones, and to focus only on the sympathetic cases of infertile couples exercising their reproductive rights. But why, if the single cases are so innocent, should multiplying their performance be so off-putting? (Similarly, why do others object to people's making money from that practice if the practice itself is perfectly acceptable?) The so-called science-fiction cases—say, *Brave New World*—make vivid the meaning of what looks to us, mistakenly, to be benign. They reveal that what looks like compassionate humanitarianism is, in the end, crushing dehumanization.

V.

Wheather or not they share my reasons, most people, I think, share my conclusion: that human cloning is unethical in itself and dangerous in its likely consequences, which include the precedent that it will establish for designing our children. Some reach this conclusion for their own good reasons, different from my own: concerns about distributive justice in access to eugenic cloning; worries about the genetic effects of asexual "inbreeding"; aversion to the implicit premise of genetic determinism; objections to the embryonic and fetal wastage that must necessarily accompany the efforts; religious opposition to "man playing God." But never mind why: the overwhelming majority of our fellow Americans remain firmly opposed to cloning human beings.

For us, then, the real questions are: What should we do about it? How can we best succeed? These questions should concern everyone eager to secure deliberate human control over the powers that could re-design our humanity, even if cloning is not the issue over which they would choose to make their stand. And the answer to the first question seems pretty plain. What we should do is work to prevent human cloning by making it illegal.

We should aim for a global legal ban, if possible, and for a unilateral national ban at a minimum—and soon, before the fact is upon us. To be sure, legal bans can be violated; but we certainly curtail much mischief by outlawing incest, voluntary servitude, and the buying and selling of organs and babies. To be sure, renegade scientists may secretly undertake to violate such a law, but we can deter them by both criminal sanctions and monetary penalties, as well as by removing any incentive they have to proudly claim credit for their technological bravado.

Such a ban on clonal baby-making will not harm the progress of basic genetic science and technology. On the contrary, it will reassure the public that scientists are happy to proceed without violating the deep ethical norms and intuitions of the human community. It will also protect honorable scientists from a public backlash against the brazen misconduct of the rogues. As many scientists have publicly confessed, free and worthy science probably has much more to fear from a strong public reaction to a cloning fiasco than it does from a cloning ban, provided that

the ban is judiciously crafted and vigorously enforced against those who would violate it....

I now believe that what we need is an all-out ban on human cloning, including the creation of embryonic clones. I am convinced that all halfway measures will prove to be morally, legally, and strategically flawed and—most important—that they will not be effective in obtaining the desired result. Anyone truly serious about preventing, human reproductive cloning must seek to stop the process from the beginning. Our changed circumstances, and the now evident defects of the less restrictive alternatives, make an all-out ban by far the most attractive and effective option.

Here's why. Creating cloned human children ("reproductive cloning") necessarily begins by producing cloned human embryos. Preventing the latter would prevent the former, and prudence alone might counsel building such a "fence around the law." Yet some scientists favor embryo cloning as a way of obtaining embryos for research or as sources of cell and tissues for the possible benefit of others. (This practice they misleadingly call "therapeutic cloning" rather than the more accurate "cloning for research" or "experimental cloning," so as to obscure the fact that the clone will be "treated" only to exploitation and destruction, and that any potential future beneficiaries and any future "therapies" are at this point purely hypothetical.)

The prospect of creating new human life solely to be exploited in this way has been condemned on moral grounds by many people—including *The Washington Post*, President Clinton, and many other supporters of a woman's right to abortion—as displaying a profound disrespect for life. Even those who are willing to scavenge so-called "spare embryos"—

those products of in vitro fertilization made in excess of peoples reproductive needs, and otherwise likely to be discarded—draw back from creating human embryos explicitly and solely for research purposes. They reject outright what they regard as the exploitation and the instrumentalization of nascent human life. In addition, others who are agnostic about the moral status of the embryo see the wisdom of not needlessly offending the sensibilities of their fellow citizens who are opposed to such practices.

But even setting aside these obvious moral first impressions, a few moments reflection show why an anti-cloning law that permitted the cloning of embryos but criminalized their transfer to produce a child would be a moral blunder. This would be a law that was not merely permissively "pro-choice" but emphatically and prescriptively "anti-life." While permitting the creation of an embryonic life it would make it a federal offense to try to keep it alive and bring it to birth. Whatever one thinks of the moral status or the ontological status of the human embryo, moral sense and practical wisdom recoil from having the government of the United States on record as requiring the destruction of nascent life and, what is worse, demanding the punishment of those who would act to preserve it by (feloniously!) giving it birth.

But the problem with the approach that targets only reproductive cloning (that is, the transfer of the embryo to a woman's uterus) is not only moral but also legal and strategic. A ban only on reproductive cloning would turn out to be unenforceable. Once cloned embryos were produced and available in laboratories and assisted-reproduction centers, it would be virtually impossible to control what was done with them. Biotechnical experiments take place in laboratories, hidden from

public view, and, given the rise of high-stakes commerce in biotechnology, these experiments are concealed from the competition. Huge stockpiles of cloned human embryos could thus be produced and bought and sold without anyone knowing it. As we have seen with in vitro embryos created to treat infertility, embryos produced for one reason can be used for another reason: today "spare embryos" once created to begin a pregnancy are now used in research, and tomorrow clones created for research will be used to begin a pregnancy.

Assisted reproduction takes place within the privacy of the doctor-patient relationship, making outside scrutiny extremely difficult. Many infertility experts probably would obey the law, but others could and would defy it with impunity, their doings covered by the veil of secrecy that is the principle of medical confidentiality. Moreover, the transfer of embryos to begin a pregnancy is a simple procedure (especially compared with manufacturing the embryo in the first place), simple enough that its final steps could be self-administered by the woman, who would thus absolve the doctor of blame for having "caused" the illegal transfer. (I have in mind something analogous to Kevorkian's suicide machine, which was designed to enable the patient to push the plunger and the good "doctor" to evade criminal liability.)

Even should the deed become known, governmental attempts to enforce the reproductive ban would run into a swarm of moral and legal challenges, both to efforts aimed at preventing transfer to a woman and—even worse—to efforts seeking to prevent birth after transfer has occurred. A woman who wished to receive the embryo clone would no doubt seek a judicial restraining order, suing to have the law overturned in the name of a constitutionally protected interest in her own reproductive choice to clone. (The cloned child would be born before the legal proceedings were complete.) And should an "illicit clonal pregnancy" be discovered, no governmental agency would compel a woman to abort the clone, and there would be an understandable storm of protest should she be fined or jailed after she gives birth. Once the baby is born, there would even be sentimental opposition to punishing the doctor for violating the law—unless, of course, the clone turned out to be severely abnormal.

For all these reasons, the only practically effective and legally sound approach is to block human cloning at the start, at the production of the embryo clone. Such a ban can be rightly characterized not as interference with reproductive freedom, nor even as interference with scientific inquiry, but as an attempt to prevent the unhealthy, unsavory, and unwelcome manufacture of and traffic in human clones.

VI.

Some scientists, pharmaceutical companies, and bio-entrepreneurs may balk at such a comprehensive restriction. They want to get their hands on those embryos, especially for their stem cells, those pluripotent cells that can in principle be turned into any cells and any tissues in the body, potentially useful for transplantation to repair somatic damage. Embryonic stem cells need not come from cloned embryos, of course; but the scientists say that stem cells obtained from clones could be therapeutically injected into the embryo's adult "twin" without any risk of immunological rejection. It is the promise of rejection-free tissues for transplantation that so far has been the most successful argument in favor of experimental cloning. Yet new discoveries have shown that we can probably obtain the same benefits without em-

bryo cloning. The facts are much different than they were three years ago, and the weight in the debate about cloning, for research should shift to reflect the facts.

Numerous recent studies have shown that it is possible to obtain highly potent stem cells from the bodies of children and adults—from the blood, bone marrow, brain, pancreas, and, most recently, fat. Beyond all expectations, these non-embryonic stem cells have been shown to have the capacity to turn into a wide variety of specialized cells and tissues. (At the same time, early human therapeutic efforts with stem cells derived from embryos have produced some horrible results, the cells going wild in their new hosts and producing other tissues in addition to those in need of replacement. If an in vitro embryo is undetectably abnormal—as so often they are—the cells derived from it may also be abnormal.) Since cells derived from our own bodies are more easily and cheaply available than cells harvested from specially manufactured clones, we will almost surely be able to obtain from ourselves any needed homologous transplantable cells and tissues, without the need for egg donors or cloned embryonic copies of ourselves. By pouring our resources into *adult* stem cell research (or, more accurately, "nonembryonic" stem cell research), we can also avoid the morally and legally vexing issues in embryo research. And more to our present subject, by eschewing the cloning of embryos, we make the cloning of human beings much less likely.

A few weeks ago an excellent federal anti-cloning bill was introduced in Congress, sponsored by Senator Sam Brownback and Representative David Weldon. This carefully drafted legislation seeks to prevent the cloning of human beings at the very first step, by prohibiting somatic cell nuclear transfer to produce embryonic clones, and provides substantial criminal and monetary penalties for violating the law. The bill makes very clear that there is to be no interference with the scientific and medically useful practices of cloning DNA fragments (molecular cloning), with the duplication of somatic cells (or stem cells) in tissue culture (cell cloning), or with whole-organism or embryo cloning of non-human animals. If enacted, this law would bring the United States into line with the current or soon-to-be-enacted practices of many other nations. Most important, it offers us the best chance—the only realistic chance—that we have to keep human cloning from happening, or from happening much.

Getting this bill passed will not be easy. The pharmaceutical and biotech companies and some scientific and patient-advocacy associations may claim that the bill is the work of bio-Luddites: anti-science, a threat to free inquiry, an obstacle to obtaining urgently needed therapies for disease. Some feminists and pro-choice groups will claim that this legislation is really only a sneaky device for fighting *Roe* v. *Wade*, and they will resist anything that might be taken even to hint that a human embryo has any moral worth. On the other side, some right-to-life purists, who care not how babies are made as long as life will not be destroyed, will withhold their support because the bill does not take a position against embryo twinning or embryo research in general.

All of these arguments are wrong, and all of them must be resisted. This is not an issue of pro-life versus pro-choice. It is not about death and destruction, or about a woman's right to choose. It is only and emphatically about baby design and manufacture: the opening skirmish of a long battle against eugenics and against a post-

human future. As such, it is an issue that should not divide "the left" and "the right"; and there are people across the political spectrum who are coalescing in the efforts to stop human cloning. (The prime sponsor of Michigan's comprehensive anti cloning law is a pro-choice Democratic legislator.) Everyone needs to understand that, whatever we may think about the moral status of embryos, once embryonic clones are produced in the laboratories the eugenic revolution will have begun. And we shall have lost our best chance to do anything about it.

As we argue in the coming weeks about this legislation, let us be clear about the urgency of our situation and the meaning of our action or inaction. Scientists and doctors whose names we know, and probably many others whose names we do not know are today working to clone human beings. They are aware of the immediate hazards, but they are undeterred. They are prepared to screen and to destroy anything that looks abnormal. They do not care that they will not be able to detect most of the possible defects. So confident are they in their rectitude that they are willing to ignore all future consequences of the power to clone human beings. They are prepared to gamble with the well-being of any live-born clones, and, if I am right, with a great deal more, all for the glory of being the first to replicate a human being. They are, in short, daring the community to defy them. In these circumstances, our silence can only mean acquiescence. To do nothing now is to accept the responsibility for the deed and for all that follows predictably in its wake.

I appreciate that a federal legislative ban on human cloning is without American precedent, at least in matters technological. Perhaps such a ban will prove ineffective; perhaps it will eventually be shown to have been a mistake. (If so, it could later be reversed.) If enacted, however, it will have achieved one overwhelmingly important result, in addition to its contribution to thwarting cloning: it will place the burden of practical proof where it belongs. It will require the proponents to show very clearly what great social or medical good can be had only by the cloning of human beings. Surely it is only for such a compelling case, yet to be made or even imagined, that we should wish to risk this major departure—or any other major departure—in human procreation.

Americans have lived by and prospered under a rosy optimism about scientific and technological progress. The technological imperative has probably served us well, though we should admit that there is no accurate method for weighing benefits and harms. And even when we recognize the unwelcome outcomes of technological advance, we remain confident in our ability to fix all the "bad" consequences—by regulation or by means of still newer and better technologies. Yet there is very good reason for shifting the American paradigm, at least regarding those technological interventions into the human body and mind that would surely effect fundamental (and likely irreversible) changes in human nature, basic human relationships, and what it means to be a human being. Here we should not be willing to risk everything in the naïve hope that, should

things go wrong, we can later set them right again.

Some have argued that cloning is almost certainly going to remain a marginal practice, and that we should therefore permit people to practice it. Such a view is shortsighted. Even if cloning is rarely undertaken, a society in which it is tolerated is no longer the same society- any more than is a society that permits (even small-scale) incest or cannibalism or slavery. A society that allows cloning, whether it knows it or not, has tacitly assented to the conversion of procreation into manufacture and to the treatment of children as purely the projects of our will. Willy-nilly, it has acquiesced in the eugenic re-design of future generations. The humanitarian superhighway to a Brave New World lies open before this society.

But the present danger posed by human cloning is, paradoxically, also a golden opportunity. In a truly unprecedented way, we can strike a blow for the human control of the technological project, for wisdom, for prudence, for human dignity. The prospect of human cloning, so repulsive to contemplate, is the occasion for deciding whether we shall be slaves of unregulated innovation, and ultimately its artifacts, or whether we shall remain free human beings who guide our powers toward the enhancement of human dignity. The humanity of the human future is now in our hands.

Cloning:
Potential Benefit

DAN W. BROCK

INTRODUCTION

The world of science and the public at large were both shocked and fascinated by the announcement in the journal *Nature* by Ian Wilmut and his colleagues that they had successfully cloned a sheep from a single cell of an adult sheep. Scientists were in part surprised, because many had believed that after the very early stage of embryo development at which differentiation of cell function begins to take place, it would not be possible to achieve cloning of an adult mammal by nuclear transfer. In this process, the nucleus from the cell of an adult mammal is inserted into an ennucleated ovum, and the resulting embryo develops following the complete genetic code of the mammal from which the inserted nucleus was obtained. But some scientists and much of the public were troubled or apparently even horrified at the prospect that if adult mammals such as sheep could be cloned, then cloning of adult humans by the same process would likely be possible as well....

The response of most scientific and political leaders to the prospect of human cloning, indeed of Dr. Wilmut as well, was of immediate and strong condemnation. In the United States, President Clinton immediately banned federal financing of human cloning research and asked privately funded scientists to halt such work until the newly formed National Bioethics Advisory Commission could review the "troubling" ethical and legal implications.... Around the world similar immediate condemnation was heard, as human cloning was called a violation of human rights and human dignity.

A few more cautious voices were heard, both suggesting some possible benefits from the use of human cloning in limited circumstances and questioning its too quick prohibition, but they were a clear minority. In the popular media, nightmare scenarios of laboratory mistakes resulting in monsters, the cloning of armies of Hitlers, the exploitative use of cloning for totalitarian ends as in Huxley's *Brave New World*, and the murderous replicas of the film *Blade Runner*, all fed the public controversy and uneasiness. A striking feature of these early responses was that their strength and intensity seemed to far outrun the arguments and reasons offered in support of them—they seemed often to be "gut level" emotional reactions rather than considered reflections on the issues. Such reactions should not be simply dismissed, both because they may point us to important considerations otherwise missed and not easily articulated, and because they often have a major impact on public policy. But the formation of public policy should not ignore the moral reasons and arguments that bear on the practice of human cloning—these must be articulated in order to understand and inform people's more immediate emotional responses. This paper is an effort to articulate, and to evaluate critically, the main moral considerations and arguments for and against human cloning....

Moral Arguments in Support of Human Cloning

A. Is There a Moral Right to Use Human Cloning?

What moral right might protect at least some access to the use of human cloning? Some commentators have argued that a commitment to individual liberty, as defended by J. S. Mill, requires that individuals be left free to use human cloning if they so choose and if their doing so does not cause significant harms to others, but liberty is too broad in scope to be an uncontroversial moral right. Human cloning is a means of reproduction (in the most literal sense), and so the most plausible moral right at stake in its use is a right to reproductive freedom or procreative liberty. Reproductive freedom includes not only the familiar right to choose not to reproduce, for example by means of contraception or abortion, but also the right to reproduce. The right to reproductive freedom is properly understood to include as well the use of various artificial reproductive technologies, such as in vitro fertilization (IVF), oocyte donation, and so forth. The reproductive right relevant to human cloning is a negative right, that is, a right to use assisted reproductive technologies without interference by the government or others when made available by a willing provider. The choice of an assisted means of reproduction, such as surrogacy, can be defended as included within reproductive freedom, even when it is not the only means for individuals to reproduce, just as the choice among different means of preventing conception is protected by reproductive freedom. However, the case for permitting the use of a particular means of reproduction is strongest when that means is necessary for particular individuals to be able to procreate at all. Sometimes human cloning could be the only means for individuals to procreate while retaining a biological tie to the child created, but in other cases different means of procreating would also be possible.

It could be argued that human cloning is not covered by the right to reproductive freedom, because whereas current assisted reproductive technologies and practices covered by that right are remedies for inabilities to reproduce sexually, human cloning is an entirely new means of reproduction; indeed, its critics see it as more a means of manufacturing humans than of reproduction. Human cloning is a different means of reproduction than sexual reproduction, but it is a means that can serve individuals' interest in reproducing. If it is not covered by the moral right to reproductive freedom, I believe that must be not because it is a new means of reproducing, but instead because it has other objectionable moral features, such as eroding human dignity or uniqueness. We shall evaluate these other ethical objections to it below....

Accepting a moral right to reproductive freedom that includes the use of human cloning does not settle the moral issue about human cloning, however, since there may be other moral rights in conflict with this right, or serious enough harms from human cloning to override the right to use it; this right can be thought of as establishing a serious moral presumption supporting access to human cloning....

B. What Individual or Social Benefits Might Human Cloning Produce?

Largely Individual Benefits

... What are the principal benefits of human cloning that might give persons good reasons to want to use it?

1. Human cloning would be a new means to relieve the infertility some persons now experience. Human cloning would allow women who have no ova or men who have no sperm to produce an offspring that is biologically related to them....

It is not enough to point to the large number of children throughout the world possibly available for adoption as a solution to infertility, unless we are prepared to discount as illegitimate the strong desire many persons, fertile and infertile, have for the experience of pregnancy and for having and raising a child biologically related to them. While not important to all infertile (or fertile) individuals, it is important to many and is respected and met through other forms of assisted reproduction that maintain a biological connection when that is possible; there seems no good reason to refuse to respect and respond to it when human cloning would be the best or only means of overcoming an individual's infertility.

2. Human cloning would enable couples in which one party risks transmitting a serious heredity disease, a serious risk of disease, or an otherwise harmful condition to an offspring, to reproduce without doing so. Of course, by using donor sperm or egg donation, such hereditary risks can generally be avoided now without the use of human cloning. These procedures may be unacceptable to some couples, however, or at least considered less desirable than human cloning, because they introduce a third party's genes into reproduction, instead of giving the couple's offspring only the genes of one of them. Thus, in some cases human cloning would be a means of preventing genetically transmitted harms to offspring....

3. Human cloning a later twin would enable a person to obtain needed organs or tissues for transplantation. Human cloning would solve the problem of finding a transplant donor who is an acceptable organ or tissue match and would eliminate, or drastically reduce, the risk of transplant rejection by the host....

Such a practice has been criticized on the ground that it treats the later twin not as a person valued and loved for his or her own sake, as an end in itself in Kantian terms, but simply as a means for benefiting another. This criticism assumes, however, that only this one motive would determine the relation of the person to his or her later twin. The well-known case some years ago in California of the Ayala family, who conceived in the hopes of obtaining a source for a bone marrow transplant for their teenage daughter suffering from leukemia, illustrates the mistake in this assumption. They argued that whether or not the child they conceived turned out to be a possible donor for their daughter, they would value and love the child for itself, and treat it as they would treat any other member of their family. That one reason it was wanted was as a means to saving their daughter's life did not preclude its also being loved and valued for its own sake; in Kantian terms, it was treated as a possible means to saving their daughter, but not *solely as a means*, which is what the Kantian view proscribes.

Indeed, when people have children, whether by sexual means or with the aid of assisted reproductive technologies, their motives and reasons for doing so are typically many and complex, and include reasons less laudable than obtaining life-saving medical treatment, such as having a companion like a doll to play with, enabling one to live on one's own, qualifying for public or government benefit programs, and so forth. While these other motives for having children sometimes may not bode well for the child's upbringing and future, public policy does not assess prospective parents' motives and reasons for procreating as a condition of their doing so....

4. Human cloning would enable individuals to clone someone who had special meaning to them, such as a child who had died. There is no denying that if human cloning were available, some individuals would want to use it in order to clone someone who had special meaning to them, such as a child who had died, but that desire usually would be based on a deep confusion. Cloning such a child would not replace the child the parents had loved and lost, but rather would create a new and different child with the same genes. The child they loved and lost was a unique individual who had been shaped by his or her environment and choices, not just his or her genes, and more important, who had experienced a particular relationship with them. Even if the later cloned child could have not only the same genes but also be subjected to the same environment, which of course is in fact impossible, it would remain a different child than the one they had loved and lost, because it would share a different history with them. Cloning the lost child might help the parents accept and move on from their loss, but another already existing sibling or another new child who was not a clone might do this equally well; indeed, it might do so better, since the appearance of the cloned later twin would be a constant reminder of the child they had lost. Nevertheless, if human cloning enabled some individuals to clone a person who had special meaning to them and doing so gave them deep satisfaction, that would be a benefit to them even if their reasons for wanting to do so, and the satisfaction they in turn received, were based on confusion.

Largely Social Benefits

5. Human cloning would enable the duplication of individuals of great talent, genius, character, or other exemplary qualities. The first four reasons for human cloning considered above looked to benefits to specific individuals, usually parents, from being able to reproduce by means of human cloning. This fifth reason looks to benefits to the broader society from being able to replicate extraordinary individuals—a Mozart, Einstein, Gandhi, or Schweitzer. Much of the appeal of this reason, like much thinking both in support of and in opposition to human cloning, rests on a confused and mistaken assumption of genetic determinism, that is, that one's genes fully determine what one will become, do, and accomplish. What made Mozart, Einstein, Gandhi, and Schweitzer the extraordinary individuals they were was the confluence of their particular genetic endowments with the environments in which they were raised and lived and the particular historical moments they in different ways seized. Cloning them would produce individuals with the same genetic inheritances (nuclear transfer does not even produce 100% genetic identity, although for the sake of exploring the moral issues, I have followed the common assumption that it does). But neither by cloning, nor by any other means, would it be possible to replicate their environments or the historical contexts in which they lived and their greatness flourished. We do not know, either in general or with any particular individual, the degree or specific respects in which their greatness depended on their "nature" or their "nurture," but we do know in all cases that it depended on an interaction of them both. Thus, human cloning could never replicate the extraordinary accomplishments for which we admire individuals like Mozart, Einstein, Gandhi, and Schweitzer....

Although there is considerable uncertainty concerning most of the possible individual and social benefits of human cloning that I have discussed above, and although no doubt it may have other benefits or uses that we cannot yet envisage, I believe it is reasonable to conclude that human cloning at this time does not seem to promise great benefits or uniquely to meet great human needs. Nevertheless, a case can be made that scientific freedom supports permitting research on human cloning to go forward and that freedom to use human cloning is protected by the important moral right to reproductive freedom. We must therefore assess what moral rights might be violated, or harms produced, by research on or use of human cloning.

Moral Arguments Against Human Cloning

A. Would the Use of Human Cloning Violate Important Moral Rights?

... Is there a moral or human right to a unique identity, and if so, would it be violated by human cloning? For human cloning to violate a right to a unique identity, the relevant sense of identity would have to be genetic identity, that, is a right to a unique unrepeated genome. This would be violated by human cloning, but is there any such right?...

What is the sense of identity that might plausibly be each person['s] right to have uniquely, which constitutes the special uniqueness of each individual? Even with the same genes, two individuals, for example homozygous twins, are numerically distinct and not identical, so what is intended must be the various properties and characteristics that make each individual qualitatively unique and different than others. Does having the same genome as another person undermine that unique qualitative identity? Only in the crudest genetic determinism, a genetic determinism according to which an individual's genes completely and decisively determine everything about the individual, all his or her other non-genetic features and properties, together with the entire history or biography that will constitute his or her life. But there is no reason whatever to believe in that kind of genetic determinism, and I do not think that anyone does. Even with the same genes, as we know from the cases of genetically identical twins, while there may be many important similarities in the twins' psychological and personal characteristics, differences in these develop over time together with differences in their life histories, personal relationships, and life choices. This is true of identical twins raised together, and the differences are still greater in the cases of identical twins raised apart; sharing an identical genome does not prevent twins from each developing a distinct and unique personal identity of their own.

We need not pursue what the basis or argument in support of a moral or human right to a unique identity might be—such a right is not found among typical accounts and enumerations of moral or human rights—because even if we grant that there is such a right, sharing a genome with another individual as a result of human cloning would not violate it. The idea of the uniqueness, or unique identity, of each person historically predates the development of modern genetics and the knowledge that except in the case of homozygous twins, each individual has a unique genome. A unique genome thus could not be the grounds of this long-standing belief in the unique human identity of each person....

B. What Individual or Social Harms Might Human Cloning Produce?

There are many possible individual or social harms that have been posited by one or another commentator, and I shall only try to cover the more plausible and significant of them.

Largely Individual Harms

1. Human cloning would produce psychological distress and harm in the later twin.

This is perhaps the most serious individual harm that opponents of human cloning foresee.... No doubt knowing the path in life taken by one's earlier twin may in many cases have several bad psychological effects. The later twin may feel, even if mistakenly, that his or her fate has already been substantially laid out, and so have difficulty freely and spontaneously taking responsibility for and making his or her own fate and life. The later twin's experience or sense of autonomy and freedom may be substantially diminished, even if in actual fact they are diminished much less than it seems to him or her. Together with this might be a diminished sense of one's own uniqueness and individuality, even if once again these are in fact diminished little or not at all by having an earlier twin with the same genome. If the later twin is the clone of a particularly exemplary individual, perhaps with some special capabilities and accomplishments, he or she may experience excessive pressure to reach the very high standards of ability and accomplishment of the earlier twin. All of these psychological effects may take a heavy toll on the later twin and be serious burdens under which he or she would live....

While psychological harms of these kinds from human cloning are certainly possible, and perhaps even likely, they remain at this point only speculative, since we have no experience with human cloning and the creation of earlier and later twins. With naturally occurring identical twins, while they sometimes struggle to achieve their own identities (a struggle shared by many people without a twin), there is typically a very strong emotional bond between the twins, and such twins are, if anything, generally psychologically stronger and better adjusted than non-twins. Scenarios are even possible in which being a later twin confers a psychological benefit. For example, having been deliberately cloned with specific genes might make the later twin feel especially wanted for the kind of person he or she is. Nevertheless, if experience with human cloning confirmed that serious and unavoidable psychological harms typically occurred to the later twin, that would be a serious moral reason to avoid the practice....

2. Human cloning procedures would carry unacceptable risks to the clone.

One version of this objection to human cloning concerns the research necessary to perfect the procedure. The other version concerns the later risks from its use. Wilmut's group had 276 failures before their success with Dolly, indicating that the procedure is far from perfected, even with sheep. Further research on the procedure with animals is clearly necessary before it would be ethical to use the procedure on humans. But even assuming that cloning's safety and effectiveness is established with animals, research would need to be done to establish its safety and effectiveness for humans. Could this research be ethically done? There would be little or no risk to the donor of the cell nucleus to be transferred, and his or her informed consent could and must always be obtained. There might be greater risks for the woman to whom a cloned embryo is transferred, but these should be comparable to those associated with IVF procedures. The woman's informed consent, too, could and must be obtained.

What of the risks to the cloned embryo itself? Judging by the experience of Wilmut's group in their work on cloning a sheep, the principal risk to the embryos cloned was their failure successfully to implant, grow, and develop. Comparable risks to cloned human embryos would apparently be their death or destruction long before most people or the law consider them to be persons with moral or legal protections of life. Moreover, artificial reproductive technologies now in use, such as IVF, have a known risk that some embryos will be destroyed or will not successfully implant and will die. It is premature to make a confident assessment of what the risks to human subjects would be of establishing the safety and effectiveness of human cloning procedures, but there are no unavoidable risks apparent at this time that would make the necessary research clearly ethically impermissible.

Could human cloning procedures meet ethical standards of safety and efficacy? Risks to an ovum donor (if any), a nucleus donor, and a woman who receives the embryo for implantation would likely be ethically acceptable with the informed consent of the involved parties. But what of the risks to the human clone if the procedure in some way goes wrong, or unanticipated harms come to the clone? For example, Harold Varrnus, director of the National Institutes of Health, has raised the concern that a cell many years old from which a person is cloned could have accumulated genetic mutations during its years in another adult that could give the resulting clone a predisposition to cancer or other diseases of aging. Moreover, it is impossible to obtain the informed consent of the clone to his or her own creation, but, of course, no one else is able to give informed consent for their creation, either.

I believe it is too soon to say whether unavoidable risks to the clone would make human cloning unethical. At a minimum, further research on cloning animals, as well as research to better define the potential risks to humans, is needed.... We should not insist on a standard that requires risks to be lower than those we accept in sexual reproduction, or in other forms of assisted reproduction. It is not possible now to know when, if ever, human cloning will satisfy an appropriate standard limiting risks to the clone.

Largely Social Harms

3. Human cloning would lessen the worth of individuals and diminish respect for human life.

Unelaborated claims to this effect were common in the media after the announcement of the cloning of Dolly. Ruth Mackim has explored and criticized the claim that human cloning would diminish the value we place on, and our respect for, human life, because it would lead to persons being viewed as replaceable. As argued above, only in a confused and indefensible notion of human identity is a person's identity determined solely by his or her genes. Instead, individuals' identities are determined by the interaction of their genes over time with their environments, including the choices the individuals make and the important relations they form with other persons. This means in turn that no individual could be fully replaced by a later clone possessing the same genes. Ordinary people recognize this clearly. For example, parents of a 12-year-old child dying of a fatal disease would consider it insensitive and ludicrous if someone told them they should not grieve for their coming loss because it is possible to replace him by cloning him; it is *their child who is dying*, whom they love and value, and that child and his importance to them could never be replaced by a cloned later twin. Even if they would also come to love and value a later twin as much as their child who is dying, that would be to love and value that *different child* who could never replace the child they lost. Ordinary people are typically quite clear about the importance of the relations they have to distinct, historically situated individuals with whom over time they have shared experiences and their lives, and whose loss to them would therefore be irreplaceable.

A different version of this worry is that human cloning would result in persons' worth or value seeming diminished because we would now see humans as able to be manufactured or "handmade." This demystification of the creation of human life would reduce our appreciation and awe of it and of its natural creation. It would be a mistake, however, to conclude that a human being created by human cloning is of less value or is less worthy of respect than one created by sexual reproduction. It is the nature of a being, not how it is created, that is the source of its value and makes it worthy of respect. Moreover, for many people, gaining a scientific understanding of the extraordinary complexity of human reproduction and development increases, instead of decreases, their awe of the process and its product.

A more subtle route by which the value we place on each individual human life might be diminished could come from the use of human cloning with the aim of creating a child with a particular genome, either the genome of another individual especially meaningful to those doing the cloning or an individual with exceptional talents, abilities, and accomplishments. The child might then be valued only for his or her genome, or at least for his or her genome's expected phenotypic expression, and no longer be recognized as having the intrinsic equal moral value of all persons, simply as persons. For the moral value and respect due all persons to be seen as resting only on the instrumental value of individuals, or of individuals' particular qualities, to others would be to fundamentally change the moral status accorded to persons. Everyone would lose their moral standing as full and equal members of the moral community, replaced by the different instrumental value each of us has to others.

Such a change in the equal moral value and worth accorded to persons should be avoided at all costs, but it is far from clear that such a change would take place from permitting human cloning. Parents, for example, are quite capable of distinguishing their children's intrinsic value, just as individual persons, from their instrumental value based on their particular qualities or properties. The equal moral value and respect due all persons just as persons is not incompatible with the different instrumental value of people's particular qualities or properties. Einstein and an untalented physics graduate student have vastly different value as scientists, but share and are entitled to equal moral value and respect as persons. It would be a mistake and a confusion to conflate the two kinds of value and respect. Making a large number of clones from one original person might be more likely to foster this mistake and confusion in the public. If so, that would be a further reason to limit the number of clones that could be made from one individual.

4. Human cloning would divert resources from other more important social and medical needs.

As we saw in considering the reasons for, and potential benefits from, human cloning, in only a limited number of uses would it uniquely meet important human needs. There is little doubt that in the United States, and certainly elsewhere, there are more pressing unmet human needs, both medical or health needs and other social or individual needs. This is a reason for not using public funds to support human cloning, at least if the funds actually are redirected to more important ends and needs. It is not a reason, however, either to prohibit other private individuals or institutions from using their own resources for research on human cloning or for human cloning itself, or to prohibit human cloning or research on human cloning.

The other important point about resource use is that it is not now clear how expensive human cloning would ultimately be, for example, in comparison with other means of relieving infertility. The procedure itself is not scientifically or technologically extremely complex and might prove not to require a significant commitment of resources.

5. Human cloning might be used by commercial interests for financial gain.

Both opponents and proponents of human cloning agree that cloned embryos should not be able to be bought and sold. In a science fiction frame of mind, one can imagine commercial interests offering genetically certified and guaranteed embryos for sale, perhaps offering a catalogue of different embryos cloned from individuals with a variety of talents, capacities, and other desirable properties. This would be a fundamental violation of the equal moral respect and dignity owed to all persons, treating them instead as objects to be differentially valued, bought, and sold in the marketplace. Even if embryos are not yet persons at the time they would be purchased or sold, they would be valued, bought, and sold for the persons they will become. The moral consensus against any commercial market in embryos, cloned or otherwise, should be enforced by law, whatever public policy ultimately is created to address human cloning....

6. Human cloning might be used by governments or other groups for immoral and exploitative purposes.

In *Brave New World*, Aldous Huxley imagined cloning individuals who have been engineered with limited abilities and conditioned to do, and to be happy doing, the menial work that society needed done. Selection and control in the creation of people was exercised not in the interests of the persons created, but in the interests of society and at the expense of the persons created. Any use of human cloning for such purposes would exploit the clones solely as means for the benefit of others, and would violate the equal moral respect and dignity they are owed as full moral persons. If human cloning is permitted to go forward, it should be with regulations that would clearly prohibit such immoral exploitation.

Fiction contains even more disturbing and bizarre uses of human cloning, such as Mengele's creation of many clones of Hitler in Ira Levin's *The Boys from Brazil*, Woody Allen's science fiction cinematic spoof *Sleeper*, in which a dictator's only remaining part, his nose, must be destroyed to keep it from being cloned, and the contemporary science fiction film *Blade Runner*. Nightmare scenarios like Huxley's or Levin's may be quite improbable, but their impact should not be underestimated on public concern with technologies like human cloning. Regulation of human cloning must assure the public that even such farfetched abuses will not take place.

7. Human cloning used on a very widespread basis would have a disastrous effect on the human gene pool by reducing genetic diversity and our capacity to adapt to new conditions.

This is not a realistic concern since human cloning would not be used on a wide enough scale, substantially replacing sexual reproduction, to have the feared effect on the gene pool. The vast majority of humans seem quite satisfied with sexual means of reproduction; if anything, from the standpoint of worldwide population, we could do with a bit less enthusiasm for it. Programs of eugenicists like Herman Mueller earlier in the century to impregnate thousands of women with the sperm of exceptional men, as well as the more recent establishment of sperm banks of Nobel laureates, have met with little or no public interest or success. People prefer sexual means of reproduction, and they prefer to keep their own biological ties to their offspring.

CONCLUSION

Human cloning has until now received little serious and careful ethical attention, because it was typically dismissed as science fiction, and it stirs deep, but difficult to articulate, uneasiness and even revulsion in many people. Any ethical assessment of human cloning at this point must be tentative and provisional. Fortunately, the science and technology of human cloning are not yet in hand, and so a public and professional debate is possible without the need for a hasty, precipitate policy response.

The ethical pros and cons of human cloning, as I see them at this time, are sufficiently balanced and uncertain that there is not an ethically decisive case either for or against permitting it or doing it. Access to human cloning can plausibly be brought within a moral right to reproductive freedom, but the circumstances in which its use would have significant benefits appear at this time to be few and infrequent. It is not a central component of a moral right to reproductive freedom, and it serves no major or pressing individual or social needs. On the other hand, contrary to the pronouncements of many of its opponents, human cloning seems not to be a violation of moral or human rights. But it does risk some significant individual or social harms, although most are based on common public confusions about genetic determinism, human identity, and the effects of human cloning. Because most moral reasons against doing human cloning remain speculative, they seem insufficient to warrant at this time a complete legal prohibition of either research on or later use of human cloning. Legitimate moral concerns about the use and effects of human cloning, however, underline the need for careful public oversight of research on its development, together with a wider public debate and review before cloning is used on human beings.

THE CONTINUING DEBATE:
Cloning

What Is New

Cloning has now become almost commonplace. A company in Massachusetts will guarantee a healthy cloned calf for a price of $34,000; a California company clones cats for $10,000 each, and expects to expand its service to dogs in a few months. Mice, rabbits, goats, pigs, horses, and mules have also been successfully cloned. But human cloning remains very controversial. Almost everyone favors a ban on human reproductive cloning (even those who believe it might be acceptable in the future generally agree that present technology makes the process too dangerous). That is, almost everyone agrees that it is not a good idea presently to produce a human baby by cloning. But there is deep controversy over whether "therapeutic cloning" should be allowed. This is cloning which produces embryos that are never implanted in the womb, and which after one week are destroyed in order to harvest stem cells for research in treating such diseases as Alzheimer's, diabetes, and Parkinson, as well as for spinal cord injuries. For example, the InterAcademy Panel on International Issues, which represents scientific academies worldwide, recently called on the United Nations to ban reproductive cloning but to allow therapeutic cloning. And late in 2004, a group of Harvard university researchers—working on juvenile diabetes and Parkinson disease—sought permission from a university ethical review board to proceed with an experiment involving therapeutic cloning. In the United States, there is currently a ban on the use of federal research funds for therapeutic cloning, but the procedure is not banned, and research in the area can be pursued through private funding. However, the Bush administration is on record as strongly opposed to therapeutic cloning, and legislation banning it entirely is likely to be proposed.

Where to Find More

The National Bioethics Advisory Commission home page makes available online a remarkably good report and collection of papers on cloning (*The Report and Recommendations of the National Bioethics Advisory Commission on Cloning Human Beings*, 1997): It can be ordered from the National Technical Information Service, at *www.ntis.gov*, and it is available online at a wonderful site for researching many issues in bioethics: *www.georgetown.edu/research/nrcb/nbac/pubs.html*.

An interesting article on the cloning controversy is Richard Lewontin, "The Confusion over Cloning," *The New York Review of Books*, volume 44, number 16, October 23, 1997. See also the reactions to the article by Harold T. Shapiro, James F. Childress, and Thomas H. Murray, followed by Lewontin's reply, in "The Confusion Over Cloning: An Exchange," *The New York Review of Books*, volume 45, number 4, March 5, 1998.

A brief collection of excellent articles (from differing perspectives) can be found in Barbara MacKinnon, editor, *Human Cloning: Science, Ethics, and Public Policy* (Urbana and Chicago: University of Illinois Press, 2000). Another good collection, representing a variety of views, is Michael C. Brannigan, editor, *Ethical Issues in Human Cloning: Cross-Disciplinary Perspectives* (New York: Seven Bridges Press, 2001). Gregory E. Pence, *Who's Afraid of Human Cloning* (Lanham, Maryland: Rowman & Littlefield, 1998), is a spirited defense of cloning. Pence has also edited an anthology on cloning, containing articles both pro and con: *Flesh of My Flesh: The Ethics of Cloning Humans* (Lanham, Maryland: Rowman & Littlefield, 1998).

As on so many topics, Lawrence Hinman's Ethics Updates Website has a superb collection of material on cloning, including many links to other sites, online papers, and video lectures (as well as a link to a *Science Friday* hour long radio program—aired on January 9, 1998—that offers a very interesting discussion of cloning); go to *ethics.sandiego.edu/Applied/Bioethics.*

THE ETHICS OF MEDICAL RESEARCH IN IMPOVERISHED COUNTRIES

Must Medical Research in Impoverished Countries Follow
the Same Procedures as in Wealthy Countries or Can Different
Procedures Be Followed?

RESEARCHERS MUST FOLLOW THE SAME RESEARCH PROCEDURES AS IN WEALTHY COUNTRIES

ADVOCATE: Marcia Angell, Executive Editor (1988–1999) and Editor-in-Chief (1999–2000) of *New England Journal of Medicine*; currently Senior Lecturer in Department of Social Medicine at Harvard Medical School

SOURCE: "The Ethics of Clinical Research in the Third World," *The New England Journal of Medicine* volume 337, number 12, September 18, 1997: 847–849

RESEARCHERS CAN USE DIFFERENT RESEARCH PROCEDURES IN IMPOVERISHED COUNTRIES

ADVOCATE: Salim S. Abdool Karim, Deputy Vice-Chancellor for Research and Development at the University of Natal in Durban, South Africa; Professor in Clinical Epidemiology at the Mailman School of Public Health at Columbia University; and Director of the Centre for the AIDS Program of Research in South Africa

SOURCE: "Placebo Controls in HIV Perinatal Transmission Trials: A South African's Viewpoint," *American Journal of Public Health* volume 88, number 4, April 1998: 564–566.

Medical research has produced wonderful discoveries, but also some ethical horror stories. The Tuskegee syphilis study, running from 1932 to 1972, was designed to study the course of untreated syphilis. The research subjects, poor African-American males, were told they were receiving treatment for their disease; in fact, they received none. Within a few years after the study was launched, penicillin was recognized as a highly effective treatment for syphilis. The Tuskegee subjects were not given penicillin, and were actively prevented from obtaining this life-saving drug; instead, they were monitored as their disease followed its terrible path of disability, blindness, paralysis, insanity, and death.

There is broad agreement that the Tuskegee study was morally wrong. There is also now wide agreement about basic principles that must guide legitimate research with human subjects. Foremost is the requirement of *informed consent*: Research subjects must be informed that they are participating in a research project. They cannot, for example, be given an experimental drug under the guise of treatment. Subjects must be informed of all risks, and they must freely choose to participate. Second, studies must be well designed to yield significant scientific results. Third, subjects must not be exposed to unnecessary risks or discomfort. Fourth—this requirement is somewhat more controversial—when a researcher runs a randomized comparative study between a *control* group (research subjects who receive the current standard best treatment, or a placebo, or no treatment) and an *experimental* group (subjects who receive the drug or procedure being tested), the researcher must *not* have any prior reason to suppose that one group will fare better than the other; that is, the two groups must be in a state of *equipoise*, in which the researcher honestly does not know which group is likely to benefit more. Furthermore, if there is a standard effective treatment for the condition being tested, then the control group *must* receive that treatment rather than a placebo.

International medical research poses tough ethical issues, particularly when the research involves North American and European pharmaceutical companies running drug tests among severely impoverished populations in Africa, Asia, and Latin America. When studies are done among people with no access to treatment other than through an experimental drug study, are these subjects giving *genuine* free consent, or are their desperate circumstances used to exploit them? Is it legitimate to run drug experiments in impoverished countries if the price of the tested medication will limit its use to wealthy nations?

One fiercely debated study—and the focus of the essays by Angell and Karim—involved the testing of a new treatment procedure to prevent the transmission of HIV from infected mothers to their newborn children. At the time the studies were done in the late 1990's, there was a standard treatment process available for preventing maternal HIV transmission, and it had a success rate of some 70%. It was, however, lengthy, complex, and expensive. A number of researchers tested programs involving much smaller drug doses administered more briefly. Studies were conducted among impoverished African women with almost no access to health care. Also, the control group was given a placebo rather than the standard effective treatment. Critics of the research argued that the control group should have been given the standard treatment. Defenders of the research insisted that while the expensive treatment might be standard in wealthy countries, it certainly was not the standard in impoverished countries. Some researchers also argued that applying the equipoise requirement was inappropriate or inapplicable here because the use of a placebo gave faster and more reliable research results, and thus made a cheaper treatment more rapidly available.

POINTS TO PONDER

➤ The policy of *The New England Journal of Medicine* is not to publish studies that it regards as ethically flawed. The journal decided to publish the study on HIV transmission, though with some misgivings. Was that the right decision?

➤ Angell has been criticized for making a comparison with Tuskegee, on the grounds that her analogy is too sensational and inaccurate. Is her use of the analogy fair?

➤ Salim Karim argues that local authorities in South Africa approved the research design. Does that validate the ethical legitimacy of the research?

The Ethics of Medical Research in Impoverished Countries:
Researchers Must Follow the Same Procedures as in Wealthy Countries

Marcia Angell

An essential ethical condition for a randomized clinical trial comparing two treatments for a disease is that there be no good reason for thinking one is better than the other. Usually, investigators hope and even expect that the new treatment will be better, but there should not be solid evidence one way or the other. If there is, not only would the trial be scientifically redundant, but the investigators would be guilty of knowingly giving inferior treatment to some participants in the trial. The necessity for investigators to be in this state of equipoise applies to placebo-controlled trials, as well. Only when there is no known effective treatment is it ethical to compare a potential new treatment with a placebo. When effective treatment exists, a placebo may not be used. Instead, subjects in the control group of the study must receive the best known treatment. Investigators are responsible for all subjects enrolled in a trial, not just some of them, and the goals of the research are always secondary to the well-being of the participants. Those requirements are made clear in the Declaration of Helsinki of the World Health Organization (WHO), which is widely regarded as providing the fundamental guiding principles of research involving human subjects. It states, "In research on man [sic], the interest of science and society should never take precedence over considerations related to the well-being of the subject," and "In any medical study, every patient—including those of a control group, if any—should be assured of the best proven diagnostic and therapeutic method."

One reason ethical codes are unequivocal about investigators' primary obligation to care for the human subjects of their research is the strong temptation to subordinate the subjects' welfare to the objectives of the study. That is particularly likely when the research question is extremely important and the answer would probably improve the care of future patients substantially. In those circumstances, it is sometimes argued explicitly that obtaining a rapid, unambiguous answer to the research question is the primary ethical obligation. With the most altruistic of motives, then, researchers may find themselves slipping across a line that prohibits treating human subjects as means to an end. When that line is crossed, there is very little left to protect patients from a callous disregard of their welfare for the sake of research goals. Even informed consent, important though it is, is not protection enough, because of the asymmetry in knowledge and authority between researchers and their subjects. And approval by an institutional review board, though also important, is highly variable in its responsiveness to patients' interests when they conflict with the interests of researchers.

A textbook example of unethical research is the Tuskegee Study of Untreated Syphilis. In that study, which was sponsored by the U.S. Public Health Service and lasted from 1932 to 1972, 412 poor African-American men with untreated syphilis were followed and compared with 204 men free of the disease to determine the natural history of syphilis. Although there was no very good treatment available at the time the study began (heavy metals were the standard treatment), the research continued even after penicillin became widely available and was known to be highly effective against syphilis. The study was not terminated until it came to the attention of a reporter and the outrage provoked by front-page stories in the *Washington Star* and *New York Times* embarrassed the Nixon administration into calling a halt to it. The ethical violations were multiple: Subjects did not provide informed consent (indeed, they were deliberately deceived); they were denied the best known treatment; and the study was continued even after highly effective treatment became available. And what were the arguments in favor of the Tuskegee study? That these poor African-American men probably would not have been treated anyway, so the investigators were merely observing what would have happened if there were no study; and that the study was important (a "never-to-be-repeated opportunity," said one physician after penicillin became available). Ethical concern was even stood on its head when it was suggested that not only was the information valuable, but it was especially so for people like the subjects—an impoverished rural population with a very high rate of untreated syphilis. The only lament seemed to be that many of the subjects inadvertently received treatment by other doctors.

Some of these issues are raised by Lurie and Wolfe elsewhere in this issue of the *Journal.* They discuss the ethics of ongoing trials in the Third World of regimens to prevent the vertical transmission of human immunodeficiency virus (HIV) infection. All except one of the trials employ placebo-treated control groups, despite the fact that zidovudine has already been clearly shown to cut the rate of vertical transmission greatly and is now recommended in the United States for all HIV-infected pregnant women. The justifications are reminiscent of those for the Tuskegee study: Women in the Third World would not receive antiretroviral treatment anyway, so the investigators are simply observing what would happen to the subjects' infants if there were no study. And a placebo-controlled study is the fastest, most efficient way to obtain unambiguous information that will be of greatest value in the Third World. Thus, in response to protests from Wolfe and others to the secretary of Health and Human Services, the directors of the National Institutes of Health (NIH) and the Centers for Disease Control and Prevention (CDC)—the organizations sponsoring the studies—argued, "It is an unfortunate fact that the current standard of perinatal care for the HIV-infected pregnant women in the sites of the studies does not include any HIV prophylactic intervention at all," and the inclusion of placebo controls "will result in the most rapid, accurate, and reliable answer to the question of the value of the intervention being studied compared to the local standard of care."

Also in this issue of the *Journal,* Whalen et al. report the results of a clinical trial in Uganda of various regimens of prophylaxis against tuberculosis in HIV-infected adults, most of whom had positive tuberculin skin tests. This study, too, employed a placebo-treated control group, and in some ways it is analogous to the studies criticized by Lurie and Wolfe. In the United States it would probably be impossible to carry out such a study, because of long-standing official recommendations that HIV-infected persons with positive tuberculin skin tests receive prophylaxis against tuberculosis. The first was issued in 1990 by the CDC's Advisory Committee for Elimination of Tuberculosis. It stated that tuberculin-test-positive persons with HIV infection "should be considered candidates for preventive therapy." Three years later, the recommendation was reiterated more strongly in a joint statement by the American Thoracic Society and the CDC, in collaboration with the Infectious Diseases Society of America and the American Academy of Pediatrics. According to this statement, "... the identification of persons with dual infection and the administration of preventive therapy to these persons is of great importance." However, some believe that these recommendations were premature, since they were based largely on the success of prophylaxis in HIV-negative persons.

Whether the study by Whalen et al. was ethical depends, in my view, entirely on the strength of the preexisting evidence. Only if there was genuine doubt about the benefits of prophylaxis would a placebo group be ethically justified. This is not the place to review the scientific evidence, some of which is discussed in the editorial of Msamanga and Fawzi elsewhere in this issue. Suffice it to say that the case is debatable. Msamanga and Fawzi conclude that "future studies should not include a placebo group, since preventive therapy should be considered the standard of care." I agree. The difficult question is whether there should have been a placebo group in the first place.

Although I believe an argument can be made that a placebo-controlled trial was ethically justifiable because it was still uncertain whether prophylaxis would work, it should not be argued that it was ethical because no prophylaxis is the "local standard of care" in sub-Saharan Africa. For reasons discussed by Lurie and Wolfe, that

reasoning is badly flawed. As mentioned earlier, the Declaration of Helsinki requires control groups to receive the "best" current treatment, not the local one. The shift in wording between "best" and "local" may be slight, but the implications are profound. Acceptance of this ethical relativism could result in widespread exploitation of vulnerable Third World populations for research programs that could not be carried out in the sponsoring country. Furthermore, it directly contradicts the Department of Health and Human Services' own regulations governing U.S.-sponsored research in foreign countries, as well as joint guidelines for research in the Third World issued by WHO and the Council for International Organizations of Medical Sciences, which require that human subjects receive protection at least equivalent to that in the sponsoring country. The fact that Whalen et al. offered isoniazid to the placebo group when it was found superior to placebo indicates that they were aware of their responsibility to all the subjects in the trial.

The *Journal* has taken the position that it will not publish reports of unethical research, regardless of their scientific merit. After deliberating at length about the study by Whalen et al., the editors concluded that publication was ethically justified, although there remain differences among us. The fact that the subjects gave informed consent and the study was approved by the institutional review board at the University Hospitals of Cleveland and Case Western Reserve University and by the Ugandan National AIDS Research Subcommittee certainly supported our decision but did not allay all our misgivings. It is still important to determine whether clinical studies are consistent with preexisting, widely accepted ethical guidelines, such as the Declaration of Helsinki, and with federal regulations, since they cannot be influenced by pressures specific to a particular study.

Quite apart from the merits of the study by Whalen et al., there is a larger issue. There appears to be a general retreat from the clear principles enunciated in the Nuremberg Code and the Declaration of Helsinki as applied to research in the Third World. Why is that? Is it because the "local standard of care" is different? I don't think so. In my view, that is merely a self-serving justification after the fact. Is it because diseases and their treatments are very different in the Third World, so that information gained in the industrialized world has no relevance and we have to start from scratch? That, too, seems an unlikely explanation, although here again it is often offered as a justification. Sometimes there may be relevant differences between populations, but that cannot be assumed. Unless there are specific indications to the contrary, the safest and most reasonable position is that people everywhere are likely to respond similarly to the same treatment.

I think we have to look elsewhere for the real reasons. One of them may be a slavish adherence to the tenets of clinical trials. According to these, all trials should be randomized, double-blind, and placebo-controlled, if at all possible. That rigidity may explain the NIH's pressure on Marc Lallemant to include a placebo group in his study, as described by Lurie and Wolfe.

Sometimes journals are blamed for the problem, because they are thought to demand strict conformity to the standard methods. That is not true, at least not at this journal. We do not want a scientifically neat study if it is ethically flawed, but like Lurie and Wolfe we believe that in many cases it is possible, with a little ingenuity, to have both scientific and ethical rigor.

The retreat from ethical principles may also be explained by some of the exigencies of doing clinical research in an increasingly regulated and competitive environment. Research in the Third World looks relatively attractive as it becomes better funded and regulations at home become more restrictive. Despite the existence of codes requiring that human subjects receive at least the same protection abroad as at home, they are still honored partly in the breach. The fact remains that many studies are done in the Third World that simply could not be done in the countries sponsoring the work. Clinical trials have become a big business, with many of the same imperatives. To survive, it is necessary to get the work done as quickly as possible, with a minimum of obstacles. When these considerations prevail, it seems as if we have not come very far from Tuskegee after all. Those of us in the research community need to redouble our commitment to the highest ethical standards, no matter where the research is conducted, and sponsoring agencies need to enforce those standards, not undercut them.

The Ethics of Medical Research in Impoverished Countries:
Researchers Can Use Different Procedures in Impoverished Countries

SALIM S. ABDOOL KARIM

INTRODUCTION

The scale of the human immunodeficiency virus (HIV) epidemic in South Africa, where 0.76% of pregnant women were HIV infected in 1990 and 14.07% in 1996, highlights the importance of research to find practical and affordable interventions to curb HIV transmission. Lurie and Wolfe and Angell have raised the vexed issue under intensive discussion for some time now in South Africa of whether a placebo arm is ethical in studies of vertical transmission of HIV.

I agree with Lurie and Wolfe that researchers and research agencies from sponsoring countries should not conduct research in poor countries that would be unethical in their own countries, except under justifiable extenuating circumstances. Indeed, this is also advocated by the Council for International Organizations of Medical Sciences (CIOMS). However, the situation in South Africa is somewhat different; the funding sources for ongoing HIV vertical transmission trials, with placebo arms, are local agencies and the United Nations Program on Acquired Immunodeficiency Syndrome (UNAIDS).

One of the two large HIV perinatal transmission trials currently under way in South Africa is assessing the effect of vitamin A supplementation; the other trial is a 4-arm trial assessing a combination of zidovudine and 3TC given for a short period before, during, or after delivery.

The vitamin A study has recruited almost 400 women and is funded by the South African Department of Health and the South African Medical Research Council. The short-course combination therapy trial, known as the Petra Study, is a multicenter trial funded by UNAIDS, and about 400 women will be recruited in each of the 2 sites in South Africa. Both trials are double-blinded, randomized control trials with placebo arms, and both have been scrutinized by institutional review boards, known in South Africa as ethics committees. The vitamin A study was approved by the University of Natal Ethics Committee, and the Petra study was approved by both the University of Natal and the University of the Witwatersrand. These studies aim to find an intervention that will be affordable and implementable in a setting such as South Africa. They are critically important if the AIDS Clinical Trial Group (ACTG) 076 regimen of zidovudine, which has been shown to be effective, cannot be implemented.

IS THE ACTG 076 REGIMEN IMPLEMENTABLE IN SOUTH AFRICA?

Although South Africa is a middle income country, cost is a constraint. Program planning with detailed costing reveals that the ACTG 076 regimen is not affordable without substantial redirection and reprioritization of health care resources. Currently, approximately 1.2 million births occur each year in South Africa. Substantial new resources will be required to test pregnant women with pre- and posttest counseling. Implementing the ACTG 076 regimen for those identified to be HIV infected will require further resources to increase the number of clinic visits several fold and to provide the close clinical management required for patients on antiretroviral drugs. Although the cost of zidovudine is substantial, important contributors to the costs of implementing the ACTG regimen in South African are the health service costs. Costs associated with HIV testing and medical care will be applicable regardless of the therapeutic regimen, but those costs will not be applicable to an intervention such as vitamin A supplementation, which can be given to all pregnant women without testing for HIV infection—hence the specific relevance of the vitamin A trial to the South African situation.

In South Africa, a second constraint to implementation of the ACTG 076 regimen is the high frequency of home deliveries, particularly in rural communities. A third constraint is the high frequency of booking for antenatal care appointments that are too late for the prenatal component of the ACTG 076 regimen, making its widespread use almost impossible. Additionally, because breast-feeding is common in rural South Africa, HIV-positive women participating in the ACTG 076 regimen will have to be discouraged from breast-feeding. This could be possible only if breast-milk substitutes are provided either free or at heavily subsidized prices.

If the ACTG 076 regimen is not being implemented in this country or cannot be implemented, should it be the standard of care in the control arm of HIV vertical transmission trials in South Africa? In this commentary, I will consider some of the scientific and ethical issues in this dilemma.

OTHER TREATMENT OPTIONS FOR THE CONTROL GROUP

Fundamentally, the research question at issue is whether shorter courses of combination antiretroviral therapy or micronutrient supplementation reduce vertical transmission of HIV sufficiently to warrant their wide-scale implementation in South Africa. If these interventions are hypothesized to be as good as or better than ACTG 076, then a control arm with the ACTG 076 regimen is entirely appropriate. What if the study interventions are not as good as ACTG 076? This possibility—in stark contrast to the "more optimistic view" taken by Lurie and Wolfe—must be seriously considered in the design of the trials.

In considering each of the 3 options for the control group in these trials, the real possibility must be considered that shorter course drug regimens or micronutrient supplementation may not reduce the HIV vertical transmission rate to the same extent as the ACTG 076 regimen (e.g., they may be only half as efficacious).

Option 1: No Concurrent Control Group: Historical Data Provide the Comparison Vertical Transmission Rate

The vertical transmission rate in South Africa has been changing over time. In a cohort of 111 subjects recruited in 1990 through 1991 at King Edward VIII Hospital, the HIV vertical transmission rate was 27%, while a cohort of 180 subjects recruited at the same hospital in 1993 through 1994 had a rate of 38% (Dr D. Moodley, personal communication). If a hypothetical nonrandomized study was conducted in 1993 to 1994 with an intervention that was 33% effective, the outcome would have been an HIV vertical transmission rate of 26%. Without placebo data providing the concurrent rate of 38%, comparing the study rate of 26%

with the rate in 1990 through 1991 of 27% would have led to the conclusion that the intervention had no effect.

The vertical transmission rate is influenced by many factors, including cesarean section rates, maternal viral load, and breast-feeding rates. As these factors change over time, the HIV vertical transmission rate will also change, either increasing or decreasing depending on which factors change and to what extent. Given the changing HIV vertical transmission rate, historical comparisons may lead to spurious conclusions and are therefore not acceptable.

Option 2: A Control Group Using the ACTG 076 Regimen

If a control group uses the ACTG 076 regimen, the clinical trial may be viewed as an equivalency study. An equivalency study is informative if the study interventions are found to be as good as, or better than, the control (equivalent) intervention and if the expected outcome of the control intervention is known. However, the effect of the ACTG 076 regimen in South Africa is not known, and extrapolation based on data from other settings is fraught with problems, given differences in breast-feeding rates, sexually transmitted disease rates, cesarean section rates, levels of viral load, and other variables....

Option 3: A Placebo Control Group

A placebo control group is the only option that would enable the calculation of the absolute reduction in the HIV vertical transmission rate, regardless of the extent to which it may differ from the effect of the ACTG 076 regimen. The essential concurrent comparison HIV vertical transmission rate is available. A meaningful result would be obtained even if the effect of the study interventions were lower

than that of the ACTG 076 regimen. It would be possible to calculate whether the study interventions make any difference at all and, if so, to what extent they lower the HIV vertical transmission rate. Therefore, on scientific grounds, a placebo control group is essential.

IS A PLACEBO CONTROL GROUP ETHICALLY JUSTIFIABLE?

The starting point for all clinical trials is the assurance that trial participants will be protected from exploitation. Persons who are being recruited into a research project must be allowed to exercise their own judgment freely (autonomy) in deciding whether or not to participate in the research. Ethics committees in South Africa have a strong tradition of vigorously upholding this principle. Legally, the South African Medical Research Council has an obligation to protect and uphold the ethical standards of research in South Africa. Guidelines from the Council for International Organizations of Medical Sciences are extensively applied and the Medical Research Council's guidelines have been widely adopted in South Africa. Although institutional review has been undertaken for all the HIV perinatal transmission trials in South Africa, further steps to monitor the ethical standards of informed consent have also been voluntarily pursued by some of the research groups.

Informed and voluntary participation requires an understanding of the risks and benefits inherent in the research. In this context, participants should not be exposed to harm or undue risk, but this can be judged only in relation to a standard. The reality is that standards—in this case, the standard of care—differ across the world and even within countries; they are seldom agreed upon internationally. Although the ACTG 076 regimen of therapy is the standard of care in some countries, it is not an international standard, such as is set by the World Health Organization. Providing high-quality routine care to the control arm without providing the ACTG 076 regimen of zidovudine cannot then be construed as causing undue risk or harm to the study participants. No therapy that they may otherwise receive is being withheld from study participants. To extend this argument, if the control arm has to be afforded an external standard of care that can produce a substantial reduction in the HIV vertical transmission rate, it then cannot be justified for participants to be randomized in a study intervention arm if there is a reasonable chance that the interventions under study are not as good as the ACTG 076 regimen. It is, therefore, my opinion that the placebo control arm is ethically justifiable.

Standards of care evolve, and the acceptable standards of care will change over time. This does not mean that ethics are flexible; the consistent application of the basic principles of ethics in a world that varies markedly and changes rapidly is not inconsistent with differing standards of care being ethically acceptable in different settings or at different times.

CONCLUSION

Everyone agrees that there is an urgent need to reduce vertical transmission of HIV, and this remains the central goal of the studies in South Africa. The local imperative is to develop and demonstrate further the efficacy of an affordable and implementable intervention to reduce HIV vertical transmission. While such an intervention need not be as good as the ACTG 076 regimen of therapy, its impact on HIV vertical transmission must be known, because this information will be the basis of policy that will aim to protect hundreds of thousands of infants from becoming infected with HIV.

THE CONTINUING DEBATE:
The Ethics of Medical Research in Impoverished Countries

What Is New

The controversy over wealthy Western pharmaceutical companies carrying out drug studies in Third World countries continues. The pharmaceutical industry generates enormous profits, and bringing a new drug to market more quickly can increase profits by millions or even hundreds of millions of dollars. Studies in impoverished countries can be done more swiftly, at lower cost, and with less regulation (for example, standards for informed consent are often lower).

Under The 2000 Declaration of Helsinki, researchers are not allowed to use placebos when a standard treatment is available, and they must continue treatment of research subjects (using either the experimental drug or the standard treatment, depending on what proves best) after the research is completed. Abruptly halting effective treatment at the conclusion of a study is regarded as cruel and unfair to the research participants. Furthermore, the Helsinki Declaration requires that all study results be made public. However, compliance with the Declaration of Helsinki must be voluntary, and the U.S. Food and Drug Administration has rejected the Declaration, claiming that its requirements are arbitrary and too demanding.

Where to Find More

For a very readable but deeply disturbing account of the Tuskegee experiment, see James H. Jones, *Bad Blood: The Tuskegee Syphilis Experiment* (New York: The Free Press, 1981, 1993). An excellent collection of articles on the experiment is by Susan M. Reverby, editor, *Tuskegee's Truths: Rethinking the Tuskegee Syphilis Study* (Chapel Hill: University of North Carolina Press, 2000).

Baruch A. Brody, *The Ethics of Biomedical Research: An International Perspective* (New York: Oxford University Press, 1998) examines a wide range of research-related issues. Ruth Macklin, *Double Standards in Medical Research in Developing Countries* (Cambridge: Cambridge University Press, 2004), is a remarkably good book, covering all the major issues and providing a superb guide to the current literature. See also two excellent articles by Macklin: "After Helsinki: Unresolved Issues in International Research," *Kennedy Institute of Ethics Journal* Volume 11, number 1, 2001: 17–36; and "International Research: Ethical Imperialism or Ethical Pluralism," *Accountability in Research* volume 7, 2001: 5 9–83. A clear introduction, with special emphasis on the positions taken by major oversight and regulatory bodies, is Aurora Plomer, *The Law and Ethics of Medical Research: International Biolethics and Human Rights* (London: Cavendish Publishing, 2005).

The article that prompted much of the international drug testing debate is Peter Lurie and Sidney M. Wolfe, "Unethical Trials of Interventions to Reduce Perinatal Transmission of the Human Immunodeficiency Virus in Developing Countries," *New England Journal of Medicine* volume 337, September 18, 1997: 853–856. Critical of that article is Robert A Crouch and John D. Arras, "AZT Trials and Tribulations," *Hastings Center Report* volume 28, number 6, 1998: 26–34; that issue of *Hastings Center Report* contains a number of other articles on the dispute. See also *Bioethics* volume 12, number 4, October 1998, which focuses on that question. Alex

John London, "Equipoise and International Human-Subjects Research," *Bioethics* volume 15, number 4, 2001, discusses the equipoise requirement in the context of international research. Three years after publishing the Lurie and Wolfe article and her own editorial on the subject, Marcia Angeli wrote an excellent follow-up to the continuing debate: "Investigators' Responsibilities for Human Subjects in Developing Countries," *New England Journal of Medicine* volume 342, Number 13, March 30, 2000: 967–968. *American Journal of Public Health* volume 88, number 4, April 1998 contains excellent articles devoted to the controversy. Karin B. Michels and Kenneth J. Rothrnan, "Update on Unethical Use of Placebos in Randomized Trials," *Bioethics*, Volume 17, Number 2, 2003: 188–204, argue against the continued practice of using placebo studies in Third World research. An excellent critique of the arguments in favor of relaxed research standards in Third World countries is offered by M. H. Kottow, "Who is my Brother's Keeper?" *Journal of Medical Ethics*, volume 28, 2002: 24–27.

D. R. Cooley, "Distributive Justice and Clinical Trials in the Third World," *Theoretical Medicine*, volume 22, 2001: 151–167, argues that researchers are under no obligation to guarantee that drugs successfully tested in third world countries will ultimately be available to those who live there. Solomon R. Benatar, "Distributive Justice and Clinical Trials in the Third World," *Theoretical Medicine*, volume 22, 2001: 169–176, insists that basic principles of distributive justice require strong efforts to improve health care in the impoverished host countries.

PHYSICIAN-ASSISTED SUICIDE

Should It Be Prohibited *or* Allowed?

PHYSICIAN-ASSISTED SUICIDE SHOULD BE PROHIBITED

ADVOCATE: John D. Arras, William and Linda Porterfield Professor of Bioethics and Professor Philosophy, University of Virginia

SOURCE: "Physician-Assisted Suicide: A Tragic View," *Journal of Contemporary Health Law and Policy*, volume 13 (1997): 361–389

PHYSICIAN-ASSISTED SUICIDE SHOULD BE ALLOWED

ADVOCATE: Margaret P. Battin, Professor of Philosophy and Adjunct Professor of Internal Medicine in the Division of Medical Ethics, University of Utah

SOURCE: This recently revised version of Margaret Battin's influential essay was originally published in Bruce N. Waller, *Consider Ethics: Theory, Readings, and Contemporary Issues* (New York: Pearson Longman, 2005); the original version of the article first appeared in the *Journal of Pain and Symptom Management*, vol. 6, no. 5 (1991): 298-305.

Though stopping treatment or tube feeding for a patient in a permanently vegetative state may still provoke controversy—as in the highly publicized and politicized Florida case of Terri Schiavo, on life support in a permanently vegetative state for 15 years—the right of a competent patient to make her *own* decisions about stopping all treatment, including the removal of feeding tubes, is legally well-established; and that includes the right of competent patients to leave advance instructions to determine when treatment should stop should they become incompetent. For competent patients, currently the major controversy concerns active intervention to cause death.

There are several key terms in this controversy over euthanasia. *Passive* euthanasia occurs when a patient chooses not to initiate or continue some treatment that would extend life: for example, if a patient chooses to stop a respirator that is necessary for continued breathing, or rejects treatment for pneumonia, or refuses tube feeding. In all these cases a severely ill patient might choose a swifter death by simply stopping treatment, and the right of a competent patient to make such decisions is a well-established legal right. Beyond the legal right, few would now deny that a competent patient also has a moral right to make such treatment or nontreatment decisions for herself. But suppose I'm a competent patient suffering from a disease that will cause a slow and lingering death process, perhaps involving severe pain or dementia, and I desire a swifter means of dying. If my physician prepares a lethal drug that I then swallow on my own, that is a case of *physician-assisted suicide* (PAS). If my physician prepares a lethal dose and administers it herself (because that is my preference, or because I am not physically able to take the dose) that is active euthanasia. In The Netherlands, where active euthanasia has been practiced legally for many years, the difference between physician-assisted suicide and *active euthanasia* is considered insignificant: So long as a competent patient has made a clear and settled decision to die, then it is not important whether the physician prepares a lethal dose that the patient swallows or the physician administers the lethal dose by injection. In the United States, many regard the difference as very important. (For example, Oregon allows physician-assisted suicide but not active euthanasia.) The significance of the distinction between physician-assisted suicide and active euthanasia, and between active and passive euthanasia, is a much disputed ethical question, and you will have to draw your own conclusions.

One qualification: No one in the debate favors killing or withdrawing treatment from patients against their wishes. Some suggest that euthanasia policies might lead down a slippery slope to that end, but no one would regard that as a desirable result. To the contrary, those who favor active euthanasia favor it as a means of allowing patients to extend their autonomous control, not as a way of coercing patients.

Though the debate over euthanasia is centered on the basic question of the right of the individual to make his or her own choices vs. the role of the state in regulating behavior, the issue also raises other basic questions: How can we determine that an individual is sufficiently free and competent to make vitally important choices about life and death? And what further effects might follow from adopting a policy designed to allow individuals the right to choose the time and manner of their death?

POINTS TO PONDER

➤ On what crucial point of difference does the argument between Arras and Battin hinge?

➤ Though Arras and Battin reach very different conclusions, they also agree on some important points. Describe some of their points of agreement.

➤ Under what circumstances might Arras favor the legalization of physician-assisted suicide (PAS)?

➤ Suppose that I am severely ill but still fully competent, and suffering from a terminal disease. I can take liquids and nourishment only through intubation. Rather than extend the dying process, I choose—as the courts and Congress have affirmed is my right—to stop all feeding, have the tubes removed, take pain killers to lessen any suffering, and die of dehydration or starvation. Is there any morally relevant difference between that act (which aims at my death) and my taking a drug that will cause my death more swiftly? If I am taking such a lethal drug, is there any *moral* difference (setting aside any practical differences) between taking the drug myself and having my physician inject me with it at my request?

Physician-Assisted Suicide:
Should Be Prohibited

JOHN D. ARRAS

ARGUMENTS AND MOTIVATIONS IN FAVOR OF PAS/EUTHANASA

The philosophical case for PAS and euthanasia consists of two distinct prongs, both of which speak simply, directly, and powerfully to our commonsensical intuitions. First, there is the claim of autonomy, that all of us possess a right to self-determination in matters profoundly touching on such religious themes as life, death, and the meaning of suffering. Just as we should each be free to make important choices bearing on how we shall live our own lives, so we should be equally free in choosing the time and manner of our deaths. For some, more life will always be welcome as a gift or perhaps even as a test of faith, but for others, continued life signifies only disfiguring suffering and the unrelenting loss of everything that invested their lives with meaning and dignity, As philosopher Ronald Dworkin has eloquently argued, it is a form of *tyranny* to force someone to endure unendurable suffering at the end of life merely for the sake of someone else's values. Each of us should be free to live or die as we see fit according to our own conceptions of the meaning of life and death.

Second, PAS and/or euthanasia are merciful acts that deliver terminally ill patients from painful and protracted death. According to the utilitarian, acts are morally right insofar as they promote happiness and alleviate unhappiness, and wrong insofar as they cause or allow others to suffer needlessly. Even according to the traditional ethic of the medical profession, physicians have a solemn duty not merely to extend life whenever possible (and desirable), but also to alleviate pain and suffering whenever possible. For patients suffering from the final ravages of end-stage AIDS or cancer, a doctor's lethal prescription or injection can be, and often is welcomed as a blessed relief. Accordingly, we should treat human beings at least as well as we treat grievously ill or injured animals by putting them, at their own request, out of their misery.

These philosophical reflections can be supplemented with a more clinical perspective addressed to the motivational factors lying behind many requests to die. Many people advocate legalization because they fear a loss of control at the end of life. They fear falling victim to the technological imperative; they fear dying in chronic and uncontrolled pain; they fear the psychological suffering attendant upon the relentless disintegration of the self; they fear, in short, a bad death. All of these fears, it so happens, are eminently justified. Physicians routinely ignore the documented wishes of patients and all-too-often allow patients to die with uncontrolled pain. Studies of cancer patients have shown that over fifty percent suffer from unrelieved pain, and many researchers have found that uncontrolled pain, particularly when accompanied by feelings of hopelessness and untreated depression, is a significant contributing factor for suicide and suicidal ideation.

Clinical depression is another major factor influencing patients' choice of suicide. Depression, accompanied by feelings of hopelessness, is the strongest predictor of suicide for both individuals who are terminally ill and those who are not. Yet most doctors are not trained to notice depression, especially in complex cases such as the elderly suffering from terminal illnesses. Even when doctors succeed in diagnosing depression, they often do not successfully treat it with readily available medications in sufficient amounts.

Significantly, the New York Task Force found that the vast majority of patients who request PAS or euthanasia are capable of being treated successfully both for their depression and their pain, and that when they receive adequate psychiatric and palliative care, their requests to die usually are withdrawn. In other words, patients given the requisite control over their lives and relief from depression and pain usually lose interest in PAS and euthanasia.

With all due respect for the power of modern methods of pain control, it must be acknowledged that a small percentage of patients suffer from conditions, both physical and psychological, that currently lie beyond the reach of the best medical and humane care. Some pain cannot be alleviated short of inducing a permanent state of unconsciousness in the patient, and some depression is unconquerable. For such unfortunate patients, the present law on PAS/euthanasia can represent an insuperable barrier to a dignified and decent death.

OBJECTIONS TO PAS/EUTHANASIA

Opponents of PAS and euthanasia can be grouped into three main factions. One strongly condemns both practices as inherently immoral, as violations of the moral rule against killing the innocent. Most members of this group tend to harbor distinctly religious objections to suicide and euthanasia, viewing them as violations of God's dominion over human life. They argue that killing is simply wrong in itself, whether or not it is done out of respect for the patient's autonomy or out of concern for her suffering. Whether or not this position ultimately is justifiable from a theological point of view, its imposition on believers and nonbelievers alike is incompatible with the basic premises of a secular, pluralistic political order.

A second faction primarily objects to the fact that physicians are being called upon to do the killing. While conceding that killing the terminally ill or assisting in their suicides might not always be morally wrong for others to do, this group maintains that the participation of physicians in such practices undermines their role as healers and fatally compromises the physician-patient relationship.

Finally, a third faction readily grants that neither PAS nor active euthanasia, practiced by ordinary citizens or by physicians, are always morally wrong. On the contrary, this faction believes that in certain rare instances early release from a painful or intolerably degrading existence might constitute both a positive good and an important exercise of personal autonomy for the individual. Indeed, many members of this faction concede that should such a terrible fate befall them, they would hope to find a thoughtful, compassionate, and courageous physician to release them from their misery. But in spite of these important concessions, the members of this faction shrink from endorsing or regulating PAS and active euthanasia due to fears bearing on the social consequences of liberalization. This view is based on two distinct kinds of so-called "slippery slope" arguments: one bears on the inability to cabin PAS/euthanasia. within the confines envisioned by its proponents, the other focuses on the likelihood of abuse, neglect, and mistake.

An Option Without Limits

The first version of the slippery slope argument contends that a socially sanctioned practice of PAS would in all likelihood prove difficult, if not impossible, to contain within its originally anticipated boundaries. Proponents of legalization usually begin with a wholesomely modest policy agenda, limiting their suggested reforms to a narrow and highly specified range of potential candidates and practices. "Give us PAS," they ask, "not the more controversial practice of active euthanasia, for presently competent patients who are terminally ill and suffering unbearable pain." But the logic of the case for PAS, based as it is upon the twin pillars of patient autonomy and mercy, makes it highly unlikely that society could stop with this modest proposal once it had ventured out on the slope. As numerous other critics have pointed out, if autonomy is the prime consideration, then additional constraints based upon terminal illness or unbearable pain, or both, would appear hard to justify. Indeed, if autonomy is crucial, the requirement of unbearable suffering would appear to be entirely subjective. Who is to say, other than the patient herself, how much suffering is too much? Likewise, the requirement of terminal illness seems an arbitrary standard against which to judge patients' own subjective evaluation of their quality of life. If my life is no longer worth living, why should a terminally ill cancer patient be granted PAS but not me, merely because my suffering is due to my "non-terminal" Arterio Lateral Sclerosis ("ALS") or intractable psychiatric disorder?

Alternatively, if pain and suffering are deemed crucial to the justification of legalization, it is hard to see how the proposed barrier of contemporaneous consent of competent patients could withstand serious erosion. If the logic of PAS is at all similar to that of forgoing life-sustaining treatments, and we have every reason to think it so, then it would seem almost inevitable that a case soon would be made to permit PAS for incompetent patients who had left advance directives. That would then be followed by a "substituted judgment" test for patients who "would have wanted" PAS, and finally an "objective" test would be developed for patients (including newborns) whose best interests would be served by PAS or active euthanasia even in the absence of any subjective intent.

In the same way, the joint justifications of autonomy and mercy combine to undermine the plausibility of a line drawn between PAS and active euthanasia. As the authors of one highly publicized proposal have come to see, the logic of justification for active euthanasia is identical to that of PAS. Legalizing PAS, while continuing to ban active euthanasia, would serve only to discriminate unfairly against patients who are suffering and wish to end their lives, but cannot do so because of some physical impairment. Surely these patients, it will be said, are "the worst off group," and therefore they are the most in need of the assistance of others who will do for them what they can no longer accomplish on their own.

None of these initial slippery slope considerations amount to knock-down objections to further liberalization of our laws and practices. After all, it is not obvious that each of these highly predictable shifts (e.g., from terminal to "merely" incurable, from contemporaneous consent to best interests, and from PAS to active euthanasia), are patently immoral and unjustifiable. Still, in pointing out this likely slippage, the consequentialist opponents of PAS/euthanasia are calling on society to think about the likely consequences of taking the first tentative step onto the slope. If all of the extended practices predicted above pose substantially greater risks for vulnerable patients than the more highly circumscribed initial liberalization proposals, then we need to factor in these additional risks even as we ponder the more modest proposals.

The Likelihood of Abuse

The second prong of the slippery slope argument argues that whatever criteria for justifiable PAS and active euthanasia ultimately are chosen, abuse of the system is highly likely to follow. In other words, patients' who fall outside the ambit of our justifiable criteria will soon be candidates for death. This prong resembles what I have elsewhere called an "empirical slope" argument, as it is based not on the close logical resemblance of concepts or justifications, but rather on an empirical prediction of what is likely to happen when we insert a particular social practice into our existing social system.

In order to reassure skeptics, the proponents of PAS/euthanasia concur that any potentially justifiable social policy in this area must meet at least the following three requirements. The policy would have to insist: first, that all requests for death be truly voluntary; second, that all reasonable alternatives to PAS and active euthanasia must be explored before acceding to a patient's wishes; and, third, that a reliable system of reporting all cases must be established in order to effectively monitor these practices and respond to abuses. As a social pessimist on these matters, I worry, given social reality as we know it, that all three assumptions are problematic.

With regard to the voluntariness requirement, we pessimists contend that many requests would not be sufficiently voluntary. In addition to the subtly coercive influences of physicians and family members, perhaps the most slippery aspect of this slope is the highly predictable failure of most physicians to diagnose reliably and treat reversible clinical depression, particularly in the elderly population. As one geriatric psychiatrist testified before the New York Task Force, we now live in the "golden age" of treating depression, but the "lead age" of diagnosing it. We have the tools, but physicians are not adequately trained and motivated to use them. Unless dramatic changes are effected in the practice of medicine, we can predict with confidence that many instances of PAS and active euthanasia will constitute abuses of the original criterion of voluntariness.

Second, there is the lingering fear that any legislative proposal or judicial mandate would have to be implemented within the present social system marked by deep and pervasive discrimination against the poor and members of minority groups. We have every reason to expect that a policy that worked tolerably well in an affluent community like Scarsdale or Beverly Hills, might not work so well in a community like Bedford-Stuyvesant or Watts, where your average citizen has little or no access to basic primary care, let alone sophisticated care for chronic pain at home or in the hospital. There is also reason to worry about any policy of PAS initiated within our growing system of managed care, capitation, and physician-incentives for delivering less care. Expert palliative care no doubt is an expensive and time-consuming proposition, requiring more, rather than less, time spent just talking with patients and providing them with humane comfort. It is highly doubtful that the context of physician-patient conversation within this new dispensation of "turnstile medicine" will be at all conducive to humane decisions untainted by subtle economic coercion.

In addition, given the abysmal track record of physicians in responding adequately to pain and suffering, we also can confidently predict that in many cases all reasonable alternatives will not have been exhausted. Instead of vigorously addressing the pharmacological and psycho-social needs of such patients, physicians no doubt will continue to ignore, undertreat, or treat patients in an impersonal manner. The result will be more depression, desperation, and requests for physician-assisted death from patients who could have been successfully treated. The root causes of this predictable lapse are manifold, but include such factors as the inaccessibility of decent primary care to over thirty-seven million Americans. Other notable causes are: an appalling lack of training in palliative care even among primary care physicians and cancer specialists, discrimination in the delivery of pain control and other medical treatments on the basis of race and economic status; various myths shared by both physicians and patients about the supposed ill effects of pain medications; and, restrictive state laws on access to opioids.

Finally, with regard to the third requirement, pessimists doubt that any reporting system would adequately monitor these practices. A great deal depends here on the extent to which patients and practitioners will regard these practices as essentially private matters to be discussed and acted upon within the privacy of the doctor-patient relationship. As the Dutch experience conclusively has demonstrated, physicians will be extremely loath to report instances of PAS and active euthanasia to public authorities, largely for fear of bringing the harsh glare of publicity upon the patients' families at a time when privacy is most needed. The likely result of this predictable lack of oversight will be society's inability to respond appropriately to disturbing incidents and long-term trends. In other words, the practice most likely will not be as amenable to regulation as the proponents contend.

THREE APPROACHES TO SOCIAL POLICY

... Central to any serious evaluation of competing policy approaches to PAS and euthanasia is the distinction between the morality of individual acts and the wisdom of social policy. Much of the debate in the popular media is driven by the depiction of especially dramatic and poignant instances of suffering humanity, desperate for release from the painful thrall of terminal illness. Understandably, many of us are prompted to respond: "Should such a terrible fate ever befall me, I certainly would not want to suffer interminably; I would want the option of an early exit and the help of my trusted physician in securing it." The problem, however, lies in getting from such compelling individual cases to social policy. The issue is not simply, "What would I want?," but rather, what the best social policy is, all things considered. Social pessimists warn that we cannot make this jump from individual case to policy without endangering the autonomy and the very lives of others, many of whom are numbered among our most vulnerable citizens....

A Policy of Prudent (Legal) Restraint and Aggressive (Medical) Intervention

In contrast to the judicial approach, which totally vindicates the value of patient autonomy at the expense of protecting the vulnerable,... my own preferred approach to a social policy of PAS and euthanasia conceives of this debate as posing essentially a "tragic choice." It frankly acknowledges that whatever choice we make, whether we opt for a reaffirmation of the current legal restraints or for a policy of legitimation and regulation, there are bound to be "victims." The victims of the current policy are easy to identify: they are on the news, the talk shows, the documentaries, and often on Dr. Kevorkian's roster of so-called "patients." The victims of legalization, by contrast, will be largely hidden from view; they will include the clinically depressed eighty-year-old man who could have lived for another year of good quality if only he had been adequately treated, and the fifty-year-old woman who asks for death because doctors in her financially stretched HMO cannot, or will not, effectively treat her unrelenting, but mysterious, pelvic pain. Perhaps eventually, if we slide far enough down the slope, the uncommunicative stroke victim, whose distant children deem an earlier death to be a better death, will fall victim. There will be others besides these, many coming from the ranks of the uninsured and the poor. To the extent that minorities and the poor already suffer from the effects of discrimination in our health care system, it is reasonable to expect that any system of PAS and euthanasia will exhibit similar effects, such as failure to access adequate primary care, pain management, and psychiatric diagnosis and treatment. Unlike Dr. Kevorkian's "patients," these victims will not get their pictures in the papers, but they all will have faces and they will all be cheated of good months or perhaps even years.

This "tragic choice" approach to social policy on PAS/euthanasia takes the form of the following argument, with four basic steps. First, the number of "genuine cases" justifying PAS, active euthanasia, or both, will be relatively small. Patients who receive good personal care, good pain relief, treatment for depression, and adequate psycho-social supports tend not to persist in their desire to die.

Second, the social risks of legalization are serious and highly predictable. They include the expansion of these practices to nonvoluntary cases, the advent of active euthanasia, and the widespread failure to pursue readily available alternatives to suicide motivated by pain, depression, lack of access to good medical care, and hopelessness.

Third, rather than propose a momentous and dangerous policy shift for a relatively small number of "genuine cases"—a shift that would surely involve a great deal of persistent social division and strife analogous to that involved in the abortion controversy—we should instead attempt to redirect the public debate toward a goal on which we can and should all agree, namely the manifest and urgent need to reform the way we die in America. Instead of launching a highly divisive and dangerous campaign for PAS, we should attack the problem at its root with an ambitious program of reform in the areas of access to primary care and the education of physicians in palliative care. At least as far as the "slippery slope" opponents of PAS and euthanasia are concerned, we should thus first see to it that the vast majority of people in this country have access to adequate, affordable, and nondiscriminatory, primary and palliative care. At the end of this long and arduous process, when we finally have an equitable, effective, and compassionate health care system in place, one that might be compared favorably with that in the Netherlands, then we might well want to reopen the discussion of PAS and active euthanasia.

Finally, there are those few unfortunate patients who truly are beyond the pale of good palliative, hospice, and psychiatric care. The opponents of legalization can take limited solace from the fact that many such patients still will be able to find compassionate physicians who, like

Dr. Timothy Quill, will ultimately be willing, albeit in fear and trembling, to "take small risks for people [they] really know and care about." Such actions will continue to take place within the privacy of the patient-physician relationship, however, and thus will not threaten vulnerable patients and the social fabric to the same extent as would result from full legalization and regulation.

To be sure, this kind of continuing covert PAS unfortunately will not be subject to regulation, but the threat of possible criminal sanctions and revocation of licensure will continue to serve, for the majority of physicians, as powerful disincentives to abuse the system. Moreover, as suggested earlier, it is highly unlikely that the proposals for legalization would result in truly effective oversight.

CONCLUSION

Instead of conceiving this momentous debate as a choice between, on: the one hand, legalization and regulation with all of their attendant risks, and on the other hand, the callous abandonment of patients to their pain and suffering, enlightened opponents must recommend a positive program of clinical and social reforms. On the clinical level, physicians must learn how to really listen to their patients, to unflinchingly engage them in sensitive discussions of their needs and the meaning of their requests for assisted death, to deliver appropriate palliative care, to dis-

tinguish fact from fiction in the ethics and law of pain relief, to diagnose and treat clinical depression, and finally, to ascertain and respect their patients' wishes for control regarding the forgoing of life-sustaining treatments. On the social level, opponents of PAS must aggressively promote major initiatives in medical and public education regarding pain control, in the sensitization of insurance companies and licensing agencies to issues of the quality of dying, and in the reform of state laws that currently hinder access to pain relieving medications.

In the absence of an ambitious effort in the direction of aggressive medical and social reform, I fear that the medical and nursing professions will have lost whatever moral warrant and credibility they might still have in continuing to oppose physician-assisted suicide and active euthanasia. As soon as these reforms are in place, however, we might then wish to proceed slowly and cautiously with experiments in various states to test the overall benefits of a policy of legalization. Until that time, however, we are not well served as a society by court decisions allowing for legalization of PAS. I hope and trust that the Supreme Court will strike them down. Finally, I hope that continued sober reflection on the likely consequences of PAS and euthanasia will prompt John Fletcher to revive his earlier well-founded skepticism regarding the current social risks of these practices.

Physician-Assisted Suicide: Should Be Allowed

Margaret P. Battin

DEALING WITH DYING IN THE UNITED STATES

In the United States, we have come to recognize that the maximal extension of life-prolonging treatment in... late-life degenerative conditions is often inappropriate. Although we could keep the machines and tubes—the respirators, intravenous lines, feeding tubes—hooked up for extended periods, we recognize that this is inhumane, pointless, and financially impossible. Instead, as a society we have developed a number of mechanisms for dealing with these hopeless situations, all of which involve withholding or withdrawing various forms of treatment.

Some mechanisms for withholding or withdrawing treatments are exercised by the patient who is confronted by such a situation or who anticipates it. These include refusal of treatment, the patient-executed Do Not Resuscitate (DNR) order, the Living Will, and the Durable Power of Attorney. Others are mechanisms for decision by second parties about a patient who is no longer competent or never was competent, reflected in a long series of court cases from *Quinlan, Saikewicz, Spring, Eichner, Barber, Bartling, Conroy, Brophy,* the trio *Farrell, Peter,* and *Jobes,* to *Cruzan.* These cases delineate the precise circumstances under which it is appropriate to withhold or withdraw various forms of therapy, including respiratory support, chemotherapy, dialysis, antibiotics in intercurrent infections, and artificial nutrition and hydration. Thus, during the past quarter-century, roughly since *Quinlan*

(1976), the U.S. has developed an impressive body of case law and state statutes that protects, permits, and facilitates the characteristic American strategy of dealing with end-of-life situations. These cases provide a framework for withholding or withdrawing treatment when physicians and family members believe there is no medical or moral point in going on. This has sometimes been termed *passive euthanasia*; more often, it is simply called *allowing to die.*

Indeed, "allowing to die" has become ubiquitous in the United States. For example, a 1988 study found that of the 85% of deaths in the United States that occurred in health care institutions, including hospitals, nursing homes, and other facilities, about 70% involved electively withholding some form of life-sustaining treatment. A 1989 study found that 85–90% of critical care professionals said they were withholding or withdrawing life-sustaining treatments from patients who were "deemed to have irreversible disease and are terminally ill." A 1997 study of limits to life-sustaining care found that between 1987–88 and 1992–93, recommendations to withhold or withdraw life support prior to death increased from 51% to 90% in the intensive-care units studied. Rates of withholding therapy such as ventilator support, surgery, and dialysis were found in yet another study to be substantial, and to increase with age. A 1994/95 study of 167 intensive-care units—all the ICUs associated with U.S. training programs in critical care medicine or pulmonary and critical care medicine—found that in 75% of deaths, some form of care was withheld or withdrawn. It has been estimated that 1.3 million American deaths a year follow decisions to withhold life support, this is a majority of the just over 2 million American deaths per year.

In recent years, the legitimate use of withholding and withdrawing treatment has increasingly been understood to include practices likely or certain to result in death. The administration of escalating doses of morphine in a dying patient, which, it has been claimed, will depress respiration and so hasten death, is accepted under the (Catholic) principle of double effect provided the medication is intended to relieve pain and merely foreseen but not intended to result in death; this practice is not considered killing or active hastening of death. The use of "terminal sedation," in which a patient dying in pain is sedated into unconsciousness while artificial nutrition and hydration are withheld, is also recognized as medically and legally acceptable; it too is understood as a form of "allowing to die," not active killing. With the single exception of Oregon, where physician-assisted suicide became legal in 1997, withholding and withdrawing treatment and related forms of allowing to die are the only legally recognized ways we in the United States go about dealing with dying. A number of recent studies have shown that many physicians—in all states studied—do receive requests for assistance in suicide or active euthanasia and that a substantial number of these physicians have complied with one or more such requests; however, this more direct assistance in dying takes place entirely out of sight of the law. Except in Oregon, *allowing to die*, but not causing to die, has been the only legally protected alternative to maximal treatment legally recognized in the United States; it remains

America's—and American medicine's-official posture in the face of death.

DEALING WITH DYING IN THE NETHERLANDS

In the Netherlands, although the practice of withholding and withdrawing treatment is similar to that in the United States, voluntary active euthanasia and physician assistance in suicide are also available responses to end-of-life situations. Active euthanasia, understood as the termination of the life of the patient at the patient's explicit and persistent request, is the more frequent form of directly assisted dying and most discussion in the Netherlands has concerned it rather than assistance in suicide, though the conceptual difference is not regarded as great: many cases of what the Dutch term *voluntary active euthanasia* involve initial self-administration of the lethal dose by the patient but procurement of death by the physician, and many cases of what is termed *physician-assisted suicide* involve completion of the lethal process by the physician if a self-administered drug does not prove fully effective. Although until 2001 they were still technically illegal under statutory law, and even with legalization remain an "exception" to those provisions of the Dutch Penal Code which prohibit killing on request and intentional assistance in suicide, active euthanasia and assistance in suicide have long been widely regarded as legal, or rather *gedoogd*, legally "tolerated," and have in fact been deemed justified (not only non-punishable) by the courts when performed by a physician if certain conditions were met. Voluntary active euthanasia (in the law, called "life-ending on request") and physician-assisted suicide are now fully legal by statue under these guidelines. Dutch law protects the physician who performs euthanasia or provides assistance in suicide from prosecution for homicide if these guidelines, known as the conditions of "due care," are met.

Over the years, the guidelines have been stated in various ways. They contain six central provisions:

1. that the patient's request be voluntary and well-considered;
2. that the patient be undergoing or about to undergo intolerable suffering, that is, suffering which is lasting and unbearable;
3. that all alternatives acceptable to the patient for relieving the suffering have been tried, and that in the patient's view there is no other reasonable solution;
4. that the patient have full information about his situation and prospects;
5. that the physician consult with a second physician who has examined the patient and whose judgment can be expected to be independent;
6. that in performing euthanasia or assisting in suicide, the physician act with due care.

Of these criteria, it is the first that is held to be central: euthanasia may be performed only at the *voluntary* request of the patient. This criterion is also understood to require that the patient's request be a stable, enduring, reflective one—not the product of a transitory impulse. Every attempt is to be made to rule out depression, psychopathology, pressures from family members, unrealistic fears, and other factors compromising voluntariness, though depression is not in itself understood to preclude such choice. Euthanasia may be performed *only* by a physician, not by a nurse, family member, or other party....

In general, pain alone is not the basis for deciding upon euthanasia, since pain can, in most cases, be effectively treated; only a third of Dutch physicians think that adequate pain control and terminal care make euthanasia redundant, and that number has been dropping. Rather, the "intolerable suffering" mentioned in the second criterion is understood to mean suffering that is intolerable in the patient's (rather than the physician's) view, and can include a fear of or unwillingness to endure entluistering, that gradual effacement and loss of personal identity that characterizes the end stages of many terminal illnesses. In very exceptional circumstances, the Supreme Court ruled in the Chabot case of 1994, physician-assisted suicide may he justified for a patient with non-somatic, psychiatric illness like intractable depression, but such cases are extremely rare and require heightened scrutiny.

In a year, about 35,000 patients seek reassurance from their physicians that they will be granted euthanasia if their suffering becomes severe; there are about 9,700 explicit requests, and about two-thirds of these are turned down, usually on the grounds that there is some other way of treating the patient's suffering. In 14% of cases in 1990, the denial was based on the presence of depression or psychiatric illness.

In the Netherlands, many hospitals now have protocols for the performance of euthanasia; these serve to ensure that the legal guidelines have been met. However, euthanasia is often practiced in the patient's home, typically by the general practitioner who is the patient's long-term family physician. Euthanasia is usually performed after aggressive hospital treatment has failed to arrest the patient's terminal illness; the patient has come home to die, and the family physician is prepared to ease this passing. Whether practiced at home or in the hospital, it is believed that euthanasia usually takes place in the presence of the family members, perhaps the visiting nurse, and often the patient's pastor or priest. Many doctors say that performing euthanasia is never easy but that it is something they believe a doctor ought to do for his or her patient when the patient genuinely wants it and nothing else can help.

Thus, in the Netherlands a patient who is facing the end of life has an option not openly practiced in the United States, except Oregon: to ask the physician to bring his or her life to an end. Although not everyone in the Netherlands does so—indeed, over 96% of people who die in a given year do not do so in this way—it is a choice legally recognized and widely understood....

OBJECTIONS TO THE DUTCH PRACTICE

The Dutch practice of physician-performed active voluntary euthanasia and physician-assisted suicide... raises a number of ethical issues, many of which have been discussed vigorously both in the Dutch press and in commentary on the Dutch practices from abroad. For one thing, it is sometimes said that the availability of physician-assisted dying creates a disincentive for providing good terminal care. There is no evidence that this is the case; on the contrary, Peter Admiraal, the anesthesiologist who has been perhaps the Netherlands' most vocal defender of voluntary active euthanasia, insists that pain should rarely or never be the occasion for euthanasia, as pain (in contrast to suffering) is comparatively easily treated. In fact, pain is the primary reason for the request in only about 5% of cases. Instead, it is a refusal to endure the final stages of deterioration, both mental and physical, that primarily motivates the majority of requests.

It is also sometimes said that active euthanasia violates the Hippocratic Oath.

The original Greek version of the Oath does prohibit the physician from giving a deadly drug, even when asked for it; but the original version also prohibits the physician from performing surgery and from taking fees for teaching medicine, neither of which prohibitions has survived into contemporary medical practice. At issue is whether deliberately causing the death of one's patient—killing one's patient, some claim—can ever be part of the physician's role. "Doctors must not kill," insist opponents, but Dutch physicians often say that they see performing euthanasia—where it is genuinely requested by the patient and nothing else can be done to relieve the patient's condition—as part of their duty to the patient, not as a violation of it. As the 1995 nationwide report commented, "a large majority of Dutch physicians consider euthanasia an exceptional but accepted part of medical practice." Some Dutch do worry, however, that too many requests for euthanasia or assistance in suicide are refused—only about 1/3 of explicit requests are actually honored. One well-known Dutch commentator points to another, seemingly contrary concern: that some requests are made too early in a terminal course, even shortly after diagnosis, when with good palliative care the patient could live a substantial amount of time longer. However, these are concerns about how euthanasia and physician-assisted suicide are practiced, not about whether they should be legal at all.

The Dutch are also often said to be a risk of starting down the slippery slope, that is, that the practice of voluntary active euthanasia for patients who meet the criteria will erode into practicing less-than-voluntary euthanasia on patients whose problems are not irremediable and perhaps by gradual degrees will develop into terminating the lives of people who are elderly, chronically ill, handicapped, mentally retarded, or otherwise regarded as undesirable. This risk is often expressed in vivid claims of widespread fear and wholesale slaughter—claims based on misinterpretation of the 1,000 cases of life-ending treatment without explicit, current request, claims that are often repeated in the right-to-life press in both the Netherlands and the U.S. although they are simply not true. However, it is true that in recent years the Dutch have begun to agonize over the problems of the incompetent patient, the mentally ill patient, the newborn with serious deficits, and other patients who cannot make voluntary choices, though these are largely understood as issues about withholding or withdrawing treatment, not about direct termination.

What is not often understood is that this new and acutely painful area of reflection for the Dutch—withholding and withdrawing treatment from incompetent patients—has already led in the United States to the emergence of a vast, highly developed body of law: namely, that long series of cases beginning with *Quinlan* and culminating in *Cruzan*. Americans have been discussing these issues for a long time and have developed a broad set of practices that are regarded as routine in withholding and withdrawing treatment from persons who are no longer or never were competent. The Dutch see Americans as much further out on the slippery slope than they are because Americans have already become accustomed to second- party choices that result in death for other people. Issues involving second-party choices are painful to the Dutch in a way they are not to Americans precisely because *voluntariness* is so central in the Dutch understanding of choices about dying. Concomitantly, the Dutch see the Americans' squeamishness about first-

party choices—voluntary euthanasia, assisted suicide—as evidence that we are not genuinely committed to recognizing voluntary choice after all. For this reason, many Dutch commentators believe that the Americans are at a much greater risk of sliding down the slippery slope into involuntary killing than they are.

OBJECTIONS TO THE AMERICAN PRACTICE

The... Dutch and American practices... occur within similar conditions—in industrialized nations with highly developed medical systems where a majority of the population die of illnesses exhibiting characteristically extended downhill courses—but the issues raised by the American response to this situation—relying on withholding and withdrawal of treatment-may be even more disturbing than those of the Dutch.... We Americans often assume that our approach is "safer" because, except in Oregon, it involves only letting someone die, not killing them; but it, too, raises very troubling questions.

The first of these issues is a function of the fact that withdrawing and especially withholding treatment are typically less conspicuous, less pronounced, less evident kinds of actions than direct killing, even though they can equally well lead to death. Decisions about nontreatment have an invisibility that decisions about directly causing death do not have, even though they may have the same result, and hence there is a much wider range of occasions in which such decisions can he made. One can decline to treat a patient in many different ways, at many different times—by not providing oxygen, by not instituting dialysis, by not correcting electrolyte imbalances, and so on—all of which will cause the patient's death. Open medical killing also brings about death, but is much more overt and conspicuous. Consequently, letting die offers many fewer protections. In contrast to the standard slippery-slope argument, which sees killing as riskier than letting die, the more realistic slippery-slope argument warns that because our culture relies primarily on decisions about nontreatment and practices like terminal sedation construed as "allowing to die," grave decisions about living or dying are not as open to scrutiny as they are under more direct life-terminating practices, and hence are more open to abuse. Indeed, in the view of one influential commentator, the Supreme Court's 1997 decision in effect legalized active euthanasia, voluntary and nonvoluntary, in the form of terminal sedation, even as it rejected physician-assisted suicide.

Second, reliance on withholding and withdrawal of treatment invites rationing in an extremely strong way, in part because of the comparative invisibility of these decisions. When a health care provider does not offer a specific sort of care, it is not always possible to discern the motivation; the line between believing that it would not provide benefit to the patient and that it would not provide benefit worth the investment of resources in the patient can be very thin. This is a particular problem where health care financing is decentralized, profit-oriented, and non-universal, as in the United States, and where rationing decisions without benefit of principle are not always available for easy review.

Third, relying on withholding and withdrawal of treatment can often be cruel. Even with Hospice or with skilled palliative care, it requires that the patient who is dying from one of the diseases that exhibits a characteristic extended, downhill course (as the majority of patients in the developed world all do) must, in effect, wait to die until the absence of a certain treatment will cause death. For instance, the cancer patient who forgoes chemotherapy or surgery does not simply die from this choice; he or she continues to endure the downhill course of the cancer until the tumor finally destroys some crucial bodily function or organ. The patient with amyotrophic lateral sclerosis who decides in advance to decline respiratory support does not die at the time this choice is made but continues to endure increasing paralysis until breathing is impaired and suffocation occurs. Of course, attempts are made to try to ameliorate these situations by administering pain medication or symptom control at the time treatment is withheld—for instance, by using opiates and paralytics as a respirator is withdrawn—but these are all ways of disguising the fact that we are letting the disease kill the patient rather than directly bringing about death. But the ways diseases kill people can be far more cruel than the ways physicians kill patients when performing euthanasia or assisting in suicide....

THE CONTINUING DEBATE:
Physician-Assisted Suicide

What Is New

Currently the state of Oregon (under the *Oregon Death with Dignity Act*, passed in 1994 by a small margin, and then reaffirmed in 1997 by sixty percent of the voters) allows physician-assisted suicide, though the issue continues in the courts. Attorney General John Ashcroft issued a directive asserting that the act violates the Controlled Substances Act, and that participating physicians would risk criminal prosecution and loss of their licenses. However, Ashcroft's directive was recently struck down by the 9th U.S. Circuit Court of Appeals, which ruled that Ashcroft had overstepped his authority and interfered in an issue that belonged to the state. Thus physician-assisted suicide is currently allowed in Oregon, although the Bush Administration has asked the Supreme Court to hear an appeal of the 9th Court decision. The Netherlands, after long allowing active euthanasia on the basis of Dutch judicial decisions, recently passed legislation giving formal legislative approval of active euthanasia, and establishing clear guidelines for its use.

Where to Find More

Ethics Updates provides (*ethics.sandiego.edu/*) extensive online resources on the question of euthanasia, including videos, links to other sites, recorded radio discussions, and full text articles taking a wide range of positions. The full text of the Supreme Court's ruling in *Washington v. Glucksberg and Vacco v. Quill* can be found at *www.Oyez.org*. It is also available at Ethics Updates, along with a number of Amicus Briefs on the subject. For more information concerning the key Supreme Court cases, see Bryan Hilliard, *The U.S. Supreme Court and Medical Ethics* (St. Paul: Paragon House, 2004).

F. M. Kamm presents a well-crafted argument in favor of euthanasia and physician-assisted suicide: "A Right to Choose Death?" Originally published in *Boston Review*, it is available online at *bostonreview.net/BR22.3/Kamm.html*, and also at Ethics Updates.

James Rachels' brief paper, "Active and Passive Euthanasia," was originally published in *New England Journal of Medicine*, 292 (1975), and has been widely anthologized. Rachels argues that there is no moral difference between allowing a patient to die and causing the patient's death. Rachels' ideas are expanded in his book, *The End of Life: Euthanasia and Morality* (New York: Oxford University Press, 1986).

Edmund D. Pellegrino's "Distortion of the Healing Relationship," in *Ethical Issues in Death and Dying*, second edition, Tom L. Beauchamp and Robert M. Veatch, editors (Upper Saddle River, N.J., Prentice-Hall: 1996) is a good brief argument against active euthanasia. For a longer examination of the arguments against euthanasia, see David C. Thomasma and Glenn C. Graber, *Euthanasia: Toward an Ethical Social Policy* (New York: Continuum, 1990).

Margaret P. Battin has an excellent book on the subject: *The Least-Worth Death: Essays in Bioethics at the End of Life* (New York: Oxford University Press, 1994). Ronald Dworkin's *Life's Dominion: An Argument about Abortion, Euthanasia, and Individual Freedom* (New York: Alfred A. Knopf, 1993) is careful and reflective, and treats all sides on these difficult issues with respect and fairness. Susan Wolf's "Gender, Feminism, and Death: Physician-Assisted Suicide and Euthanasia," in *Feminism & Bioethics: Beyond Reproduction*, edited by Susan M. Wolf (New York: Oxford University Press, 1996) raises doubts about active euthanasia, and offers original insights on an old issue. An excellent recent debate is found in Gerald Dworkin, R. G. Frey, and Sissela Bok, *Euthanasia and Physician-Assisted Suicide* (Cambridge: Cambridge University Press, 1998).

Active euthanasia has been openly practiced in the Netherlands for many years, originally authorized by judicial rulings. The Dutch experience with euthanasia has been closely watched, and one of the best sources for examining the issue from the Dutch perspective is a book edited by David C. Thomasma, Thomasine Kimbrough-Kushner, Gerrit K. Kimsma, and Chris Ciesielski-Carlucci, eds., *Asking To Die: Inside the Dutch Debate about Euthanasia* (Dordrecht: Kluwer Academic Publishers, 1998).

There are many good anthologies on euthanasia, including: Bonnie Steinbock and Alastair Norcross, editors, *Killing and Letting Die*, 2nd Ed. (New York: Fordham University Press, 1994); Margaret Battin, Rosamond Rhodes, and Anita Silvers, eds. *Physician-Assisted Suicide: Expanding the Debate* (London: Routledge, 1998); Loretta M. Kopelman and Kenneth A. De Ville, eds., *Physician-Assisted Suicide: What Are the Issues?* (Dordrecht: Kluwer, 2001); and Robert F. Weir, editor, *Physician-Assisted Suicide* (Bloomington: Indiana University Press, 1997).

CAPITAL PUNISHMENT

Is It Appropriate for Some Crimes *or* Should It Be Abolished?

CAPITAL PUNISHMENT IS APPROPRIATE FOR SOME CRIMES

ADVOCATE: Walter Berns, Resident Scholar, American Enterprise Institute; Professor Emeritus and formerly John M. Olin University Professor, Georgetown University

SOURCE: "The Morality of Anger," from his book *For Capital Punishment: Crime and the Morality of the Death Penalty* (New York: Basic Books, 1979)

CAPITAL PUNISHMENT SHOULD BE ABOLISHED

ADVOCATE: Stephen Nathanson, Professor of Philosophy, Northeastern University

SOURCE: "The Death Penalty as a Symbolic Issue," excerpted from chapter 11 of his book, *An Eye for an Eye? The Morality of Punishing by Death* (Totowa, N.J.: Rowman & Littlefield, 1987): 131-146

It is hardly surprising that an issue debated for many centuries has generated a variety of arguments, both pro and con. The classic argument for capital punishment is retributive: Blood deserves blood; those who commit murder deserve to die, and justice is not done when a murderer is allowed to live. The retributive argument plays a prominent role in the history of the capital punishment debate, and it was the argument favored by Immanuel Kant. Its justification is stated plainly by Igor Primoratz:

> Capital punishment ought to be retained where it obtains, and reintroduced in those jurisdictions that have abolished it, although we have no reason to believe that, as a matter of deterrence, it is any better than a very long prison term. It ought to be retained, or reintroduced, for one simple reason: that justice be done in cases of murder, that murderers be punished according to their just deserts. (*Justifying Legal Punishment*, Atlantic Highlands, N.J.: Humanities International, 1989, p. 159)

A more sophisticated version of this argument gives capital punishment a symbolic or expressive function: Capital punishment is the strongest and most appropriate way for society to express its deep abhorrence of the most awful crimes. The argument that capital punishment is an effective deterrent of crime is perennially popular, though it can offer little in the way of empirical support for its claims. Those opposing capital punishment argue that capital punishment may have an expressive function, but that it expresses the wrong message: that killing is a solution, and that reform is impossible. They also argue that capital punishment is a cruel and unusual punishment, and that it has bad effects on those involved in the terrible machinery of execution. Recently, two arguments against capital punishment have come to the forefront: first, that capital punishment is administered in a capricious or arbitrary or racially discriminatory manner; and second, that because of many flaws in our system of justice and the honest mistakes of eyewitnesses, the danger of wrongly executing an innocent prisoner has become unacceptably high. (The large number of convicted prisoners—including many on death row—who have been freed after new evidence has established their innocence gives strong support to this line of abolitionist argument).

POINTS TO PONDER

> Based on the high number of mistaken convictions that have been overturned during the last decade—many for prisoners on death row—there seems little doubt that if capital punishment continues, the state will wrongly execute some innocent persons along with those who are guilty. *If* that is true, is that a sufficient reason to halt capital punishment?

> The United States is the only Western industrialized country that still practices capital punishment; it also has one of the highest homicide rates of any Western industrialized country. Do those facts have any bearing on the question of capital punishment?

> Walter Berns insists that "the criminal law must be made awful, by which I mean inspiring, or commanding 'profound respect or reverential fear.' It must remind us of the moral order by which alone we can live as *human* beings, and in America... the only punishment that can do this is capital punishment." Assuming that the death penalty does command "reverential fear," is that an appropriate goal for a democratic society to have toward its laws, or is it more appropriate to a monarchical or tyrannical society?

> If one *accepts* Berns view that the law requires some punishment that is "awful" and awe-inspiring, is it possible that the nature of such punishment might change over time? Centuries ago only lengthy torture—drawing and quartering, or crucifying—could inspire such "awe"; eventually capital punishment, without torture, seemed sufficient to count as ultimate punishment. Might life without parole now (or in the future) play such an awe-inspiring role?

> Nathanson writes that "Berns' romantic vision of the death penalty cannot withstand confrontation with the actual practice of executions. The actual history of the death penalty [including racism and arbitrary application, and now sometimes accompanied by youthful parties near the prison gates] is scarcely an ennobling spectacle." If Berns conceded that many of the details surrounding executions are tawdry rather than ennobling, could he still argue that the death penalty serves the purpose he lays out for it?

Capital Punishment:
It Is Appropriate for Some Crimes

Walter Berns

Anger is expressed or manifested on those occasions when someone has acted in a manner that is thought to be unjust, and one of its bases is the opinion that men are responsible, and should be held responsible, for what they do. Thus, anger is accompanied not only by the pain caused by him who is the object of anger, but by the pleasure arising from the expectation of exacting revenge on someone who is thought to deserve it. We can become angry with an inanimate object (the door we run into and then kick in return) only by foolishly attributing responsibility to it, and we cannot do that for long, which is why we do not think of returning later to revenge ourselves on the door. For the same reason, we cannot be more than momentarily angry with an animate creature other than man; only a fool or worse would dream of taking revenge on a dog. And, finally, we tend to pity rather than to be angry with men who—because they are insane, for example—are not responsible for their acts. Anger, then, is a very human passion not only because only a human being can be angry, but also because it acknowledges the humanity of its objects: it holds them accountable for what they do. It is an expression of that element of the soul that is connected with the view that there is responsibility in the world; and in holding particular men responsible, it pays them that respect which is due them as men. Anger recognizes that only men have the capacity to be moral beings and, in so doing, acknowledges the dignity of human beings. Anger is somehow connected

with justice, and it is this that modern penology has not understood; it tends, on the whole, to regard anger as merely a selfish passion.

It can, of course, be that; and if someone does not become angry with an insult or an injury suffered unjustly, we tend to think he does not think much of himself. But it need not be selfish, not in the sense of being provoked only by an injury suffered by oneself. There were many angry men in America when President Kennedy was killed; one of them—Jack Ruby—even took it upon himself to exact the punishment that, if indeed deserved, ought to have been exacted by the law. There were perhaps even angrier men when Martin Luther King was killed, for King, more than anyone else at the time, embodied a people's quest for justice; the anger—more, the "black rage"—expressed on that occasion was simply a manifestation of the great change that had occurred among black men in America, a change wrought in large part by King and his associates in the civil rights movement: the servility and fear of the past had been replaced by pride and anger, and the treatment that had formerly been accepted as a matter of course or as if it were deserved was now seen for what it was, unjust and unacceptable. King preached love but the movement he led depended on anger as well as love, and that anger was not despicable, being neither selfish nor unjustified. On the contrary, it was a reflection of what was called solidarity and may more accurately be called a profound caring for others, black for other blacks, white for blacks, and, in the world King was trying to build, American for other Americans. If men are not saddened when someone else suffers, or angry when someone else suffers unjustly, the implication is that they do not care for anyone other than themselves or that they lack some quality that befits a man. When we criticize them for this, we acknowledge that they ought to care for others. If men are not angry when a neighbor suffers at the hands of a criminal, the implication is that their moral faculties have been corrupted, that they are not good citizens.

Criminals are properly the objects of anger, and the perpetrators of terrible crimes—for example, Lee Harvey Oswald and James Earl Ray—are properly the objects of great anger. They have done more than inflict an injury on an isolated individual; they have violated the foundations of trust and friendship, the necessary elements of a moral community, the only community worth living in. A moral community, unlike a hive of bees or a hill of ants, is one whose members are expected freely to obey the laws and, unlike a tyranny, are trusted to obey the laws. The criminal has violated that trust, and in so doing has injured not merely his immediate victim but the community as such. He has called into question the very possibility of that community by suggesting that men cannot be trusted freely to respect the property, the person, and the dignity of those with whom they are associated. If, then, men are not angry when someone else is robbed, raped, or murdered, the implication is that there is no moral community because those men do not care for anyone other than themselves. Anger is an expression of that caring, and society needs men who care for each other, who share their pleasures and their pains, and do so for the sake of the others. It is the passion that can cause us to act for reasons

having nothing to do with selfish or mean calculation; indeed, when educated, it can become a generous passion, the passion that protects the community or country by demanding punishment for its enemies. It is the stuff from which heroes are made.

THE IMMORALITY OF ABOLITION

A moral community is not possible without anger and the moral indignation that accompanies it....

The abolitionists are the moralists, their opponents (the "hang-hards") the immoralists; they respect human life, the others show disdain for it; they recognize man's dignity, the others are blind to every human consideration. This is what the abolitionists say, but the opposite is closer to the truth. Abe Fortas, writing after he stepped down from the Supreme Court,... says that the "essential value," the value that constitutes the "basis of our civilization," is a "pervasive, unqualified respect for life." This unqualified respect for life forbids us, he says, to take anyone's life, even a murderer's life. But even a moment's reflection shows that our respect for life is not and has never been "unqualified." We send men into battle knowing that some of them will lose their lives. By what right do we do this? By what right deriving from the "basis of our civilization" do we expect citizens to stand ready to give their lives for their country? Well, in fact, by the same right that led Lincoln to believe, or at least to hope, that Mrs. Bixby might be consoled by "the thanks of the Republic [her sons] died to save" or to hope that she might derive a "solemn pride" for having "laid so costly a sacrifice upon the altar of freedom." Similar considerations led the Founders in 1776 to pledge their "lives"—as well as their "fortunes" and their "sacred honor"—to the cause of our independent establishment as a nation. The men who founded this country, as well as its greatest defenders, thought that what was essential was not *that* one live but *how* one lives,...

Then Justice Brennan, still on the Court, says the death penalty does not "comport with human dignity" because it treats "members of the human race as nonhumans, as objects to be toyed with and discarded." On the contrary, it treats them as responsible moral beings. Did not Washington refuse to commute Major André's death sentence, and did not André go to his death with dignity? And was this not also true of the American spy, Nathan Hale, whose statue stands in the Yale Yard, with hands tied behind the back and head held high, presumably as an inspiration to the undergraduates who are supposed to look upon their country—"for God, for Country, and for Yale"—as something worth dying for? The legendary Hale regretted that he could die only once for it. The British did not toy with him, any more than the Americans toyed with André; in fact, by executing Hale the British provided his countrymen, then and since, with a standard against which to measure the greatness of his deeds. If we cannot say Hale achieved dignity by being put to death, we can say he achieved it by his willingness to serve his country at the risk of death, and the reality of that risk is a measure of his greatness in American eyes. By way of claiming dignity for his own position, Justice Brennan also says that the authors of the cruel and unusual clause of the Eighth Amendment intended to forbid all punishments that do not comport with human dignity, and that the death penalty does not comport with human dignity because it is too severe, and that it is too severe because it causes death. Of course it does. But, as Brennan knows, the authors of the Eighth Amendment were not opposed to it, and, therefore, could

not have regarded it as too severe, and, therefore, could not have regarded it as incompatible with human dignity. Brennan concludes by saying that "even the vilest criminal remains a human being possessed of human dignity," which is cited as evidence of Brennan's humanism. But what sort of humanism is it that respects equally the life of Thomas Jefferson and Charles Manson, Abraham Lincoln and Adolf Eichmann, Martin Luther King and James Earl Ray? To say that these men, some great and some unspeakably vile, equally possess human dignity is to demonstrate an inability to make a moral judgment derived from or based on the idea of human dignity. Understood as Brennan understands it, the term should be dropped from the debate; it is meaningless, empty, as empty as the morality he and his abolitionist colleagues espouse....

THE MORAL NECESSITY OF CAPITAL PUNISHMENT

... What can a dramatic poet tell us about murder? More, probably, than anyone else, if he is a poet worthy of our consideration, and yet nothing that does not inhere in the act itself. In *Macbeth*, Shakespeare shows us murders committed in a political world by a man so driven by ambition to rule that world that he becomes a tyrant. Is that a true account of a great but unbridled ambition? He shows us also the consequences, which were terrible, worse even than Macbeth feared. The cosmos rebelled, turned into chaos by his deeds. He shows a world that was not "benignly indifferent" to what we call crimes and especially to murder, a world constituted by laws divine as well as human, and Macbeth violated the most awful of those laws. Because the world was so constituted, Macbeth suffered the torments of the great and the damned, torments far beyond the "practice" of any physician.

Will all great Neptune's ocean wash
  this blood
Clean from my hand? No, this my
  hand will rather
The multitudinous seas incarnadine,
Making the green one red.

He had known glory and had deserved the respect and affection of king, countrymen, army, friends, and wife; and he lost it all. At the end he was reduced to saying that life "is a tale/Told by an idiot, full of sound and fury,/Signifying nothing"; yet, in spite of the horrors provoked in us by his acts, he excites no anger in us. We pity him; even so, we understand the anger of his countrymen and the dramatic necessity of his death. *Macbeth* is a play about ambition, murder, tyranny; about horror, anger, vengeance, and, perhaps more than any other of Shakespeare's plays, justice. Because of justice, Macbeth has to die, not at his own hand—he will not "play the Roman fool, and die/On [his] own sword"—but at the hand of the avenging Macduff. The dramatic necessity of his death would appear to rest on its moral necessity. Is that right? Does this play conform to our sense of what a murder means? Lincoln thought it was "wonderful."...

[Shakespeare's account of murder is true] to our natural moral sense of what a murder is and what are the consequences that attend it. Shakespeare shows us vengeful men because there is something in the souls of men—men then and men now—that requires such crimes to be revenged. Can we imagine a world that does not take its revenge on the man who kills Macduff's wife and children? (Can we imagine the play in which Macbeth does not die?) Can we imagine a people that does not hate murderers? To ask these questions is to ask whether we can imagine a world without Shakespeare's poetry,

because that poetry is a reflection of the moral sense we have, and it would be impossible on the basis of the moral sense that the abolitionists insist we ought to have....

CONCLUSION

There is a sense in which punishment may be likened to dramatic poetry or the purpose of punishment to one of the intentions of a great dramatic poet (and Shakespeare is clearly the greatest in our language).... In *Macbeth* the majesty of the moral law is demonstrated to us; as I said, it teaches us the awesomeness of the commandment, thou shalt not kill. In a similar fashion, the punishments imposed by the legal order remind us of the reign of the moral order; not only do they remind us of it, but by enforcing its prescriptions, they enhance the dignity of the legal order in the eyes of moral men, in the eyes of those decent citizens who cry out "for gods who will avenge injustice." Reenforcing the moral order is especially important in a self-governing community, a community that gives laws to itself.

That the American legal order must, in the eyes of its citizens, have this dignity is the substance of Madison's argument in the Forty-ninth *Federalist*. In it he was responding to Jefferson's suggestion that there be conventions of the people whenever "any two of the three branches of government," by extraordinary majorities, shall concur in the opinion that the Constitution should be amended. Madison opposed this suggestion; he saw that these appeals, especially if they were to be frequent, would "deprive the government of that veneration which time bestows on everything, and without which perhaps the wisest and freest governments would not possess the requisite stability." Government rests on opinion, he went on, and the strength of opinion in each individual depends in part on the extent to which he supposes others to share it and in part on its venerableness. Such factors would not matter in a "nation of philosophers"; among such a people a "reverence for the laws would be inculcated by the voice of enlightened reason." But there can be no nation of philosophers, or even one governed by philosophers, and any real government, even "the most rational" government, "will not find it a superfluous advantage to have the prejudices of the community on its side."

I can illustrate Madison's point, and show its relevance to capital punishment, by saying first that if the laws were understood to be divinely inspired or, in the extreme case, divinely given, they would enjoy all the dignity that the opinions of men can attach to anything and all the dignity required to insure their being obeyed by most of the men living under them. Like Duncan in the opinion of Macduff, they would be "the Lord's anointed," and they would be obeyed even as Macduff obeyed the laws of the Scottish kingdom.... But the laws of the United States are not of this description; in fact, among the proposed amendments that became the Bill of Rights was one declaring, not that all power comes from God, but rather "that all power is originally vested in, and consequently derives from the people"; and this proposal was dropped only because it was thought to be redundant: the Constitution's Preamble said essentially the same thing, and what we know as the Tenth Amendment reiterated it. So Madison proposed to make the Constitution venerable in the minds of the people, and Lincoln... went so far as to say that a "political religion" should be made of it. They did this not because the Constitution and the laws made pursuant to it could not be supported by "enlightened reason," but because they feared en-

lightened reason would be in short supply; they therefore sought to augment it. The laws of the United States would be obeyed by some men because they could hear and understand "the voice of enlightened reason," and by other men because they would regard the laws with that "veneration which time bestows on everything."

But, as our history attests, this is only conditionally true. The Constitution is surely regarded with veneration by us—so much so that Supreme Court justices have occasionally complained of our habit of making "constitutionality synonymous with wisdom," or wisdom synonymous with constitutionality—but the extent to which it is venerated and its authority accepted depends on the compatibility of its rules with our moral sensibilities, for the Constitution, despite its venerable character, is not the only source of these moral sensibilities. There was even a period before slavery was abolished by the Thirteenth Amendment when the Constitution was regarded by some very moral men as an abomination: William Lloyd Garrison called it "a convenant with death and an agreement with Hell," and there were honorable men holding important political offices and judicial appointments who refused to enforce the Fugitive Slave Law even though its constitutionality had been affirmed. In time this opinion spread far beyond the ranks of the original Abolitionists until those who held it comprised a constitutional majority of the people, and slavery was abolished. But Lincoln knew that more than amendments were required to make the Constitution once more worthy of the veneration of moral men. This is why, in the Gettysburg Address, he made the principle of the Constitution an inheritance from "our fathers," and asked the living generation to dedicate themselves to the cause that the Gettysburg dead had left "unfinished," so that generations yet unborn might enjoy a "new birth of freedom." For the same reason, in his Second Inaugural he called upon the nation to see in the Civil War the expiation demanded by a just God for the sin of slavery. As Harry V. Jaffa has shown, the Constitution had not only to be cleansed of its aspects of slavery, but, if it were once again to be an object of veneration, it would have to be exalted, its dignity enhanced. This Lincoln sought to do and this, I think, he accomplished. That it should be so esteemed is, as I said before, especially important in a self-governing nation that gives laws to itself, because it is only a short step from the principle that the laws are merely a product of one's own will to the opinion that the only consideration that informs the law is self-interest; and this opinion is only one remove from lawlessness. A nation of simply self-interested men will soon enough perish from the earth.

It was not an accident that Lincoln spoke as he did at Gettysburg or that he chose as the occasion for his words the dedication of a cemetery built on a portion of the greatest battlefield of the Civil War.... His words at Gettysburg serve to remind Americans in particular of what Hegel said people in general needed to know, and could be made to know by means of war and the sacrifices demanded of them in wars, namely, that their country is something more than a "civil society" the purpose of which is simply the protection of individual and selfish interests.

Capital punishment, like Shakespeare's dramatic and Lincoln's political poetry (and it is surely that, and was understood by him to be that) serves to remind us of the majesty of the moral order that is embodied in our law and of the terrible consequences of its breach. The law must not be understood to be merely statute that we

enact or repeal at our will and obey or disobey at our convenience, especially not the criminal law. Wherever law is regarded as merely statutory, men will soon enough disobey it, and they will learn how to do so without any inconvenience to themselves. The criminal law must possess a dignity far beyond that possessed by mere statutory enactment or utilitarian and self-interested calculations; the most powerful means we have to give it that dignity is to authorize it to impose the ultimate penalty. The criminal law must be made awful, by which I mean, awe-inspiring, or commanding "profound respect or reverential fear." It must remind us of the moral order by which alone we can live as *human* beings, and in our day the only punishment that can do this is capital punishment.

That was not always the case. In the beginning, banishment was considered the equal to the death penalty in severity and significance: Cain was not put to death but, instead, was banished "from the presence of the Lord" to become a "fugitive and vagabond" on the earth, unfit to live in the human community—or, as Justice Felix Frankfurter once said respecting certain American criminals, unfit "to remain in the communion of our citizens." But he said that in a dissenting opinion; the Court's majority said that Americans may no longer be banished or punished by being deprived of their citizenship. They may voluntarily renounce their citizenship, but imposed as punishment, expatriation is unconstitutionally cruel and unusual. Citizenship, said Chief Justice Warren, is the right to have rights, and Congress may not deprive anyone of that right, no matter what duties he shirks or what crimes he commits. Even a traitor who levies war against the United States is entitled to remain a citizen of the United States if, for some reason (perhaps because he is uncertain who is going to win that war), he wishes to do so. The essence of American citizenship, as the Warren Court saw it, consists in the right to keep one's options open, so to speak.... The justices may not know it, but this understanding of the rights and duties of American citizenship owes much to Beccaria, who devoted the chapter following his chapter on the death penalty to "banishment and confiscations," and in the course of it said that the "loss of possessions is a punishment greater than that of banishment."

Beccaria opposed both banishment and capital punishment because he understood that both were inconsistent with the principle of self-interest, which was the basis of the political order he favored. If a man's first or only duty is to himself, of course he will prefer his money to his country; he will also prefer his money to his brother. In fact, he will prefer his brother's money to his brother, and a people of this description, or a country that understands itself in this Beccarian manner, can put the mark of Cain on no one. For the same reason, such a country can have no legitimate reason to execute its criminals, or, indeed, to punish them in any manner. What would be accomplished by punishment in such a place? Punishment arises out of the demand for justice, and justice is demanded by angry, morally indignant men; its purpose is to satisfy that moral indignation and thereby promote the law-abidingness which, it is assumed, accompanies it. But the principle of self-interest denies the moral basis of that indignation.

Not only will a country based solely on self-interest have no legitimate reason to punish; it may have no need to punish. It may be able to solve what we call the crime problem by substituting a law of contracts for a law of crimes. According to

Beccaria and Hobbes's social contract, men agree to yield their natural freedom to the "sovereign" in exchange for his promise to keep the peace. As it becomes more difficult for the sovereign to fulfill his part of the contract, there is a demand that he be made to pay for his nonperformance. From this come compensation or insurance schemes embodied in statutes whereby the sovereign (or state), being unable to keep the peace by punishing criminals, agrees to compensate its contractual partners for injuries suffered at the hands of criminals, injuries the police are unable to prevent. The insurance policy takes the place of law enforcement and the *posse comitatus*, and John Wayne and Gary Cooper give way to Mutual of Omaha. There is no anger in this kind of law and none (or no reason for any) in the society. The principle can be carried further still. If we ignore the victim (and nothing we do can restore his life anyway), there would appear to be no reason why—the worth of a man being his price, as Hobbes put it—coverage should not be extended to the losses incurred in a murder. If we ignore the victim's sensibilities (and what are they but absurd vanities?), there would appear to be no reason why—the worth of a woman being *her* price—coverage should not be extended to the losses incurred in a rape. Other examples will, no doubt, suggest themselves.

This might appear to be an almost perfect solution to what we persist in calling the crime problem, achieved without risking the terrible things sometimes done by an angry people. A people that is not angry with "criminals" will not be able to deter crime, but a people fully covered by insurance has no need to deter crime: they will be insured against all the losses they can, in principle, suffer. What is now called crime can be expected to increase in volume, of course, and this will cause an increase in the premiums paid, directly or in the form of taxes; but it will no longer be necessary to apprehend, try, and punish criminals.... There is this difficulty: as Rousseau put it, to exclude anger from the human community is to concentrate all the passions in a "self-interest of the meanest sort," and such a place would not be fit for human habitation.

When, in 1976, the Supreme Court declared death to be a constitutional penalty, it decided that the United States was not that sort of country; most of us, I think, can appreciate that judgment. We want to live among people who do not value their possessions more than their citizenship, who do not think exclusively or even primarily of their own rights, people whom we can depend on even as they exercise their rights, and whom we can trust, which is to say, people who, even in the absence of a policeman, will not assault our bodies or steal our possessions, and might even come to our assistance when we need it, and who stand ready, when the occasion demands it, to risk their lives in the defense of their country. If we are of the opinion that the United States may rightly ask of its citizens this awful sacrifice, then we are also of the opinion that it may rightly impose the most awful penalty; if it may rightly honor its heroes, it may rightly execute the worst of its criminals. By doing so, it will remind its citizens that it is a country worthy of heroes.

Capital Punishment:
It Should Be Abolished

STEPHEN NATHANSON

The debate about the morality of the death penalty is one of those recurring questions that seems to have a life of its own. Shifts in public opinion, actions by legislatures, or decisions by courts may sometimes appear to put the issue to rest, but somehow the debate retains its vigor. Why is this?

The first and perhaps most important reason is the obvious one that lives are at stake. Death penalty opponents cannot accept defeat because the operation of the death penalty means that people will die. Some of those who die ought not to be executed, even if we accept the criteria of death penalty supporters. They may be innocent, or they may have acted wrongly but not from deep-seated malice or cruelty. To let the issue rest is to allow these errors to occur without challenge. Likewise, for death penalty supporters who believe that executions are a superior deterrent, it is the lives of potential victims that are at stake. They too cannot rest when public policy runs contrary to their views.

Second, because the stakes are high, people's feelings are deeply engaged by the issue, and they are motivated to continue the struggle. The taking of lives—whether by murder or by legal execution—is a "gut" issue, not in the sense that we cannot reason about it but rather in the sense that we are deeply affected by killings and feel strongly about the views we hold. Given the strong feelings aroused by the issue, neither side is willing to accept defeat.

Finally, the question whether we ought to punish by death is a question with great symbolic meaning. For people on both sides, whether we impose or refrain from imposing the death penalty seems to say something about our values, about the kind of people we are, about the nature of our society. The death penalty debate is in part a field on which we champion some of our most central social and ethical ideals. We think that retaining or abolishing the death penalty conveys an important message, and we want it to be the right message.

One might think that symbolic messages are even more difficult to reason about than the other questions we have considered, but there is no obvious reason why assessing these messages is beyond our ability. If they are an important component of the debate, we should try to confront them directly....

THE MORALITY OF ANGER

The symbolic importance of the death penalty is strongly emphasized by Walter Berns in his defense of the death penalty. In discussing the symbolism of punishing by death, Berns stresses the moral significance of anger. He writes:

> If... men are not angry when someone else is robbed, raped, or murdered, the implication is that no moral community exists, because those men do not care for anyone other than themselves. Anger is an expression of that caring, and society needs men who care for one another.... [Anger] is the passion that can cause us to act for reasons having nothing to do with selfish or

mean calculation: indeed, when educated, it can become a generous passion, the passion that protects the community or country by demanding punishment for its enemies.

Berns wants to vindicate anger because he regards it as an expression of concern for others, and he fears that society is being undermined by a lack of other-directed concerns. He criticizes liberal political theory for what he sees as a capitulation to self- interest. Anger shows that we are not simply self-interested individuals joined together in a marriage of convenience. Instead, we are a community of people who share common concerns and recognize common values.

Berns is certainly correct that anger may reveal important virtues in people, especially if a failure to be angry arises either from callousness or indifference. Nonetheless, whatever virtues are displayed by anger, everyone would agree that the actions that flow from anger must be controlled. The expression of anger needs to be limited by moral constraints, and the reasons for these constraints are moral and not simply pragmatic or self-interested.

A person whose family has been killed in an automobile accident caused by the carelessness of another driver may be angry enough to kill the driver. The anger shows the depth of the person's caring for other human beings, but it does not provide a justification for killing the driver. Virtually everyone would agree that execution for carelessness is too severe a response. While some negative response to destructive and harmful actions is appropriate, it does not follow that anything done in the name of righteous anger is morally right.

I know of no one who denies that anger and outrage are the appropriate responses to the murder of innocent human beings. Nor do I know of anyone who argues that murderers should not be punished at all. The question is whether punishing by death is morally required. That we may feel angry enough to kill someone does not imply that doing so would be morally legitimate.

So, one can sympathize and agree with much of Berns' message, but that message does nothing to support the appropriateness of using death as a punishment. To favor severe but lesser punishments is in no way to express indifference or callousness toward the deaths of murder victims. The anger and grief that we feel about these deaths do not give us a license to kill.

Indeed, at the level of symbolism, one would think that it was important to convey the message that strong feelings of anger or hatred do not by themselves justify the taking of life. In a society where the strength of one's passions became a justification for harming others (and not just a potential excuse or mitigating factor), those whom we care about would be more rather than less threatened. It would be a mistake to convey to people that killing in anger is a morally acceptable act.

AFFIRMING THE MORAL ORDER

Berns is critical of liberal political theorists because they emphasize that government is a humanly created instrument. He believes that if people regard laws as conveniences for improving life, then they will not take them seriously enough. They will feel free to disobey the law when obedience is inconvenient. Part of the appeal of the death penalty for Berns is that it suggests that the law possesses a transcendent value. "Capital punishment," he writes,

> serves to remind us of the majesty of the moral order that is embodied in our law and of the terrible consequences of its breach. The law must

not be understood to be merely statute that we enact or repeal at our will and obey or disobey at our convenience, especially not the criminal law.... The criminal law must be made awful, by which I mean, awe-inspiring... It must remind us of the moral order by which alone we can live as *human* beings, and in our day the only punishment that can do this is capital punishment.

For Berns, permitting the state to punish by death is a means of affirming the moral order and its embodiment in the law.

Berns is correct about one point here. The law must support the moral order in the sense that it must provide appropriate punishments for particular crimes. Morality is subverted when terrible crimes go unpunished or are punished very leniently, since these responses would suggest that the crimes are not really serious. One of the worst implications of the statistics that show fewer death sentences for murders of black victims is that this undermines the value of the lives of black citizens and sends a permissive signal to people about the killing of blacks.

In the same way, however, the disproportionate number of blacks who have been executed for killing whites seriously calls into question Berns' notion that the actual practice of the death penalty affirms the moral order. Berns' romantic vision of the death penalty cannot withstand confrontation with the actual practice of executions. The actual history of the death penalty is scarcely an ennobling spectacle.

Thinking about the actual practice of executions as opposed to a romanticized vision of what punishment might be leads to the most serious problem with Berns' view of the symbolism of executions. Berns wants to see the moral order reaffirmed, but he equates this order with the

legal system. He does not want us to view the law "merely [as] statute that we enact or repeal at will." Yet, that is precisely what the law is. While the moral order does not shift with the votes of a legislature, the legal order does. All too frequently, the legal order itself runs quite counter to what morality would require. Bernss does the cause of morality no service by offering a blanket sanctification of the law.

Surely Berns is correct in his view that the nature and content of the law is a serious matter, but it is doubtful that we need to kill people in order to convey that message. Moreover, by revering the law when it does not deserve reverence, we help to perpetuate injustice. A critical and sober view of the law may do more to affirm the moral order than an attitude of awe or exaggerated respect. The critic who sees the flaws of the legal system and wants to limit its powers may be as committed to the moral order as Berns and may indeed have a better way to make the legal system conform to the moral order.

There are, then, several flaws in Berns' argument. He nowhere shows that the death penalty is necessary to producing the right moral attitude toward the law. He ignores the reality of the death penalty and the messages that its actual—as opposed to its idealized—workings convey. Finally, he supports a reverential and uncritical view of the law that is not likely to help us to improve the legal order.

THE SYMBOLISM OF ABOLISHING THE DEATH PENALTY

What is the symbolic message that we would convey by deciding to renounce the death penalty and to abolish its use?

I think that there are two primary messages. The first is the most frequently emphasized and is usually expressed in terms of the sanctity of human life, although I think we could better express it in terms of respect for human dignity. One way we express our respect for the dignity of human beings is by abstaining from depriving them of their lives, even if they have done terrible deeds In defense of human well-being, we may punish people for their crimes, but we ought not to deprive them of everything, which is what the death penalty does.

If we take the life of a criminal, we convey the idea that by his deeds he has made himself worthless and totally without human value. I do not believe that we are in a position to affirm that of anyone. We may hate such a person and feel the deepest anger against him, but when he no longer poses a threat to anyone, we ought not to take his life.

But, one might ask, hasn't the murderer forfeited whatever rights he might have had to our respect? Hasn't he, by his deeds, given up any rights that he had to decent treatment? Aren't we morally free to kill him if we wish?

These questions express important doubts about the obligation to accord any respect to those who have acted so deplorably, but I do not think that they prove that any such forfeiture has occurred. Certainly, when people murder or commit other crimes, they do forfeit some of the rights that are possessed by the law-abiding. They lose a certain right to be left alone. It becomes permissible to bring them to trial and, if they are convicted, to impose an appropriate—even a dreadful—punishment on them.

Nonetheless, they do not forfeit all their rights. It does not follow from the vileness of their actions that we can do anything whatsoever to them. This is part of the moral meaning of the constitutional ban on cruel and unusual punishments. No matter how terrible a person's deeds, we may not punish him in a cruel and unusual way. We may not torture him, for example. His right not to be tortured has not been forfeited. Why do these limits hold? Because this person remains a human being, and we think that there is something in him that we must continue to respect in spite of his terrible acts.

One way of seeing why those who murder still deserve some consideration and respect is by reflecting again on the idea of what it is to *deserve* something. In most contexts, we think that what people deserve depends on what they have done, intended, or tried to do. It depends on features that are qualities of individuals. The best person for the job deserves to be hired. The person who worked especially hard deserves our gratitude. We can call the concept that applies in these cases *personal* desert.

There is another kind of desert, however, that belongs to people by virtue of their humanity itself and does not depend on their individual efforts or achievements. I will call this impersonal kind of desert *human* desert. We appeal to this concept when we think that everyone deserves a certain level of treatment no matter what their individual qualities are. When the signers of the Declaration of Independence affirmed that people had inalienable rights to "life, liberty, and the pursuit of happiness," they were appealing to such an idea. These rights do not have to be earned by people. They are possessed "naturally," and everyone is bound to respect them.

According to the view that I am defending, people do not lose all of their rights when they commit terrible crimes. They still deserve some level of decent treatment simply because they remain living, functioning human beings. This level of moral desert need not be earned, and it cannot be forfeited. This view may sound controversial, but in fact everyone who believes that cruel and unusual punishment should be forbidden implicitly agrees with it. That is, they agree that even after someone has committed a terrible crime, we do not have the right to do anything whatsoever to him.

What I am suggesting is that by renouncing the use of death as a punishment, we express and reaffirm our belief in the inalienable, unforfeitable core of human dignity.

Why is this a worthwhile message to convey? It is worth conveying because this belief is both important and precarious. Throughout history, people have found innumerable reasons to degrade the humanity of one another. They have found qualities in others that they hated or feared, and even when they were not threatened by these people, they have sought to harm them, deprive them of their liberty, or take their lives from them. They have often felt that they had good reasons to do these things, and they have invoked divine commands, racial purity, and state security to support their deeds.

These actions and attitudes are not relics of the past. They remain an awful feature of the contemporary world. By renouncing the death penalty, we show our determination to accord at least minimal respect even to those whom we believe to be personally vile or morally vicious. This is, perhaps, why we speak of the sanctity of human life rather than its value or worth. That which is sacred remains, in some sense, untouchable, and its value is not dependent on its worth or usefulness to us. Kant expressed this ideal of respect in the famous second version of the Categorical Imperative: "So act as to treat humanity, whether in thine own person or in that of any other, in every case as an end withal, never as a means only."...

THE MORALITY OF RESTRAINT

I have argued that the first symbolic meaning conveyed by a renunciation of

the death penalty is that human dignity must be respected in every person. To execute a person for murder is to treat that person as if he were nothing but a murderer and to deprive him of everything that he has. Therefore, if we want to convey the appropriate message about human dignity, we will renounce the death penalty....

[There is a] second important message conveyed by the renunciation of punishing by death. When we restrain ourselves and do not take the lives of those who kill, we communicate the importance of minimizing killing and other acts of violence. We reinforce the idea that violence is morally legitimate only as a defensive measure and should be curbed whenever possible.

We can see the point of this message by contrasting it with Walter Berns' emphasis on the morality of anger. Without discounting all that Berns says, it seems to me that the death penalty supports the morality of anger in an unacceptable way. It suggests that if someone's acts have provoked you to be very angry, then you may legitimately act violently against that person. The morality of restraint, on the other hand, requires that one control one's anger and allows one to attack another person only defensively. Anger by itself provides no justification for violence.

When the state has a murderer in its power and could execute him but does not, this conveys the idea that even though this person has done wrong and even though we may be angry, outraged, and indignant with him, we will nonetheless control ourselves in a way that he did not. We will not kill him, even though we could do so and even though we are angry and indignant. We will exercise restraint, sanctioning killing only when it serves a protective function.

Why should we do this? Partly out of a respect for human dignity. But also because we want the state to set an example of proper behavior. We do not want to encourage people to resort to violence to settle conflicts when there are other ways available. We want to avoid the cycle of violence that can come from retaliation and counter-retaliation. Violence is a contagion that arouses hatred and anger, and if unchecked, it simply leads to still more violence. The state can convey the message that the contagion must be stopped, and the most effective principle for stopping it is the idea that only defensive violence is justifiable. Since the death penalty is not an instance of defensive violence, it ought to be renounced.

We show our respect for life best by restraining ourselves and allowing murderers to live, rather than by following a policy of a life for a life. Respect for life and restraint of violence are aspects of the same ideal. The renunciation of the death penalty would symbolize our support of that ideal....

THE CONTINUING DEBATE:
Capital Punishment

What Is New

A case concerning capital punishment shows up in the Supreme Court almost every session. In 2005 a question before the court (in *Roper v. Simmons*) will be whether executing sixteen- and seventeen-year-old children should be prohibited on the grounds of cruel and unusual punishment. In a 1989 case, *Stanford v. Kentucky*, the court ruled in favor of allowing the execution of juveniles, leaving the United States as the only country in the world—other than possibly Somalia, where the law is not altogether clear—to permit such executions. Since the Court has ruled in the past that what is considered cruel and unusual punishment can change as opinion in the U.S. changes, it is interesting to note that current polls indicate that only one third of Americans support capital punishment for juvenile crimes. In fact, while a majority of Americans support capital punishment (around 64%), that is significantly lower than the high of approximately 80% that was reached in 1994, and the lowest since 1978. When respondents are given a choice between the death penalty and life without parole, there is an almost even split: 50% favor the death penalty and 46% favor life imprisonment. (Gallup Poll News Service, June 2, 2004)

Where to Find More

Full transcripts of all U.S. Supreme Court cases dealing with capital punishment can be found at *www.Oyez.org*. For further study of key Supreme Court death penalty cases, a good source is Barry Latzer, *Death Penalty Cases: Leading U.S. Supreme Court Cases on Capital Punishment* (Woburn, MA: Butterworth-Heinemann, 1997).

Franklin E. Zimring and Gordon Hawkins, *Capital Punishment and the American Agenda* (Cambridge: Cambridge University Press, 1986) places capital punishment within a world setting and draws the historical and sociological background for use of capital punishment in the United States.

Michael A. Mello has been a defense lawyer involved in death row cases for many years; his very readable book on the subject is *Dead Wrong: A Death Row Lawyer Speaks out Against Capital Punishment* (Madison: The University of Wisconsin Press, 1997) Barry Scheck, Peter Neufeld and Jim Dwyer, *Actual Innocence* (New York: Doubleday, 2000) examines the death penalty in light of the many mistaken convictions that have recently been overturned (many involving prisoners on death row).

Three books offer interesting debates on the subject. E. Van den Haag and J. P. Conrad, *The Death Penalty: A Debate* (New York: Plenum, 1983) focuses on the death penalty, as do Louis P. Pojman and Jeffrey Reiman in *The Death Penalty: For and Against* (Rowman & Littlefield, 1998); for a fascinating debate that places the issue in a much larger context, see Jean Hampton and Jeffrie Murphy, *Forgiveness and Mercy* (Cambridge: Cambridge University Press, 1988).

Among the many anthologies are Hugo Adam Bedau, *The Death Penalty in America*, 3rd edition (New York: Oxford University Press, 1982); J. Feinberg and H. Gross, eds., *Punishment: Selected Readings* (Belmont, Cal.: Dickinson, 1975); Carol Wekesser, ed., *The Death Penalty: Opposing Viewpoints* (San Diego, Cal.: Greenhaven Press, 1991); Robert M. Baird and Stuart E. Rosenbaum, *Punishment and the Death*

Penalty: The Current Debate (Amherst, N. Y.: Prometheus Books, 1995); James R. Acker, Robert M. Bohm and Charles S. Lanier, *America's Experiment with Capital Punishment* (Durham, N.C.: Carolina Academic Press, 1998); and Austin Sarat, ed., *The Killing State: Capital Punishment in Law, Politics, and Culture* (New York: Oxford University Press, 1999).

For arguments opposing capital punishment, see Charles Black, *Capital Punishment: The Inevitability of Caprice and Mistake*, 2nd Edition (New York: W. W. Norton, 1976); and Thomas W. Clark, "Crime and Causality: Do Killers Deserve to Die?" *Free Inquiry*, February/March 2005: 34–37. The pro capital punishment view can be found in Walter Berns, *For Capital Punishment: Crime and the Morality of the Death Penalty* (New York: Basic Books, 1979); and Ernest van den Haag, "In Defense of the Death Penalty: A Legal-Practical-Moral Analysis," *Criminal Law Bulletin*, vol. 14 (1978): 51–68.

The Ethics Updates Website has links to other sites, full-text online articles, video discussions, and audio recordings of relevant radio programs; check particularly the link to excellent resources provided by the documentary series *Frontline*. Go to *ethics.sandiego.edu/Applied/Death Penalty*.

CAMPAIGN FINANCE REFORM

Destruction of Freedom *or* Promotion of Democracy?

DESTRUCTION OF FREEDOM

ADVOCATE: Bobby Burchfield, partner in the law firm Covington and Burling

SOURCE: "Enemies of the First Amendment," *Weekly Standard,* October 11, 1999: 23–25

PROMOTION OF DEMOCRACY

ADVOCATE: Ronald Dworkin, Sommer Professor of Law and Philosophy, NYU; and Quain Professor of Jurisprudence at University College, London

SOURCE: "The Curse of American Politics," *New York Review of Books,* October 17, 1996: 19–24

Arizona Senator Barry Goldwater was a revered conservative leader, and a fierce critic of government regulation. But he was also profoundly concerned with the dangers of massive amounts of money corrupting the democratic process: "Our nation is facing a crisis of liberty if we do not control campaign expenditures. Unlimited campaign spending eats at the heart of the democratic process." The perils of great wealth translating into political power have long been recognized: As Supreme Court Justice Louis Brandeis stated, "We can have a democratic society or we can have great concentrated wealth in the hands of a few. We cannot have both."

The cost of running a competitive political campaign has risen to staggering levels. In 2004, the average (mean) cost of a winning House campaign exceeded one million dollars; for a winning Senate campaign, in excess of six and a half million dollars (data from The Campaign Finance Institute, *www.campaignfinanceinstitute.org*). The enormous cost of campaigns has two obvious effects. First, it eliminates from realistic consideration candidates who are not wealthy or do not have wealthy backers. Second, it gives wealthy contributors privileged access to and influence over elected members of government: successful politicians must stay on congenial terms with those who provide the essential cash.

Limiting campaign contributions raises its own problems. If I have great wealth, why should my freedom to spend on campaigns be denied? If I wish to spend my money in television ads promoting a particular cause (such as pro-life or pro-choice), restrictions seem to limit my freedom to express my own ideas and ideals and arguments. On the other hand, some argue that my wealth may make my voice so loud that opposing views are overwhelmed: My right to freedom of speech does not include the right to shout so loudly that all other voices are drowned out.

Buckley v. Valeo, 424 U.S. 1 (1976), is the pivotal U.S. Supreme Court decision for issues of campaign finance reform. The Court ruled that individual contributions to a specific candidate could be limited; however, no limits could be imposed on contributions to organizations that might use the money to support candidates indirectly (for example, by spending money to support an issue that is closely identified with a particular candidate), and no limits could be imposed on the amount of money a wealthy individual can spend on his or her own campaign. The court also struck down any overall limit on campaign spending. In a strong dissent to the majority ruling, Justice White stated:

> Elections are not to turn on the difference in the amounts of money that candidates have to spend. This seems an acceptable purpose and the means chosen a commonsense way to achieve it. The Court nevertheless holds that a candidate has a constitutional right to spend unlimited amounts of money, mostly that of other people, in order to be elected. The holding perhaps is not that federal candidates have the constitutional right to purchase their election, but many will so interpret the Court's conclusion in this case.

Those who oppose campaign finance reform regard the Buckley decision as a great victory for free speech (in the form of financial contributions); advocates of campaign finance reform see it as an enormous roadblock. Both sides agree that prospects for campaign finance reform are profoundly influenced by the Buckley decision.

POINTS TO PONDER

> If you are restricted in how much money you can spend in a political campaign, in support of a candidate, or in support of or opposition to an issue, *is* that a restriction of your free speech?
> Almost everyone agrees that some restrictions on free speech are legitimate: in the classic example, you cannot yell "Fire!" in a crowded theater. If we assume for the purposes of argument that restricting campaign contributions and expenditures *is* a restriction on free speech, is it a *legitimate* restriction on free speech?
> The Supreme Court's Buckley decision (which Burchfield supports and Dworkin opposes) claims that reducing the amount of money spent on campaigns reduces the quantity of political speech and the range of issues discussed, and thus lowers the quality of political debate. There are two claims involved: First, that reducing the amount of money spent in campaigns reduces the quantity of political speech; Second, that such a reduction would result in lowering the quality of political debate. Do you agree with both of those claims? Neither? Could you consistently *agree* with the first and *reject* the second?

Campaign Finance Reform: Destruction of Freedom

BOBBY R. BURCHFIELD

For those who decry the amount and role of money in politics, the problem has an obvious solution: Simply outlaw certain campaign donations and strictly limit spending. To accomplish this, however, reformers must get around a long line of court decisions holding that restrictions on political giving and spending suppress political dialogue and thus violate the First Amendment's guarantee of free speech.

Fortunately for the country, there is no way around the First Amendment. The essential provisions of all campaign finance proposals—and that includes the Shays-Meehan bill passed by the House on September 14 and the less sweeping McCain-Feingold bill now pending in the Senate—inevitably fetter the political debate that is basic to our system of government.

Both the case for campaign finance regulation and this core obstacle remain essentially what they were when Congress passed the Federal Election Campaign Act of 1971 and extensively revised it in 1974. Congress recognized that the goals of regulation advocates—"leveling the playing field" by equalizing resources available to candidates, reducing the total amount of money in politics, and eliminating the reality or appearance of *quid pro quo* corruption—could be achieved only through a vast regulatory regime. The post-Watergate reforms attempted to regulate all activity that "influences a federal election" by imposing disclosure requirements, contribution limits on donations to parties and federal candidates, and spending limits on candidates and independent groups.

Even before they were fully implemented, large portions of the 1974 reforms were struck down by the Supreme Court as offensive to the First Amendment. In its landmark *Buckley v. Valeo* decision in 1976, the Supreme Court ruled that restrictions on political giving and spending have the direct effect of limiting core political speech. "The Act's contribution and expenditure limits," the Court held, "operate in an area of the most fundamental First Amendment activities." Since virtually all means of mass communication require money, limits on campaign spending "necessarily" reduce the number of issues discussed and the quality of the debate. The Court found it "beyond dispute" that campaign regulation was motivated at least in part by the desire to limit communication.

Buckley made clear that the only governmental interest in campaign finance sufficient to override these First Amendment concerns is the need to prevent "corruption," which the Court defined as the giving of dollars for political favors—essentially bribery. The Court unequivocally rejected efforts to reduce or equalize candidate spending as "wholly foreign" to the First Amendment. *Buckley* also emphasized the critical importance of letting both donors and spenders know what activities are subject to regulation. To provide notice to donors and spenders, the Court crafted the "express-advocacy standard"—that is, only speech that "expressly advocates the election or defeat of a clearly identified candidate" can be regulated.

Specifically, the *Buckley* Court upheld limits on the contributions individuals can make to candidates and parties for express advocacy in federal elections. (Corporations and unions had been barred from making federal political contributions for decades.) The limits—$1,000 in gifts to a candidate each election cycle and $20,000 each year to a political party for federal election activity—were deemed narrowly tailored to serve the compelling government interest of eliminating actual or apparent corruption. Disclosure requirements for giving and spending for express advocacy also withstood challenge.

But perhaps more important is what the Court refused to allow. *Buckley* struck down all efforts to limit the amount candidates, parties, and interest groups can spend.

Since the moment *Buckley* was decided, campaign regulation advocates have attacked it. Common Cause, the Brennan Center for Justice (named, ironically, for the principal author of the *Buckley* opinion), and other pro-regulation groups unabashedly call for *Buckley* to be overruled. In a case currently pending before the Supreme Court, senators John McCain and Russell Feingold, joined by other congressional advocates of tighter regulation, have called the constitutional protections elucidated in *Buckley* a "straitjacket" preventing their proposed reforms. They are absolutely right. But it is the reforms that are defective, not the Court's understanding of the First Amendment.

An important by-product of the reforms of the early 1970s is the distinction between "hard" and "soft" money, hard money being money raised subject to the limitations of the Federal Election Campaign Act, soft money being everything else. Under current law, political parties are allowed to accept both soft and hard money, so long as they keep them in separate accounts and do not use soft money

for express advocacy. The current wave of reform proposals aims to stamp out soft money—that is, to bring all political party spending under the regulatory net. The central feature of the Shays-Meehan bill, thus, is a ban on the solicitation or acceptance of soft money by national political parties. The bill would allow national parties to accept only fully regulated hard money.

But the Shays-Meehan bill would do much more. It would effectively prohibit preelection political advertising by corporations, unions, and other groups. Under *Buckley*, dozens of courts have rebuffed federal and state efforts to regulate corporate and union advertisements that do not urge the election or defeat of a clearly identified candidate. No problem. The House bill simply redefines express advocacy to encompass any "communication" on radio or television that *mentions* a candidate within 60 days of an election. Only hard money could be used to fund such advertisements—meaning, in disregard of settled First Amendment law, that corporations, unions, and other interest groups could not fund them. Shays-Meehan, in other words, would make it illegal for Common Cause, which raises all its money outside the Federal Election Campaign Act's restrictions, to pay for a radio advertisement on October 1 in an election year saying "Support the Shays-Meehan Bill." Virtually no one expects this provision to withstand constitutional scrutiny.

But the House bill would impose new restrictions on hard money as well. It would overrule the Supreme Court's 1996 decision in *Colorado Republican Federal Campaign Committee*, under which political parties have a First Amendment right to spend any amount of hard money to advocate the election or defeat of a particular candidate, so long as they do not coordinate that spending with the candidate. The House bill would prohibit such "independent expenditures" favoring a candidate if the political party also engages in any coordinated activity with the candidate—which it always does.

Finally, Shays-Meehan would punish any candidate who spent more than $50,000 of his *own money* on his campaign by denying him party funds. The Supreme Court held in *Buckley* that a candidate can spend as much of his own money as he likes, since he obviously cannot corrupt himself. Apparently members of Congress, a great many of whom first won election by spending from their personal or family fortunes, are now so secure in their huge fund-raising advantage over challengers that they are willing to impose the $50,000 limit on all who run for office.

Days after the House passed the Shays-Meehan bill, senators McCain and Feingold introduced a pared-down version in the Senate. In its present form, the McCain-Feingold legislation would prohibit soft money donations to national political parties and provide some fairly meaningless protection for a small class of workers against use of their union dues for political activities. Commendably, McCain-Feingold abjures many of the offensive features of the House bill. It would not regulate speech by corporations, unions, and other groups; it would not limit independent expenditures by political parties; and it would not bar individuals from financing their own campaigns.

Even without those odious provisions, however, McCain-Feingold flunks the constitutional test. Like the House bill, it would prohibit the Republican and Democratic national committees and their affiliated congressional campaign committees from accepting soft money.

Unable to justify this provision by citing instances of bribery advocates of the soft money ban must argue that soft money donations create the appearance of corruption.

Donors, they say, receive unequal "access" or "influence" in the legislative process. But this argument is specious. The largest soft money donation to the Republican National Committee during the 1998 election cycle was $500,000, a lot of money, to be sure, but only .28 percent of the RNC's total receipts during that cycle. The largest soft money donation to the Democratic National Committee during the same cycle was $250,000, or .21 percent of its receipts. These donations cannot legally be earmarked to aid any specific candidate. Can anyone credibly argue that the RNC or DNC pressures its officeholders to change positions on issues—inevitably alienating other donors—to increase its receipts by a few tenths of a percent?

The tobacco companies, reformers cry, use soft money to buy influence. But during the 1998 cycle, while Congress was considering legislation that would have imposed hundreds of billions of dollars in additional taxes on the tobacco industry, the tobacco companies' donations to Republican party committees declined by almost 20 percent, from $5,232,789 during the 1996 cycle to $4,225,611. It is lobbying expenditures by tobacco companies that rose, reaching $77,474,400 in the 1998 cycle, eighteen times their soft money donations.

The fact is that special interests rely on lobbying, not soft-money donations, to obtain influence. During the 1998 cycle, the top ten corporate soft money donors gave the national parties $12,002,390—and spent $104,176,042 on lobbying. To believe that eliminating soft money donations to political parties would equalize access to legislators is simply naive.

Not only does the soft money ban, then, target a nonexistent problem, it also offends the Constitution in several respects. The Republican and Democratic parties are national parties. In addition to candidates for federal office, they help candidates for governor, state legislator, and mayor. And when they aid state and local candidates, they must comply with state law. Thirty states currently allow corporate contributions to parties; thirty-seven allow union contributions. Simply put, each of these states has made a sovereign legislative judgment about how campaigns for state office will be financed. Like the House bill, McCain-Feingold would summarily overrule those state judgments. It would impose existing federal contribution limits on national party participation in state and local elections, and would create a new federal contribution limit for state political parties. As policy, this is yet another instance of Congress imposing its will on the states. As law, it is an open assault on the Constitution's federal structure and on the powers reserved to the states by the Tenth Amendment.

Finally, the soft money ban would restrict the ability of political parties to engage in pure issue debate—about taxes, health care, gun control, and so on. The Supreme Court made clear in *Buckley* that speakers have an unfettered First Amendment right to discuss issues, using money from any source.

Clearly unconstitutional, a ban on soft money spending by political parties would also be ineffectual: It would simply cause corporations and unions to redirect their soft money resources—from donations to parties, which are fully disclosed, to independent issue advertising, which is not. Corporations and unions would remain free to mount blistering attacks on any candidate by name based on his character or voting record. So long as their speech did not expressly advocate the candidate's election or defeat, it would be constitutionally protected.

Senators McCain and Feingold appear to recognize that the restrictions on corporate and union issue speech in the House bill are unconstitutional. They are perfectly willing, however, to place political parties at a severe disadvantage in relation to such special interests. To join the issue debate at all, parties would have to divert their hard money from direct candidate support. The unavoidable effect of a soft money ban for parties would thus be an abridgment of the parties' political speech and a violation of their right to equal protection.

If restricting issue speech by corporations and unions, personal spending by candidates, and independent spending by parties is so clearly offensive to the First Amendment, why do campaign finance reformers keep trying to do it? The short answer is, they have to. Campaign finance regulation that addresses only party and candidate activity is doomed to fail, since political donors will inevitably use their resources to engage in independent speech that does not expressly advocate any candidate's election. Such speech is fundamental to our democracy. It encompasses virtually every public policy discussion on the air and in print—and is fully protected by the First Amendment.

The reformers know this. As they recently told the Supreme Court in a brief, the giant free speech "loophole" thwarts all efforts at "meaningful" reform. Why else would reform advocates ranging from House minority leader Dick Gephardt to presidential candidate Bill Bradley advocate amending the Constitution to clear away the First Amendment as an obstacle to increased regulation?

But free speech is not a loophole, it is the oxygen of democracy. Plainly overreaching, the regulatory scheme constructed by the House would certainly fail the test of constitutionality. McCain and Feingold, though intending to be more deferential to the Constitution, would leave open the means of evading their restrictions. Either way, the effort to ban soft money is doomed to fail.

Campaign Finance Reform:
Promotion of Democracy

RONALD DWORKIN

1.

America is worried about its democracy in this election year. The power of money in our politics, long a scandal, has now become a disaster. Elections are fought mainly on television, in a battle of endless and hugely expensive political ads, and candidates are trapped in spiraling arms races of fund-raising, desperately trying to raise more than their opponents. *The New York Times* estimates that the 1996 presidential race will cost between $600 million and $1 billion, that it now takes at least $5 million to run a successful Senate campaign—in some states as much as $30 million—and that even a seat in the House can cost $2 million....

The sheer volume of money raised and spent is not the only defect in contemporary American politics. The national political "debate" is now directed by advertising executives and political consultants and conducted mainly through thirty-second, "sound bite" television and radio commercials that are negative, witless, and condescending; these ads, in the view of the authors of a recent book, *Going Negative*, drive political moderates into not voting, leaving the field to partisans and zealots. Television newscasts, from which most Americans now learn most of what they know about candidates and issues, are more and more shaped by rating wars, in which network and local news bureaus are pressed to provide entertainment rather than information or analysis, and by feature reporters, whose definition of success is to become celebrities themselves, with

huge salaries and lecture fees, and public recognition that often dwarfs that of the politicians they supposedly cover....

But money is the biggest threat to the democratic process. The time politicians must spend raising money in endless party functions and in more personal ways—not only during an election campaign but while in office, preparing for the next election—has become an increasingly large drain on their attention. Senator Tom Harkin of Iowa complained in 1988, "As soon as a Senator is elected here, that Senator better start raising money for the next election 6 years down the pike. Everyone here does it, and to deny that is to deny the obvious and to deny what is also on the record." The great corporate contributors are not altruists or even political ideologues—the largest of them contribute to both parties—but businessmen anxious to influence policy or at least, as many corporate executives put it, to insure special "access" to high officials to put the case for their interests.

2.

Money is not only the biggest problem, but in good part the root of other problems as well. If politicians had much less to spend on aggressive, simple-minded television spots, for example, political campaigns would have to rely more on reporters and on events directed by nonpartisan groups, like televised debates, and political argument might become less negative and more constructive. Money is, moreover, also the easiest problem to solve, at least in theory. A free society cannot dictate the tone its politicians adopt or the kind of arguments they offer the public, or what political news or scandal reporters do or do not print, or how carefully television commentators analyze what the candidates have offered or opposed. But a free society can—or so it would seem—limit the amount of money that candidates or anyone else may spend on political campaigns. Every European democracy does this and Europeans are amazed that we do not. But the Supreme Court has held that we may not, that limiting political expenditures by law would be an unconstitutional denial of free speech, in violation of the First Amendment.

Following the Watergate scandals, Congress enacted the 1974 Electoral Reform Act, which set upper limits, or "caps," on any congressional candidate's expenditures. But in its 1976 decision in *Buckley v. Valeo*, the Supreme Court declared those limits unconstitutional. The Court did approve other provisions of the 1974 legislation, which imposed limits on the amounts that individuals and groups can contribute to political parties and campaigns. These permitted individuals to contribute up to $1,000 per election to a federal candidate up to $20,000 a year to a political party, and up to $5,000 to a PAC. They also permitted PACs to donate $50,000 a year to each federal candidate they support, with no limit on the total number of candidates they choose. The Court said that though these constraints limit the political activity of potential contributors in one respect. they leave them free to spend as much of their own money as they wish supporting the candidates or policies they favor in other ways—for example, by publishing advertisements for them not at their request—so that the constraint on their freedom of speech is minimal....

Commentators have suggested a wide variety of reforms in an attempt to restore some measure of financial sanity and equality to the political process. Some of these invite candidates voluntarily to limit total campaign expenditures in return for grants of public funds for campaigning or the provision of free television time. Presidential elections are financed through such grants—this year $61.8 million to each of the two major candidates—in return for a commitment to spend no more than that sum. And the major senatorial candidates in Massachusetts—the incumbent Senator John Kerry and Governor William Weld—agreed, starting July 1, to limit their expenditures to $6.9 million each. But candidates are not required to accept these offers—Ross Perot declined the federal grant in the 1992 presidential election and spent more of his own money than he would have received: and the use of soft money and independent party expenditures greatly reduces the force of voluntary limitations anyway. As I said, this year's presidential campaigns are expected actually to cost up to $1 billion in total, not just the $152 million paid in federal grants (including $29 million to Perot)....

Was the *Buckley* decision right in principle? If so, then it would be wrong to amend the Constitution to reverse it. It would also be wrong to try to circumvent the decision.... If it really would violate free speech for Congress to deprive the public of everything a rich candidate might wish to tell it in repeated television commercials, then it must also be wrong to induce rich candidates, by bribing them with public money, to muzzle themselves voluntarily. So the present disposition of most commentators—to accept the *Buckley* decision and then to try to evade it—seems untenable. If we think the decision a mistake, we should explain why and attempt, in one way or another, to reverse it. If we think it right, we should stop what almost every politician now seems to endorse—trying to achieve what it forbade by other means.

3.

Was the *Buckley* decision right? The Constitution's First Amendment declares that Congress "shall make no law... abridging the freedom of speech." These abstract words cannot mean that government must pass no law that prevents or punishes *any* form of speech—that would rule out laws against blackmail and fraud. Free speech must mean the freedom to speak or publish when denying that freedom would damage some other individual right that free speech protects, or when it would impair democracy itself. It is a premise of democracy, for example, that the people as a whole must have final authority over the government, not vice versa. That principle is compromised when official censorship limits the character or diversity of political opinion the public may hear or the range of information it may consider, particularly—though not exclusively—when the censorship is designed to protect government from criticism or exposure. So the Supreme Court has ruled, as in the Pentagon Papers case, that government may not prohibit the publication of material pertinent to judging its own performance. It is another premise of democracy that citizens must be able, as individuals, to participate on equal terms in both formal politics and in the informal cultural life that creates the moral environment of the community. That principle is compromised when government prohibits speech on the ground that the convictions or tastes or preferences it expresses are unworthy or degraded or offensive, or that they would be dangerous if others were persuaded to embrace them. So, particularly in recent decades, the Court has been zealous in protecting neo-Nazis, pornographers, and flag-burners from censorship inspired by such judgments.

Neither of these two principles of democracy is violated, however, by a legal restriction on campaign expenditures. Expenditure limits do not protect govermnent from criticism—incumbents, as we saw, benefit more than challengers from unlimited spending—and they do not presuppose that any political opinion is less worthy or more dangerous than any other. Nor would such limits seriously risk keeping from the public any argument or information it would otherwise have: media advertising of rich candidates and campaigns is now extremely repetitive, and the message would not change if the repetitions were fewer.

In the *Buckley* decision, however, the Court claimed another, more general, principle of democracy. It declared that since effective speech requires money in the television age, any legal limit on how much politicians can spend necessarily diminishes the overall *quantity* of political speech, and violates the First Amendment for that reason. The Court conceded that capping expenditures would permit poor candidates to compete more effectively with rich ones. But, it said, "the concept that government may restrict the speech of some elements of our society in order to enhance the relative voice of others is wholly foreign to the First Amendment." What reason might we have for accepting that view?

Two arguments are often made. The first supposes. in the spirit of John Stuart Mill's famous defense of free speech, that a community is more likely to reach wise political decisions the more political argument or appeal its citizens are able to hear or read. It is certainly true that expenditure caps would limit the quantity of political speech. If a rich politician or a well-financed campaign is prevented from broadcasting as many television ads as he or it would like, then the sum total of political broadcasts is, by hypothesis, less than it would otherwise be. Some citizens would indeed be prevented from hearing a message they might have deemed pertinent.

But since the curtailed broadcasts would almost certainly have repeated what the candidate had said on other occasions, it seems very unlikely that the repetition would have improved collective knowledge. Nothing in the history of the many democracies that do restrict electoral expense suggests that they have sacrificed wisdom by doing so. In any case, the argument that curtailing political expenditure would hinder the search for truth and justice seems so speculative—and the potential cost in those values so meager even if the argument is right—that it hardly provides a reason for forgoing the conceded gains in fairness that restricting electoral expenses would bring.

A second familiar argument is very different. It insists that the freedom of speech that really is essential to democracy—the freedom to criticize government or to express unpopular opinions, for example—is best protected from official abuse and evasion by a blanket rule that condemns any and all regulation of political speech—except, perhaps, to avoid immediate and serious violence or a national disaster. It is better for a community to forgo even desirable gains than to run the risk of abuse, and the censorship of genuinely important speech, that a less rigid rule would inevitably pose. But this argument overlooks the fact that, in this case, what we risk in accepting a rigid rule is not just inconvenience but a serious loss in the quality of the very democracy we supposedly thereby protect. It seems perverse to suffer the clear unfairness of allowing rich candidates to drown out poor ones, or powerful

corporations to buy special access to politicians by making enormous gifts, in order to prevent speculative and unnamed dangers to democracy that have not actually occurred and that no one has shown are likely to occur. We would do better to rely on our officials—and ultimately on our courts—to draw lines and make distinctions of principle, as they do in all other fields of constitutional law.

But though these two familiar arguments are easily countered, the *Buckley* decision cited another, more profound, argument—I shall call it the "individual-choice" argument—which I believe has been very influential among those who support the decision even though it is rarely articulated in full. "In the free society ordained by our Constitution," the Court said, "it is not the government, but the people individually as citizens and candidates and collectively as associations and political committees who must retain control over the quantity and range of debate on public issues in a political campaign." We must take some care to appreciate the force of that argument. I said that much of First Amendment law is grounded in the ideal of democratic self-government—that the ultimate governors of a society should be the people as a whole, not the officials they have elected. That principle does not seem to apply in the case of expenditure limitations, I said, because those limits are designed not to prevent the public from learning any particular kind of information or hearing any particular kind of appeal but, on the contrary, to enhance the diversity and fairness of the political debate.

But the individual-choice argument insists that instead of that apparently admirable goal justifying the constraint, it explains what is *wrong* with it, because any attempt to determine the character of the political debate by legislation violates an important democratic right—the right of each individual citizen to make up his own mind about what information or message is pertinent to his decision how to use his vote. Should he watch as much of his favorite candidate or party as possible, to solidify or reinforce convictions he holds intuitively, or in order to arm himself for political arguments with other citizens? Or should he watch all candidates, including those whose personality or views he knows he detests, when he would rather do something else? Should he take an interest in negative ads that deride an opponent's character? Or should he try to follow complex political argument crammed full of statistics he knows can be manipulated?

Some people, including many who now press for expenditure limits and other reforms, have their own clear answer to such questions. They endorse a highminded, "civic republican" ideal of democratic discourse. They imagine a nation of informed citizens giving equal time and care to all sides of important issues, and deliberating thoughtfully about the common good rather than their own selfish interests. But the individual-choice argument insists that those who accept that ideal have no right to impose it on others, and are therefore wrong to appeal to it as justification for coercive measures, like expenditure caps, that deny people the right to listen to whatever political message they want, as often as they want. In a genuine democracy, it insists, the structure, character, and tone of the public political discourse must be determined by the combined effect of individual choices of citizens making political decisions for themselves, not by the edicts of self-styled

arbiters of political fairness and rationality. If we want to bring American politics closer to civic republican ideals, we must do so by example and persuasion, not by the coercive force of expenditure caps or other majoritarian rules.

It might seem natural to object to this argument that, in the real world we live in, people cannot make their own decisions about which political messages to watch or listen to anyway, because those decisions are made for them by rich or well-financed candidates whose advertisements dominate programming. But that objection is less powerful than it might at first seem. There is little evidence that citizens who take an active interest in politics could not discover the statements and positions of any serious candidate—that is, of any candidate who would have any significant chance of winning if every voter knew his views in great detail—if they were willing to make the effort to do so. Of course it is true, as Senator Bradley said, that voters are much more likely to be convinced by advertisements constantly shown during commercial breaks in popular programming than by the less expensive campaigning that poorer candidates can afford. If that were *not* true, then candidates who spent fortunes on such advertising would be wasting their money. But it does not decrease the freedom of a voter to choose for himself which candidate to watch when one candidate is on television constantly and another only rarely, provided that the voter can find the latter's message if he searches. And it would be unacceptably paternalistic to argue that a voter should not be allowed to watch what he wants to because he is too likely to be convinced by it.

It is also true, as I said, that many potential candidates decide not to run because they are likely to lose when money dominates politics. But we must distinguish between two reasons a poor candidate might have for that decision. He might fear that voters would not learn of his existence or policies, because he has too little money to spend on publicizing them, or he might fear that even if voters did learn, he would lose anyway, because the weight of money and advertisement on the other side would make his good ideas seem terrible ones.

The appropriate remedy for the first danger, according to the individual-choice argument, is some form of subsidy for poorer candidates—direct grants to those whose opponents spend more than a specified limit, for example, or free television time for poorer candidates on special cable channels created or used for that purpose, or in specified network slots paid for from a national fund. (Nothing in the Supreme Court's decisions would bar such government subsidies.) And according to the individual-choice argument, the second danger—that even candidates subsidized in such a way could not match the advertising power of those with enormous resources—is not one that a democracy can address through expenditure limits, because government would then be denying citizens the broadcasts they wished to watch on the ground that they should not want to watch them, or that they are too likely to be persuaded by them. Once again, these are obviously impermissible grounds for any constraints on speech.

4.

I emphasize the apparent strength of the individual-choice argument not to support that argument, but to make its structure plainer, and to suggest that we must confront it at a more basic level, by rejecting the conception of democratic self-government on which it is based. Citizens play two roles in a democracy. As voters they are, collectively, the final referees or judges of political contests. But they also participate, as individuals, in the contests they collectively judge: they are candidates, supporters, and political activists; they lobby and demonstrate for and against government measures, and they consult and argue about them with their fellow citizens. The individual-choice argument concentrates exclusively on citizens in the first role and neglects them in the second. For when wealth is unfairly distributed and money dominates politics, then, though individual citizens may be equal in their vote and their freedom to hear the candidates they wish to hear, they are not equal in their own ability to command the attention of others for their own candidates, interests, and convictions. When the Supreme Court said, in the *Buckley* case, that fairness to candidates and their convictions is "foreign" to the First Amendment, it denied that such fairness was required by democracy. That is a mistake because the most fundamental characterization of democracy—that it provides self-government by the people as a whole—supposes that citizens are equals not only as judges but as participants as well.

Of course no political community can make its citizens literally their own governors one by one. I am not my own ruler when I must obey a law that was enacted in spite of my fierce opposition. But a community can supply self-government in a more collective sense—it can encourage its members to see themselves as equal partners in a cooperative political enterprise, together governing their own affairs in the way in which the members of a college faculty or a fraternal society, for example, govern themselves. To achieve that sense of a national partnership in self-government, it is not enough for a community to treat citizens only as if they were shareholders in a company, giving them votes only in periodic elections of officials. It must design institutions, practices, and conventions that allow them to be more engaged in public life, and to make a contribution to it, even when their views do not prevail. Though the question of what that means in practice is a complex one, it seems evident that at least two conditions must be met for any community fully to succeed in the ambition.

First, each citizen must have a fair and reasonably equal opportunity not only to hear the views of others as these are published or broadcast, but to command attention for his own views, either as a candidate for office or as a member of a politically active group committed to some program or conviction. No citizen is entitled to demand that others find his opinions persuasive or even worthy of attention. But each citizen is entitled to compete for that attention, and to have a chance at persuasion, on fair terms, a chance that is now denied almost everyone without great wealth or access to it. Second, the tone of public discourse must be appropriate to the deliberations of a partnership or joint venture rather than the selfish negotiations of commercial rivals or military enemies. This means that when citizens disagree they must present their arguments to one another with civility, attempting rationally to support policies they take to be in the common interest, not in manipulative, slanted, or mendacious pitches designed to win as much of the spoils of politics as possible by any means. These two requirements—of participant equality and civility—are parts of the civic republican ideal I described. But we can now defend them, not just as features of an attractive society that perceptive statesmen have the right to impose on everyone, but as essential conditions of fair political engagement, and hence of self- government, for all.

If we embraced that attractive account of the conditions of self-government, we would have to accept that democracy—self-government by the people as a whole—is always a matter of degree. It will never be perfectly fulfilled, because it seems incredible that the politics of a pluralistic contemporary society could ever become as egalitarian in access and as deliberative in tone as the standards I just described demand. We would then understand democracy not as a pedigree a nation earns just by adopting some constitutional structure of free elections, but as an ideal toward which any would-be democratic society must continually strive.

We would also have to accept not only that America falls short of important democratic ideals, but that in the age of television politics the shortfall has steadily become worse. The influence of wealth unequally distributed is greater, and its consequences more profound, than at any time in the past, and our politics seem daily more rancorous, ill-spirited, and divisive. So this analysis of democracy as self-government confirms—and helps to explain—the growing sense of despair about American politics that I began this essay by trying to describe. How should we respond to that despair? We must understand the First Amendment as a challenge, not a barrier to improvement. We must reject the blanket principle the Supreme Court relied on in *Buckley*, that government should never attempt to regulate the public political discourse in any way, in favor of a more discriminating principle that condemns the constraints that do violate genuine principles of democracy—that deny citizens information they need for political judgement or that deny equality of citizenship for people with unpopular beliefs or tastes, for example—but that nevertheless permits us to try to reverse our democracy's decline.

5.

Is it realistic to hope that the Supreme Court will soon overrule or modify the *Buckley* decision? If I am right, the decision was a mistake, unsupported by precedent and contrary to the best understanding of prior First Amendment jurisprudence. It is internally flawed as well: its fundamental distinction between regulating any citizen's or group's contributions to someone else's campaign, which the Court allowed, and regulating the expenditures of individuals or groups on their own behalf, which it did not, is untenable. Justice Thomas remarked in his concurring opinion in the *Colorado Republican* case last June that there is no difference in principle between these two forms of political expression. Thomas was right—why should Perot be free to spend a great fortune promoting his views in the most effective way he can—by running for president and spending a fortune on television—while one of his passionate supporters is not free to promote his own views in the most effective way he can-by contributing what he can afford to Perot's campaign.

In retrospect, at least, this untenable distinction seems a compromise designed to split the difference, allowing Congress to achieve one of its purposes—preventing the corruption that almost inevitably accompanies large-scale contributions—while still insisting on the sanctity of political speech. If so, the Court's compromise has failed, because without a direct limit on spending, any system of regulation of contributions, no matter how elaborate, will collapse, as ours has. When politics desperately needs money, and money desperately seeks influence, money and politics cannot be kept far apart.

Therefore the case for overruling *Buckley* is a strong one. The prospects for doing so are much less strong. Justices Ginzburg and Stevens made plain, in a dissenting opinion by the latter, their doubts that the First Amendment really does bar expenditure limits. But though Justice Thomas even more openly announced himself ready to revise *Buckley*, he would revise it by forbidding contribution limits as well as expenditure limits, not by allowing limits on expenditures: and, as I said, he and three other Justices argued for an even stronger ban on regulating expenditures than *Buckley* imposed.

But the American public is becoming increasingly angered by the political role of money. Even in 1992, before the new explosion in campaign contributions, a poll of registered voters likely to vote showed that 74 percent agreed that "Congress is largely owned by the special interest groups." and that 84 percent endorsed the statement that "special interest money buys the loyalty of candidates." If that dissatisfaction continues to grow, and the public understands that the *Buckley* decision prevents the most direct attack on the problem, the pressure for overruling it would intensify. If the decision were overruled, the way might be opened for a new system of regulation banning, for example, political commercials in breaks in ordinary programming, as other democracies do, and providing free television time, out of public funds, for longer statements by the candidates themselves.

In any case, even if *Buckley* remains, we should feel no compunction in declaring the decision a mistake, and in attempting to avoid its consequences through any reasonable and effective device we can find or construct. The decision did not declare a valuable principle that we should hesitate to circumvent. On the contrary, it misunderstood not only what free speech really is but what it really means for free people to govern themselves.

THE CONTINUING DEBATE:
Campaign Finance Reform

What Is New

The amount of money spent by the 2004 presidential and congressional campaigns exceeded four billion dollars, up a billion dollars since the 2000 campaign, and almost double what was spent in 1996. In 2002 the McCain-Feingold bill, which aimed at restricting soft money contributions to political parties, was signed into law (rather reluctantly—he had opposed the bill) by President Bush. The bill was challenged in court, but its major provisions were upheld by the Supreme Court in December 2003 (by a 5 to 4 vote). The Court majority stated that "There is substantial evidence in these cases to support Congress' determination that contributions of soft money give rise to corruption and the appearance of corruption." However, much of the "soft" money that would have gone to candidates and political parties has been channeled to "issue" ads, that do not fall under the ban but clearly support or attack candidates. (The notorious "Swift Boat Veterans" ads in the 2004 Presidential Campaign are the clearest example.) As the amount of money spent on campaigns continues to increase, voter confidence in the electoral process continues to decline. How to restore integrity to the electoral process without placing undue limits on free speech and free advocacy remains a difficult but pressing question.

Where to Find More

The Goldwater quote in the introduction to this topic came from Susan Manes, "Up for Bid: A Common Cause View," in an anthology edited by Margaret Latus Nugent and John R. Johannes, *Money, Elections, and Democracy* (Boulder, Colorado: Westview Press, 1990).

Two excellent essays on the problems for democracy caused by great differences in wealth are Harry Brighouse, "Political Equality and the Funding of Political Speech," *Social Theory and Practice*, 21 (1995), 473–500; and David Copp, "Capitalism versus Democracy: The Marketing of Votes and the Marketing of Political Power," in John Douglas Bishop, editor, *Ethics and Capitalism* (Toronto: University of Toronto Press, 2000): 81–101. The opposing view is represented by conservative economist Milton Friedman, in Milton Friedman and Rose D. Friedman, *Free to Choose: A Personal Statement* (New York: Harcourt Brace Jovanovich,1980). A detailed account of the issue is presented in a very readable book by Kevin Phillips, *Wealth and Democracy* (New York: Broadway Books, 2002).

A particularly good collection of essays, exploring various views on campaign finance reform, is Anthony Corrado, Thomas E. Mann, Daniel R. Ortiz, Trevor Potter, and Frank J. Sorauf, editors, *Campaign Finance Reform: A Sourcebook* (Washington, D.C.: Brookings Institution Press, 1997). Annelise Anderson, editor, *Political Money: Deregulating American Politics*, contains essays primarily (but not exclusively) opposing campaign finance reform. An excellent article on campaign finance reform is Daniel R. Ortiz, "The Democratic Paradox of Campaign Finance Reform," *Stanford Law Review*, Volume 50, Issue 3 (February 1998): 893–914. *Buckley Stops Here: Loosening the Judicial Stranglehold on Campaign Finance Reform* (New York: The Century Foundation Press) is the Report of the Twentieth Century Fund Working Group on

Campaign Finance Litigation, a group of legal scholars who lay out the case for overturning the *Buckley* decision. The text of the majority decision and the minority dissent in *Buckley* v. *Valeo*, 424 U.S. 1 (1976) can be found at *www.oyez.org*.

Philip M. Stern, *The Best Congress Money Can Buy* (New York: Pantheon Books, 1988) is a disturbing account of the corrupting influence of campaign money on the operations of Congress.

JURY NULLIFICATION

Should a Jury Member Follow Her Convictions *or* Follow the Law?

FOLLOW HER CONVICTIONS

Advocate: Jeffrey Abramson, Louis Stulber Distinguished Professor of Law and Politics, Brandeis University

Source: *We, the Jury: The Jury System and the Ideal of Democracy*, Chapter 2 (Cambridge, Mass.: Harvard, 2000)

FOLLOW THE LAW

Advocate: Erick J. Haynie, Attorney with Perkins Coie, Portland, Oregon

Source: "Populism, Free Speech, and the Rule of Law: The 'Fully Informed' Jury Movement and its Implications," *The Journal of Criminal Law & Criminology*, volume 88, number 1, 1998

When you serve on a jury in the United States, the judge may give you the following instruction:

> Members of the jury, it will be your duty to find from the evidence what the facts are. You and you alone will be the judges of the facts. You will then have to apply to those facts the law as the court will give it to you. You must follow that law whether you agree with it or not.

Through most of U.S. history, the courts followed the British tradition: juries could decide that a law (or its particular application) was unjust, and thus legitimately return a verdict of not guilty even if the jury thought the defendant had violated the law. Of course juries in the United States still sometimes refuse to convict when they believe that a law is unjust, and juries clearly have the *power* to do that; but for several decades (with the exception of Indiana and Maryland) juries are officially not *supposed* to do so.

It's easy to find cases where we might like the result of jury nullification (for example, juries that refused to convict those who violated the Fugitive Slave Act by helping escaped slaves); but it is equally easy to find results that are profoundly disturbing (for example, the notorious refusal of Southern all-white juries to convict for white defendants civil rights violations and even murders of black people). Because jury nullification is often favored by those who oppose current laws, the arguments in favor of jury nullification brings together a remarkably varied cast of characters.

Sometimes jury nullification occurs when jurors reject a specific law: Jury nullification of laws requiring the return of fugitive slaves is a clear example. But jury nullification can also occur when jurors believe that the law is legitimate but special circumstances make conviction unjust. An example (shown on *Frontline*) occurred in the criminal trial of Leroy Reid in Milwaukee Superior Court. Reid was a convicted felon who had served his time, been released, and for many years had no further violations. Borderline retarded, Reid desperately wanted to find work. He sent money to a mail order "detective school" which gave him a "private detective badge," and in pursuing his "career goal" Reid bought a small caliber pistol. This was prior to the Brady bill, so there were no background checks; Reid wrote some random numbers on the required form, but could not read enough to understand and complete the form. One day Reid proudly showed a deputy sheriff his receipt from the purchase of his pistol. The deputy instructed Reid to go home and bring the pistol to the Sheriff's office and turn it in; Reid did so, and was promptly arrested and charged with violating a recently passed Wisconsin statute making it a felony for a convicted felon to knowingly possess a firearm. Of course Reid had no idea that he was violating the law; but knowing that he was in violation of the law was not required: All that was necessary for Reid to be in violation of the law was that he be a convicted felon, that he possess a firearm, and that he knows he possesses a firearm; and Reid clearly met all three conditions. When the case went to the jury they unanimously found Reid not guilty, believing that in this special case a conviction would be unjust.

POINTS TO PONDER

> ➤ If you were on the jury that tried Leroy Reid, what verdict would you favor?
> ➤ A standard argument *against* jury nullification is that in a democracy laws should be decided by *all* the people, through our elected representatives, and not by some small group of jurors. What do you think of that argument?
> ➤ Another argument against jury nullification is that every defendant has the right to be tried under the same law. If jurors in Miami do not like a law and decide to nullify it while jurors in Jacksonville favor and uphold the law, then defendants in Jacksonville and Miami are not being treated equally. Is that a strong argument against jury nullification?
> ➤ Haynie argues that if a juror is informed of a right of nullification, then the juror will believe that she fashioned the law that condemns, and that will be an "extreme burden for the jurors' psyche." If you were serving on a criminal jury, would being informed of a right of jury nullification make your decision to acquit or convict *more* or *less* psychologically burdensome, or would it have no effect?

Jury Nullification:
A Jury Member Should Follow Her Convictions

JEFFREY ABRAMSON

... Philosophically, jury nullification is a close cousin to the theory of civil disobedience. In our own time, Martin Luther King, Jr., was a leading advocate for the view that individuals have a "moral responsibility to disobey unjust laws." But King accepted the state's authority to punish his acts of lawbreaking. In fact, willingness to accept punishment was a sign that the disobedience was a challenge to a particular unjust law and not to the state as a whole.

Jury nullification takes the classic theory of civil disobedience one step further by inviting the jury not to punish justified acts of lawbreaking. If the jury agrees that the broken law is unjust, then, say proponents of nullification, it should acquit rather than convict the defendant. The jury should also acquit when it finds the broken law just but agrees that enforcing it against the particular defendant on trial would be unjust.

Jury nullification is an appealing doctrine, promising to give meaning to the sometimes empty phrase "verdicts rendered according to conscience." Authorized to nullify, a jury might move from merely finding that the defendant violated the law to further deliberation about the ethical claims raised by acts of civil disobedience; instead of mechanically convicting because the law has been broken, the nullifying jury would have to consider the justice of the cause for which the law was violated. Sometimes the causes are grand, as was the case when juries deliberated whether to enforce the Fugitive Slave Law against those who helped runaway slaves

attain freedom. At other times, the tension between law and conscience concerns lesser matters, such as enforcing liquor laws during Prohibition. But, for anyone who takes seriously the jury as a bridge between community values and the law, jury nullification is a strong plank. In essence, nullification empowers jurors to appeal to fundamental principles of justice over and above the written law.

There is, however, a vicious side to jury nullification that Americans know all too well. The moral case for this right foundered and sank over the issue of race. In the South especially, all-white juries repeatedly refused to convict whites charged with murdering blacks or civil rights workers of any race. Few bothered to use the word "nullification" to describe the horror of the not guilty verdicts for Emmett Till's or Viola Liuzzo's murderers, but it was also no secret that the verdicts flew in the face of both the evidence and the law. As the sociologist Gunnar Myrdal noted in his classic study of American racism, the Southern all-white jury became a shield for local racism and a prime obstacle to enforcement of national civil rights legislation. The obstacle was all the more solid because, in our trial system, a not guilty verdict is final and unreviewable.

This is not just a story about the distant past. In Mississippi in the late 1960s, a former Ku Klux Klan leader accused of plotting to murder a black leader reportedly told an associate, "Don't worry.... No jury in Mississippi would convict someone over killing a nigger." The KKK leader was tried twice, the jury deadlocking each time. In 1979, Ku Klux Klan gunmen opened fire on marchers in an anti-Klan rally in Greensboro, North Carolina, organized by the Communist Workers' Party. Five marchers died. An all-white jury (including one juror who said, "It's less of a crime to kill communists") found the gunmen not guilty on all charges. The not guilty verdict barred any state retrial of the Klansmen on the same charges. (The Klansmen were subsequently tried in federal court on separate federal civil rights charges, but an all-white jury acquitted the defendants again in 1984.)

Episodes such as the Greensboro and Mississippi trials undercut any innocent faith in nullification to pardon defendants. Once we grant jurors the right to set conscience above law, we have to live with consciences we admire as well as those we despise. As one critic put it, an "invitation to jurors to vote their consciences is inevitably an invitation to greater parochialism.... Local biases... are legitimated and activated..., immuniz[ing] criminal acts visited upon members of society's 'discrete and insular minorities.'"

Stripped of moral stature by its service to racism, the doctrine of nullification is in virtual eclipse today. Only two states, Indiana and Maryland, recognize the doctrine and require judges, upon the request of a defendant, to apprise the jury of its right to disregard the law in favor of an acquittal.

In every other state and in the federal system, the doctrine has passed into history. In California, Operation Rescue jurors heard, as all California jurors hear, that they had "a duty to apply the law as I give it to you to the facts as you determine them." The Massachusetts *Trial Juror's Handbook* states that the jury "decides the facts... [but] does *not* decide the rules of

law to be applied to the facts in the case....The judge tells the jury the proper rules of law required to resolve the case." Pennsylvania's *Handbook for Jurors* is similar: "It is the jury's function to determine what facts are established by competent evidence [but it] is the judge's responsibility to tell... the jury the proper rules of law required to resolve the case.... [The] judge instructs the jury on the law which must guide and govern." During deliberations, "the jury is free to determine the procedures it will follow... as long as the judge's instructions are followed."

In some federal courts, the jury is greeted with an even more explicit statement of its duty to follow the law:

Ladies and gentlemen: You now are the jury in this case and I want to take a few minutes to tell you something about your duties as jurors....
It will be your duty to decide from the evidence what the facts are. You, and you alone, are the judges of the facts. You will hear the evidence, decide what the facts are, and then apply those facts to the law which I will give to you. That is how you will reach your verdict. *In doing so you must follow that law whether you agree with it or not* [emphasis added].

These instructions illustrate the strict division of labor between judges deciding questions of law and juries deciding questions of fact. But, for all its familiarity, the idea that jurors must have nothing to do with the law marked a fundamental shift, a deep decline, in the democratic functions the jury once exercised in England and America. Well into the nineteenth century, criminal juries frequently (and civil juries occasionally) were instructed that the judge's statement of the law was not binding on them, that they could determine for themselves what the law was. Juries in England used this authority to become the first to extend legal protection to Quakers assembled in peaceable worship. Juries in the American colonies found that newspapers had a lawful right to print "true" criticisms of government long before legislatures recognized truth as a defense in seditious libel cases. And up until the Civil War, defendants charged with violating the Fugitive Slave Law appealed to juries to judge the law invalid. Well-known examples such as these illustrate the substantial contributions that juries, equipped with the right to decide questions of law, once made to upholding civil liberties.

The fact/law distinction, so starkly posed in judges' instructions to juries today, is, however, a fiction that seldom corrals the behavior of actual jurors. Even critics of jury nullification concede that criminal juries have the raw power to pardon lawbreaking because there is no device for reversing a jury that insists on acquitting a defendant against the law. Opponents of jury nullification therefore fall back on a technical distinction between the conceded power to nullify and the denied right to nullify. They insist on this distinction because it has one major practical implication: judges should not instruct juries about nullification because it is not a power jurors have any lawful right to exercise.

Much of the debate over jury nullification is about this formal issue of whether to instruct or not. Defenders of jury nullification argue in favor of open instruction; anything less misleads the jury about the full extent of its powers and may produce convictions a jury knowing about nullification would have rejected as unjust. Jurors who grudgingly convict because they mistakenly believe that they have no choice may feel deceived if they learn after trial that they had the power to acquit.

Critics retort that nullification instructions conflict with instructions to jurors that they are duty-bound to apply the law whether they accept it or not. Officially informing jurors that they have the power to nullify would confuse them; it would also threaten the unpartiality of justice with the anarchy of conscience, as jurors pick and choose against whom to enforce the law. Open instruction might even encourage jurors to nullify, by portraying nullification as a right rather than a power. The present arrangement of keeping mum about nullification may be hypocritical, but it ensures that jurors will nullify only in extreme cases of conflict between law and conscience.

The debate over nullification instructions is important, but it sometimes obscures the overriding fact that jurors continue to nullify, whether officially instructed about their options or not. Ultimately, I think all sides must admit that verdicts according to conscience are so deeply entwined with popular images of the jury that jurors follow their conscience rather than the law in a good many cases, and the more visible cases at that....

[J]ury nullification lives on, even when officially banished from the approved list of jury rights. But its life is secret because jurors are discouraged from openly deliberating about the justice of enforcing the law and are no doubt forced frequently into smuggling their views on the justice of law into "approved debate" about the evidence or facts. But, if jurors continue to nullify on the sly. would we not do better to recognize in theory what jurors do in practice? Would not the quality of the debate about law versus justice be better if jurors were told that such debate was part of their function, that we cherish trial by jury precisely because we expect ordinary citizens to repudiate laws, or instances of law enforcement, that are repugnant to their consciences? These are the questions I wish to pursue, by revisiting the history of jury nullification.

NULLIFICATION'S RISE AND FALL

Jury nullification grew out of a general claim that jurors have the right to decide all questions of law necessary to reach a verdict. According to this broad claim, jurors have the right to disregard judicial instructions and arrive at their own resolution of all contested matters of law at trial.

Jurors' right to decide questions of law gives them considerably greater authority than jury nullification itself requires. The right to nullify is narrow, permitting jurors only the right not to apply the law. The crucial significance of this restriction is that juries can nullify only to acquit, never to convict. By contrast, the right to decide questions of law entitles jurors to apply their own interpretation of the law to either the detriment or the benefit of a defendant.

Logically speaking, it is possible to defend jury nullification while rejecting the notion that juries have any general right to decide questions of law. After all, it is one thing for a judge to tell the jury what the applicable law is; it is quite another for the judge to require the jury to apply the law. But historically, jury nullification was debated as one example of the broader claim that jurors decided questions of law. The classic arguments came into English law in the middle of the seventeenth century, made by dissenting groups such as Levellers or Quakers on trial for treason, seditious libel, unlawful assembly, or disturbance of the peace. Defendants appealed to the jury to be "judges of the law," never quite specifying whether they were calling upon the jury to reject English law as unjust (to nullify it) or simply to find them innocent under existing laws (despite judicial instructions to the contrary). At any rate, the right of juries to decide questions of law became a rallying cry for political and religious minorities throughout the seventeenth century; in the colonies it turned local juries in times of crisis into centers of resistance to parliamentary law....

In virtually every jurisdiction's handbook for jurors, the same mechanical description appears: find the facts, and reach a verdict by applying whatever the judge says about the law to those facts.

But the search for a strict division of labor between jury and judge creates a number of practical problems for trials today. First,... the division of labor does not hold up well in practice. The more we emphasize the remoteness of law from the experience of the average juror, the less credible it is that jurors receive sudden enlightenment on legal matters simply by listening to the judge's furious, quick-paced, jargon-laced set of instructions.

For instance, if I do not understand what differentiates murder from manslaughter in Massachusetts, I am unlikely to suddenly understand it because a judge instructs that murder requires malice and that malice does not require any ill-will toward the victim but includes a deliberate purpose to injure without legal excuse or palliation. Nor were jurors in the Bernhard Goetz trial likely to understand from the judge's instructions whether Goetz acted lawfully in self-defense, if he *mistakenly* thought he was facing deadly attack. In a Philadelphia racketeering trial in 1993, several jurors said that they did not believe the defendant guilty but voted to convict because they mistakenly thought a hung jury was unacceptable.

Legal realist critics have pointed out since the beginning of the century that modern jury procedures mask a charade: we have judges go through the motions of instructing jurors on the law and tell them they must abide by the instructions, but we suspect that jurors do not fathom the instructions and fall back on their own gut reactions or common sense in deciding how the case should come out. To anyone who has ever witnessed a judge instructing a jury, it is clear that our system does not even pretend that the instructions are meaningful. Rarely are jurors even provided with written copies of the instructions; little attempt is made to translate jargon into common language. Most annoying of all, juror questions about the instructions are usually rebuffed with verbatim rereadings of the same instructions.

The second difficulty, as our predecessors appreciated, is that the world outside the courtroom does not neatly divide questions of fact from questions of law. When we ask jurors to decide, as a matter of fact, whether the defendant acted with malice, we are asking them to make a complicated assessment of the nature of the defendant's mental state—an inquiry far different from finding facts in the who did what, when, and where sense. To label the defendant's behavior malicious is partly to find the historical facts, but it is also to render a judgment about its blameworthiness. Juries are constantly presented with these mixed questions that jump the artificial law/fact boundary. This is true in negligence cases, where juries decide the fact of whether a defendant's behavior fell below the behavior expected of a reasonable person. It is true in obscenity cases, where juries apply "contemporary community standards" to decide the fact of whether the work in question is pornographic. So here too, against official theory, we have to admit that juries do what we say they are not equipped to do: they decide what the law means by "negligence" or "obscenity" or even "murder."

The practical impossibility of abiding by the fact/law distinction casts a new light on the earnest attempts of American law to stamp out the tradition of jury nullification. History teaches us that jurors escape from all kinds of legal straitjackets designed to restrain conscientious acquittals in criminal trials.

And this is the way it ought to be. Many of the arguments that the Supreme Court laid down in *Sparf* stripping juries of any right to decide legal questions, have no relevance to what jury nullification is about—the right to set aside the law only to acquit, never to convict. As a doctrine, jury nullification poses no threat to the accused; it is in fact the time-honored way of permitting juries to leaven the law with leniency.

To permit juries to show mercy by not enforcing the law in a given case is hardly to destroy the fabric of a society under law. Indeed, putting pressure on jurors to convict against their conscience would seem to threaten the integrity of the law far more seriously. Our current system, in which we tell jurors they must apply the law in every case no matter how unjust the results seem to them, opens the chasm between law and popular beliefs that the jury system exists to prevent.

This is not to deny that jury nullification sometimes goes badly... There is no denying, as the Supreme Court said in another context, that "the power to be lenient is the power to discriminate." It is for this reason that the Massachusetts affiliate of the American Civil Liberties Union (ACLU) took a firm stance against a bill, introduced in the state legislature in 1991, that would have amended the jury trial handbook to inform jurors that they could acquit "according to their conscience" if they felt "the law as charged by the judge is unjust or wrongly applied to the defendant(s)." The ACLU chapter believed that "jurors often manage to control their own strong prejudices because the judge tells them they must." Its fear was that jury nullification would be an open invitation for jurors to unleash their prejudices in the name of conscience.

The ACLU affiliate's stance against jury nullification is a succinct expression of the collapsed faith in the virtue of jurors that drives the declining role of jurors at trial. In that group's judgment, jury nullification encourages jurors not to rise above law to consult fundamental justice but to fall below law into brute bias. One is left to wonder whether the rejection of jury nullification is not a rejection of the idea of the jury altogether.

Suppose we were to inform jurors that nullification is an option. Is the Massachusetts chapter of the ACLU right to fear dire consequences—a sudden bursting of prejudice through legal dikes? In the two states that do instruct about nullification—Indiana and Maryland—judges have not detected any dramatic rise in the frequency of nullification. Alan Scheflin and Jon Van Dyke, the leading scholars of jury nullification, reported recently on an empirical study where the effect of jury nullification instructions on mock jurors depended on the issue involved. Juries given nullification instructions were not more likely to acquit a college student charged with driving drunk and killing a pedestrian; in fact, they were less likely to acquit than juries given standard instructions. On the other hand, receiving a nullification instruction did increase the number of mock juries that acquitted a nurse charged with the mercy killing of a terminally ill cancer patient. It is encouraging that nullification instructions left the mock jurors able to distinguish the merits of pardoning the nurse and not acquitting the drunk driver.

In 1983, a California murder trial demonstrated the dwarfing of deliberation that comes from denying juries the right to nullify. A seventeen-year-old shot and killed a marijuana-growing farmer during a botched attempt to rob crops from the farm. In accordance with the felony murder rule, the judge instructed the jury that a killing committed during armed robbery was to be considered first-degree murder. After deliberating some time, the jury returned to ask the judge whether it was compelled to find the defendant guilty of first-degree murder if it found that the killing occurred during an armed robbery. At this point, there was only one forthright answer; the jury should have been apprised of its power to nullify.

Clearly, the jury was struggling with the issue of the harsh consequences of the felony murder rule and was searching for a way to convict the defendant of less than first-degree murder. In reacting this way to the felony murder rule, the jury was not behaving strangely but rather in tune with sentiments that had caused many other states to abandon the rule by 1983. But the judge remained silent about nullification and simply repeated the instruction that felony murder is first-degree murder. Even if the judge was not originally obliged to volunteer information about nullification, surely he answered incorrectly when the jury broached the issue on its own. An entire line of deliberation was cut off, or at least it appears to have been cut off, because the jury returned a first-degree murder conviction.

Whether such a verdict represented the jury's considered and independent judgment of justice in the case, we will never know. We do know that the California Supreme Court upheld the conviction but reduced the punishment to that for second-degree murder, finding the punishment of first-degree murder to be so "grossly disproportionate to the offense" in the case as to constitute cruel and unusual punishment. Thus, the Court ended up reaching exactly the judgment the jury was not permitted to make....

Either openly displayed or hidden, nullification remains a timeless strategy for jurors seeking to bring law into line with their conscience. This reconciliation is what the jury system is about, for better or worse. Official disapproval of jury nullification may drive it underground,... But, as long as we have juries, we will have nullification and verdicts according to conscience. Some of those verdicts will outrage us, others will inspire us. But always nullification will give us the full drama of democracy, as citizen-jurors assume on our behalf the task of deliberating about law in relation to justice.

Jury Nullification:
A Jury Member Should Follow the Law

ERICK J. HAYNIE

The Drawbacks of Nullification Instructions and FIJA Advocacy

Courts and commentators offer five primary reasons why juries are not explicitly instructed on their nullification powers.

1. Rule of Law v. Rule of Men

At the core of American constitutional jurisprudence is the notion that ours is a government of laws, not of men. Under the rule of law, citizen behavior is regulated not according to the passions and prejudices of human beings, but according to objective, published laws formally sanctioned by elected representatives through a pre-ordained process. As a federal judge sitting at criminal law aptly observed in 1941:

> Our American system represents the collective wisdom, the collective industry, the collective common sense of people who for centuries had been seeking freedom, freedom from the tyranny of government actuated or controlled by the personal whims and prejudices of kings and dictators. The result is a government founded on principles of reason and justice, a government of laws and not of men.

Because nullification instructions give juries affirmative permission to ignore applicable legislative definitions of culpable conduct, such instructions undermine the rule of law. This reality was explained long ago in the Supreme Court's landmark decision of *Sparf & Hansen v. United States*, which addressed the issue of jury nullification in the federal court system. Holding that it is the right and duty of the trial judge to instruct the jury to follow the law, the Court wrote that:

> Public and private safety alike would be in peril if the principle be established that juries in criminal cases may, of right, [be told to] disregard the law as expounded to them by the court, and become a law unto themselves. Under such a system, the principal function of the judge would be to preside and keep order while jurymen, untrained in the law, would determine questions affecting life, liberty, or property according to such legal principles as, in their judgement, were applicable to the particular case being tried.... We must hold firmly to the doctrine that in the courts of the United States it is the duty of juries in criminal cases to take the law from the court, and apply that law to the facts as they find them to be from the evidence.

The Ninth Circuit has criticized nullification arguments by counsel as violative of the rule of law in even stronger terms:

> If we... allow lawyers to appeal for jury nullification at will and indefinitely, and if we grant defendants a Sixth Amendment right to explain themselves in legally irrelevant terms—then we move to a "system" in which the loudest voice carries the day, in which the phrase "order

in the court" literally has no meaning, and in which the [rule of] law has about as much force as the Cheshire Cat's grin.

Stated another way, the principal danger in giving juries an affirmative option to ignore the criminal law is that the jury is thereby transformed from a *fact-finding* into a *law-making* body In so doing, nullification instructions convert juries into junior varsity legislatures whose decisions undermine the impartial determination of justice based on published law. Thus, explicit nullification instructions would convey "an implied approval that runs the risk of degrading the legal structure [below the level of integrity requisite for true freedom, for an ordered liberty that protects against anarchy as well as tyranny." By refusing to allow the nullification power to be explained to juries, courts better ensure that jurors use the nullification power sparingly, departing from the rule of law only where their own conscience naturally compels a veto of a judge's instructions.

2. Due Process

A second and related reason courts refuse nullification instructions is that they would frustrate due process. As the venerable Latin maxim *nullum crimen sine lege, nulla poena sine lege* provides, there shall be "no crime without law, nor punishment without law." This maxim rings true today in the constitutional due process requirement that criminal liability and punishment be based only "upon a prior legislative enactment of a prohibition expressed with adequate precision and clarity." As the Supreme Court has stated, "[l]iving under a rule of law entails various suppositions, one of which is that [all persons] are entitled to be informed as to what the State commands or forbids." By

affirmatively authorizing juries to assign moral blame inconsistent with the law, nullification instructions confuse juries and increase the odds that a defendant will be convicted of conduct he is not on notice to avoid.

Nullification instructions also frustrate due process by thwarting a defendant's "fundamental right" to a fair, impartial trial by jury. The Sixth Amendment guarantees every criminal defendant a trial based exclusively on the evidence of record, in accordance with the law, and free from outside influences. By making the jury the "finder of law" as well as fact, however, nullification instructions encroach upon the promise of due process. For what better way to ensure a verdict outside the law than to instruct jurors that they may ignore it.

3. Democracy

Closely related to their damaging effect on due process and the rule of law, nullification instructions also run contrary to democratic principles. As the D.C. Circuit observes, "[a]ny arguably salutary functions served by inexplicable jury acquittals would be lost if that prerogative were frequently exercised... [for] calling attention to that power could encourage the substitution of individual standards for openly developed community rules." Indeed, the ultimate effect of nullification instructions is simply to give twelve "randomly selected individuals with no constituency but themselves" an open invitation to frustrate the policies of Congress or the state legislatures, whose laws in all probability will "reflect the majority's view." The undemocratic force of nullification instructions is particularly strong given that it takes not twelve but one nullifying juror to prevent conviction of a man guilty of the crime charged beyond a reasonable doubt.

Nullification instructions are also inherently undemocratic because they frustrate the right of the people to insure that those who violate their laws do not go without punishment. Furthermore, jurors who are forced into the unaccustomed role of making macro-social choices would undoubtedly tend to "overlook the broader implications of their decisions."

4. The Inappropriateness of Juror Legislators

An additional rationale for denying nullification instructions is that juries are not competent to make the law. First, it is highly questionable whether jurors should be instructed to "make" the law when a legislative body has already done the job for them. Congress and the state legislatures have superior expertise, resources and perspective to make macro-social decisions. Congress and the state legislatures also have greater access to relevant information, and much more time to reach a well-reasoned decision than does "a group of twelve citizens of no particular distinction snatched away from their primary vocations" to spend a couple of days in court. Secondly and more importantly, it is utterly unfair to thrust upon jurors a duty of criminal law-making. As the D.C. Circuit explains, "[t]o tell [a juror] expressly of [his] nullification prerogative... is to inform him, in effect, that it is he who fashions the rule that condemns. That is an overwhelming responsibility, an extreme burden for the jurors' psyche."

5. Inconsistent Application of Laws

The final reason courts deny nullification instructions is that allowing jury nullification would lead to inconsistent application of laws: If nullification instructions were allowed, local, state and federal penal laws would never be uniformly applied. Rather, their application would depend entirely on the idiosyncrasies of particular

juries. For this reason, nullification instructions pose the greatest threat to the fair and consistent application of federal criminal laws—laws with which local biases may be in greater conflict. As the Supreme Court noted in *Sparf*:

> If a petit jury can rightfully exercise this power [of nullification] over one statute of Congress, they must have an equal right and power over any other statute, and indeed over all the statues; for no line can be drawn, no restriction imposed, on the exercise of such power; it must rest in discretion only. If this power be once admitted, petit jurors will be superior to the national legislature.... *The doing of certain acts will be held criminal, and punished in one state, and similar acts may be held innocent, and even approved and applauded, in another.*

Indeed, nullification instructions are ultimately an invitation to greater parochialism in the jury decision-making process. By legitimizing local biases, nullification instructions run the risk of immunizing "criminal acts visited upon members of society's 'discrete and insular minorities....'" In the 1960s, for example, jury nullification was used by some Southern juries to shield local racial preferences and block enforcement of federal civil rights legislation.

6. Nullification Policies of the States: Conclusion

This discussion has identified the major reasons courts, while recognizing the power of juries to nullify the law, nonetheless refuse to allow juries to be explicitly informed of this power. To some, this arrangement is hypocritical. To others, it is outrageous. Nevertheless, it strikes a necessary balance in a system based on the rule of law and which also refuses to police the minds of jurors to ensure the legal propriety of their decisions.

IV. CONCLUSION

For over 100 years, federal and state courts have striven to preserve due process and the rule of law by refusing to *explicitly instruct* juries on their *de facto* nullification powers. With the rise of the Fully Informed Jury Association, however, a growing number of jurors arrive at the courthouse with some awareness of this power. The FIJA movement thus poses a serious threat to the democratic and impartial administration of criminal justice; for by slipping *de facto* nullification instructions through the back door of the jury room, FIJA greatly increases the odds that the jury will render its verdict inconsistent the criminal law.

Worse yet, little can be done to counteract the movement. Despite the various remedial actions that might be taken to dilute FIJA's potency, the Sixth Amendment clearly grants the criminal jury unreviewable and almost absolute discretion in

making its decisions. Indeed, it is precisely the *absolute power* vested in the criminal jury that makes the FIJA movement so penetrating. For a jury that is taught the legal reality that, no matter the facts of the case, an acquittal verdict is unreviewable and a guilty verdict will be given much deference on appeal, will also understand that it has nearly absolute power to determine questions of life, liberty, and property however it pleases. At that point, law is no more. Statutes become mere "suggestions" that jurors (and their lobbyists) can rewrite to see that particular groups or political causes win. In short, the "fully informed jury" is none other than a law unto itself, and indeed has "more power than Congress, the President, and the Supreme Court."

And so time will march on until either FIJA withers into nothingness or the rule of law comes to have "about as much force as the Cheshire Cat's grin." True lovers of liberty will fear the latter over the former. Anarchy is no better friend of freedom than an overreaching government.

THE CONTINUING DEBATE:
Jury Nullification

What Is New

In San Francisco in early 2003, Ed Rosenthal was convicted in federal court on federal charges of marijuana cultivation and conspiracy to grow and distribute marijuana. Jurors did not know that Rosenthal was growing marijuana for the relief of patients suffering from cancer, cerebral palsy, and other severe illnesses, and that his activities (though in violation of federal law) were legal under California's Compassionate Use Statute (which California voters had passed as proposition 215), and that Rosenthal had been deputized by the city of Oakland to provide medical marijuana for patients unable to grow their own. Jurors were told by the judge that they must follow the law, and under the provisions of the federal Controlled Substances Act Rosenthal was clearly guilty. After they learned more details of the case (which had been kept from them during the trial), six of the jurors called a press conference to denounce the verdict. The foreman of the jury also concluded that the jury reached the wrong verdict, and said that although none of the jurors were aware of jury nullification; he believes that if they had known the verdict would have been not guilty.

In both Maryland and Indiana, jury nullification is recognized as a right of juries; however, in neither state are juries instructed that they have such a right. The Indiana Constitution states that "In all criminal cases whatever, the jury shall have the right to determine the law and the facts." In 2003 a case was appealed to the Indiana Supreme Court on the grounds that the trial judge refused to tell the jury of its right of nullification. The Indiana Supreme Court rejected the appeal and affirmed the decision of the trial judge raising questions about what sort of right the jury has if they cannot be informed of it. Also in 2003, a bill was introduced in the New Hampshire Legislature that would have required judges to instruct jurors they have a right to find a defendant not guilty even when there is sufficient evidence to establish guilt under the law. The bill passed the New Hampshire House by vote of 220–149, but failed in the Senate.

Where to Find More

In *Sparf and Hansen v. U.S.*, (1894), the U.S. Supreme Court ruled that judges need not tell jurors of their power to nullify law by judging both fact and law. Justices Gray and Shiras wrote a strong dissent. This case can be found at *www.Oyez.org*.

Alan W. Scheflin, "Jury Nullification: The Right to Say No," *Southern California Law Review* 45, 168–226 (1972) is an excellent source for the legal history of jury nullification.

Paula Di Perna, in *Juries on Trial: Faces of American Justice* (New York: Dembner Books, 1984), offers a very readable history of the idea of jury nullification in U.S. and British courts, so does William L. Dwyer, *In the Hands of the People: The Trial Jury's Origins, Triumphs, Troubles and Future in American Democracy* (New York: St. Martin's Press, 2002).

Richard St. John argues against jury nullification in "License to Nullify: The Democratic and Constitutional Deficiencies of Authorized Jury Lawmaking," *Yale Law*

Journal, volume 106, June, 1997, pp. 2563–2597. Nancy J. King, "Silencing Nullification Advocacy Inside the Jury Room and Outside the Courtroom," *University of Chicago Law Review*, volume 65, pp. 433–501, is an excellent study of the current law and jury nullification controversies. The Fully Informed Jury Association (FIJA), a nonprofit organization promoting the principle of jury nullification, can be found at *www.fija.org*.

THE MILITARY DRAFT

THE MILITARY DRAFT:
Restore the Draft *or* Continue with an All-Volunteer Armed Forces?

RESTORE THE DRAFT

ADVOCATE: William A. Galston, Saul I. Stern Professor of Civic Engagement and Director of both the Institute for Philosophy and Public Policy and the Center for Information and Research on Civic Learning and Engagement at the School of Public Affairs, University of Maryland

SOURCE: *Philosophy & Public Policy Quarterly*, volume 23, number 3 (Summer 2003): 8–13

CONTINUE WITH AN ALL-VOLUNTEER ARMED FORCES

ADVOCATE: Robert K. Fullinwider, a fellow at the Institute for Philosophy and Public Policy at the School of Public Affairs, University of Maryland

SOURCE: *Philosophy & Public Policy Quarterly*, volume 23, number 3 (Summer 2003): 2–7

The draft (also called "conscription," although "draft" is generally preferred in the U.S.) was a very contentious issue during the Vietnam War, and during other wars as well. There were massive Civil War draft riots, particularly in New York City, and during World War I some 3 million young men refused to register.

Opposition to the draft usually focuses on two issues: First, is the draft fair? Are the wealthy and well-connected able to avoid service while others bear the risks? During the Civil War, wealthy persons who wished to avoid military service could either pay a commutation fee of $300 (a substantial sum at that time) or hire a replacement (who was likely to be poor). A popular slogan among Union soldiers was "Rich man's war, poor man's fight." During the Vietnam conflict, wealthy and upper middle class young men were often able to avoid the draft (for example, those enrolled in college were exempted from the draft), while the poor and lower middle class made up a disproportionate share of the military.

The second source of opposition concerns the war itself: Is the military enterprise to which soldiers are being drafted a just and legitimate cause? During the Vietnam War, for example, many who were subject to the draft believed that the war between North and South Vietnam was essentially a civil war in which the United States was an unwelcome and illegitimate intruder.

Some who are most reluctant to employ U.S. military forces in foreign countries are most favorable toward a draft, while some of those most eager to use military force are strongly opposed to a draft, preferring to rely exclusively on a volunteer army. For those most inclined to use military force, a draft involves more people directly in the risks of warfare, and thus often intensifies opposition to unpopular wars. Those more inclined toward the use of military force may believe that professional soldiers are less likely to balk at being sent to war because successful military action is often a swift path to military career advancement. Both sides may see drafters as more willing to report war crimes and atrocities, while professional soldiers—feeling more loyalty to their professional comrades, and being more concerned with their own military career advancement—will be less likely to make such stories public.

An argument in favor of conscription—offered here by William Galston—is that service to country is a good thing, both inherently good and likely to have good effects on both individual character (developing leadership abilities and fortitude) and the character of the country (particularly developing its sense of unity). Galston also argues that having an all-volunteer professional military force weakens the commitment to active citizenship, causes a gap between military personnel and civilians, and contributes to economic and social stratification. He proposes a system of universal service to the country for all capable eighteen-year-old citizens, with an option between full-time civilian and military service. Robert Fullinwider responds that the all-volunteer force is neither the source nor the solution of the problems identified by Galston, and that the details of any system of universal conscription will cause difficulties. Thus Fullinwider concludes that any use of the draft should be a last resort for supplying essential military manpower.

POINTS TO PONDER

➤ Fullinwider notes that "nothing undermines [military] unit morale and cohesion like the presence of malcontents, troublemakers, and malingerers—and a draft will deliver up plenty of each." There are obvious disadvantages to having malcontents in the military; but are there any advantages, also?

➤ Galston's claim that universal service will have good effects on those who serve is a common theme sounded by many supporters of the draft. What effects on individual soldiers do you believe would be likely to result from universal compulsory military service? Are they, on balance, positive? Would they be positive for citizens of a democratic society?

➤ In 1917 George Nasmyth stated: [quoted by Eliot A. Cohen]:

> The whole object of military training is to secure instantaneous obedience without thought, to make men a part of an autocratic military machine, so that if he is ordered to sink the *Lusitania* or destroy the city of Louvain, he will obey instantly and unquestioningly. Surely unthinking obedience is far removed from the self-imposed discipline, that respect for laws because they have been enacted by common consent for the welfare of the people.

How serious is this as an objection to compulsory universal service? Suppose we agreed with Nasmyth that military service is incompatible with the values of a free democratic society, and we also believe that a military force is necessary. Would that imply we ought *not* to have a draft, and instead rely on an all-volunteer professional force? Or would it imply the opposite: that since military service has a corrupting effect, it should be divided among all, rather than concentrated on a few?

The Military Draft:
It Is Time to Restore the Draft

WILLIAM A. GALSTON

In the run up to the war against Iraq, an op-ed by congressional representative Charles Rangel (D-NY) rekindled a debate about the military draft; unexpectedly, because most scholars and an overwhelming majority of senior military leaders regarded this matter as settled. The Vietnam-era draft was regarded as arbitrary and unfair, and it was held responsible for dissension within the military as well as the wider society.

In the immediate wake of its disaster in Vietnam, the United States made an historic decision to end the draft and institute an All-Volunteer Force (AVF). On one level, it is hard to argue with success. The formula of high quality volunteers, combined with intensive training and investment in state of the art equipment has produced by far the most formidable military in history. Evidence suggests that the military's performance, especially since 1990, has bolstered public trust and confidence....

These gains in institutional performance and public confidence are impressive and significant, but they hardly end the discussion. As every reader of Machiavelli (or the Second Amendment) knows, the organization of the military is embedded in larger issues of citizenship and civic life. It is along these dimensions that the decision in favor of the AVF has entailed significant costs. First, the AVF reflects, and has contributed to the development of, what I call *optional citizenship,* the belief that being a citizen involves rights without responsibilities and that we need do for our country only what we choose to do.

Numerous studies have documented the rise of individual choice as the dominant norm of contemporary American culture, and many young people today believe being a good person—decent, kind, caring, and tolerant—is all it takes to be a good citizen. This dutyfree understanding of citizenship is comfortable and undemanding; it is also profoundly mistaken.

Second, the AVF contributes to what I call *spectatorial citizenship*—the premise that good citizens need not be active but can watch others doing the public's work on their behalf. This spectatorial outlook makes it possible to decouple the question of whether *we* as a nation should do *X* from the question of whether *I* would do or participate in *X*. In a discussion with his students during the Gulf War, philosophy professor Cheyney Ryan was struck by "how many of them saw no connection between whether the country should go to war and whether they would... be willing to fight in it." A similar disconnect exists today. Young adults have been more supportive of the war against Iraq than any other age group (with more than 70 percent in favor), but recent surveys have found an equal percentage would refuse to participate themselves.

As a counterweight to this decoupling, Ryan proposes what he calls the Principle of Personal Integrity: You should only endorse those military actions of your country in which you yourself would be willing to give your life. The difficulty is that integrity does not seem to require this kind of personal involvement in other public issues. For example, a citizen of integrity can favor a costly reform of the welfare system without being required to serve as a welfare caseworker. Presumably it is enough if citizens are willing to contribute their fair share of the program's expenses. So one might ask: why is it not enough for citizens to contribute their fair share to maintain our expensive military establishment? Why should integrity require direct participation in the case of the military but not in other situations? This raises the question, to which I shall return, of when monetary contributions are morally acceptable substitutes for direct participation, and why.

Finally, the AVF has contributed to a widening gap between the orientation and experience of military personnel and that of the citizenry as a whole. To be sure, this is an empirically contested area, but some facts are not in dispute. First, since the inauguration of the AVF, the share of officers identifying themselves as Republican has nearly doubled, from 33 to 64 percent. (To be sure, officers were always technically volunteers, but as I can attest from personal experience, the threat of the draft significantly affected the willingness of young men to volunteer for officer candidacy.) Second, and more significantly, the share of elected officials with military experience has declined sharply. From 1900 through 1975, the percentage of members of Congress who were veterans was always higher than in the comparable age cohort of the general population. Since the mid-1990s, the congressional percentage has been lower, and it continues to fall.

Lack of military experience does not necessarily imply hostility to the military. Rather, it means ignorance of the nature of military service, as well as diminished capacity and confidence to assess critically the claims that military leaders make. (It is no accident that of all the post-war presidents, Dwight Eisenhower was clearly the most capable of saying no to the military's strategic assessments and requests for additional resources.)

For these reasons, among others, I believe that as part of a reconsideration of the relation between mandatory service and citizenship, we should review and revise the decision we made thirty years ago to institute an all-volunteer armed force. I hasten to add that I do not favor reinstituting anything like the Vietnam-era draft. It is hard to see how a reasonable person could prefer that fatally flawed system to today's arrangements. The question, rather, is whether feasible reforms could preserve the gains of the past thirty years while enlisting the military more effectively in the cause of civic renewal....

[Judge Richard] Posner contends that "Conscription could be described as a form of slavery, in the sense that a conscript is a person deprived of the ownership of his own labor." If slavery is immoral, so is the draft. In a similar vein, [Robert] Nozick once contended that "taxation of earnings from labor is on a par with forced labor." (If Nozick were right, then the AVF that Posner supports, funded as it is with tax dollars, could also be described as on a par with forced labor.)

Both Posner's and Nozick's arguments prove too much. If each individual's ownership of his or her own labor is seen as absolute, then society as such becomes impossible, because no political community can operate without resources, which must ultimately come from *someone*. Public choice theory predicts, and all of human history proves, that no polity of any size can subsist through voluntary contributions alone; the inevitable free riders must be compelled by law, backed by force, to ante up.

Posner might object, reasonably enough, that this argument illustrates the difference between taxation and conscription: while political community is inconceivable without taxation, it is demonstrably sustainable without conscription. It is one thing to restrict self-ownership of labor out of necessity, but a very different matter to restrict it out of choice. The problem is that this argument proves too little. Posner concedes that "there are circumstances in which military service is an obligation of citizenship." But there are no circumstances in which slavery is an obligation of citizenship. Moreover, it is not morally impermissible to volunteer for military service. But it is impermissible, and rightly forbidden, to voluntarily place oneself in slavery. Therefore, slavery and military service differ in kind, not degree. And if there are circumstances in which military service is an obligation of citizenship, then the state is justified in enforcing that obligation through conscription, which is not impermissible forced labor, let alone a form of slavery. QED. For the purposes of this article, then, I will suppose that a legitimate government would not be exceeding its rightful authority if it chose to move toward a more mandatory system of military recruitment.

Celebrating the cash nexus: four thought experiments.

But this is not the end of the argument, because Posner has another arrow in his quiver. He rejects the claim, advanced by Michael Sandel and other communitarians, that substituting market for nonmarket services represents a degrading "commodification" of social and civic life. Indeed, Posner celebrates what communitarians deplore. "Commodification promotes prosperity," he informs us, "and prosperity alleviates social ills." Moreover, commodification enables individuals to transform burdensome obligations into bearable cash payments: middle-aged couples can purchase both care for their children and assisted living for their parents, and so forth.

Posner charges that communitarian theory is incapable of drawing a line between matters that rightly belong within the scope of the market and those that do not. Posner's celebration of the cash nexus is exposed to precisely the same objection. Rather than scoring rhetorical points, I will offer a series of examples designed to help delimit the proper sphere of nonmarket relations.

Paying people to obey the law.

Suppose we offered individuals a "compliance bonus"—a cash payment at the end of each year completed without being convicted of a felony or significant misdemeanor. It is not hard to imagine situations in which the benefits of this policy (measured in reduced enforcement costs) would outweigh the outlays for bonuses. What (if anything) is wrong with this?

My answer: at least two things. First, it alters for the worse the expressive meaning of law. In a legitimate order, criminal law represents an authoritative declaration of the behavior the members of society expect of one another. The authoritativeness of the law is supposed to be a sufficient condition for obeying it, and internalizing the sense of law as authoritative is supposed to be a sufficient motive for obedience. To offer compliance payments is to contradict the moral and motivation sufficiency of the law.

Second, payment for compliance constitutes a moral version of Gresham's law: lower motives will tend to drive out higher, and the more comfortable to drive out the more demanding. When those who are inclined to obey the law for its own sake see others receiving compensation, they are likely to question the reasonableness of their conduct and to begin thinking of themselves as suckers. Most would end up accepting payment and coming to resemble more closely those who began by doing so.

Paying citizens for jury duty.

Consider the analogy (or disanalogy) between national defense and domestic law enforcement. The latter is divided into two subcategories: voluntary service (there is no draft for police officers) and mandatory service (e.g., jury duty). Our current system of military manpower is all "police" and no "jury." If we conducted domestic law enforcement on our current military model we'd have what might be called "The All-Volunteer Jury," in which we'd pay enough to ensure a steady flow of the jurors the law enforcement system requires to function.

There are two compelling reasons not to move in this direction. First, citizens who self-select for jury duty are unlikely to be representative of the population as a whole. Individuals who incur high opportunity costs (those who are gainfully employed, for example) would tend not to show up. The same considerations that militate against forced exclusion of racial and ethnic groups from jury pools should weigh equally against voluntary self-exclusion based upon income or employment status. (We should ask ourselves why these considerations do not apply to the composition of the military.)

Second, it is important for all citizens to understand that citizenship is an *office*, not just a *status*. As an office, citizenship comprises matters of both rights and duties—indeed, some matters that are both. Service on juries is simultaneously a right, in the sense that that there is a strong presumption against exclusion, and a duty, in the sense that there is a strong presumption against evasion. To move jury duty into the category of voluntary, compen-

sated acts would be to remove one of the last reminders that citizenship is more than a legal status.

Paying foreigners to do our fighting for us.

Consider: we might do as well or better to hire foreigners (the All-Mercenary Armed Forces) as kings and princes did regularly during the eighteenth century. The cost might well be lower, and the military performance just as high. Besides, if we hire foreigners to pick our grapes, why not hire them to do our fighting?

There is of course a practical problem, discussed by Machiavelli among others: a pure cash nexus suggests the mercenaries' openness to opportunistic sideswitching in response to a better offer, as happened in Afghanistan. In addition, what Abraham Lincoln called the "last full measure of devotion" would be less likely to be forthcoming in the handful of extreme situations in which it is required.

Beyond these practical considerations lies a moral intuition: even if a mercenary army were reliable and effective, it would be wrong, even shameful, to use our wealth to get non-citizens to do our fighting for us. This is something we ought to do for ourselves, as a self-respecting people. I want to suggest that a similar moral principle does some real work in the purely domestic sphere, among citizens.

Paying other citizens to do our fighting for us.

Consider military recruitment during the Civil War. In April 1861 President Lincoln called for, and quickly received, 75,000 volunteers. But the expectation of a quick and easy Union victory was soon dashed, and the first conscription act was passed in March, 1863. The act contained two opt-out provisions: an individual facing conscription could pay a fee of $300 to avoid a specific draft notice; and an individual could avoid service for the entire war by paying a substitute to volunteer for three years.

This law created a complex pattern of individual incentives and unanticipated social outcomes, such as anti-conscription riots among urban workers. Setting these aside, was there anything wrong in principle with these opt-out provisions? I think so. In the first place, there was an obvious distributional unfairness: the well off could afford to avoid military service, while the poor and working class could not. Second, even if income and wealth had been more nearly equal, there would have been something wrong in principle with the idea that dollars could purchase exemption from an important civic duty.

THE LEGACY OF THE AVF: ECONOMIC AND SOCIAL STRATIFICATION

We can now ask: What is the difference between the use of personal resources to opt *out* of military service and the impact of personal resources on the decision to opt *in*? My answer: as both a practical and a moral matter, less than the defenders of the current system would like to believe. To begin with, the decision to implement an AVF has had a profound effect on the educational and class composition of the U.S. military. During World War Two and the Korean War—indeed, through the early 1960s—roughly equal percentages of high school and college graduates saw military service, and about one third of college graduates were in the enlisted (that is, non-officer) ranks. Today, enlisted men and women are rarely college graduates, and elite colleges other than the service academies are far less likely to produce military personnel of any rank, officer or

enlisted. As a lengthy *New York Times* feature story recently put it, today's military "mirrors a working-class America." Of the first twenty-eight soldiers to die in Iraq, only one came from a family that could be described as well off.

Many have argued that this income skew is a virtue, not a vice, because the military extends good career opportunities to young men and women whose prospects are otherwise limited. There is something to this argument, of course. But the current system purchases social mobility at the expense of social integration. Today's privileged young people tend to grow up hermetically sealed from the rest of society. Episodic volunteering in soup kitchens does not really break the seal. Military service is one of the few experiences that can.

In an evocative letter to his sons, Brookings Institution scholar Stephen Hess reflects on his experiences as a draftee and defends military service as a vital socializing experience for children from fortunate families. His argument is instructive: "Being forced to be the lowest rank..., serving for long enough that you can't clearly see 'the light at the end of the tunnel,' is as close as you will ever come to being a member of society's underclass. To put it bluntly, you will feel in your gut what it means to be at the bottom of the heap.... Why should you want to be deprived of your individuality? You shouldn't, of course. But many people are, and you should want to know how this feels, especially if you someday have some responsibility over the lives of other people." It is a matter, not just of compassion, but of respect: "The middle class draftee learns to appreciate a lot of talents (and the people who have them) that are not part of the lives you have known, and, after military duty, will know again for the rest of your lives. This will come from being thrown together with—and having to depend on—people who are very different from you and your friends."

A modern democracy, in short, combines a high level of legal equality with an equally high level of economic and social stratification. It is far from inevitable, or even natural, that democratic leaders who are drawn disproportionately from the upper ranks of society will adequately understand the experiences or respect the contributions of those from the lower. Integrative experiences are needed to bring this about. In a society in which economic class largely determines residence and education and in which the fortunate will not willingly associate with the rest, only nonvoluntary institutions cutting across class lines can hope to provide such experiences. If some kind of sustained mandatory service does not fill this bill, it is hard to see what will.

THE IMPORTANCE OF UNIVERSAL SERVICE

The inference I draw from this analysis is far from original: to the extent that circumstances permit, we should move toward a system of universal eighteen-month service for all high school graduates (and in the case of dropouts, all eighteen year olds) who are capable of performing it. Within the limits imposed by whatever ceiling is imposed on military manpower, those subject to this system would be able to choose between military and full-time civilian service. (If all military slots are filled, then some form of civilian service would be the only option.) The cost of fully implementing this proposal (a minimum of $60 billion per year) would certainly slow the pace of implementation and might well impose a permanent ceiling on the extent of implementation. The best response to these constraints would be a lottery to which all are exposed and

from which none except those unfit to serve can escape.

It might be argued that a program of this sort would have little if any effect on the armed forces, which would continue to draw their manpower from the current stream of volunteers. That may be the case if the military does not expand during the next decade. But there are reasons to believe that it will. It is fast becoming evident that that the post-war occupation of Iraq will take more troops and last longer than administration officials had predicted. As an interim response, the military has already moved away from the all-volunteer principle. The US Marine Corps has frozen enlistments for all of the 175,000 personnel currently on active duty. Marines whose period of voluntary enlistment has expired are required to remain in the service, on active duty, until the freeze expires. Other services have imposed similar if more limited freezes. It is likely, moreover, that the prospect of being sent to Iraq as part of a vulnerable long-term occupation force will depress voluntary enlistments, especially in the Army and Marines.

There is evidence suggesting that movement toward a less purely voluntary system of military and civilian service could pass the test of democratic legitimacy. For example, a 2002 survey sponsored by the Center for Information and Research on Civic Learning and Engagement (CIRCLE) found 60 percent-plus support for such a move across lines of gender, race and ethnicity, partisan affiliation, and ideology. Still, it is plausible that intense opposition on the part of young adults and their parents could stymie such a change. Assuming that this is the case, there are some feasible interim steps that could yield civic rewards. Let me mention just two.

First, we could follow the advice of former secretary of the navy John Lehman and eliminate the current bias of military recruiters in favor of career personnel and against those willing to serve for shorter periods. As Lehman puts it, we should "actively seek to attract the most talented from all backgrounds with service options that allow them to serve their country... without having to commit to six to ten years' active duty." He makes a strong case that this change would markedly increase the number of young men and women from elite colleges and universities who would be willing to undergo military service.

Second, the Congress could pass legislation sponsored by senators John McCain (R-AZ) and Evan Bayh (D-IN) that would dramatically expand AmeriCorps (the Clinton-era national and community service program) from its current level of 50,000 to 250,000 fulltime volunteers each year. Survey evidence shows overwhelming (80 percent-plus) support for the basic tenet of this program, that young people should have the opportunity to serve full-time for a year or two and earn significant post-service benefits that can be used for higher education and advanced technical training. As Sen. McCain rightly puts it, "one of the curious truths of our era is that while opportunities to serve ourselves have exploded...[,] opportunities to spend some time serving our country have dwindled." In this context, the ongoing resistance to AmeriCorps in some quarters of Congress verges on incomprehensible.

It would be wrong to oversell the civic benefits that might accrue from the revisions to the AVF that I propose, let alone the more modest steps I have just sketched. Still, some of our nation's best social scientists see a link between World War Two-era military service and that generation's subsequent dedication to our nation's civic life. If reconsidering a decision about military manpower made three decades ago could yield even a fraction of this civic improvement, it would be well worth the effort.

The Military Draft:
We Should Have an All-Volunteer Armed Forces

ROBERT K. FULLINWIDER

In his brief for restoring military conscription, Bill Galston attributes to the All-Volunteer Force two significant civic costs. The all-volunteer policy of raising military forces permits the flourishing of citizenship-without-responsibility, he claims, and "has contributed to a widening gap between the orientation and experience of military personnel and that of the citizenry as a whole."

As to the second cost, Galston misidentifies its cause. An "experience gap" is a function of numbers. If a large proportion of Americans serves under arms decade after decade, eventually a large percentage of the civilian population will have military experience. If a very small number serves, an "experience gap" will become a prominent feature of the civilian world. It doesn't matter what mechanism—conscription or volunteering—generates the big or small numbers. Currently, the military takes in 250,000 recruits a year. Given our total population of 290 million, this intake (and consequent outflow) is miniscule. Small force size is the cause of any present and future "experience gap."

As to the first cost, why does Galston impute it to the all-volunteer policy of military recruitment? There are any number of historical and structural features of American life that might lead some young Americans to believe citizenship is duty-free or too casually to endorse military action. However, suppose the existence of the AVF does contribute to these outcomes. Despite this unfortunate side-effect, the soundness of the all-volunteer policy is determined by its effectiveness in producing a first-class military force, and Galston concedes that on this score the all-volunteer policy has been an "impressive" success.

Nevertheless, he wants, while preserving "the gains [in military effectiveness] over the past thirty years," to tamper with the all-volunteer policy by "enlist[ing] the military more effectively in the cause of civic renewal." He would reinstate conscription and make it universal for eighteen-year-olds, although he leaves vague the operational details of the new policy of forced service and the effects it would have on the uniformed services. These details and effects matter a lot, as I will show below.

PHILOSOPHICAL FOUNDATIONS

Galston [argues that] society may legitimately coerce military service *in the nation's defense*. I agree that society may do so when such coercion is necessary. However, under current circumstances, our nation's military defense is being met without coercion. Coercion would add nothing to it. In fact, the universal service scheme Galston proposes reaches far beyond the simple propositions Mill adduces on behalf of conscription to defend "society or its members from injury and molestation." Galston needs premises that support *conscription to promote a social experiment*. Why? Because almost all of those conscripted under his plan will end up working in some inner city homeless shelter or tutoring first-graders how to read or engaging in some similar task that by no stretch of the imagination can be called "defense of the nation." In being forced to undertake these "duties," young people will learn, Galston hopes, that citizenship is not free and that rights bring responsibilities. Moreover, they will experience a kind of "civic socialization," the rich and privileged sons and daughters of America no longer "hermetically sealed from the rest of society" but laboring alongside the lower classes. For a brief time in forced service, upper, middle, and lower class kids will experience intensely a kind of equality they will not know most of their lives. However, that this forced service will actually civically profit those who bear it or successfully teach the right lessons in responsibility is highly speculative. This is why I said Galston needs a philosophical defense not of conscription to defend the nation but of conscription to promote a social experiment.

PRACTICAL DIFFICULTIES

Galston limns military service as one of the few experiences that can yield the civic socializing he wants, but a close reading of his essay shows that military service is *not* what his coerced servers will be experiencing. He proposes, ideally, a universal draft of eighteen-year-olds. The draftees can choose between military or civilian service. However, if all military slots are already filled, he notes parenthetically, then civilian service will be the only option available to new conscripts.

Now, since the military services have met their accession needs over the last two decades through volunteers, a coercive universal service scheme piggybacked onto the present system would seem to yield no increase in military experience and, thus, no increase in egalitarian shoulder-rubbing. Of course, no coercive scheme can actually be piggy-backed onto the present system without *altering* it, and that is why Galston needs to put some operational de-

tails of his draft on the table and discuss their effects.

If we are to have the draft Galston envisages, here are some basic changes we might expect. First, we have to reconstitute the central bureaucracy of the Selective Service System and reestablish the roughly 4,000 local draft boards around the country. Second, we have to be prepared to put people in jail. For good reasons and silly ones, plenty of conscripts will resist. Their resistance cannot be allowed to succeed if the whole coercive scheme is not to be undermined. Third, we have to be prepared for gender inequities. Suppose there *were* some slots in the military the new draftees could take. Those slots could be filled only on an 8 to 1 ratio, men to women. This ratio represents the current gender configuration of the military and no one in the services or Congress wants to change it. Under Galston's draft, some women will complain that they are disproportionately and unfairly excluded from their preferred choice, military service.

Fourth, we have to be prepared to put in place a set of exemptions and deferments. Galston insists that only the unfit (physically and mentally) will be exempted from service under his plan but this is surely not feasible (and further, this exempted group itself will turn out to be very large if *military* standards are imposed; the single largest group of young men of draft-age who did not serve in the Vietnam War era were those who failed their preinduction physicals). For example, a new high school graduate may be an unmarried mother of a small child or the financial mainstay of a household with ill or disabled parents or a crucial income-earner in a family already below the poverty line. There can be no politically feasible conscription that does not exempt on the basis of hardship (and it is worth recalling that ten times as many young men received hardship exemptions from the Vietnam draft as received student deferments). There will be clamor for other exemptions, as well. For example, young Mormons go on extended tours of foreign missionary work after high school; Congress will undoubtedly be asked by the Mormon Church to exempt these young people from Galston's draft or at least defer their service. Other groups will make their claims, as well.

More important from the military's point of view will be way in which a draft will threaten enlistment standards. Galston asserts that the AVF policy has had a profound effect on the educational composition of the services and he is right, but not in the way he suggests. The eighteen-year-olds recruited into today's military are far better educated than their civilian counterparts. This is because the military can be selective. It can turn away not only unqualified but *minimally* qualified applicants and accept only those who meet a much higher standard. Newspaper stories periodically observe that the AVF has to work hard to meet its recruiting goals. What the stories don't mention is that the services have to work hard because they set their standards so high. They recruit, with few exceptions, only high school graduates, and among those the services look for kids who score above average on the Armed Forces Qualifying Test (more than two-thirds of enlistees do). The services would have far less trouble recruiting if they lowered standards—especially if they lowered them to the level prevailing in the conscription years Galston looks back on fondly. And lower its standards the military might have to do if Galston's conscription plan goes into effect. If the new conscripts are to be given a choice of service, military or civilian, it will be polit-

ically difficult to deny the military option to those who are *minimally* (though not exceptionally) qualified to serve.

THE REAL MESSAGE OF COERCED SERVICE

As part of his philosophical defense of coerced service, Galston notes the expressive dimension of the law. The law not only tells us what to do, it sends messages as well. What message will Galston's draft send?

It won't be the message World War II conscription sent. In World War II, America was in a fight to the death against fascism in both its German and Japanese variants. Between 1941 and 1945, ten million men were drafted and twenty million served overall—this out of a national population of 140,000,000. The great majority of able-bodied men under thirty bore arms. Those who remained on the home front—men, women, and children—did their part. Women went into the factories; children collected scrap. Everyone submitted to rationing and regimentation. Consequently, the conscription law's expressive effect was unmistakably a message of social duty and needed sacrifice.

Galston's draft law is unlikely to send any such message because its rationale is so transparently didactic. His law will more likely come across as a meddling busybody, disdaining the life courses young adults might choose for themselves (with civic and service components incorporated in any number of legitimate ways) and insisting that all of them submit to the particular pattern the government thinks best for their civic souls.

Galston claims to eschew any policy like the Vietnam-era draft. This is a wise move, since that draft was thoroughly discredited by the time it ended in 1973. However, the basic flaw in that draft was not that it gave some college kids deferments or led to an active force skewed toward the lower middle classes. Indeed, the Vietnam-era draft had far fewer loopholes than the 1950s draft Galston admires. (For example, Galston notes that the conscription of the 1950s brought college graduates into the enlisted ranks, thus producing the social mixing he desires. However, he doesn't say how many of these graduates stayed in uniform and for how long. In the 1950s, a drafted college graduate could get right back out of the service by teaching in a public school, and some not insubstantial number did.)

What discredited the Vietnam-era draft more than anything else was its expressive content. Let me explain. By 1968, although America's active-duty military numbered 3.6 million, Selective Service was filling slots from a national population of 200 million, a population disproportionately bulging right at the youth end, as the leading edge of the baby boom was slamming its way through high school. Nearly 27 million men came of draft age during the Vietnam War but 16 million of them—more than half—never served at all. Of that number, four million were lottery escapees—men put in the lottery pool after 1969 but lucky enough to possess lottery numbers that excluded them from the annual draft calls. (Incidentally, these lottery escapees amounted to eight times the number of college kids given student deferments.) Small draft calls from a large target population made conscription look not like a mechanism of universal service but like a booby-prize for the unlucky few. *That* was the expressive effect of the Vietnam-era draft.

If a draft is to teach a lesson in universal duty, it needs to approach universality itself, as it did in World War II and in the

early stages of the Cold War. This is no doubt why Galston wants to conscript all eighteen-year-olds. However, he concedes that shanghaiing into service a sizeable portion of the four million kids who turn eighteen each year might take a considerable bite out of the public fisc and dampen voter enthusiasm for a fully universal conscription. "The best response" to this state of affairs, writes Galston, is limited conscription using a lottery—in other words, the best response is reinstating the very feature of the Vietnam-era draft that divided youth into the unlucky few and the lucky many.

CONSCRIPTION PROPERLY BOUNDED

Galston suggests that the country's current military engagements may require more manpower than current enlistments provide. If manpower shortages arise, the military will be loathe to return to a draft until other options fail. The impressive success of the AVF that Galston refers to arises out of three facts—first, that the men and women who make up the services' platoons, companies, and battalions want to be there; second, that they are well-educated, committed, disciplined, and trainable; and third, that they serve long enough to become highly proficient at their jobs. The American military is an expeditionary force, designed to fight overseas, using complex weaponry and sophisticated tactics. Even in the infantry, it needs soldiers who can master an array of technical tasks. Short-termers (which is what draftees would be) would barely learn their craft before finishing their active duty. Moreover, nothing undermines unit morale and cohesion like the presence of malcontents, troublemakers, and malingerers—and a draft will deliver up plenty of each. Under conscription, the Army cannot reward bad behavior with a discharge—otherwise coerced service wouldn't work. It has to keep bad eggs in the barracks or in the brig.

Even so, if the Army truly needs not 70,000 but 140,000 or 280,000 recruits a year and can't meet this need through voluntary enlistments, then the country may have to resort to a draft. It might be a draft short on the civic lessons desired by Galston but it would be one justified on the grounds set out by Mill.

Further, if the country decided that defense against domestic terror attacks requires the creation of a substantial new homeland "light" military force (e.g., soldiers trained to stand guard around every nuclear power plant, chemical factory, airport, train station, power grid, hydroelectric dam, hospital, and government office in the country), then something approaching universal conscription might be appropriate. The point is, the question of conscription should be settled on grounds of national defense, not determined by hoped-for civic by-products.

POSTSCRIPT: A COMMENT ON CLASS

Galston laments the absence of the college-educated from the ranks. Privileged youth currently escape the burden of service, he says, and this is bad for America.

Others likewise see the AVF through the prism of "class." Unfortunately, much of the discussion of the military's class structure is built on an implicit class bias. For example, consider a recent policy report by Marc Magee and Steven J. Nider, "Citizen Soldiers and the War on Terror," for the Progressive Policy Institute. In their report, Magee and Nider praise legislation passed last year that will make available a "citizen soldier" option in which individuals can enlist for an 18-month tour of duty in one of the armed services and then serve a further period in the Individ-

ual Ready Reserves, the Peace Corps, or Americorps.

The new short-term option, Magee and Nider believe, "would appeal especially to college-educated youths, who are now dramatically underrepresented in" the military.

The creation of a citizen soldier enlistment track marks the most important change in America's military recruitment policies since the draft was ended. The introduction of the all-volunteer force in 1974 ushered in an era of military recruitment that targeted people primarily interested in cash, job security, or technical training. The citizen soldier track adds a civic dimension to this economic model.

Instead of using a recruitment strategy "based exclusively on economic incentives," write Magee and Nider, the new track will allow "the nation's most fortunate sons and daughters" to act on their duty to contribute to America's defense.

Here we see the germs of a charge that has been thrown at the AVF since its beginnings—that it amounts to a "mercenary" force. (One recent example: John Gregory Dunne, essayist and novelist, gives voice in the May 29, 2003 issue of the *New York Review of Books* to the claim that the AVF is a "Hessian force of the unlettered and underprivileged.") Do we want people to do our fighting who enter service motivated exclusively by the prospect of financial gain? That's how mercenary armies are formed. Can we honor what Magee and Nider call our "civic ethic of equal sacrifice" by turning the job of defense over to mere hired hands?

This "mercenary" charge has been around since the AVF was created. What merit does it have? None. It is true that military pay was raised after the draft ended, because military recruiters had to begin competing in an open job market. Today, a private in the Army with less than two years service earns almost $1,100 a month basic pay. Factor in the free food, housing, and medical care he receives by living on base, and this is not a bad income for a twenty year old with only a high school diploma. Moreover, the private may get an up-front cash bonus for enlisting and be eligible to receive quite substantial college tuition benefits at the end of his term. All in all, the military offers an attractive option for many youth. But this is not an option open to the truly "unlettered and underprivileged." As we've already seen, the services set a high bar for admission. Those who fill the enlisted ranks of the AVF come principally from lower middle- and middle-class blue collar and white collar families. They are high school graduates with good grades, good entry-test scores, and capable of college work. Indeed, many of those who leave service after their initial term of enlistment go straight on for a baccalaureate using the tuition benefits they've earned.

A decent wage and prospects of future financial rewards: do these make a recruit a mercenary? Where is the evidence that no "civic dimension" weighs in the choices of current recruits? Where is the evidence that enlistees in the AVF are motivated "exclusively" by financial inducements rather than by a mix of patriotic feeling, desire for adventure, and a wish for an occupation both socially meaningful and personally challenging, all of this leavened by an attractive economic package to boot? Where is the evidence that members of the AVF are Hessians who would abandon their Army, Air Force, or Navy jobs to serve in the Canadian, Libyan, German, Venezuelan, or Chinese armies for higher wages and bonuses? There is none. Indeed, the "mercenary" charge is not an induction from empirical evidence, and never has been, but a deduction from unstated prejudices. The deduction moves from the fact that economic incentives offered by the military play a role in enlistments to the conclusion that enlistees are mercenaries. There's a missing premise here. What is it? That people for whom economic incentives make a difference are mercenaries? This can hardly be the right premise, as the report by Magee and Nider so ironically illustrates. After initially characterizing the AVF policy as targeting people "primarily interested" in money and relying "exclusively on economic incentives," they extol the new "citizen soldier" option that will, they hope, appeal to upper middle-class and college-educated youth. Part of that appeal, however, turns out to be *cash*—a $5,000 cash bonus or an $18,000 education grant to pay off tuition loans! Now, if upper-class youth aren't turned into mercenaries by accepting substantial bundles of cash, how are lower middle-class youth nevertheless compromised by the military's financial compensation packages?

Consider this further fact. The military maintains a substantial officer corps, largely composed of graduates from the service academies or from college ROTC programs. These graduates are not individuals who've taken a vow of poverty. The cadets and midshipmen at the academies gain a free college education; many ROTC students receive substantial scholarships. A newly commissioned lieutenant begins with more than twice the basic pay of a private. While a Master Sergeant with fifteen years experience and a family of four takes home $53,000 in RMC (regular military compensation, which includes basic pay, food and housing allowances, and tax advantages), a Lt. Colonel with fifteen years experience and a family of four takes home $95,000. To the critics of the AVF like Magee and Nider, the Sergeant is part of a tainted volunteer system relying "exclusively" or "primarily" on economic incentives. Yet, except for rare moments in our history, the officer corps has always been all-volunteer. If the Sergeant is a mercenary, why then isn't the Lt. Colonel a super-mercenary? The critics of the AVF never draw this conclusion. Why not? It begins to look like the missing premise in the "mercenary" argument is some piece of class snobbery: for lower-class kids the money is all that counts, while for upper-class kids the money merely eases the way for them to act on selfless motives of service and duty. What else explains the dual attitude Magee and Nider take toward the regular enlistee and the "citizen soldier," the latter drawn (they hope) from "the ranks of the best educated and most well-off citizens," while the former comes from an average American family?

Magee and Nider, like many critics of the AVF, focus on the enlisted ranks and then treat them as the whole military. For example, they claim that college-educated youth are dramatically underrepresented in the AVF. However, the college-educated are underrepresented only in the enlisted ranks, not in the officer corps. Nearly every commissioned officer is a college graduate. Magee and Nider lament the fact that only 6.5 percent of active duty enlistees have had some college experience, by contrast to 46 percent of the general population. However, when you add in the officer corps, the percentage of active duty military personnel *in total* with some college experience jumps to 21 percent. Indeed, 15 percent of the military have a bachelor's degree or higher, a figure not terribly out of line with the civilian world, where 26 percent of individuals twenty-five or older possess at least a baccalaureate.

The low percentage of bachelor's degrees in the enlisted ranks is a matter of concern only if we think the military will perform better by having college-trained privates and corporals serving under high-school-educated sergeants. Even Galston's universal draft wouldn't supply the services with more college-educated privates, only more college-bound ones.

THE CONTINUING DEBATE:
The Military Draft

What Is New

While Galston favors a system of universal eighteen-month service for all eighteen year olds and Fullinwider favors conscription only in the event of national military emergency, they each recognize that there are other alternatives. Galston suggests that military recruiters might be encouraged to seek volunteers for shorter periods, rather than concentrating on finding those wanting a military career. Fullinwider considers a new program that would recruit volunteers to serve a relatively brief eighteen month tour of military duty followed by a period of nonmilitary service (such as the Peace Corps). Would either of those options be workable? Are there other options that are better? Are there other options that might satisfy both Galston and Fullinwider?

While there has not been an active draft in the United States in several decades—though young men are still required to register with the Selective Service—the U.S. military actions in Afghanistan and Iraq have clearly stretched the U.S. military resources quite thin, and recently calls for a draft have been renewed. Though neither major political party favors resumption of a draft, several experts have suggested that any increase in military involvement around the world would require the use of a draft, and others have recommended a draft on other grounds. U.S. Representative Charles Rangel of New York City (a liberal Democrat, and himself a decorated war hero) recently proposed legislation to reinstate the draft, on the grounds that the burdens of military service are now being borne disproportionately by those from lower economic strata. The legislation was sponsored in the Senate by Republican Senator Chuck Hagel of Nebraska, whose argument for the bill focused on the importance of involving young people in active service to their country. Shortly before the 2004 election, the bill—without hearings having been held, and with the opposition of the original sponsors of the bill who wanted hearings and further deliberation before any vote—was brought before the Congress and soundly defeated. The vote in the House was 402 to 2. Politicians widely believed that supporting a draft would be a very unpopular political stance.

At present, there is little active political support for a military draft; however, wars in Afghanistan and Iraq have stretched the U.S. all-volunteer armed forces very thin, and some branches of the military report increased difficulty with recruiting. Many believe that any further military action—and the U.S. has a very tense relationship with Syria, Iran, and North Korea—would require a draft to provide sufficient soldiers.

Where to Find More

Ben Schiffrin, in "Recent Developments: Universal National Service Act," *Harvard Journal on Legislation*, Volume 41, Number 1, Winter 2004: 337–349, argues against any form of required national service that deprives young people of choices, advocating instead that we make programs sufficiently attractive to draw great numbers of applicants. In favor of a National Service requirement are E.J. Dionne, Jr. and Kayla Meltzer Drogosz, in "The Promise of National Service: A (Very) Brief History of an Idea," in Policy Brief #120, 2003, The Brookings Institution. It can be found at *www.brook.edu/printme.wbs?page=/comm/policybriefspb120.htm* Dionne and Drososz, along with Robert E. Litan, have also edited a collection of essays on the issue of national service: *United We Serve: National Service and the Future of Citizenship* (New York: Brookings Institution Press, 2003).

The Cato Institute, a conservative/libertarian organization, opposes the draft; a strong statement of arguments against the draft can be found in a paper by Doug Bandow, a senior fellow at the Institute. Entitled "Fixing What Ain't Broke: The Renewed Call for Conscription," it is No. 351 in the Institute's *Policy Analysis* series, published August 31, 1999; it is available online at *http://www.cato.org/*.

Eliot A. Cohen, *Citizens and Soldiers: The Dilemmas of Military Service* (Ithaca, N.Y.: Cornell University Press, 1985), offers an insightful analysis of both the historical dimensions and contemporary issues in conscription policies. An excellent collection of articles on various issues related to conscription is edited by Robert K. Fullinwider, *Conscripts and Volunteers: Military Requirements, Social Justice, and the All-Volunteer Force* (Totowa, N.J.: Rowman & Allanheld, 1983).

ACTS OF TERRORISM:
Always Morally Wrong *or* Sometimes Morrally Justified?

ALWAYS MORALLY WRONG

ADVOCATE: C. A. J. (Tony) Coady, Australian Research Council Senior Research Fellow in Philosophy at the University of Melbourne

SOURCE: "Terrorism, Just War and Supreme Emergency," in C. A. J. (Tony) Coady and Michael O'Keefe, editors, *Terrorism and Justice: Moral Argument in a Threatened World* (Melbourne University Press, 2002).

SOMETIMES MORALLY JUSTIFIED

ADVOCATE: Gabriel Palmer-Fernandez, Professor, Department of Philosophy and Religion and Director, Dale Ethics Center, Youngstown State University

SOURCE: "Terrorism, Innocence, and Justice," *Philosophy & Public Policy Quarterly*, Spring 2005

The destruction of New York City's Twin Towers and the simultaneous attack on the Pentagon brought the question of terrorism sharply into focus for most Americans. Of course this was by no means the first terrorist attack on American soil–the Oklahoma City bombing was a horrific terrorist attack years before, and (depending on one's definition of terrorism) the massacre of a village of women and children at Wounded Knee, many years earlier, might also fall within the category. This brings up a very difficult question about terrorism: How should we define it? It is always important to have clear definitions that do not prejudge important ethical issues, but it is particularly important when dealing with terrorism. Suppose that a government directed its armed forces to make a missile attack against an office building in another country; would that count as a terrorist attack? There is no reason to believe that the Saudi government had any knowledge of or involvement in the attack on the Twin Towers; but *if* the Saudi citizens who hijacked the airliners and attacked the Twin Towers had been military personnel acting under orders of the Saudi government, would that still have been a terrorist attack? The answers to those questions will depend, obviously, on how "terrorism" is defined. And definitions are not always neutral: Under the preferred U.S. State Department definition of terrorism, official acts by states can never count as terrorist acts. Such special definitions lead some to believe that what counts as terrorism will always depend on the perspective we adopt, as in the poem by Roger Woddis:

> Throwing a bomb is bad,
> Dropping a bomb is good;
> Terror, no need to add,
> Depends on who's wearing the hood.

If intelligent discussion of terrorism is possible, it must start with some reasonable definitions.

Terrorism often involves the killing of innocent people. Is terrorism, then, always an unjustified wrong? That conclusion is not quite so obvious. After all, we know that making war on a country will involve the killing of innocents; but most people believe that war is sometimes justified. If it is sometimes acceptable to kill innocents for the political purposes of war, why would it never be acceptable to kill innocents for the political purposes of a terrorist group—for example, if the terrorist group is seeking recognition of what it regards as its legitimate claim for territorial independence as a sovereign country? Or suppose a country is under foreign occupation, perhaps a very brutal occupation. Those who want to throw off the occupation typically cannot declare war against their occupiers: they have no resources for raising or equipping armies. If it is wrong for them to plant a bomb in a city of the occupying country in a terrorist strike aimed at forcing the occupier to leave, how could it be right for a nation to bomb the city of an enemy that is attempting to forcibly conquer and occupy that nation? Some suggest that terrorism aims at the deaths of innocents, while warfare does not. But often "terrorists" send warnings to evacuate a building before it is blown up; and in any case, the carpet bombing of European cities during World War Two and North Vietnam cities and villages during the Vietnam conflict—not to mention the bombing of Hiroshima and Nagasaki—makes that a difficult distinction to defend.

POINTS TO PONDER

➤ Could any act of the revolutionary "insurgents" of the American colonies against the British "occupation" legitimately be classified as "terrorist" by the British?

➤ Suppose two terrorist groups make similar attacks against similar targets: both destroy office buildings containing government and military offices, along with civilian offices, and both attacks kill government officials, military officers, and civilians. One attack is aimed at a brutal occupying regime that is carrying out mass murder, while the latter attack is aimed at an occupying regime following more humane practices. In your view, *might* the former attack be justified while the latter is wrong? Or must they be considered morally equal, because both involve the killing of innocents?

➤ Suppose that a *dictatorship*, in which the citizens have little or no voice in the government wages an aggressive and unjust war against the peaceful country of Tranqua; and from the other side Tranqua is unjustly attacked by a *democracy* in which citizens have substantial control over government actions. Would people in Tranqua be more justified in launching terrorist attacks against the citizens of the democracy than against the citizens of the dictatorship?

Acts of Terrorism:
Always Morally Wrong

C. A. J. COADY

WHAT IS TERRORISM?

Defining terrorism is a hazardous task. It has been estimated that there are well over one hundred different definitions of terrorism in the scholarly literature. This disarray reflects the highly polemical contexts in which the term is used so that the act of defining can become a move in a campaign rather than an aid to thought. Consider some influential definitions picked out by the Terrorism Research Center in the United States.

1. 'Terrorism is the use or threatened use of force designed to bring about political change' (Brian Jenkins).
2. 'Terrorism constitutes the illegitimate use of force to achieve a political objective when innocent people are targeted' (Walter Laqueur, *The Age of Terrorism*).
3. 'Terrorism is the premeditated, deliberate, systematic murder, mayhem, and threatening of the innocent to create fear and intimidation in order to gain a political or tactical advantage, usually to influence an audience' (James M. Poland, *Understanding Terrorism*).
4. 'Terrorism is the unlawful use or threat of violence against persons or property to further political or social objectives. It is usually intended to intimidate or coerce a government, individuals or groups, or to modify their behaviour or politics' (Vice-Presidents Task Force, 1986).
5. 'Terrorism is the unlawful use of force or violence against persons or property to intimidate or coerce a government, the civilian population, or any segment thereof, in furtherance of political or social objectives' (FBI Definition)

We might note that Jenkins's definition has the consequence that all forms of war are terrorist. Whatever verdict we give on war, it is surely just confusing to equate all forms of it, including the armed resistance to Hitler, with terrorism. More interestingly, several of the definitions make use of the idea of unlawful or illegitimate violence, but this seems to fudge too many questions about what is wrong with terrorism. The idea of the illegal simply raises the issue of what and whose laws are being broken—armed internal resistance to Hitler by German citizens would arguably have been justified, yet it would certainly have been against German law. And the adjective illegitimate needs unpacking in terms of what makes this or that use of force illegitimate.

Rather than further reviewing the varieties of definition, I propose to concentrate on one key element in common responses to and fears about terrorism, namely the idea that it involves 'innocent' victims. This element features in several of the quoted definitions. It was recently overtly invoked by Yasser Arafat's condemnation of terrorism when he said: 'no degree of oppression and no level of desperation can ever justify the killing of innocent civilians. I condemn terrorism, I condemn the killing of innocent civilians, whether they be Israeli, American or Palestinian'. It also usefully provides a point of connection with the moral apparatus of just war theory, specifically the principle of discrimination and its requirement of non-combatant immunity. Of course, terrorism does not always take place in the context of all-out international war, but it usually has a warlike dimension. I will define it as follows: 'the organised use of violence to target noncombatants ("innocents" in a special sense) for political purposes'.

This definition has several contentious consequences. One is that states can themselves use terrorism, another is that much political violence by non-state agents will not be terrorist. As to the former, there is a tendency, especially among the representatives of states, to restrict the possibility of terrorist acts to non-state agents. But if we think of terrorism, in the light of the definition above, as a tactic rather than an ideology, this tendency should he resisted, since states can and do use the tactic of attacking the innocent. This is why allegations of terrorism against Israeli government forces in parts of Palestine during the anti-terrorist campaign in 2002 made perfect sense, even if the truth of the claims was contentious.

Some theorists who think terrorism cannot be perpetrated by governments are not so much confused as operating with a different definition. They define terrorism, somewhat in the spirit of the FBI definition, as the use of political violence by non-state agents against the state. Some would restrict it to violence against a democratic state. This is the way many political scientists view terrorism. Call this the political definition to contrast with the tactical definition.

A further consequence of the tactical definition is that it implies a degree of purposiveness that terrorism is thought to lack. Some theorists have claimed that terrorism is essentially 'random', others that it is essentially 'expressive'. In both cases,

the claim is that a reference to political purposes is inappropriate. In reply, it can be argued that talk of terrorism as random is generated by the genuine perception that it does not restrict its targets to the obvious military ones, but this does not mean that it is wild and purposeless. Indeed, most terrorists think that the best way to get certain political effects is to aim at 'soft' non-combatant targets. Similarly, there can be no doubt that many terrorist attacks are expressive and symbolic, involving the affirmation of the attitude: 'We are still here; take notice of us'. Yet the expressive need not exclude the purposive. So terrorist acts can be, and usually are, both expressive and politically purposive. It is a further question whether these purposes are particularly realistic. The idea that terrorist acts are merely expressive is partly sustained by the belief that when viewed as purposive the acts are basically futile. The futility is often real enough, but purposive acts abound that are in fact futile. Note that I am not *defining* terrorism as immoral: it needs discussion and some background moral theory to show that it is immoral.

THE JUST WAR TRADITION

It is time to say a few words about the just war tradition that provides much of that background. Its development has been strongly influenced by Catholic philosophers and theologians in the West, but also by people of quite different commitments, such as Aristotle, Grotius, Locke, and in modern times Michael Walzer, a nonreligious Jew. There are also parallel lines of thought in the ancient Chinese philosophical traditions. This is not surprising, because, unless one takes the view that war is entirely beyond moral concern or that it is simply ruled out by morality, then one has to give some account of what can morally justify it. Just war theories constitute a major line of response to this need; another is provided by utilitarian thinking, and another by the so-called realist tradition. In the just war tradition, this account has two key divisions—the *jus ad bellum* and the *jus in bello*. The former tells us the conditions under which it can be right to resort to war, the latter is concerned to guide us in the permissible methods by which we should wage a legitimate war.

Under the *jus ad bellum* it is common to list the following conditions:

1. War must be declared and waged by legitimate authority.
2. There must be a just cause for going to war.
3. War must be a last resort.
4. There must be reasonable prospect of success.
5. The violence used must be proportional to the wrong being resisted.

Under the *jus in bello* there are basically two governing principles:

1. *The Principle of Discrimination*—this limits the kind of kind of violence that can be used, principally by placing restrictions on what count as legitimate targets.
2. *The Principle of Proportionality*—this limits the degree of response by requiring that the violent methods used do not inflict more damage than the original offence could require.

There are clearly many difficulties with these conditions, but equally clearly they make initial intuitive sense. In this brief discussion, I shall concentrate on the Principle of Discrimination since it is the principle most relevant to my approach to terrorism. As Janna Thompson has noted... in developing Coates's comments on terrorism, the approach embodied in what I have called 'the political definition' could also connect with just

war theory through a particular interpretation of the requirement of legitimate authority.

Moral restrictions on how one conducts oneself in war are apt to be met with incredulity. 'You do what needs to be done to win' is a common response. There is a certain appeal in this pragmatic outlook, but it flies in the face not only of just war thinking but of many common human responses to war. The concept of an atrocity, for instance, has a deep place in our thinking. Even that very tough warrior, the US war ace General Chuck Yeager writes in his memoirs that he suffered genuine moral revulsion at orders to commit 'atrocities' that he was given and complied with in World War II. He was especially 'not proud' of his part in the indiscriminate strafing of a 50 square mile area of Germany that included mainly non-combatants.

A major part of the discrimination principle concerns the immunity of non-combatants from direct attack. This is a key point at which utilitarian approaches to the justification of war tend to clash with the classical just war tradition. Either they deny that the principle obtains at all, or, more commonly, they argue that it applies in virtue of its convenience. The former move is associated with the idea that war is such 'hell' and victory so important that everything must be subordinated to that end, but even in utilitarian terms it is unclear that this form of ruthlessness has the best outcomes, especially when it is shared by the opposing sides. Hence, the more common move is to argue that the immunity of non-combatants is a useful rule for restricting the damage wrought by wars. Non-utilitarians (I shall call them 'intrinsicalists' because they believe that there are intrinsic wrongs, other than failing to maximise good outcomes) can agree that there are such extrinsic reasons for the immunity rule, but they will see this fact as a significant additional reason to conform to the principle. Intrinsicalists will argue that the principle's validity springs directly from the reasoning that licenses resort to war in the first place. This resort is allowed by the need to resist perpetrators of aggression (or, on a broader view, to deal with wrongdoers), and hence it licenses violence only against those who are agents of the aggression.

This prohibition on attacking the non-perpetrators (noncombatants or the innocent as they are often called) has been a consistent theme in the just war tradition. So John Locke says in Chapter XV of his *Second Treatise of Civil Government* that a conqueror with a just cause 'gets no power' over those among the enemy populace who are innocent of waging the war. As Locke puts it: 'they ought not to charged as guilty of the violence and injustice that is committed in an unjust war any farther than they actually abet it'.

It is nonetheless understandable that various questions have been raised about the making of the combatant/non-combatant distinction in the context of modern war. The first point of clarification is that when we classify people as non-combatants or innocents we do not mean that they have no evil in their hearts, nor do we mean that combatants are necessarily full of evil thoughts. The classification is concerned with the role the individual plays in the chain of agency directing the aggression or wrongdoing. And it is agency not mere cause, that is important since the soldier's aged parents may be part of the causal chain that results in his being available to fight without their having any agent responsibility for what the soldier is doing. The combatant may he coerced to fight, but is still prosecuting the war, even if the greater blame lies with those who coerce. On the other hand, young schoolchildren may be enthusiastic about their country's war, but are not prosecuting it. Neither are the farmers whose products feed the troops, for they would feed them (if they'd buy) whatever their role. It should be added that the combatant/non-combatant distinction is not equivalent to the soldier/civilian distinction even though they overlap considerably. Some civilians, such as political leaders and senior public servants, will be legitimate targets if they are actively directing or promoting unjust violence whether or not they wear uniforms or bear arms.

But even when these distinctions are made there seems room not only for doubt about the application of the distinction to various difficult categories of person such as slave labourers coerced to work in munitions factories but also its applicability at all to the highly integrated citizenry of modern states. Some people say that it is surely anachronistic to think of contemporary war as waged between armies; it is really nation against nation, economy against economy, peoples against peoples. But although modern war has many unusual features, its 'total' nature is more an imposed construction than a necessary reflection of changed reality. Even in World War II not every enemy citizen was a combatant. In any war, there remain millions of people who are not plausibly seen as involved in the enemy's lethal chain of agency. There are, for instance, infants, young children, the elderly and infirm, lots of tradespeople and workers, not to mention dissidents and conscientious objectors. This challenge to the distinction requires there to be no serious moral difference between shooting a soldier who is shooting at you and gunning down a defenceless child who is a member of the same nation as the soldier. The conclusion is perhaps sufficiently absurd or obscene to discredit the argument.

In fact, there has been a remarkable change on this issue in the strategic doctrine and military outlook of many major powers since the end of the Cold War. It is now common to pay at least lip service to the principle, as evidenced by certain restraint shown or announced during the Gulf War, and the bombing of Serbia, and by the widespread condemnation of Russian brutality in Chechnya. The rhetoric, at least, of the recent US-led war in Afghanistan is also respectful of the distinction. The real question is not so much whether it is immoral to target non-combatants (it is), but how 'collateral' damage and death to non-combatants can be defended. This was always a problem in just war theory, often solved by resort to some form of the principle of double effect. This allowed for the harming of non-combatants in some circumstances as a foreseen but unintended side-effect of an otherwise legitimate act of war. The 'circumstances' included the proportionality of the side-effect to the intended outcome. Not everyone agrees with the principle (and this is not the place to discuss it in detail), but the conduct of war in contemporary circumstances is morally impossible unless the activities of warriors are allowed to put noncombatants at risk in certain circumstances. Some modification to the immunity principle to allow indirect harming seems to be in line with commonsense morality in other areas of life, and to be necessitated by the circumstances of war. If it is not available, then pacifism, as Holmes has argued, seems the only moral option.

The tactical definition of terrorism faces the problems already discussed concerning the meaning of the term 'non-combatant', but even more acutely. In guerilla war, for instance, insurgents may not be easily identifiable as combatants, and will seek to enlist or involve the vil-lagers and local inhabitants in the campaign, thereby blurring their status as non-combatants. On the other hand, many state officials who are not directly prosecuting the campaign against the insurgents may he plausibly viewed as implicated in the grievances the revolutionaries are seeking to redress. There are certainly problems here, but they do not seem insurmountable. In the heat and confusion of battle, it may be difficult and dangerous to treat even children as non-combatants, especially where children are coerced or seduced into combatant roles (as is common in many contemporary conflicts). Nonetheless, a premeditated campaign of bombing regional hospitals to induce civilian lack of co-operation with rebels is in palpable violation of the *jus in bello*. So are the murder of infants, and the targeting of state officials, such as water authorities or traffic police, whose roles are usually tangentially related to the causes of the conflict. It is true that some ideologies purport to have enemies so comprehensive as to make even small children and helpless adults 'combatants'. Western advocates of strategic bombing of cities in the name of 'total war' share with the Islamic fanatics who incorporate American air travellers and sundry citizens of Manhattan into their holy targets a simplistic and Manichaean vision of the world. This vision is at odds with the just war tradition's attempt to bring some moral sanity to bear upon the use of political violence.

WAR, TERRORISM AND 'SUPREME EMERGENCY'

Is terrorism wrong? Given just war theory and the tactical definition, the answer is clearly yes. And if one takes the principle of non-combatant immunity to invoke an absolute moral prohibition, as just war thinkers have commonly done, then it is always wrong. Yet many contemporary moral philosophers, sympathetic to just war thinking, are wary of moral absolutes. They would treat the prohibition as expressing a very strong moral presumption against terrorism and the targeting of non-combatants, but allow for exceptions in extreme circumstances. So, Michael Walzer thinks that in conditions of 'supreme emergency' the violation of the normal immunity is permissible in warfare, though only with a heavy burden of remorse. He thinks the Allied terror bombing of German cities in World War II (in the early stages) was legitimated by the enormity of the Nazi threat. John Rawls has recently endorsed this view while condemning the bombings of Hiroshima and Nagasaki. If this concession is allowed to states, it seems mere consistency to allow it to non-state agents on the same terms. The general reluctance to do so suggests that such categories as 'supreme emergency' may mask contestable political judgements.

Let us look more carefully at this. The idea of exemptions from profound moral constraints has taken many different forms in contemporary moral philosophy. Some of these are closely associated with the philosophy of utilitarianism. In its simplest form, act utilitarianism, and certain allied forms of thought, hold that all moral constraints are simply 'rules of thumb' that can and should he overruled if calculations of the overall outcomes of so doing show that it is productive of more general happiness than sorrow. This seems to me a deeply misguided view of ethics, but I cannot offer a full-scale rebuttal here. Its principal defect in connection with terrorism is that, in essence, it doesn't allow that the profound moral constraints against killing the innocent are really profound at all. That is why it calls them 'rules of thumb', along with all sorts of

other shorthand adages in the moral life. In connection with terrorism, the more interesting exemption questions arise for those, like Walzer, who *do* think the restriction profound. Such people don't believe that ordinary calculations of utility can possibly override these sorts of constraints. Nonetheless, they think that certain circumstances can allow the regrettable but morally painful choice to violate such deep norms. Those who think this are sometimes operating in the tradition of what has come to be called 'dirty hands'.

The basic idea, we may here take from the tradition, plausibly traceable to Machiavelli, is that certain necessities of life may require the overriding of profound and otherwise 'absolute' moral prohibitions in extreme situations. Walzer's defence of the terror bombing of German cities in World War II in terms of 'supreme emergency' is clearly in the tradition, and provides a useful focus for discussing its relevance to terrorism. Walzer does not defend the bombing unequivocally. He thinks that, though it was morally wrong as a violation of the principle of discrimiflation, it was justified by the plea of supreme emergency in the early stages of the war. In the later stages, however, it was just plain morally criminal, since an Allied victory could he reasonably foreseen on the basis of morally legitimate targeting and fighting. The bombing of Dresden was therefore an outright atrocity, though the bombing of other German cities up to 1942 was not. He is clear that the bombing in this earlier phase was a violation of the principle of discrimination, and at one point calls it 'terrorism'. It was morally wrong and implies guilt, but had to be done.

Walzer's use of the category 'supreme emergency' here is based on the idea that the need to defeat Nazi Germany was no ordinary necessity. Hitler's victory would have been a dire blow to civilisation. The enormity of his regime and its practices was such that his extended empire would have been a disaster for most of the people living under its sway. In addition, the threat of Hitler's victory was present and urgent, and the bombing of German cities aimed directly at the civilian populations was the only offensive weapon the British had.

Now, two things are worth noting about this characterisation. The first is that some of the matters that Walzer factors into this dire judgement on Germany's war efforts were not factors that were known to Churchill and his advisers or influenced the decision to use strategic bombing. Hitler was known to be anti-Semitic and to have persecuted Jews and political opponents, but not to have a program of genocide in hand. So part of the legitimation deployed by Walzer is largely *post facto*. Second, Walzer makes the issue of Germany's possible victory a matter of supreme emergency but not that of Japan. Japan's war, he claims, was 'a more ordinary sort of military expansion, and all that was morally required was that they be defeated, not that they be conquered and totally overthrown'. This is part of his argument against the atomic bombing of Hiroshima and Nagasaki. He denies that this was required by 'supreme emergency', partly because Japan was no longer in a position to win the war so the threat was no longer imminent, and partly because the Japanese did not represent the same danger to civilisation as their Nazi allies. He thinks it mere utilitarianism that the atomic bombs were (allegedly) needed to end the war more quickly with less loss of life, and argues that an ordinary (rather than an unconditional) surrender would have been the morally licit path to ending the war.

A CRITIQUE OF THE SUPREME EMERGENCY DEFENCE

I hold no brief for the doctrine of unconditional surrender, but Walzer's relatively benign view of Japanese aggression is hard to take seriously. I feel inclined to say: 'Tell that to the Chinese'. In the Japanese invasion of China in the 1930s it is soberly estimated that more than 300,000 Chinese civilians were massacred in Nanking alone in a racist rampage of raping, beheading and bayoneting that lasted six weeks. Nor was the racist and anticivilisational behaviour of the Japanese warriors much better in the rest of South-East Asia during the war. Those directly threatened with a Japanese victory in Asia and the Pacific would clearly have had a much sounder case for talking of 'supreme emergency' than Walzer allows. Had they had the capacity to terrorise Japanese cities (as the Americans later did), then it would seem that supreme emergency would have licensed their attacking the innocent. But if this is so, then it is hard to resist the suspicion that 'supreme emergency' is too elastic to do the job required. So elastic, indeed, that whenever you are engaged in legitimate self-defence and look like losing you will be able to produce plausible reasons of 'supreme emergency' for attacking the innocent.

A further curiosity of Walzer's argument is that it is presented primarily as an argument available to states and their representatives. This is not exclusively true of the tradition of the 'dirty hands' debate (it is less true of Weber, for instance) but it is a pronounced emphasis of Walzer's treatment. This is particularly surprising, given that Walzer derives the term 'dirty hands' from Sartre's play of the same name, which is concerned with the supposed necessity for revolutionaries to violate morality in pursuit of their cause. But, if we think only of the connotations of 'supreme emergency', it is not at all obvious that the issue can be so restricted. Palestinian resistance groups, for example, can mount a powerful case that they face a hostile power bent upon subordination and dispossession to a degree that threatens not only their lives but their way of life. Even the various groups around Osama bin Laden may well see themselves as qualifying for this exemption. No doubt it can be argued that there are various delusions and mistakes in their outlooks, but the history of warfare is replete with similar delusions and mistakes.

In his discussion of 'supreme emergency' Walzer makes explicit his pro-state bias: 'Can soldiers and statesmen override the rights of innocent people for the sake of their own political communities? I am inclined to answer the question affirmatively, though not without hesitation and worry'. And he goes on to speak of nations in a way that identifies political communities and nations. Of course, even Walzer's language here leaves logical space for the idea that nations or political communities can be driven by necessity, even where they do not possess a state or have been deprived of one. Yet it is clear that recourse by such people or their real or imagined leaders to 'supreme emergency' is far from his mind.

My own view is that the supreme emergency story suffers from grave defects whether it is offered as an exemption on behalf of a state, or some less established political community, or a group claiming to represent either. The first problem is that it under-values the depth and centrality of the prohibition on killing the innocent. In spite of Walzer's agonising about the need to acknowledge that we have violated an important moral restraint by our bombing or other terror tactic, he locates the prohibition on attacking non-combatants within what he calls 'the war convention'. Although, there is some unclarity about what he means by this, the terminology suggests that the prohibition is itself somehow merely conventional. On the contrary, it is, as I have argued, basic to what makes it legitimate to wage a just war at all. More generally the prohibition on intentionally killing innocent people functions in our moral thinking as a sort of touchstone of moral and intellectual health. To suspend this, because of necessity or supreme emergency, is to bring about an upheaval in the moral perspective. The situation is, I think, rather like that supposed by the philosopher W. V. O. Quine to operate with empirical and scientific knowledge. Quine thinks that no propositions, even those of logic, are beyond revision or abandonment, but some are more deeply entrenched in our way of thinking and responding to the world than others, and so less revisable. Some indeed may be so deeply entrenched that we cannot imagine what it would be like to have to give them up. Ludwig Wittgenstein makes some similar suggestions in his book *On Certainty*, but explicitly includes many ordinary empirical propositions in the central core. My suggestion is that some of our moral beliefs have an analogous position in the framework of our moral thinking. Rejection of them leads to an unbalance and incoherence in moral thought and practice parallel (though different in kind) to the rejection of entrenched propositions in empirical and theoretical thinking.

My second point is that the primacy of the political community that lies behind much of the dirty hands debate is highly suspect. Walzer admits of individuals that they can never attack innocent people to aid their self-defence. He then adds: 'But communities, in emergencies, seem to have different and larger prerogatives. I am not sure that I can account for the difference, without ascribing to communal life a kind of transcendence that I don't believe it to have'. Walzer goes on to try to locate the 'difference' in the supposed fact that 'the survival and freedom of political communities... are the highest values of international society'. Maybe they are the highest values of international society, but this is hardly surprising if one construes international society as a society of political communities, namely recognised states. What is needed, at the very least, is an argument that locates the survival and freedom of political communities as the highest *human* value, and one that is capable of justifying the overriding that 'supreme emergency' requires. I doubt that any such argument exists. Certainly, it is not enough to point to the undoubted value of political life for there are many other values that are equally, if not more, significant.

A third consideration against the dirty hands story in its 'supreme emergency' form is that admission of this exemption is likely to generate widespread misuse of it. On Walzer's own account the 'legitimate' resort to terror in the early stages of World War II led rapidly to its illegitimate use thereafter. It is surely plain enough that the widespread resort to state terror in various contexts has been justified in ways that parallel Walzer's apologetic, and non-state agents are not slow to follow suit. We surely do better to condemn the resort to terrorism outright with no leeway for exemptions, be they for states, revolutionaries or religious zealots.

MORAL RESPONSE

Finally what sorts of violent responses to terrorism can be morally legitimate? The first thing to say of this is that the use of terrorism to combat terrorism should be ruled out. Attacking the innocent is illicit when used by non-state groups and it is wrong when used by states in response. Two wrongs do not make a right. Second, the use of violence to capture or even kill terrorists is legitimate if it accords with the conditions of the *jus ad bellum* that govern the morality of resort to war. One of the crucial conditions most relevant here, and especially relevant to the present 'war against terrorism', is whether the exercise is likely to achieve success. Here it is difficult to know what success amounts to. Venting of rage or grief is hardly sufficient. Bringing the agents of terrorist attack to justice or destroying them would seem a legitimate aim, as would diminishing the future prospect of terrorist attacks. At the time of writing, it is unclear whether the war in Afghanistan has fulfilled these aims. A further campaign of violence against the nations classified by President Bush as forming an 'axis of evil' looks even more problematic from this point of view. It is also doubtful whether it would satisfy the conditions of last resort and proportionality. Finally, and more generally, massive aerial bombardments to aid the military overthrow of ugly regimes is likely to be politically and morally inadequate as a response to terrorism. The paradigm of state-against-state warfare is ill adapted to the threat of terrorists like al-Qaeda since such terrorists are not state-based, are relatively independent of the host nations they infest, and breed on the oppression and injustice in the international order that remain unaddressed by campaigns of violence. Bombing campaigns like that in Afghanistan inevitably produce alarmingly high numbers of non-combatant casualties and damage to civilian infrastructure. Even where these are not directly intended, their scale can betray an immoral indifference to innocent life.

Acts of Terrorism:
Sometimes Morally Justified

GABRIEL PALMER-FERNANDEZ

On May 21, 1856 proslavery forces from Missouri attacked the antislavery town of Lawrence, Kansas. They looted stores, burned buildings, and assaulted residents. Three days later, John Brown, proclaiming himself the servant of the Lord, and his group of antislavery fighters sought revenge by killing five proslavery farmers along the Pottawatomie Creek. At the Doyle farm, James and his two sons were hacked to death. Mrs. Doyle, a daughter, and a fourteen-year-old son were spared. Brown and his fighters then moved on to a second farm, where Allen Wilkinson was taken prisoner, and finally to a third where William Sherman was executed. The attack on Lawrence and the killings at Pottawatomie Creek sparked a guerilla war between proslavery and antislavery forces in Missouri and Kansas. It lasted several months and cost nearly two hundred lives.

Brown's campaign against slavery won him many supporters in the North, particularly among a group of wealthy New Englanders. With their help, Brown moved to Virginia where he hoped to start a slave rebellion. In 1859 he raided the United States armory in Harper's Ferry and held some sixty hostages. He was defeated, arrested and charged with inciting a slave insurrection, murder, and treason. In a plea for Brown's life, Henry David Thoreau said, Brown "was like the best of those who stood on Concord Bridge.... You who pretend to care for Christ crucified, consider what you are about to do to him who offered himself to be the savior of four millions of men." On December 1859, Brown was hanged. But in the North, church services and public meetings glorified his deeds. Ralph Waldo Emerson, for example, said that Brown's execution would "make the gallows glorious as the cross." Some years later, in an address given at Harper's Ferry, Frederick Douglass praised Brown's unequalled dedication to the cause of abolition by saying, "I could live for the slave, but he could die for him."

The activities of John Brown and his militia have been repeated countless times throughout the world, particularly in the past few decades. Men and women organize themselves into a group and engage in acts of violence for a political objective. Sometimes they wish to have their own separate homeland or defeat a foreign aggressor—the IRA in Ireland, ETA in Spain, Irgun in Israel, Tamil Tigers in Sri Lanka, FLN in Algeria, Hezbollah in Palestine. At other times they wish to overturn an unjust, tyrannical government and establish, as the Constitution of the United States declares, a "more perfect union." Such violence is almost always illegal. No state or system of law could long endure should it tolerate private violence, even for an important political objective. By almost all accounts, it is irregular violence, like vigilante justice, often biased in its own favor. Even when it elicits our sympathies, we regret if not fear this kind of violence. How, then, shall we think of John Brown? Was he a criminal, murderer, traitor, a religious zealot who killed and held hostage ordinary people? Was he a martyr whose selfless sacrifice contributed to the liberation of millions of children, women, and men from slavery?

I. TERRORISM

One response is that John Brown killed innocent civilians. That makes him a murderer. It doesn't matter that he was motivated by a strong sense of justice, abolishing that horrible institution of slavery. That is a view that is well established in international law and that long tradition of moral reasoning called the just war theory. Among the important provisions of that theory is the principle of noncombatant immunity. It says that civilians are innocent and on that account they are to be spared the ravages of war. They are immune from deliberate attack, and killing them is, as Elizabeth Anscombe puts it, "always murder." But what is the meaning of innocence in war? Why may we kill soldiers but never the ordinary citizen? Were Douglass, Thoreau and Emerson wrong about making Brown's "gallows glorious as the cross"? Was Brown, in today's language, a terrorist or a freedom fighter?

We do well first to come to some conceptual understanding of terrorism. What is it? How does it differ from other forms of political violence? When we define terrorism we need to be careful not to confuse the conceptual with the moral issues. Some writers do just that, giving a definition of terrorism that makes terrorism always by its very nature an immoral activity. This makes any disagreement about the morality of terrorism a disagreement about its nature. Although it is difficult, we can distinguish one from the other.

In a recent article, C. A. J. Coady gives the following definition: terrorism is "the organized use of violence to target noncombatants ('innocents' in a special sense) for a political objective." At first sight this seems a very useful definition. It covers a broad range of relevant phenomena and

allows us to distinguish political from criminal violence, and more important to recognize that terrorism is a tactic used not only by nonstate groups (Aum Shinrikyo, al-Qaida, KKK), but also by states themselves as a way of governing their citizens. Such an understanding is compatible with much of the history of terrorism. For example, the first English-language use of the word dates from 1795 and, like the French use that appeared a few years earlier, describes a mode of governing aimed to suppress political dissent. Examples of state terrorism abound: the mass-drowning and massacre of helpless prisoners during The Reign of Terror under Robespierre in France; executions in the former Soviet Union under Stalin and in Haiti under "Papa Doc" Duvalier; the killing fields under Pol Pot in Cambodia; or the recent wave of torture, rapes, and arbitrary arrests in Equatorial Guinea, to name a few.

Coady's definition captures this important dimension of terrorism. However, there are a few problems with it. First, it does not address an important development in the history of terrorism. The emergence of anarchist movements in Russia, France, Spain, Italy, and the United States in the nineteenth century brought a new type of violence not by states but, as we say today, "from below," intended to bring about political change. Terrorism in this period referred to a way of fighting rather than governing and was largely restricted to the assassination of high political figures. There was during this period hardly a trace of indiscriminate violence or the desire to intimidate and create fear in a civilian population for a political objective. On the contrary, a crucial feature of terrorism during this period was the attempt to arouse the spirit of revolt by highly selective violence and assassinations. This understanding of terrorism continued well into the twentieth century. For example, in Hardman's entry in the *Encyclopedia of the Social Sciences*, published in 1934, indiscriminate violence was not yet a defining feature of terrorism: "Terrorist acts are directed against persons who as individuals, agents or representatives of authority interfere with the consummation of the objectives of group."

Now, contemporary terrorism differs from its predecessors in an important way. Perhaps as early as 1940, it emerged as a way of fighting by acts of indiscriminate violence with the goal of intimidating, creating fear, and undermining the morale of a population. The paradigm case is the intentional indiscriminate aerial bombardment of German cities during World War II, where it was thought that subjecting large segments of the population to the terror of aerial bombardment would produce domestic unrest and widespread opposition to the war. The use of terror by revolutionary or insurgent groups (as some in Iraq today) differs from indiscriminate aerial bombardment only in degree, not in kind. Both aim for the same objective, to undermine civilian morale for the sake of arousing political opposition, and employ the same means, random killing and other acts of indiscriminate violence.

Second, contemporary terrorism is not restricted solely to targeting persons. Several groups have emerged in the past decades that strike only at property. Radical elements of the environmental and animal rights movements have engaged in a wide range of violent actions aimed to change social policies and practices that pollute water and air, and destroy forests and animal species. In the 1980s, for example, some of these groups spiked trees in public lands in Maine, Maryland, and North Carolina, others firebombed research facilities at Oregon State, Michigan State and Washington State universities, and still others sabotaged and sunk whaling vessels in Iceland.

The above concerns can easily be incorporated in Coady's definition. However, it has a further problem: by his account, terrorism targets the noncombatant—the ordinary civilian. This is problematic because there are many cases of killing soldiers that have a strong resemblance to terrorism. Consider the suicide bombing on October 1983 in Beirut that killed 241 American soldiers and 58 French paratroopers, or the identical attack on the U.S. military barracks at Khobar Towers in Saudi Arabia on June 1996. What about killing soldiers on leave as they dine with their families, or go to the grocery store, or drink a beer at the local bar? Or soldiers sent on humanitarian missions after natural disasters, like the recent tsunami in South Asia? Not the happiest way of putting it, but perhaps if we distinguish between soldiers, who are military personnel not in a condition of war, and combatants who are soldiers in war, we can understand why killing the French paratrooper or American soldier in Beirut and killing him on the battlefield are very different things. Combatants are soldiers in war. They are legitimate targets and killing them is an act of war. But soldiers (not in war) are much closer to civilians and killing them is an act of terror.

I propose, then, the following definition of the core feature of terrorism. Terrorism is the organized use of violence against civilians or their property, the political leadership of a nation, or soldiers (who are not combatants in a war) for political purposes. On this account, Robespierre, Stalin, Pol Pot, the radical environmentalists, the suicide bombers in Beirut and Saudi Arabia were terrorists. So, too, was John Brown. They killed civilians or destroyed their property or held hostages for a political purpose. We need now to determine whether what John Brown and other terrorists do is immoral. To do so, I first take up the question of innocence.

II. INNOCENCE

For Coady and many other writers, terrorism is immoral because it deliberately kills persons who are illegitimate targets, persons who are, Coady says, innocent in a special sense, and those persons who are innocent in a special sense are the noncombatants. But these terms—*illegitimate targets, innocence,* and *noncombatants*—do not jibe. Furthermore, conflating them, as Coady does, confuses the conceptual and moral issues in terrorism. It smuggles the moral appraisal of terrorism into its definition, motivating the unavoidable conclusion that terrorism is, by definition, immoral.

The distinction between legitimate and illegitimate targets of attack has a long history. For example, the Hebrew Bible contains at least one passage that spares children and women from death in war, as well as livestock and fruit-bearing trees (Deuteronomy 20). The fourteenth century text by Honoré Bonet, *Tree of Battles,* explicitly prohibits the killing of ploughmen, laborers, pilgrims, and clerics (so too the ox and the ass) because, Bonet writes, "they have no concern with war." They lack responsibility for, and so are illegitimate targets of, war. In the sixteenth century the word "innocent" came into use to describe the civilian or noncombatant. "The basis of war is a wrong done," writes the Spanish theologian Victoria. "But a wrong is not done by an innocent person. Therefore war may not be used against him." For Victoria, innocents include children, women, old men, peasants, farmers, foreign travelers, literary men, clerics, and "the rest of the peaceable population." All

of them, Victoria says, must be "presumed innocent" unless they bear arms and pose a danger. But for Victoria soldiers in war can also be innocent when, for example, they fight "in good faith" or when their cause is just, or when they have been defeated. And these soldiers, he says, "may not be killed.... Not even one of them." Killing any one of them is on par with killing children, women, and old men.

When Coady says that noncombatants are innocent in a "special sense," it is not that understanding he has in mind. For him, innocence refers to the role one plays in the prosecution of a war. Noncombatants are innocent in the special sense that they do not bear arms, are not directly engaged in the prosecution of a war, and do not pose a danger of imminent death to enemy combatants. But this notion of innocence makes no moral sense, for at least two reasons. First, it assumes that the role of the civilian is much like that of the medieval serf who toils the soil now for this lord and later for another, as the knightly class competed for honor, status, glory, and land. If there is any moral sense to the notion of innocent civilian it is here that we find it: harmless persons alienated from the source of political power lacking any responsibility for the war. Under the political conditions of the time, there were no conscripts, volunteers, or citizen-soldiers. Armies consisted of hired guns of foreign mercenaries with little if any loyalty to a nation, but to the spoils and other material rewards of war. For them, war was not a political act or a form of public service. Civilians were immune from war only because they would later provide the source of labor the victor would need to profit from the newly conquered land. They were property, much like Bonet's ox and ass.

But the nature of war changed dramatically with the French Revolution. Political power went from the monarchy to the people. Consequently, war was no longer the king's or the knight's concern. It became the people's business. "The young men shall fight," the French National Convention declared in 1793, "married men shall forge weapons and transport supplies; women will make tents and clothes and will serve in the hospitals; the children will make up old linen into lint; the old men will have themselves carried into the public square to rouse the courage of the fighting men, to preach hatred of kings and the unity of the Republic." To assume that civilians are passive bystanders who, as Bonet puts it, "have no concern with war," fails to recognize that for modern democracies war is a complex institution in which civilians play a crucial role. They provide not only the public spirit essential for war, but also the material necessities for success.

Second, if civilians cannot be killed in war because they are innocent, we must recognize that innocents are always killed in war—not civilians, but morally innocent soldiers. Coady alludes to this point when he says that what is important is "the role the individual plays in the chain of agency directing the aggression or wrongdoing." Those who are in that chain directing aggression or wrongdoing are guilty and may (perhaps must) be killed. Some soldiers will surely be in that chain. But others fighting on behalf of justice and acting in self-defense are innocent and morally may not be killed. Suppose you unjustly attack me and I defend myself. Though I use lethal force against you, I am innocent of any aggression or wrongdoing. You do not have open to you to say that because I employ lethal force against you, you may do likewise and that killing me would not be wrong. Now, there are many soldiers who fit this description—innocent combatants fighting a war of

self-defense. There will also likely be very many innocent combatants in totalitarian regimes whose leadership is guilty of aggression or wrongdoing, for example, forced conscripts in Baathist Iraq under Hussein in the 1991 Persian Gulf War. They were more cannon fodder than anything else. Combatants of totalitarian states hardly have any responsibility for the wars they fight and even when they fight an unjust war (like Hussein's aggression against Kuwait in 1990) seem more like Bonet's serf, ox or ass having no responsibility for the war. But civilians of democratic nations are not like Bonet's serf, mere property used now by this lord and then the other, or combatants of totalitarian regimes removed from the source of political power. Citizens of democratic states fighting an unjust war have a measure of responsibility for the injustice. Are they, therefore, legitimate targets of attack?

III. JUSTICE

There are many things any one of us may not have caused but which were nonetheless under our power to influence or control. Insofar as such things were under our power, we share some responsibility for them. And if such things bring harm to others, we are (partially) responsible for the harm. Suppose you endorse a political candidate by voting for him. This candidate declares that once elected he'll balance the federal budget by (among other things) slashing college financial aid, adversely affecting, discriminating against, harming, say, Chicanos and African-Americans, but not white Americans. Are you by voting for that candidate responsible for discrimination, for the harm? Surely not, you will say, since you did not cause the policy nor wish to discriminate against Chicanos or African-Americans. But still you support him. He's your man in Washington. Four more years! That view of responsibility is very short sighted. It fails to see that government policies in a democracy are joint ventures. They are never the result of any one individual, but of many acting in concert for a common purpose. In such ventures, individuals play a necessary role by endorsing, contributing, or participating in them. By playing a necessary role in any one of those ways, each individual shares responsibility for the venture.

Those statements invite some general queries: What is the responsibility of citizens for their government's actions? Suppose a democratic regime, like ours, wages an unjust war. Just who is responsible? Are we morally responsible for the injustice of that war? Are we legitimate targets of deliberate attack? Would killing any one of us be an act of injustice?

Coady, the law of war, and the just war theory are firm in the opinion that regardless of the injustice of a government's actions, civilians are immune from deliberate attack. Individuals can lose their immunity in a number of ways, for example, by becoming soldiers, working for the war machine, or bearing arms. War is, however, never an individual, private, or personal enterprise. It is not something you or I do. But something we do together for a common purpose. It is a joint venture, a national activity. If we are engaged in grave injustice, say, a war of aggression, do those who endorse, contribute, or participate in the venture, as soldiers or civilians, lose their immunity from attack? How shall we think about this?

Suppose there is a gang of thieves headed by George and Tony in competition for territory and resources with another gang, headed by Boris and Jose. George and Tony decide to eliminate the competition and send their best hit men

to kill Boris and Jose. Of course, Boris and Jose can defend themselves by killing the hit men, who are engaged in a criminal, immoral activity. But may they also kill those who sent them, George and Tony? After all, the hit men can botch their mission and then George and Tony will send their second best. Would it not be preferable for Boris and Jose to remove the danger by killing George and Tony rather than the hit men? Or do we say that since George and Tony are not bearing arms only the hit men may be killed? Who is responsible for the danger imposed on Boris and Jose?

In a democratic system like ours, given the possibility of free action, civilians bear a high burden of responsibility. When we support an unjust war, does it really make any sense to say that we are immune from attack because we are not bearing arms? Do we say only our soldiers can be killed, even when we, and not they, are responsible for an illegal and unjust proceeding? Are those who support an unjust war really innocent?

The fact is that not everyone will support an unjust war. And so, we have to distinguish between those who do and are therefore morally responsible, like George and Tony, and those who do not, who may not be killed because they are innocent of injustice. But it seems correct to say that George and Tony along with those who support, encourage, and send out the troops to wage an illegal and unjust war may morally be killed. If we take the idea of democratic popular sovereignty really seriously, then it is difficult to avoid that conclusion.

But there's at least one problem here: those who would attack a people waging an unjust war may kill only the guilty, otherwise they commit murder. Yet, there is no practical way by which one can do that. Bombs and bullets cannot read the bumper stickers on our cars that say "Not In My Name" and "Regime Change Begins At Home"; bombs and bullets do not know that some of us have organized antiwar demonstrations and that we know and have declared that this is an immoral, illegal, and criminal war. Nonetheless, suppose in some (very rare) circumstances the guilty can be distinguished from the innocent. When possible, then, the guilty may morally be killed.

We might, however, retreat from this view, even when we agree that it is correct. Perhaps morality is not always the best guide. Sometimes it demands too much. In the present case, it demands (at least permits) killing those responsible for grave injustice, the guilty. Of them, there will be very many and most of them will be found among the civilian population. But for the sake of reducing the carnage of war, we might let most of the guilty go free and restrict legitimate targets of attack to soldiers in war. But we do so not because civilians are innocent. Rather we do so because without limiting the range of legitimate targets to soldiers, there would be no room for war in this world. That might be a very good thing. But in the world as I know it, we must make some room for various forms of political violence as they can secure important moral goods—insurrection and revolution, for example, to free the slave and defeat tyrants, and war to defend the nation against those who would unjustly attack us.

THE CONTINUING DEBATE:
Speech Codes

What Is New

Terrorist attacks have a long history and a wide variety of perpetrators, and the following is merely a sample (depending always on how one defines terrorism). A 1979 attack on the Grand Mosque in Mecca, Saudi Arabia, killed 250 and wounded 600; in1980 El Salvador, U.S. supported death squads killed 4 nuns, an archbishop, and in the village of El Mozote executed 800. Sixty-three died in a 1983 attack on the U.S. Embassy in Beirut, and a few months later 300 were killed in attacks on U. S. and French bases there. In 1985 a bomb destroyed an Air India 747, killing 329; 259 died in the 1988 bombing of Pan American Airlines Flight 103, and the next year the bombing of UTA flight 772 killed 170. In 1994 a Jewish extremist machine-gunned Moslem worshipers at a mosque in Hebron, killing 29 and wounding 150; also in 1994, 86 died in an attack on a Jewish Center in Buenos Aires, Argentina. The following year a Sarin nerve gas attack in Tokyo killed 12 and injured 5,700; and U.S. right-wing extremists bombed the Federal Building in Oklahoma City, killing 166 and injuring hundreds. 1966 saw an attack in Colombo, Sri Lanka, which killed 90 and injured more than 1,400. In 1977, 58 tourists were killed at the Hatshpsut Temple near Luxor, in Egypt; and a paramilitary group killed 46 at a church in Acteal, Chiapas, Mexico. In 1998 an attack on the U. S. Embassy in Nairobi, Kenya killed almost 300 and injured 5,000. The early years of the twenty-first century have seen a steep increase in terrorism: The September 11, 2001 attacks killed more than 3,000; suicide bombings occurred throughout Israel, and many more in Iraq; more than 200 were killed in a car bomb attack in Bali, Indonesia. A commuter train, a theater, and a school were among targets attacked in Russia; a commuter train attack in Spain killed almost 200 and wounded 1,500. Though natural disasters are often more deadly (think of the Indian Ocean Tsunami in 2005), and diseases particularly so, terrorist attacks evoke a profound sense of vulnerability or even helplessness.

Where to Find More

A good starting point is Michael Walzer, *Just and Unjust Wars: A Moral Argument with Historical Illustrations* 3rd Edition (New York: Basic Books, 2000). Obviously not everyone agrees with Walzer, but he sets out the basic issues quite clearly.

A number of distinguished philosophers grapple with the issues related to terrorism in R. G. Frey and Christopher W. Morris, editors, *Violence, Terrorism, and Justice* (Cambridge: Cambridge University Press, 1991). Walter Reich, editor, *Origins of Terrorism: Psychologies, Ideologies, Theologies, States of Mind* (Cambridge: Cambridge University Press, 1990), contains interesting perspectives, including an essay by psychologist Albert Bandura. *Ethics in International Affairs*, edited by Andrew Valls (Lanham, Maryland: Rowman & Littlefield, 2000), has excellent articles on terrorism as well as on just war theory and global justice. Catherine Besteman's *Violence: A Reader* (New York: New York University Press, 2002) contains some good pieces not found elsewhere. The essays in James P. Sterba, editor, *Terrorism and International Justice* (New York: Oxford University Press, 2003) place the issue of terrorism in a larger global context. C. A. J. (Tony) Coady and Michael O'Keefe, editors, *Terrorism and*